DIODORUS SICULUS
THE PERSIAN WARS TO THE FALL OF ATHENS

DIODORUS SICULUS
THE PERSIAN
WARS TO THE
FALL OF ATHENS
BOOKS 11–14.34
(480 – 401 BCE)

*Translated, with Introduction
and Notes, by Peter Green*

 UNIVERSITY OF TEXAS PRESS, AUSTIN

Requests for permission to reproduce material from this work should be
sent to:
    Permissions
    University of Texas Press
    P.O. Box 7819
    Austin, TX 78713-7819
    www.utexas.edu/utpress/about/bpermission.html

♾ The paper used in this book meets the minimum requirements of
ANSI/NISO Z39.48-1992 (R1997) (Permanence of Paper).

Library of Congress Cataloging-in-Publication Data
Diodorus, Siculus.
    [Bibliotheca historica. Books 11–14. English]
    The Persian wars to the fall of Athens : books 11–14.34 (480–401 BCE) /
Diodorus Siculus ; translated, with introduction and notes by Peter
Green. — 1st ed.
    p.   cm.
    Includes bibliographical references and index.
    ISBN 978-0-292-71939-2 (cloth : alk. paper) — ISBN 978-0-292-72125-8
(pbk. : alk. paper)
    1. Greece—History—Athenian supremacy, 479–431 B.C.
2. Greece—History—Persian Wars, 500–449 B.C.   3. Greece—
History—Peloponnesian War, 431–404 B.C. I. Green, Peter,
1924– II. Title.
    PA3965.D4E5   2009
    938—dc22
                                       2009025758

CONTENTS

PREFACE

In a recent review (BMCR 2007.02.48) of a volume of Italian articles devoted to Diodorus Siculus, Catherine Rubincam—a scholar who has done as much as anyone to upgrade Diodorus' abysmal reputation—described him, crisply, as "the historian whose work every modern historian of ancient Greece must use, while fervently wishing this could be avoided." Use him they certainly must. His is the only connected ancient narrative of the period from the Persian Wars to the early conflicts of Alexander's successors. Without what survives of his work, we should know virtually nothing—to take two obvious examples—about the history of ancient Sicily or the reign of Philip II of Macedon. His chronological markers, book after book, despite their incidental errors, underlie much of our modern dating of ancient events; did they not exist, our knowledge of the Athenian archon list (to look no further) would be in tatters. It might be thought that modern scholarship would take all that this late, plodding, scissors-and-paste historian could give them and be thankful. Instead, a tradition developed in the nineteenth century of treating him as a mental defective: when he said what critics wanted to hear, that was due to his mindlessly copying a good source; when he did not, that was the result of his own stupidity.[1]

There have been several unfortunate results of this general reaction. Large numbers of serious historical difficulties that Diodorus' text raised were shelved or ignored on the grounds that this historian could not be taken seriously. Until recently the text of the *Bibliotheke* was studied only for what it might be able to tell us about its supposed sources. Lastly, no one in England or America has chosen to translate it in the last half-century, presumably out of fear of being associated with the mindlessness of its author. It is really astonishing, considering the crucial periods covered by the surviving books, that in fact the only English-language version available is that provided by the

---

1. Those interested in pursuing this sad historigraphical trail in detail should read the introduction to Green 2006.

Loeb Classical Library. Thus, what I have primarily set out to do is to fill a serious gap.

The aim of the present work (which will be followed by a companion volume taking the narrative as far as the death of Alexander, which closes Book 17) is to provide a new translation that treats Diodorus as a minor, but perfectly sane, universal historian; is cognizant of recent scholarship; and handles his text with an eye not only on the manuscript tradition but also always on the many historical problems that are to be found in his pages. Further, while Diodorus' style is unremarkable, it is not—as might be assumed on occasion from the Loeb versions—leaden, and I have done my best to replicate his always clear, and often brisk, narrative prose.

In certain cases I have retained Greek terms when no sufficiently precise English equivalent exists or when the common translation carries misleading overtones. These are as follows: (i) *barbaros,* pl. *barbaroi.* Commonly rendered as "barbarians," which carries over-pejorative implications. From Herodotus onward, the term covered those, mainly Thracians or Asiatics, whose speech was unintelligible. The recent habit of translating *barbaroi* as "foreigners" ignores the fact that Greek has a perfectly good term for foreigners, that is, *xenoi:* there is a distinction between the two. (ii) *demos,* the voting members of a democratic or populist community, acting in assembly. (iii) *proxenos,* the representative of one city or state in another. Often translated as "consul," but this is wrong: a *proxenos* was a citizen, and resident, of the host community rather than of the community he represented. (iv) *stadion,* pl. *stadioi,* the distance (roughly 200 yards) and name of the main Olympic footrace. (v) *tyrannos:* this term causes endless trouble. Essentially it defines any ruler who obtains power otherwise than through succession or election; it does not per se imply despotism or moral condemnation, though latterly (for the most part due to the strictures of Hellenistic philosophers) it came to have much the same implications that "tyranny" does to the modern reader. *Tyrannis* is the abstract term for the rule of a *tyrannos.* (vi) *stasis,* civic conflict, ranging from factional rivalry to outright civil war.

Green (2006) covers the period to the outbreak of the Peloponnesian War (431) in much greater detail and depth, with full documentation and commentary. The translation of Diodorus in that volume has occasionally been improved or corrected, while the spelling of proper names has—much against my natural inclination—been Latinized for easier general access through linkage to other works; but otherwise the present volume, which covers 480 to 401, offers radically reduced notes, and an introduction that distils the essence of my earlier, more technical presentation, that was aimed, in the first instance, at fellow-professionals.

Thus, unlike my earlier study, this version does not pretend to offer a commentary in depth (I have not, for example, seriously explored the *Bibliotheke's* chronographical difficulties but have merely noted their impact as they occur). My model has been, from the start, the excellent translation of Justin by Yardley and Develin: a short, general introduction and a translation accompanied by minimal running notes designed to clarify the text and historical background, for an audience of students, teachers, and some general readers who may enjoy the *Bibliotheke,* for a change, as it is seldom read (most scholars merely consult isolated passages): an unbroken narrative covering the most momentous century of Hellenic history, in the Italo-Sicilian West as well as on the Greek mainland and in Asia Minor. My bibliography is mostly a guide to further reading in English-language sources, except for those works of foreign scholarship that I have used to clarify various issues and cite for the benefit of fellow-academics.

For the benefit of general readers who may not be acquainted with the history of the period, I give here a brief guide to reading the present volume. For the Persian Wars, it pays to have Herodotus at hand: the most useful translation currently available is Marincola 2003. For background, use Green 1996, Lazenby 1993 (which contradict each other throughout), and Cartledge 2006. The period between the Persian and the Peloponnesian wars is briefly covered by Thucydides (best translation, Lattimore 1998): back up with French 1971, Kagan 1969, Meiggs 1972, Badian 1993, and Green 2006. The Peloponnesian War itself: Thucydides throughout (Lattimore 1998), with Kagan 1974, 1981, and 1987 as backup. The Thirty: Xenophon's *Hellenica* (Cawkwell 1978), with Krentz 1982 and Strauss 1987 for background. For Sicily and Italy during the period covered by this volume (except for the Athenian invasion of 415–413), Diodorus is virtually the sole ancient text. Backup is from Finley 1968, Freeman 1891–1894 (if you can find a copy), Caven 1990, Green 2006.

My use of available Greek texts has been eclectic. Where possible, I have relied primarily on the new—and newly edited—French Budé series: Haillet for Book 11, Casevitz 1972 (with reservations) for Book 12, Bonnet and Bennett for Book 14. For Book 13 I went back to Vogel's now elderly (1893) Teubner and Oldfather's 1950 Loeb, the latter being (with one or two interesting deviations) virtually a reprint of Vogel. At the same time there are quite a few places in Books 11, 12, and 14 where I prefer Vogel's or Oldfather's earlier readings to those of the Budé editors. Luckily, there are comparatively few textual cruxes (the main problem is lacunas), and where they exist, I have added a brief explanatory note. Only in such notes, where exact readings are crucial, have I sometimes printed the original Greek, and these words have always been transliterated as well as translated.

I have also used several conventional signs in the text: < > indicates the insertion of an emendation or the filling of a lacuna in Diodorus' Greek; [ ] indicates the insertion of editorial or explanatory matter that is *not* a part of the text; { } indicates text that in my opinion does not belong and should be deleted; and † † are signs enclosing a clearly corrupt word in the text for which no compelling replacement has been found. To save space, cross-references to other authors or to other parts of Diodorus' text are indicated by insertions in square brackets, for example, [Hdt. 7.89–95]; in Diodorus' case with arrowheads (< >) indicating whether the reference is forward, for example, [>14.10], or back, for example, [<12.65].

As before, I must acknowledge the enormous help I have had from my predecessors in the business of reestablishing Diodorus as a source to be studied in his own right and not sidelined as a mere brainless copyist: above all, John Marincola, Catherine Rubincam, and Kenneth Sacks, whose work continues to inspire me, not least in those dark moments when Diodorus seems to have taken me over forever, and I remember that originally I began investigating him only as a preliminary to working on my commentary to Herodotus, now for too long on that traditional back burner. It is some compensation that my ideas on the Greco-Persian wars, the Pentecontaetia, and the Peloponnesian War have been sharpened as a result of my pursuit of Diodorus, though any real insights I have gained have been largely due to what I have learned as I went from friends and colleagues such as Ernst Badian, John Buckler, Paul Cartledge, and Simon Hornblower. The anonymous readers for UT Press pointed out numerous anomalies: I am grateful to them both for their lynx-eyed ability to spot faults and also for their (mostly) acceptable solutions. My wife, as always, has been professionally tolerant of my odd obsession with this minor historian, to the point of encouraging me to see him through (as a necessary precondition, I suspect, for returning full time to Herodotus). As usual, the Interlibrary Loan team of the University of Iowa filled my requests with exemplary speed and efficiency: behind my necessarily brief notes much research, inevitably, lies concealed.

Finally, a confession. In the course of translating so much of Diodorus, I have, I must admit, become rather fond of him. I know his faults as well as anyone—not least the stereotyped phrases he trots out, time and again, to describe a battle or the moral values he attaches to his major characters, both pro and con. But his personality is companionable, and in serving him as best I can I feel I am at least making some amends for the mean and contemptuous aspersions on his intellect, judgment, and historical vision that scholars have so freely expressed over the last century and a half. Armchair scissors-and-paste historian he may be, but (not least in return for much precious information that only he provides) at least he deserves better treatment than that.

ABBREVIATIONS

Ael.	Aelian [Claudius Aelianus], freedman, Second Sophistic writer, c. 160–c. 235 CE
	VH *Varia Historia*
Aesch.	Aeschylus of Athens, Greek tragedian, c. 525/4–c. 456/5 BCE
	Pers. *Persians*
Aeschin.	Aeschines, Athenian orator, c. 397–c. 322 BCE
Andoc.	Andocides, Athenian orator, c. 440–c. 390 BCE
App.	Appian[os] of Alexandria, Greek historian, *fl.* 2nd century CE
	BC *Bella Civilia*
Arist.	Aristotle of Stagira, Greek philosopher, 384–322 BCE
	Ath. Pol. *Athenaion Politeia*
	Pol. *Politics*
	Rhet. *Rhetoric*
Aristoph.	Aristophanes, Athenian comic playwright, c. 455–386 BCE
	Acharn. *Acharnians*
	Kn. *Knights*
Athen.	Athenaeus of Naucratis, Greek essayist, *fl.* c. 200 CE
CAH	*Cambridge Ancient History*
Cic.	M. Tullius Cicero, orator and statesman, 106–43 BCE
	De Orat. *De Oratore*
	Rep. *De Re Publica*
	ii Verr. *In Verrem* Actio Secunda
CQ	*Classical Quarterly*
Ctes.	Ctesias of Cnidos, Greek doctor and historian at the court of Artaxerxes II, late 5th century BCE
Diels[5]	H. Diels, *Die Fragmente der Vorsokratiker.* 5th ed. Berlin 1934–1937

Diog. Laert.	Diogenes Laertius, Greek biographer, ?3rd century CE
Dion. Hal.	Dionysius of Halicarnassus, Greek critic and historian, late 1st century BCE

AR	*Antiquitates Romanae*
Ep. ad Pomp.	*Epistula ad Cn. Pompeium*

Front.	Sextus Iulius Frontinus, consul and governor of Britain, military writer, c. 40–103/4 CE

Hdt.	Herodotus of Halicarnassus, Greek historian, c. 485–c. 420 BCE
Hell. Oxy.	*Hellenica Oxyrhynchia*

IG	*Inscriptiones Graecae* (Berlin 1873–)
Isocr.	Isocrates, Athenian orator and educator, 436–338 BCE

Just.	Justin [M. Iunianus Iustinus], Latin epitomator, 2nd century CE or later

Liv.[y]	T. Livius Patauinus, Roman historian, 59 BCE–c. 17 CE
LSJ	A *Greek-English Lexicon. 9th ed.* H.G. Liddell, R. Scott, rev. H.S. Jones. Oxford 1940
Lycurg.	Lycurgus, Athenian statesman, c. 390–c. 325/4 BCE

In Leocr.	*In Leocratem*

Lys.	Lysias, Attic orator, ?459/8–c. 380 BCE

Nep.	Cornelius Nepos, Roman biographer, c. 110–24 BCE

Alcib.	*Alcibiades*
Lys.	*Lysander*
Them.	*Themistocles*

OCD	*Oxford Classical Dictionary.* 3rd ed. Oxford 1996

Paus.	Pausanias of Magnesia-ad-Sipylum, travel writer, *fl.* c. 150 CE
Pind.	Pindar[os] of Boeotia, Greek lyric poet, 518–?438/7 BCE

Ol.	*Olympian Odes*
Pyth.	*Pythian Odes*

Plat.	Plato of Athens, philosopher, c. 429–347 BCE

Apol.	*Apology*
Ep.	*Epistulae*
Menex.	*Menexenus*

Plut.   Plutarch of Chaeroneia, Greek biographer and essayist,
c. 50 – c. 120 CE

Alcib.	*Alcibiades*
Arist.	*Aristeides*
Artax.	*Artaxerxes*
Cim.	*Cimon*
Dion	*Dion*
Lys.	*Lysander*
Mor.	*Moralia*
Nic.	*Nicias*
Per.	*Pericles*
Sol.	*Solon*
Them.	*Themistocles*
Tim.	*Timoleon*

Polyaen.   Polyaenus, Macedonian military writer, 2nd century CE

Polyb.   Polybius, Greek historian, c. 200 – c. 118 BCE

schol.   scholiast, scholia

Soph.   Sophocles, Athenian tragedian, c. 496/5 – 405 BCE
    OC   *Oedipus at Colonus*

Strab.   Strabo of Amaseia, Greek geographer, c. 64 BCE – c. 20 CE

Suet.   Suetonius [C. Suetonius Tranquillus], Roman biographer and
chief secretary to Hadrian, ?69 – 140 CE
    Div. Iul.   *Divus Iulius*

Thuc.   Thucydides son of Olorus, Athenian historian, c. 460 – c. 403
BCE

Varr.   Marcus Terentius Varro, Roman polymath (116 – 27 BCE); also
used to indicate the "Varronian" (Republican) calendar

Xen.   Xenophon son of Gryllus, Athenian general and writer,
c. 430 – c. 355 BCE
    Anab.   *Anabasis*
    Hell.   *Hellenica*

DIODORUS SICULUS
THE PERSIAN WARS TO THE FALL OF ATHENS

INTRODUCTION

Few people apart from professional ancient historians know anything about Diodorus Siculus, and even ancient historians for the most part consult his text rather than read it. Those who have heard of him probably repeat the one cliché he invariably elicits, carefully fostered by generations of academics: that he is an unimaginative copyist only as good as his current source. Yet Diodorus provides us with our only connected narrative of the period from the Persian Wars to the internecine conflicts between Alexander's immediate successors; without him we would know virtually nothing of the early history of Sicily and South Italy and much less about Athens in the mid 5th century or the career of Philip of Macedon. For these reasons alone—not to mention his contribution to the chronography of the ancient world—he would be worth our careful attention.

When we seek details about the man himself, we are, as so often with ancient authors, almost entirely dependent on incidental information furnished by his own work. There are only two external references, both placing him firmly in the last years of the Roman Republic. St. Jerome, in his version of Eusebius' *Chronicle,* identifies 49 BCE as the year in which Diodorus acquired public fame. An entry in that late Byzantine lexicon the *Suda* informs us that he "lived in the time of Augustus Caesar and earlier."[1] In fact, as we shall see, he probably died before, or very soon after, Octavian's victory at Actium in 31/0 BCE.

Diodorus Siculus was born about 90 BCE in Agyrium (modern Agíra), a small town in northeast Sicily ("Siculus" in his title means "the Sicilian").

---

1. See R. Helm, *Eusebius Werke: Siebenter Band: Die Chronik der Hieronymus,* 2nd ed. (Berlin 1956) 1:155: "Diodorus Siculus Graecae scriptor historiae clarus habetur" ("Diodorus Siculus, writer of Greek history, regarded as famous"), and *Suda* (no. D 1152 Adler) s.v. Diodoros.

He was proud of his birthplace and refers to it frequently. The earliest date he provides relating to his own activities is the 180th Olympiad (60/59–57/6 BCE), during which, he tells us (1.44.1), he began his period of residence in Egypt. Can we place his arrival date more precisely? He witnessed (1.83.8–9) the lynching of one member of a Roman mission who accidentally killed a cat; this incident took place, he tells us, before the recognition of Ptolemy XII Auletes as a "friend" of Rome. We know that this recognition, achieved through massive bribery, was negotiated by Caesar and Pompey in 59 (Suet. *Div. Iul.* 54.3). It thus seems clear that Diodorus' arrival in Alexandria is to be dated in 60 or early 59, while the purpose of his residence was almost certainly research in preparation for the composition of his *Bibliotheke,* in particular the opening books with their emphasis on early myth.

He was still there in 55—at 1.44.4 he remarks that the Ptolemaic dynasty had, at the time of writing, lasted 276 years—but at some point prior to 45[2] he began a prolonged period of residence (1.4.2–3) in Rome. How long this lasted is uncertain: it is possible that late in life he retired to Agyrium and died there. One of the few inscriptions from his birthplace (*IG* xiv 588) is the gravestone of "Diodorus son of Apollonius." The name is common, but the coincidence remains striking.

When did Diodorus die? The latest historical event he mentions is Octavian's expropriation of the Greek inhabitants of Tauromenium (modern Taormina) in 36 BCE (App. *BC* 5.109–111). Since he refers to the Ptolemies as the latest rulers of Egypt, and makes no allusion to Octavian's takeover of Egypt after Actium, it is evident that he was not editing his work for publication later than 31/0 BCE, and it is unlikely that he lived much longer.

What else can we deduce about his personality or his career? All the evidence suggests that his entire adult life was occupied in researching and writing the *Bibliotheke:* he himself claims (1.4.1–2) to have devoted thirty years to the task, including a period of travel for purposes of autopsy. Since no patron receives the customary encomium in his surviving text, it is a fair assumption that Diodorus was a gentleman of private means. If this means that he was a Sicilian landowner, the civil wars of the late Roman republic did not treat him kindly. He was a young man during Verres' notorious administration of Sicily (73–71 BCE), when Agyrium suffered from extortion as well as overtaxation. Many property owners sought redress in Rome for ruined estates and illegal expropriations (Cic. ii *Verr.* 2.91–100, etc.).

After a brief (and much debated) period of entitlement to some form of

---

2. We know this date because of his claim (12.26.1) to have seen the Rostra outside the Senate: it was in 45 that Caesar had them removed.

citizenship (Green 2006, 6), in 36 Sicily was taken over by Octavian, who subjected the island to worse indignities than even Verres had inflicted, including not only a 1,600-talent indemnity but also mass confiscations of property and relocation of the inhabitants. Agyrium lay at the center of the area that had supported Sextus Pompeius and was thus the target of Octavian's especial animus. Many lost their property, and not a few their lives, to new Roman colonists, especially Octavian's veterans. Was Diodorus one of these? His repeated advocacy of humanity and moderation in the treatment of victims by the powerful is suggestive; and as we shall see, it is extremely likely that he died before his revision of the *Bibliotheke*'s text was half complete.

Details he lets fall about his character and outlook hint at a rather solitary personality. Like many historians in antiquity, he presents himself as conventionally religious (while at the same time obsessed with Tyche: Fortune, Fate), and he repeatedly asserts that the prime purpose of history is as an instrument for moral improvement. He relishes occasions on which he can plausibly point to divine vengeance overtaking the impious. He also, however, has an antiquarian's taste for the oddities of myth, and raps other historians for not paying sufficient attention to this area. Ostensibly, the reason for this, he claims, is the variety of good moral lessons myths inculcate. In fact, he obviously enjoys them for their own sake. Like Herodotus, he has a passion for marvels (*thaumata*) and a weakness for fascinating digressions, while simultaneously taking Herodotus himself to task for inaccuracies and overcredulity. Unlike Herodotus, he gives the impression of disliking and mistrusting women. All in all, he does not reveal overmuch about himself.

THE *BIBLIOTHEKE*

The *Bibliotheke,* or "Library" (sometimes referred to by later writers as the "Historical Library"), is oddly titled; modern scholars often refer to it, without ancient justification, as Diodorus' *Universal History.* The latter is a fair description but not what the ancient world knew it as. Did Diodorus so call it, modestly, from the numerous works on which he drew to complete his narrative? Did he perhaps also have in mind the great Alexandrian Library (where he surely worked) and its tradition of the *catalogue raisonné* and description (*pinax*) of books on a specific topic? Impossible to tell.

Self-deprecating though the author may have been about his originality, he nevertheless planned on a vast scale. Six books (1–6, probably in his original plan the first of seven hexads: see below) dealt with mythical matters prior to the Trojan War: these books, exceptionally, are not subsumed to a chronographical pattern, since, he explains (1.5.1), for this early period no reliable chronological data existed. (He obviously, and rightly, distrusted the kind of witness provided by the Marmor Parium of 264 BCE, which confidently provided the firm date of 1531/0 for the quarrel between Ares and Poseidon over the Areopagus.[3]) For him as for many, the Trojan War formed a kind of stepping-stone between the mythic past and increasingly documentable history: on the near side of it, chronographical criteria apply.

We possess, regrettably, only fragments, for the most part anecdotal, of Books 6–10. But with Book 11 (the first in this volume), covering Xerxes' invasion in 480 BCE, we are introduced to the three-strand chronographical system Diodorus employs for the rest of the *Bibliotheke*. Every year he correlates his narrative with (i) the Athenian eponymous archon; (ii) the quadrennial Olympic athletic contests (together with the victor in the *stadion*); (iii) the consular Fasti at Rome. Our own BCE/CE chronographical axis is so taken for granted that we "forget just how much synchronistic work our predecessors going back to the Renaissance had to do in order for us to be able to say something like 'Xerxes invaded Greece in 480 BCE'" (Feeney, 12). So, in what we take for granted as 480, Diodorus pinpoints the year as that in which Calliades was archon, when the consuls were Spurius Cassius and Proculus Verginius Tricostus, and the 75th Olympiad took place.

Diodorus did not create this system from scratch, though he made it more thoroughly universal than most. He used the *Chronicle* composed in verse (to aid memorization) by Apollonius of Athens (c. 180–110 BCE). He borrowed the use of Olympiads and Athenian archons from the Sicilian historian Timaeus of Tauromenium (c. 350–260 BCE), and the deliberate "interweaving" (*symplokê*) of synchronicities from Polybius (c. 200–c. 118 BCE). The latter, in particular the use of the Roman Fasti, led him into frequent error, most often through ignorance of nonconsular *interregna* when working out consular years: for example, in Books 11–12 we find consuls misdated by six or seven years (those cited for 480 actually belong in 486). He also tends (Green 2006, 12) "to blur midsummer distinctions between archon-years [which ran from July to June] when narrating events through a campaigning season, and to write achronic introductions, or postscripts, covering an extended period, under the rubric of one specific year."

The *Bibliotheke* was originally planned in forty-two books, comprising seven hexads, and terminating in 46/5 BCE with Caesar's quadruple triumph

---

3. See Feeney, 80–81.

and appointment as Dictator.[4] (Fifteen of these books [1–5, 11–20] survive intact; for the rest, we have extracts and fragments only.) But at some point Diodorus changed his mind, breaking the narrative off in 60/59, at the beginning of the Gallic Wars. As we have seen, he had little reason to love Octavian; but he must have seen, in the years immediately before Actium, that it would be more prudent, whichever way the conflict went, to cut his Caesarian narrative short, even if that meant spoiling his hexadic structure by losing two final books. In any event, he did not eliminate all traces of his original schema: his total count of 1,138 years from the Trojan War to (allegedly) the outbreak of the Gallic Wars (a date he gets right) takes us not to 60/59 but to 46/5 (1.4.7). In all probability, he died before he had time to revise this and other details: there are passages in Books 11–17 (commented on ad loc.) that read like rough first drafts, sometimes even like alternative notes jotted down from different sources.

As Diodorus knew, the idea of writing "universal history," encouraged by the steadily widening horizons of the Mediterranean world, had been around for a long time. As he also knew (and pointed out, 1.3.2–3) earlier attempts had not, for a variety of reasons (mostly omissions: the mythic past, the affairs of *barbaroi*) been successful. No one had come close to the scale of world events he proposed to encompass. Herodotus' survey of the provinces of the Achaemenid empire had pointed the way. Isocrates' notion of Panhellenism as a cooperative Greek venture against the *barbaroi* had built on this earlier work. Ephorus of Cyme (c. 405–330 BCE), one of Diodorus' main sources, covered a wide sweep (he began with the Dorian invasion and had got as far as Philip II's siege of Perinthos when he died), divided his work into books with prefaces, stressed moral improvement as a major reason for writing history, and seems (perhaps on this account) to have sought out ad hominem scandals when in search of political motivation.

This grubbing after what a later critic[5] nicely described as "all the secrets of seeming virtue and unrecognized vice" was brought to a fine art by Theopompus of Chios (? 378/7–c. 320 BCE) in his *Philippic History,* which excoriated the Macedonian court with invective that owed not a little to the Cynic diatribe. We have already noticed the work of Timaeus of Tauromenium, both his chronographical innovations and his massive *Sicilian History:* both utilized by Diodorus, who also took over with some enthusiasm his moral trope of divine intervention overtaking evildoers. Some of Timaeus' faults, categorized with venom by Polybius (12.3–4, 25E–G, 27–28), recur as regular

---

4. See Green 2006, App. A, 237–241, and sources there cited, in particular Rubincam.
5. Dion. Hal. *Ep. ad Pomp.* 6 (p. 394 Usher).

charges against universal historians, Diodorus included: uncertain autopsy, lack of military experience, ignorance of geography, overdependence on earlier written sources, fictional reported speeches, local patriotic allegiances. In Diodorus' case, such accusations (true in certain cases) have been consistently and systematically overdone.

The two major factors that really opened up the whole concept of universal history, however, were Alexander's eastern conquests (which disrupted old accepted notions by totally changing the face of the inhabited world, the *oikouménê*) and the meteoric rise of Rome, in half a century, to the status first of a world power and second, by Diodorus' day, to that of the only Mediterranean power that counted. Roman *imperium,* in fact, became the central unifying element, both geographically and chronologically, of the entire universalist methodology: we can watch all the strands being interwoven (*symplokê* again) in Polybius' narrative (which Diodorus clearly knew and used), along with the notorious fallback of Tyche (Fate, Fortune, the random factor) to account for the embarrassing ease with which Rome had risen to dominance over the Hellenic world. Diodorus also borrows from Polybius (38.6.1–7), who perhaps was inspired by Herodotus, the device of using regular digressions to ease the reader's intellectual concentration.

All these traits are consummated in the work of Posidonius of Apamea (c. 135 – c. 51 BCE), the great Stoic polymath, who began his *History* in 146, the year in which both Corinth and Carthage fell, as a direct sequel to Polybius. In Posidonius we see the emergence of that seamless cosmic *sympatheia* between microcosm and macrocosm, with Tyche governing all human actions—all that happens is fated to happen—where Roman *imperium* and the cosmic order become virtually indistinguishable, paving the way for a succession of emperors to be assimilated without trouble to the divine pantheon. As early as Ovid's day the worldview thus delineated had become a commonplace: *Romanae spatium est Urbis et orbis idem* ("The city of Rome's dimensions are the same as the world's"; *Fasti* 2.683). It is thus not surprising that Posidonius' entire approach is that of a moral philosopher or that Diodorus could envision universal history as a succession of object lessons in virtue and vice.

The *Bibliotheke* indeed reveals Diodorus as in every respect a typical product, intellectually and historiographically, of the late Hellenistic age, distinguished only by the scope of his universalist ambitions. Herodotus, Ephorus, Timaeus, Polybius, and Posidonius—together, in all likelihood, with others whose work has failed to survive—all, as we have seen, left their mark on him. He also refers, in the course of his surviving text, to Thucydides, Xenophon, Theopompus, Philistus, and Hieronymus of Cardia. The long popular theory that he knew few, if any, of these at first hand (e.g., that his acquaintance with

Herodotus was limited to references in Ephorus) is, at best, a gross exaggeration. The texts of the great classics were easily available; it would be extraordinary had he *not* read them as part of his basic education.

Diodorus also gives evidence of understanding many of the key principles of historiography that had been evolved by his day (Green 2006, 25). He emphasizes the need, where possible, for autopsy (3.11.3) and for a proper consideration of antecedent causes, topography, and social background as a basis for narrative exposition (18.5.1). Selectivity (4.5.2), proper proportion (4.5.4), careful examination of detail (4.46.5), and the need to compare and evaluate variant sources (2.32.1) are all stressed. Though he is not above inserting lengthy speeches himself (see, e.g., 13.20.1–32.6), in what may be a swipe at Thucydides he objects to them being made a substitute for analysis (20.1–2.2). He is aware of the distortions produced by ethnic prejudice (3.34.6). His rationalization of myth (3.52.1–3) is in an intellectual tradition that goes back to the best thinkers of the 5th century. Unimaginative he may be, but a mindless idiot he most certainly is not.

BOOK 11: 480–451 B.C.E.

1. The preceding book, the tenth overall, concluded with the events of the year immediately prior to Xerxes' crossing into Europe and the public speeches delivered in the General Assembly of the Hellenes at Corinth to discuss an alliance between Gelon [of Syracuse] and the Greeks [481; all dates are B.C.E. unless otherwise noted].[1] In the present book we shall fully narrate the subsequent course of events, beginning with Xerxes' expedition against the Hellenes and concluding with the year before the Athenians' expedition to Cyprus commanded by Cimon [451].

[2] When Calliades was archon in Athens [480/79], the Romans elected [Varr. 486] Spurius Cassius [Vicellinus] and Proculus Verginius Tricostus [Rutilus] consuls.[2] The 75th Olympiad, in which Astylos of Syracuse won the *stadion*, was celebrated at Elis.[3] It was in this year that Xerxes launched his expedition against Greece, for the following reason. [3] The Persian Mardonius was Xerxes' cousin and kinsman by marriage, and because of his intelligence and bravery, enjoyed high esteem among his fellow-countrymen. This man, being high in his own conceit and at the peak of his youthful

---

1. The embassy was to solicit Gelon's aid against Persia. Gelon had seized Syracuse in 491 and had immense reserves of wealth and manpower. He refused to help, ostensibly because denied a share in the command, in fact because he was already threatened by Carthage. His victory at Himera (480) made him virtual lord of all Sicily: 11.20–26.

2. For Diodorus' chronology, see Introduction, p. 4. The discrepancy between his archontic (correct) and his consular dates is due to his consulting consular Fasti that did not list various interregna when there were no consuls. Diodorus is thus here seven years ahead of the Roman (Varronian) chronology and so remains until ch. 41.1. From ch. 48.1 until ch. 91.1, the gap is reduced to six years, at which point it increases to seven once more.

3. The actual celebration of the 75th Olympiad coincided with the defense of Thermopylae (Hdt. 7.206), one alleged reason for Sparta's allies sending only advance parties up north at the time.

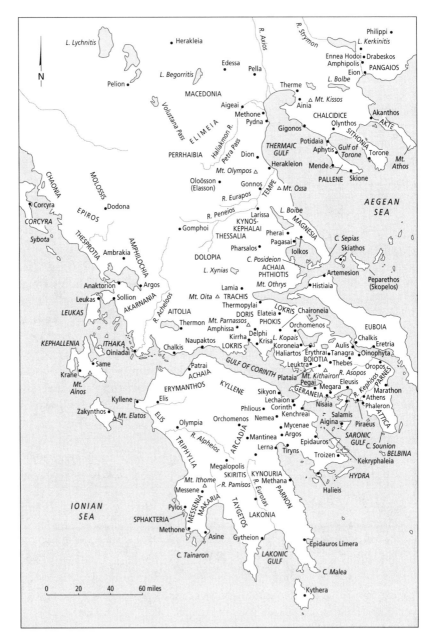

Map 11.1. Mainland Greece

strength, passionately desired to command a great military expedition. He therefore persuaded Xerxes that he should enslave the Greeks, who had always been in a state of enmity with the Persians. [4] Xerxes was convinced by him and determined to uproot all the Greeks from their homeland. He therefore sent envoys to the Carthaginians to propose a joint undertaking and made an agreement with them, that while he campaigned against the mainland Greeks of Hellas, the Carthaginians should simultaneously raise a large force and subdue those Greeks living in Sicily and southern Italy [>II.20.I]. [5] In compliance with this treaty, the Carthaginians raised large sums of money and hired mercenaries from Italy and Liguria as well as from Galatia and Spain, conscripting in addition to these forces citizen-soldiers from throughout Libya, as well as from Carthage itself. Finally, having spent three whole years in nonstop preparations, they mustered over 300,000 men and a fleet of two hundred vessels [Hdt. 7.165].

2. Xerxes meanwhile, vying with the vigorous efforts of the Carthaginians, surpassed them in all his preparations, as well as in the number of peoples over whom he ruled. He started building ships throughout the entire coastal region subject to him: in Egypt, Phoenicia, and Cyprus, as well as Cilicia, Pamphylia, and Pisidia, not to mention Lycia, Caria, Mysia, the Troad, the cities on the Hellespont, Bithynia, and Pontus. During the three years that he, like the Carthaginians, spent on his preparations, he put into commission more than 1,200 warships [Hdt. 7.89–95]. [2] In this task he was helped by his father Darius, who before he died had himself been assembling powerful armaments; for having been beaten by the Athenians at Marathon [490] (Datis being the commander on that occasion), he continued to bear a grudge against them because of their victory. Darius, however, when on the point of crossing [the Hellespont] against the Greeks, was caught short by death. Thereupon Xerxes, moved both by his father's plans and the recommendations of Mardonius, as was stated earlier, decided to make war on the Greeks.[4]

[3] When everything had been readied for his expedition, he ordered his admirals to assemble their fleets at Cyme and Phocaea, while he himself, after marshaling the infantry and cavalry contingents from all the satrapies, set out from Susa. On reaching Sardis, he dispatched heralds to Greece, with orders to visit every Greek city-state and demand earth and water of the in-

---

4. Marathon: Burn 236–257; Lazenby 45–80; Green 1996, 30–40. Darius' preparations up to his death in 486: Hdt. 7.1. Causes of Xerxes' invasion: Hdt. 7.8; Thuc. 1.18.2; Lys. 2.27.

habitants.[5] [4] He then divided his forces, sending ahead sufficiently large detachments both to bridge the Hellespont and to dig a channel through the Athos peninsula at its narrowest point: thus not only making the passage safe and short for his armies but also (he hoped) dumbfounding the Hellenes with the vastness of his achievements [Hdt. 7.22–24]. As a result, those who were detailed for the implementation of these tasks were soon well on the way to completing them, since such a swarm of laborers had been pressed into service. [5] When the Greeks became aware of the size of the Persian expeditionary force, they dispatched 10,000 hoplites into Thessaly to occupy the passes by Tempe: the Spartan contingent was commanded by Euaenetus, and the Athenian by Themistocles. These two dispatched envoys to the <neighboring>[6] states, asking them to send troops to share in the defense of the passes, since they were eager for every Greek city-state to take part in the defense and make common cause with them in this war against the Persians. [6] However, since both the Thessalians and most of the other Greeks who lived in the area of the passes had given earth and water to Xerxes' envoys at the time of their visit, the Greek generals, seeing that the defense of Tempe was a lost cause,[7] withdrew to their own territories.

3. At this point it may be profitable to identify those of the Hellenes who chose to side with the *barbaroi,* in the hope that the shame here visited upon them may, by the sheer force of its condemnation, deter any <future>[8] traitors to the cause of common freedom. [2] The Aenianians, Dolopians, Malians, Perrhaebians, and Magnesians were already lined up with the *barbaroi* while the defense force was still stationed at Tempe; the Phthiotic Achaeans, the Locrians, the Thessalians, and most of the Boeotians went over to them as

---

5. I.e., in token of their complete submission. Darius had made similar demands in 491 (Hdt. 6.48–49), when both the Athenians and the Spartans had killed the Persian heralds delivering the demand (Hdt. 7.133): Xerxes therefore excepted them from his new mission.

6. It seems clear from the context that the epithet *plésiochōrous* ("neighboring") has dropped out here: cf. 3.6.

7. The most pressing reason for withdrawal (Plut. *Them.* 7.1–2) was the discovery that the Tempe position could be turned via at least two passes, those of Petra and Volustana.

8. Vogel 1890, correctly in my opinion, emended the tense of the Greek verb from aorist (*genoménous*) to future (*genêsoménous*): the deterrent is aimed at future generations. But of course in Diodorus' day the Greeks had no "common freedom"; it looks as though Diodorus simply appropriated the opinion of his 4th-century source (probably Ephorus), for whom the phrase still had very real meaning, and there was urgent need for the deterrent.

soon as it had pulled out. [3] The Greeks who were in joint session at the Isthmus [of Corinth] voted to make those Hellenes who voluntarily supported the Persian cause pay a tithe to the gods once the war was won and to send envoys to those who were taking no action, exhorting them to join in the struggle for their common freedom. [4] Some of the latter wholeheartedly threw in their lot with the alliance; but others procrastinated for a considerable time, with concern for nothing but their own safety, and closely watching the outcome of the war.[9] The Argives sent ambassadors to the allied congress, announcing that they would join the alliance if offered a share of the command. [5] To whom the delegates responded in plain terms that if the Argives thought it worse to have a Greek general than a barbarian master, they were right to remain inactive; but if they aspired to take over the leadership of the Hellenes, they should (said the delegates) have performed deeds deserving of such an honor before applying for it. Afterwards, when ambassadors from Xerxes came to Greece demanding earth and water, all the states [included in the alliance] made very clear their enthusiasm for the cause of common freedom.

[6] When Xerxes was informed that the Hellespont had been bridged and a channel dug through Athos, he set out from Sardis and marched for the Hellespont; and when he reached Abydos, he led his forces across the connecting bridge into Europe. During his advance through Thrace, he recruited numerous troops from the Thracians themselves and other neighboring Greeks. [7] When he reached the city called Doriscus, he summoned his naval forces there, so that both fleet and army were assembled in one place. He also conducted a roll call of the entire expeditionary force: his land forces totaled more than 800,000 men, while the full count of his warships was more than 1,200, of which three hundred and twenty were Greek, with the Greeks supplying the crews and the Great King the vessels. All the rest were listed as *barbaroi*: of these the Egyptians supplied two hundred, the Phoenicians three hundred, the Cilicians eighty, the Pamphylians forty, the Lycians the same; and in addition to these the Carians provided eighty and the Cypriots one hundred and fifty. [8] Of the Greeks, the Dorians from the coast of Caria, together with the Rhodians and the Coans, sent forty ships; the Ionians, together with the Chians and Samians, provided one hundred, the Aeolians, together with the Lesbians and the men of Tenedos, forty; the Hellespontines and those settled along the coast of Pontus, eighty; and the islanders fifty, for the Great King had brought over to his side all islands within the area bounded by the Cyanean Rocks, Cape Sunium, and Cape Triopion. [9] The total I have enu-

---

9. In particular Corcyra (11.15.1) and Gelon (Hdt. 7.163–164).

merated consisted entirely of triremes; there were also 850 horse transports and 3,000 triakonters. Thus was Xerxes occupied with the tallying of his forces at Doriscus.[10]

4. When reports reached the Greek delegates [at the Isthmus] that the Persian forces were near, they voted for the immediate dispatch of the fleet to Artemisium in Euboea, seeing that this site was well placed for resisting the enemy, and of an adequate hoplite force to Thermopylae, to occupy the passes at their narrowest point ahead of the *barbaroi,* and block their further advance into Greece; for they were eager to include those who had chosen the cause of the Hellenes within their defense line and to safeguard their allies to the best of their ability.[11] [2] The commander-in-chief was Eurybiades the Lacedaemonian, and the contingent dispatched to Thermopylae was led by the Spartan king Leonidas, a man who prided himself on his own courage and generalship. When he took up his command, he proclaimed that only a thousand men should follow him on this campaign. [3] The ephors told him that this was altogether too small a force to take against a mighty armament, and ordered him to take more troops. To them he replied, behind closed doors, that for stopping the *barbaroi* getting through the passes they might be few, but for the action to which they were now bound they were many. [4] Finding his response enigmatic and unclear, the ephors demanded of him whether he thought he was leading his men on some unimportant mission. He replied that officially he might be leading them to the defense of the passes, but in fact to die for the cause of common freedom. If a thousand men were to march [north], Sparta would gain greater renown by their deaths; but if the Lacedaemonians took the field in full force, Lacedaemon would perish utterly, since not one man there would dare to cut and run in order to save his own life.[12] [5] The contingent was therefore made up of one thousand Lacedaemonians, including three hundred Spartiates [citizen-warriors]: these, together with three thousand other Greeks, were now ordered to Thermopylae.

---

10. Cf. the full account in Hdt. 7.53–100, with *CAH* 4 534–538.

11. Cf. Hdt. 7.175–177 and the Troezen Decree (Green 1996, 98–114): both make it clear that this was to be an amphibious holding operation.

12. Cf. Plut. *Mor.* 866B–D. This is clearly an ex post facto rationalization of Leonidas' sacrificial defeat after the pass had been turned. Leonidas in fact took an advance force of no more than 1,000 Lacedaemonians because it was thought that they, together with 3,000 Greek allies, would be sufficient to hold the pass till major reinforcements arrived. See Hdt. 7.205–206, and 202–203 for a breakdown of the contingents at Thermopylae.

[6] So Leonidas with his four thousand troops advanced to Thermopylae. Now the Locrians living near the passes had given earth and water to the Persians and were under an obligation to occupy these passes before the Greeks; but when they heard that Leonidas was coming to Thermopylae, they had second thoughts and went over to the Greeks. [7] Thus there also arrived at Thermopylae a thousand Locrians, the same number of Malians, not much short of a thousand Phocians, together with up to four hundred Thebans of the opposition (for the inhabitants of Thebes were split into opposing parties as regards their alliance with the Persians). These Greeks mustered with Leonidas, then, to the number stated above, busied themselves in and around Thermopylae, awaiting the arrival of the Persians.

5. After the tallying of his forces, Xerxes advanced with the entire land army, while as far as the city of Acanthus the whole fleet sailed alongside the line of march. From there the ships were piloted through the channel that had been dug for them, safely and speedily, into the sea beyond. [2] When [Xerxes] reached the Malian gulf, however, he found that the enemy had already occupied the passes. So, after enrolling the forces [waiting for him] there, he then summoned his allies from Europe, who were not much short of 200,000 men, so that the overall number of his troops was now not less than 1,000,000, not counting the naval complement. [3] The total figure of those who served as crews aboard his warships, together with those who transported his commissariat and other supplies, was at least as great as those already mentioned, so that the common reports of the multitudes assembled by Xerxes should occasion no surprise, with their claims that perennial rivers were drunk dry by the never-ending columns of troops [Hdt. 7.109] and that the seas were hidden by the sails of his vessels. Certainly the greatest military forces of any for which historical records have survived were those that marched with Xerxes.

[4] When the Persians had set up camp by the Sperchcius River, Xerxes sent messengers to Thermopylae, who were to find out [Hdt. 7.208] the attitude of the [Greeks there] to the war against him. He also instructed them to make the following proclamation: "King Xerxes orders everyone to surrender their arms, to go back under safe conduct to their native country, and to be allies of the Persians; and if they do this," the proclamation continued, "he will grant them more and better land than that they now possess." [5] But when Leonidas and his companions heard what the messengers had to say, they replied that if they were to be the King's allies, they would be more use to him fully armed, and if they were compelled to wage war against him, they would do battle for freedom all the better through keeping their weapons; and

as for the lands he promised to give them, it was a tradition with the Greeks to gain lands not by cowardice but by valor [>11.28.1–2].

6. Having heard from his messengers what replies the Greeks made, the King summoned Demaratus,[13] a Spartan who had come to [the Persian court] when exiled from his own country; and after a mocking dismissal of the replies, asked the Laconian: "Will these Hellenes flee faster than my horses? Will they dare to face such vast armaments in battle?" [2] To which, they say, Demaratus replied: "You yourself do not lack knowledge of Greek bravery, for you use Greek troops to reduce any of the *barbaroi* who revolt. Do not, therefore, suppose that men who fight better than Persians on behalf of your rule will be less ready to risk their lives against the Persians for the sake of their own freedom." But Xerxes laughed Demaratus to scorn, and ordered him to remain in attendance, so that he might watch the Lacedaemonians in full flight.

[3] Xerxes then advanced with his forces against the Greeks at Thermopylae. He stationed the Medes ahead of all other peoples, either because he ranked them first for courage or through a desire to destroy them all; for the Medes still retained their pride, since it was only recently [550/49] that their ancestral supremacy had been toppled [by Cyrus the Great]. [4] It so happened that there were among the Medes brothers and sons of those who had died at Marathon; Xerxes made this fact known to them, in the belief that they would thus <be sharpened in their desire>[14] for vengeance against the Greeks. So the Medes, after being deployed in this manner, fell upon those defending Thermopylae; but Leonidas was well prepared, and massed the Greeks in the narrowest part of the pass.

7. A fierce battle then[15] took place. Since the *barbaroi* had the Great King as observer of their fighting spirit, while the Greeks were mindful of their freedom and were being urged on in the conflict by Leonidas, the result was a quite extraordinary struggle. [2] Since the battle line was shoulder to shoulder, the fighting hand-to-hand, and the combatants in dense array, for

---

13. For Demaratus, Eurypontid king of Sparta (reigned 515–491) and the circumstances of his exile from Sparta on a trumped-up charge of illegitimacy organized by his Agiad co-king and rival Cleomenes, see Hdt. 6.50–70.

14. The Greek of 6.4 is badly corrupted in Diodorus' MSS: I follow Haillet's very persuasive reconstruction.

15. According to Hdt. 7.210.1, only after Xerxes had waited four days, in the expectation that the Greeks would cut and run.

a long time the issue hung in the balance. But the Greeks had the advantage, both in their bravery and in the great size of their shields, and so the Medes were gradually forced back: large numbers of them were killed, and not a few wounded. A contingent of Cissians and Sacae, specially picked for valor, who had been posted as reinforcements for the Medes, now took their place in the front line. Being fresh troops joining battle against exhausted opponents, for a little while they held their own; but Leonidas' men inflicted heavy casualties on them and pressed them hard, so that they too gave way. [3] The reason was that the *barbaroi* employed small shields and targets, which gave them an advantage in open terrain, allowing them to move easily. On a narrow front, however, they found it difficult to wound foemen who stood close-packed side by side, their huge shields protecting their entire bodies, while they themselves, at a disadvantage because of the lightness of their protective armor, suffered countless wounds.

[4] In the end Xerxes, seeing the whole region around the passes strewn with corpses, and the *barbaroi* failing to match the fighting spirit of the Greeks, ordered up those picked Persian troops known as the Immortals, who were reputed to rank first among their fellow-soldiers for bravery in action. But when these too retreated after no more than a brief period of resistance, and night was falling, they broke off the battle, with heavy casualties among the *barbaroi,* but only light Greek losses.

8. The next day Xerxes, since the battle had turned out contrary to his expectations, selected from all the peoples in his army those with the highest reputation for courage and daring. He then made them a speech, indicating the high expectations he had of them, and informing them that if they forced the entrance to the pass, he would give them gifts of great note, but that the penalty for retreat would be death. [2] So these troops launched a violent massed charge against the Greeks; but Leonidas and his men closed ranks, making a solid wall of their defense line, and threw themselves into the struggle with a will. So great, indeed, was their zeal that the customary rotation of troops out of the front line no longer happened: they all stayed in place, and by their unbroken endurance took out many of these elite *barbaroi.* [3] The whole day long they continued in this struggle, vying one with another: for the older soldiers challenged the vigor of the young men in their prime, while the young in turn set themselves to equal the experience and reputation of their elders. When, finally, Xerxes' elite troops too broke and fled, those *barbaroi* holding the support line formed a barrier and would not let the elite troops withdraw, so that they were forced to turn back and renew the fight [Hdt. 7.212].

[4] The King was now at a complete loss and convinced that not a man of his would dare to join battle again; but at this point there approached him a Trachinian, a native of those parts, who was familiar with the local mountainous terrain. When he came into Xerxes' presence, this man offered to guide the Persians along a certain narrow and precipitous path, which would bring those accompanying him out in the rear of Leonidas' position: the defenders, being thus surrounded and penned in, could then be destroyed without trouble.[16] [5] The King was beside himself with joy, loaded the Trachinian with rewards, and dispatched a force of 20,000 troops with him under cover of darkness.[17] But a man in the Persian camp named Tyrrhastiadas, a Cymaean by birth, a person of high principles and upright conduct, deserted from the Persian encampment that night, went to Leonidas' position, and told the Greeks (who had known nothing of it) about the Trachinian's action.

9. The Greeks, on hearing this, held a meeting about midnight to take counsel concerning the dangers now threatening them. Some, then, declared that they should abandon the pass right away and save themselves by falling back on their allies, since if they stayed where they were, they had no hope of survival. But Leonidas, the Lacedaemonian king, who was ambitious to win high glory for himself and his Spartiate warriors, ordered all other Greeks to pull out and save themselves, so that they might fight with their fellow-Hellenes in battles yet to come; but the Lacedaemonians themselves, he said, must stay behind and not abandon the defense of the pass, since it was fitting that the leaders of Hellas should be prepared to die while striving for the prize of honor.[18] [2] So all the rest departed at once, leaving Leonidas and his fellow-citizens to perform heroic and incredible deeds. Though the Lacedaemonians were few in number—of the rest Leonidas had retained only the Thespians—so that he had not more than five hundred men with him all told, he was ready to face death for the sake of Hellas.[19]

[3] After this the Persians accompanying the Trachinian, having made their

---

16. Hdt. 7.213–214 names the informant as Ephialtes of Trachis. The mountain path, known today as Anopaea (and for the most part neither narrow nor precipitous), began at the Asopus River and ended at Alpenus: Hdt. 7.215–216; cf. Paus. 1.4.2, 10.2–8.

17. These were the Immortals, under Hydarnes: 10,000 at full strength, though almost certainly, given the topography, it was a much smaller body that actually went over the mountain.

18. Diodorus omits any mention of the Phocians detached to guard the summit of Anopaea (Hdt. 7.217).

19. Herodotus (7.222) states that the Thebans as well as the Thespians remained. Thus the total force was not five hundred but nearer nine hundred to a thousand.

way round over very difficult terrain, suddenly caught Leonidas and his men from the rear. The Greeks abandoned any thought of saving themselves and instead opted for glory, with one voice calling on their commander to lead them against the enemy before the Persians learned that their own troops' encircling strategy had succeeded. [4] Leonidas welcomed his soldiers' readiness and told them to make a quick breakfast, since they would be dining in Hades. He himself took nourishment in accordance with the orders he had given, thinking that by so doing he would be able to husband his strength for a longer period and better endure in battle. Then, when they had hastily refreshed themselves and all were ready, he ordered his troops to make a raid on the Persian camp, killing all they met, and to aim for the Great King's own pavilion.

10. So they, in accordance with his commands, formed a tight column under cover of darkness and charged into the Persian encampment, with Leonidas himself at their head. The *barbaroi,* taken by surprise and not knowing what was happening, with loud shouts came running pell-mell from their tents: getting the idea that the contingent with the Trachinian had been destroyed, and the Greeks' entire force was now upon them, they panicked. [2] As a result, many fell victims to Leonidas and his men, and many more perished at the hands of their own people, who, failing to recognize them, took them for enemies, since the darkness made correct recognition impossible. The resultant confusion, which spread through the entire encampment, understandably caused considerable slaughter: with no orders from a commanding officer, no demands for the password, and a complete failure to restore reasoned thinking, the circumstances did not permit careful scrutiny, and so they kept killing one another. [3] Thus, if the King had stayed in his royal pavilion, he himself might easily have been killed by the Greeks, and the entire war would have reached a quick conclusion; but in the event, before the Greeks burst into the pavilion and slaughtered almost everyone they found still there, Xerxes had hastened out to confront the uproar. [4] So long as it remained dark, they (very understandably) ranged through the length and breadth of the encampment looking for Xerxes; but when day dawned and the whole situation became clear, the Persians, noting that the Greeks were few in number, made light of them.[20] Yet they still did not confront them face to face, through fear of their valor, but instead grouped themselves on their

20. The night raid described by Diodorus is absent from Herodotus, who places the "rain of arrows" at the Hot Gates, but confirmed in detail by Plutarch (*Mor.* 866A) and also by Justin (2.11.12–18). Most scholars dismiss it as a fabrication.

flanks and in rear of them, from where with a rain of arrows and javelins they slew them all. Such, then, was the end met by those who guarded the pass of Thermopylae with Leonidas.

11. Who would not be amazed by these men's prowess? With united determination they did not abandon the post to which Greece had assigned them, but willingly gave up their own lives for the common salvation of the Greeks, and chose rather to die with honor rather than live in ignominy. Nor could anyone doubt the sheer consternation experienced by the Persians. [2] For which of the *barbaroi* could have grasped what had taken place? Who could have foreseen that a group numbering five hundred would dare to attack a million? As a result, what man of a later age would not aspire to emulate the courageous achievement of these warriors? Rendered powerless by the magnitude of the crisis, they may have been physically beaten down but remained unconquered in spirit; and thus alone among those of whom record survives they have become more renowned in defeat than all who have won even the finest victories. Brave men should be judged not by the outcome of their deeds but rather by their intentions; [3] for the first is governed by chance, whereas it is right intention that wins esteem. Who would reckon any men braver than these, since though not numerically equaling a thousandth part of the enemy, they nevertheless dared to set their valor against such incredible multitudes? With no expectation of defeating so many tens of thousands, they still reckoned on surpassing all their predecessors in courage; and though they were fighting the *barbaroi,* they reckoned the true contest, with the prize for valor, was in competition with all those who had ever excited amazement on account of their bravery. [4] For they alone of those commemorated down the ages chose to preserve the traditions of their city-state rather than their own lives: not resentful that so great a peril hung over them but convinced that for those who practice valor, nothing could be more desirable than exposure to contests of this kind. [5] Moreover, anyone who argued that these men were also more responsible for achieving the freedom of the Greeks than the victors in subsequent battles against Xerxes would be in the right of it; for when the *barbaroi* recalled their deeds they were terror-struck, whereas the Greeks were encouraged to attempt similar acts of bravery [>16.2–3].

[6] Generally speaking, these men alone of their predecessors [and contemporaries] were immortalized because of their exceptional valor. As a result, not only historians but also numerous poets hymned their courageous deeds, including Simonides, the lyric poet, who composed a celebratory ode (*enkômion*) worthy of their valor, from which these lines are taken:

Of those who died at Thermopylae
renowned is the fortune, noble the fate:
Their grave's an altar, their memorial our mourning,
     their fate our praise.
Such a shroud neither decay
nor all-conquering time shall destroy.
This sepulcher of brave men has taken the high
renown of Hellas for its fellow-occupant, as witness
Leonidas, Sparta's king who left behind a great
memorial of valor, everlasting renown.

12. Now that we have discoursed sufficiently on the theme of these men's valor, we shall continue our narrative from the point at which we abandoned it. By gaining control of the passes in the way previously described, which gave him (as the proverb has it) a "Cadmean" victory only,[21] Xerxes had caused very few enemy casualties, while losing countless numbers of his own troops. So, having thus obtained control of the passes with his land forces, he decided to make trial now of his navy, and force the issue at sea.[22] [2] He therefore promptly sent for Megabates, the high admiral of the fleet, and ordered him to sail out against the Greek squadrons: his instructions were to make every effort, with all the ships at his disposal, to force the Greeks into a sea battle. [3] Megabates, in accordance with the King's briefing, set sail from Pydna in Macedonia towards the promontory of Magnesia known as Cape Sepias. At this point a huge storm got up, and he lost more than three hundred warships, as well as a large number of horse transports and other vessels. When the storm died down, he put to sea again, making for Aphetae in Magnesia. From there he ordered out two hundred triremes, instructing the captains to follow a roundabout sailing route, keeping Euboea to starboard, and thus to outflank the enemy.

[4] The Greeks were anchored at Artemisium in Euboea and had a total of two hundred and eighty triremes, of which one hundred and forty were Athe-

---

21. I.e., a victory in which the victor lost as much as the defeated, the name being taken from the fratricidal combat of the Seven Against Thebes (cf. Aeschylus' play of the same name), in which both Eteocles and Polynices, sons of Oedipus and thus descended from Cadmus, died.

22. In fact, the war at sea had been going on concurrently with the assault on the pass, and (Hdt. 8.15; Lys. 2.31) the battles of Artemisium and Thermopylae traditionally took place on the same day.

nian, and the remainder contributed by the other Greeks. Their admiral was Eurybiades the Spartan, but it was Themistocles the Athenian who ordered the disposition of the fleet, since on account of his sharp intelligence and strategic skill, he had the confidence not only of the Greeks throughout the fleet but also of Eurybiades himself: he was the man to whom everyone looked for guidance and whose word they eagerly accepted. [5] When a council of ships' captains was held to discuss naval strategy, all the rest advocated holding station and waiting for the enemy to attack; only Themistocles expressed the opposite opinion, demonstrating that it would be to their advantage to sail out against the enemy in a single body, with the whole fleet. He argued that in this way they would prevail, since they would be going in close formation against an enemy whose line must inevitably be broken and in disarray, with squadrons emerging from a number of harbors at some distance one from the other. Finally, the Greeks accepted Themistocles' advice and sailed against the enemy with their entire fleet.[23] [6] Now since the *barbaroi* did indeed have to put out from numerous separate harbors, to begin with Themistocles engaged with scattered groups of Persian [ships], sank a good number of them, and forced not a few others to turn tail, pursuing them landwards. Later, however, when the entire fleet had gathered, a hard-fought battle ensued: each side gained the upper hand with part of their complement, yet neither could win a total victory, and so as night fell, they broke off the engagement.

13. After this sea battle a great storm arose, which destroyed a large number of vessels riding at anchor outside the harbor, so that it seemed as though divine providence was taking the side of the Greeks, and by reducing the numbers of the *barbaroi's* fleet was making the Greek forces a fair match for them and a worthy opponent in any sea battle. Consequently, the Greeks became steadily bolder, while the *barbaroi* faced each successive conflict with increasing timidity. Despite this, when they had recovered from the effects of the shipwreck, they put out against the enemy with their whole [surviving] fleet. [2] The Greeks, their numbers now augmented by fifty [new] Athenian triremes, moved into position facing the *barbaroi*. The naval engagement that followed much resembled the skirmishes at Thermopylae; for the Persians were determined to force back the Greeks and win passage through the Euripus channel, while the Greeks were blocking the narrows and fighting to

---

23. Cf. Hdt. 8.4–9; Plut. *Them.* 7.4–6. Intelligence reconnaissance showed some Persian confusion after the storm and a reduction of strength with the detachment of two hundred triremes to outflank Euboea: these were decisive factors in shaping Greek strategy.

safeguard their allies in Euboea and beyond. A fierce battle took place, with heavy loss of vessels on both sides, and only the onset of darkness forced them to put about and return to their respective harbors. In both engagements, as is reported, the prize for conspicuous bravery went, on the Greek side, to the Athenians, and on that of the *barbaroi* to the men of Sidon.

[3] After this the Greeks, on hearing what had happened at Thermopylae, and learning besides that the Persians were advancing on Athens overland, lost heart. They therefore sailed away to Salamis and took up station there.[24] [4] Meanwhile, the Athenians, perceiving that the whole population of Athens was in imminent danger, embarked on boats their women and children, together with all useful objects for which there was room, and conveyed them to Salamis.[25] [5] The Persian admiral, on learning of the enemy's retreat, sailed for Euboea with his entire complement, where he stormed the city of the Histiaians, after which he looted and ravaged their territory.

14. Simultaneously with these events, Xerxes struck camp and marched from Thermopylae, advancing through the territory of the Phocians, sacking their cities and destroying their rural holdings. The Phocians had thrown in their lot with the Greeks, but now, seeing they were not strong enough to offer resistance, they abandoned all their cities en masse and sought refuge in the rugged terrain around Mt. Parnassos. [2] After this the King traversed the territory of the Dorians and did it no harm, since they were the Persians' allies. He left there one part of his army, with orders to march on Delphi, burn the precinct of Apollo, and pillage the votive offerings, while he himself with the rest of the *barbaroi*'s host advanced into Boeotia and set up camp there. [3] Those detailed for the robbing of the oracle had got as far as the temple of Athena of the Foreshrine [*Pronaia*] when a heavy rainstorm, accompanied by incessant thunder and lightning, unexpectedly fell from heaven. What was more, the tempest broke loose huge rocks and dropped them on the *barbaroi*'s encampment: as a result, many of the Persians perished, and all the survivors, terror-struck at this intervention by the gods, fled the region [Hdt. 8.25–34]. [4] Thus the oracle at Delphi, by some divine dispensation, escaped being plundered. The Delphians, wanting to leave for later genera-

---

24. With the amphibious Thermopylae-Artemisium line broken, Salamis was the prearranged fallback and second line of defense. Cf. Green 1996, 144–148.

25. The Troezen Decree makes clear that this main evacuation had been ordered, and taken place, two months earlier, in June: what happened now (? 24 Aug.) was a final emergency exodus of those still remaining. Cf. Hdt. 8.40–41; Plut. *Them.* 10.1–4; Green 1996, 97–105, 156–161.

tions an eternal memorial of this epiphany of the gods, set up a trophy by the temple of Athena of the Foreshrine, on which they carved the following elegiac quatrain:

> In memory of defensive action and as witness to victory
> the Delphians set me up, in gratitude to Zeus
> and Phoebus, for their repulse of the Medes' city-sacking column
> and rescue of the bronze-crowned shrine.

[5] Xerxes meanwhile, on his march through Boeotia, ravaged the territory of the Thespians and burned Plataea, which was empty of inhabitants, since the population of both cities had fled en masse into the Peloponnese. After this he pressed on into Attica, ravaging the countryside, burning the temples of the gods, and razing Athens to the ground. While the King was occupied with these matters, his fleet sailed from Euboea to Attica, sacking both Euboea itself and the Attic coast as it went.

15. About this same time, the Corcyraeans, who had fitted out sixty triremes, were waiting off the Peloponnese. The reason they themselves give for this is that they were unable to round Cape Malea; but according to certain historians, they were watching to see how the war turned out, so that, if the Persians won, they might offer them earth and water, whereas if the Greeks secured the victory, Corcyra would be credited with having offered them support. [2] The Athenians waiting on Salamis, however, when they saw Attica ablaze and heard that the precinct of Athena had been destroyed, were terribly disheartened. (Considerable panic likewise possessed those other Greeks, fugitives from every quarter, who were now crowded into the Peloponnese.) They therefore decided that all those appointed to commands should hold a joint meeting and take counsel as to what kind of site would best suit their plans for a naval engagement. [3] After many and various arguments had been put forward, the Peloponnesians—thinking solely of their own security—said that the struggle should take place at the Isthmus, since it had been strongly fortified, and thus, if the sea battle produced any setback, the losers would be able to take refuge in the Peloponnese, the handiest sanctuary available. On the other hand, if they boxed themselves up in the little island of Salamis, they would be beset by dangers from which it would be hard to rescue them. [4] Themistocles, however, urged that the naval battle should take place off Salamis, arguing that in the narrows those with fewer ships to deploy would have a great advantage over a vast fleet. He also demonstrated, in general terms, that the Isthmus would be an altogether unsuitable venue for this sea battle; for there the fight would take place in open waters, and

the Persians, having ample room to maneuver, would easily overcome a small flotilla with their countless vessels. By similarly advancing many other relevant arguments, he persuaded everyone to vote in support of the plan he had recommended.[26]

16. When finally a general decision had been taken to fight at sea off Salamis, the Greeks began making preparations to face the Persians and the challenge of battle. Eurybiades therefore, taking Themistocles with him, undertook the task of exhorting the crews and filling them with zest for the impending struggle. But the crews refused to pay any attention; in fact, since they were all in a state of panic because of the size of the Persian armaments, not a single man took the slightest notice of the commanders, since every one of them was desperate to sail away to the Peloponnese. [2] The Hellenic land forces likewise were equally terrified by the enemy's vast armaments: the loss at Thermopylae of their most distinguished fighters utterly dismayed them, while the disasters taking place in Attica before their very eyes reduced the Greeks to a state of deep despair. [3] The delegates to the Greek congress, observing the confusion of the masses and the general atmosphere of panic, voted to build a wall across the Isthmus. The work was soon completed, due to the eagerness and the vast numbers of those taking part in it. However, while the Peloponnesians were reinforcing this wall, which stretched for forty *stadioi* [about 4½ miles], from Lechaeum to Cenchreae, those waiting on events at Salamis, together with the entire fleet, were so demoralized that they no longer obeyed the orders given by their officers.

17. Themistocles, seeing that the naval commander Eurybiades could do nothing to overcome the state of mind of his forces, but also that the cramped space on Salamis might contribute largely to achieving victory, devised the following scheme. He persuaded a certain man[27] to approach Xerxes in the guise of a deserter and assure him, as certain knowledge, that the ships at Salamis were going to pull out from there and reassemble at the Isthmus. [2] So the King, believing him because of the plausibility of the news he

---

26. On this crucial debate, cf. Hdt. 8.56–63 and Plut. *Them.* 11.2–12.3. Diodorus alone mentions here the (very cogent) argument about the potential danger of being cut off on Salamis, though Herodotus (8.70) makes clear that he was well aware of it; he also emphasizes that there was general agreement on retreating to the Isthmus before the meeting was even held.

27. Sicinnus, the school escort (*paidagōgos*) of Themistocles' children. The trick is also reported by Aesch. *Pers.* 355–360, Hdt. 8.75–76.1, and Plut. *Them.* 12.3–5.

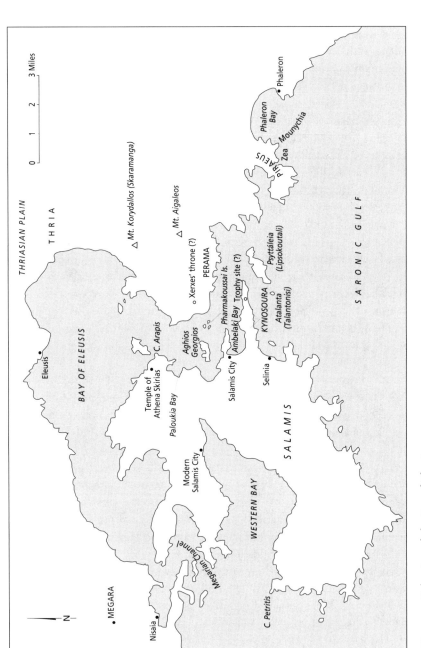

Map II.2. *Salamis and the Bay of Eleusis*

brought, hurried to prevent the Greeks' naval forces from linking up with the troops they had stationed ashore. To this end he at once dispatched the Egyptian squadron, with orders to block the channel between Salamis and the territory of the Megarid.[28] The remaining bulk of his fleet he ordered to Salamis, with instructions to join battle with the enemy and decide the issue at sea. His triremes were stationed in successive ethnic groups, so that a common language and mutual recognition might encourage them to help one another. [3] This deployment of the fleet was so arranged that the right wing was held by the Phoenicians, and the left by those Greeks who were fighting with the Persians.

The commanders of the Ionian squadrons sent a Samian over to the Greeks to inform them of all Xerxes' decisions and of his entire battle plan, and to say that they, the Ionians, planned to desert from the *barbaroi* during the course of the battle. [4] When the Samian had swum across unobserved, and had briefed Eurybiades on these matters, Themistocles, overjoyed that his stratagem had worked out as planned, rousingly encouraged the crews for the fight ahead, while the Greeks as a whole took heart from the news about the Ionians; and though circumstances were forcing them to fight at sea against their own inclinations, they came down readily from Salamis to the shore to engage in this naval battle.[29]

18. Eurybiades, Themistocles, and their staff finally completed the disposition of the [Greek] forces. The Athenians and Lacedaemonians held the left wing, which would thus be matched against the Phoenicians; for the Phoenicians enjoyed a sizable advantage both on account of their numbers and through the experience in naval matters, which they had from their ancestors. [2] The right wing went to the crews of Aegina and Megara, since these were reputed to be the most skilled sailors after the Athenians and would, it was thought, evince the best fighting spirit, since alone of the Greeks they would have no refuge anywhere should there be any setback during the battle. The center was held by the rest of the Greek forces.

So they sailed out drawn up in this manner and occupied the strait between Salamis and the shrine of Heracles; [3] and the King gave the order to

---

28. Diodorus' phrasing somewhat obscures Xerxes' strategy, in the light of Sicinnus' message, which was also to bottle up the Greek fleet in the Bay of Eleusis and prevent it escaping (cf. Hdt. 8.76; Aesch. *Pers.* 363–371; Plut. *Them.* 12.5). The other exits were at either end of the island of Psyttáleia (modern Lipsokoutali): see Hdt. 8.76 passim.

29. The story of the Samian deserter is unique to Diodorus. We do not know his source for it: it could well be true, with the Ionians hedging their bets on the outcome.

his admiral to sail against the enemy, while he himself moved to a spot directly opposite Salamis, from where he could observe the development of the battle. [4] As they sailed, the Persians could, to begin with, hold their battle line, since they had ample room; but when they came to the narrows, they were forced to pull out some of their ships, and this caused considerable confusion. [5] The admiral, who was ahead of the line and leading it, and had been the first to engage, was killed after putting up a gallant fight. When his ship sank, there was chaos in the *barbaroi*'s fleet, since those giving orders were many, but there was no agreement over the commands. In consequence, they halted the advance, backed off, and began to retreat towards open water. [6] The Athenians, perceiving the confusion among the *barbaroi,* drove ahead against the foe, ramming some of their vessels and shearing off the oar banks of others; and since their rowers could now no longer operate, many of the Persian triremes turned broadside on to the [enemy's] rams, and in consequence, again and again suffered crippling damage. Because of this they stopped backing water, instead putting about and retreating in headlong flight.

19. While the Phoenician and Cypriot vessels were being worsted by the Athenians, those of the Cilicians and Pamphylians—as well as the Lycian squadron, stationed in their rear—to begin with offered a strong resistance; but when they saw the most powerful ships in retreat, they too abandoned the struggle. [2] On the other wing a fierce engagement took place and for some while the battle hung in the balance; but the Athenians, once they had driven the Phoenicians and Cypriots ashore, turned back and pressed the *barbaroi* hard, so that they broke line and fled, losing many of their ships. [3] With such tactics, then, the Hellenes triumphed, winning a most notable naval victory over the *barbaroi.* During this battle forty Greek vessels were lost, but of the Persian fleet over two hundred, not counting those captured with their crews.[30]

[4] The King, being thus worsted against his expectations, put to death the most culpable of those Phoenicians who had first fled and threatened to visit the rest with the punishment they merited. The Phoenicians, scared by his threats, initially sought refuge further down the coast of Attica and then, as soon as it was dark, hoisted sail for Asia. [5] Now Themistocles, who was credited with responsibility for the victory, thought up another stratagem no less

---

30. The battle began early in the morning and lasted all day (Aesch. *Pers.* 384–386, 428; Hdt. 8.83). It remained long in doubt. Diodorus omits the hard-fought sweep of the island of Psyttáleia by Aristeides and the hoplites: Aesch. *Pers.* 445–471; Hdt. 8.95; Plut. *Arist.* 9.1–2.

ingenious: since the Greeks were scared of engaging in a land battle against such vast numbers of Persians, by the following device he greatly reduced the size of the Persian army. He sent his own sons' school-escort (<17.1) to Xerxes, with the message that the Greeks intended to sail [to the Hellespont] and break down his bridge [of boats]. [6] Consequently, the King, convinced by this report because of its plausibility, became panic-stricken in case he might be cut off—with the Greeks now dominant at sea—from his line of retreat back to Asia. He therefore resolved to make the crossing from Europe into Asia with all speed, leaving Mardonius in Greece with the pick of his infantry and cavalry, to the total number of not less than 400,000. In this way Themistocles, by employing the two ruses described, brought substantial benefits to the Greeks. Such was the course of events in Greece during this period.

20. Now that we have discoursed at sufficient length on events in Europe, we shall transfer our narrative to the affairs of another nation. The Carthaginians had reached an agreement with the Persians to reduce the Greeks in Sicily at the same time [as Xerxes was invading the Greek mainland], and had amassed large quantities of such materials as were useful for fighting a war.[31] And when all their preparations were complete, they chose as general Hamilcar, on the grounds that no other man among them enjoyed a higher reputation.[32] [2] He took over the command of vast forces, both naval and military, and sailed from Carthage with an army of not less than 300,000 men and more than two hundred warships, quite apart from a fleet of over 3,000 merchantmen for transporting supplies. While crossing the Libyan Sea, he was hit by a storm and lost the craft transporting his horses and chariots. When he reached port in the Sicilian harbor of Panormus,[33] he had, he said, concluded the war; for he had been afraid that the sea would save the Siceliotes from peril. [3] He spent three days resting his troops and repairing the damage that the storm had done to his ships and then advanced with his entire force against Himera, while the fleet accompanied him off shore. When he reached

---

31. Sicily at this time was divided into pro-Carthaginian (Selinous, Himera) and anti-Carthaginian (Syracuse, Acragas) tyrannies. Carthage already held several cities, including Panormus and Motyon, in the north and west of the island, and was eager to extend her power eastward, not least for commercial reasons.

32. Hamilcar (Abd-Melkart) was the grandson of Mago, the founder of the Magonid dynasty, and either king himself or a *suffete* (elected ruler, judge), noted for his "manly courage" and for his Syracusan mother: Hdt. 7.166.

33. Diodorus (himself a Sicilian) elsewhere (22.10.4) describes Panormus (Palermo) as "the finest harbor in Sicily."

the aforementioned city, he set up two encampments, one for his land forces, the other for the navy. All the warships he hauled ashore and surrounded with a deep ditch and wooden palisade. He reinforced the army's encampment by relocating it to face the city and extending it along the [line of the] naval defense works as far as the surrounding hills. [4] In general, after occupying the entire western quarter, he unloaded all the supplies from the merchant-men and then immediately sent them off again, with orders to bring grain and other goods from Libya and Sardinia. [5] He himself then took the pick of his troops and marched on the city. He routed those of the Himerans who ventured out against him, killing large numbers of them. This caused panic among the city's inhabitants. It also scared Theron, the ruler of Acragas, who with a fair-sized force was standing guard over Himera, into sending a hasty message to Syracuse, asking Gelon for immediate reinforcements.[34]

21. Gelon had similarly put his forces on the alert, and when he learned of the Himerans' plight, he force-marched from Syracuse, at the head of not less than 50,000 infantry and over 5,000 cavalry. He covered the distance in short order, and as he approached the Himerans' city he gave heart to those who until then had been dumbfounded by the might of the Carthaginians. [2] He began by making his own encampment, adapting it to the terrain outside the city, and fortifying it with a deep ditch and a palisade. He also dispatched his entire cavalry force against a number of the enemy who were roaming the region in search of easy plunder. These horsemen, appearing out of the blue to troops scattered over the countryside in no kind of order, rounded up as many prisoners as each could drive before him. When more than 10,000 captives had been thus shepherded to the city, Gelon was in high regard, and the inhabitants of Himera began to despise the enemy. [3] Gelon followed up what he had already achieved by unblocking all the gateways that Theron and his men had previously bricked up out of fear, and even built some extra ones that it might be handy to utilize in an emergency.

In general, then, Gelon—a man of outstanding generalship and subtle insight—at once began looking for a way in which, without risk to his own troops, he might outwit the *barbaroi* and utterly destroy their power. His own ingenuity was greatly helped by a stroke of pure accidental luck, through the following circumstances. [4] He had planned to set fire to the enemy's fleet;

---

34. Theron had been tyrant of Acragas (modern Agrigento) since 489. About 483/2 he drove out Terillus, then tyrant of Himera, and took over the city, aligning it with Syra-cuse. This was the immediate excuse for a Carthaginian invasion, since Terillus had been Hamilcar's guest-friend and appealed to him.

and while Hamilcar was busy in the naval encampment with the preparations for a lavish sacrifice to Poseidon, horsemen arrived from the countryside, bringing to Gelon a courier, who was delivering letters from the people of Selinos. In these letters it was written that they would send their cavalry on the day that Hamilcar in his letter had asked them to. [5] Since the day was that same one on which Hamilcar intended to offer up his sacrifice, when it arrived, Gelon sent out cavalry of his own, with orders to skirt round the immediate area and to ride up to the naval encampment at dawn, as though they were the allies sent from Selinos. Once they were inside the wooden stockade, they were to kill Hamilcar and set fire to the ships. He also sent scouts up into the hills overlooking [the city], with instructions to give the signal when they saw the horsemen actually inside the stockade. He himself mustered his forces by dawn and waited for the signal from the scouts.

22. So at sunrise the cavalry detachment rode up to the Carthaginians' naval encampment and were admitted by the guards, as supposed allies. They then galloped across to where Hamilcar was occupied with his sacrifice, killed him, and set the ships ablaze, at which point the scouts gave the signal, and Gelon advanced with his entire army, in close order, against the Carthaginian encampment. [2] The leaders of the Phoenicians in the camp at first led out their troops to resist the Siceliotes, and when the lines met, they fought fiercely. At the same time trumpets in both camps gave the signal for battle, and shouting arose from both sides in turn, each determined to outdo their adversary in the volume and loudness of their cheers. [3] The death toll was heavy, and the battle was surging to and fro: then suddenly the flames from the ships shot high into the air, and reports began to circulate of the general's death. At this the Greeks took fresh courage, and, their spirits raised both by these reports and by their hopes for victory, they assailed the *barbaroi* with increasing fury, while the Carthaginians, disheartened and giving up all hope of victory, turned tail and fled.

[4] Since Gelon had given orders to take no one alive, a mass slaughter of the fugitives ensued: before it was over no less than 150,000 of them had been butchered. The remainder who escaped got to a stronghold where at first they held out against their attackers, but the site they had occupied was waterless, and the pressure of thirst forced them to surrender to the victors. [5] Gelon, victorious in a most extraordinary battle, won first and foremost by his own generalship, gained a reputation that spread abroad not only among the Siceliotes but among all other [Greeks] as well; [6] for there is record of no man before him who employed such a stratagem, or who slew more *barbaroi* in a single onset, or took so vast a number of prisoners.

23. As a result, many writers compare this battle with that fought by the Greeks at Plataea [>34–36], and Gelon's strategy with the clever ideas of Themistocles; and because of both men's surpassing excellence, some allot first place to the one and some to the other. [2] And indeed, at a time when both Greeks and Greek Sicilians were dumbfounded by the vast size of the *barbaroi*'s forces, it was the Sicilians whose earlier victory raised the spirits of the Greek mainlanders when they heard of Gelon's triumph. As for those who held supreme command on each occasion, in the case of the Persians the Great King escaped, and a great host with him; but in that of the Carthaginians, not only did the commanding general perish but all who took part in that campaign were butchered too, and, as report has it, not a man was left alive to carry the news back to Carthage. [3] What is more, of the two most distinguished Greek commanders, Pausanias and Themistocles, the first was put to death by his own countrymen because of his arrogant ambition and treasonable dealings, while the second was forced out of Greece altogether and sought refuge with Xerxes, his most determined enemy, on whose bounty he lived until his dying day.[35] Gelon, on the other hand, after the battle stood ever higher in the esteem of the Syracusans, grew old in his kingship, and died with his popularity still undiminished. So powerful was the goodwill felt by the citizens towards him that the rule of his house continued under three further relatives.

However, now that these men's well-justified renown has been augmented by befitting encomia from us, we shall return to the continuation of our previous narrative.

24. Gelon's victory happened to take place on the same day as Leonidas' final battle against Xerxes at Thermopylae, as though heaven had deliberately arranged for the finest victory and the most famous of defeats to take place simultaneously.[36] [2] After the battle outside Himera, twenty warships managed to make their escape, being a detachment that Hamilcar had <not> hauled ashore but kept available for routine errands. For this reason, though virtually all his men were either killed or taken prisoner, these vessels put out to sea before they were noticed. They took aboard numerous fugitives, however, and being thus overburdened, they ran into a storm and were all lost.

---

35. Diodorus clearly has in mind here Thucydides' famous excursus on Pausanias and Themistocles, 1.128–138. Cf. his own excursuses at 44.1–47.8, 54.1–59.4.

36. Such coincidences are not impossible, but we should be wary of them: the "myth of simultaneity" was popular in antiquity and was used chronographically to boost the standing of the colonial Greek West in relation to the mother country. See Feeney, 49.

Only a few survivors got safely home to Carthage in a small skiff, and broke the news to the citizen body with a brief statement, to the effect that all who had made the crossing to Sicily had perished.

[3] The Carthaginians had thus, contrary to all expectation, suffered a major disaster, and were so panic-stricken that night after night they remained wakeful, guarding the city, convinced that Gelon had decided to sail against Carthage at once, with his entire armament. [4] Because of the huge number of casualties, the city went into public mourning, while privately the homes of individual citizens were filled with grief and lamentation. Some were enquiring after the fate of sons, some of brothers; while innumerable children who had lost their fathers, and were now orphans bereft of support, lamented both the death of their begetters and their own lack now of anyone to make provision for them. So the Carthaginians, fearing lest Gelon should steal a march on them by crossing over into Libya, at once dispatched to them as ambassadors plenipotentiary their most persuasive public speakers and counselors.

25. After his victory, Gelon honored with gifts the horsemen who had slain Hamilcar, and bestowed decorations for valor on those others who had displayed outstanding bravery in action. The best of the booty he kept in reserve, desiring to adorn the temples of Syracuse with the spoils; of what remained, he nailed a good deal to the most notable of the Himeran shrines, and the rest, together with the prisoners, he shared among the allies, proportionately to the number that had served under him. [2] The cities chained the captives thus divided among them and employed them as laborers on public works. An especially large number went to the Acragantines, who used them for the embellishment both of their city and of the surrounding countryside: indeed, so great was the multitude of war captives they received that many private citizens had five hundred fettered prisoners at their disposal. One supplementary reason for the vast number of these captives, in addition [the Carthaginians] having sent out so many troops, was that when the rout took place, many of the fugitives fled into the interior and particularly into the territory of the Acragantines; and since the Acragantines captured every single one of them, the city was overflowing with prisoners of war. [3] The bulk of them were turned over to the state; and it was these men who quarried the stones that went to build not only the biggest temples of the gods[37] but also the subterranean conduits used to drain off water from the city, which

37. In particular, the gigantic temple of Olympian Zeus, or Olympieum (though work on this may have begun before 480): see 13.82.1–5 for Diodorus' detailed description, based on autopsy.

are of such a size that their construction amply merits inspection — though because it was done on the cheap it tends to be underrated. The overseer of this work, a man by the name of Phaeax, used the fame of his undertaking to ensure that these underground conduits were named *phaiakes* after him. [4] The Acragantines also built an extravagant swimming pool, seven *stadioi* [c. ¾ mile] in circumference and twenty cubits [about thirty feet] deep. They piped water from both rivers and springs into it and [later] turned it into a fish pond, which supplied fish in great quantities both as food and for pleasure. Swans in abundance also settled on its surface, and the scene it presented was enchanting [>13.82.5]. In later years, however, it became silted up through neglect, and in course of time ceased to exist; [5] but the area remained fertile, and the inhabitants planted it thickly with vines and [orchard] trees of every sort, so that they drew a substantial income from it.

After dismissing the allies, Gelon led his citizen-soldiers home to Syracuse. Because of the magnitude of his achievement, he was highly regarded not only among his fellow-citizens but also throughout Sicily; for he brought with him such a mass of captives that it seemed as though all Libya had been taken prisoner by their island.

26. Also, ambassadors from those cities and rulers that had previously opposed him made haste to seek audience, begging forgiveness for past errors and assuring him that in future they would execute his every command. He showed restraint to them all and concluded alliances with them, bearing his good fortune with proper moderation: this attitude embraced not them alone but even his worst enemies, the Carthaginians. [2] For when the envoys who had been dispatched from Carthage appeared before him, and implored him with tears to show humanity in his treatment of them, he granted them peace, on condition that they paid the cost of his campaign, 2,000 talents of silver; in addition, he required them to build two temples, in which they had to deposit [copies of] the peace treaty. [3] The Carthaginians, having thus against all expectation achieved their deliverance, accepted the outlay required of them and, further, offered a gold crown to Gelon's wife Damarete, since it had been Damarete who, at their behest, did most towards achieving the peace treaty. When she received this honor, of one hundred gold talents,[38] she used it to

---

38. The talent here mentioned is not the usual measure (= c. 57½ lbs.), which would produce a crown of something over 5,700 lbs., but the Homeric gold talent of two drachms' weight, i.e., three tenths of an ounce, resulting in a crown weighing 30 oz., or just under 2 lbs.

mint a coin for circulation, the *Damarateion* that was named after her. This
was the equivalent of ten Attic drachmas and because of its weight was called
by the Sicilian Greeks a *pentekontalitron*. [4] Gelon treated all men equitably,
in the first instance because this was his natural disposition, but in no small
degree because of his eagerness to secure the loyalty of all by acts of benevolence. [5] Now he was preparing to sail to Greece with a large force and to
ally himself with the Hellenes against the Persians. When he was already on
the point of putting to sea, some men arrived from Corinth with the news
that the Greeks had won the sea battle off Salamis and that Xerxes and part
of his host had retreated from Europe. He therefore canceled his departure.
Delighted by the enthusiasm of his soldiers, he summoned an assembly, with
orders that all should attend fully armed. He himself, however, came to the assembly not only unarmed but not even wearing a tunic, and simply wrapped
in a mantle. Then, coming forward, he gave an accounting of his entire life
and of all he had done for the Syracusans. [6] At each act he mentioned, the
crowd applauded; they appeared absolutely astonished that he had presented
himself thus defenseless for anyone who might so wish to assassinate him.
In fact, so far was he from suffering the retribution due to a tyrant, that
with one voice they proclaimed him Benefactor, Savior, and King.[39] [7] It
was after these events that Gelon built notable shrines to Demeter and Corê
[Persephone] from the spoils of war and also fashioned a golden tripod worth
sixteen talents, which he set up in the sacred precinct at Delphi as a thank
offering to Apollo. He later planned to erect a temple to Demeter at Aetna,
<since none existed there>[40]; but fate cut short his life [>478: 38.7], and so
this aim remained unfulfilled.

[8] Of the lyric poets Pindar [518–438/7] was at his peak during these
times. Such, by and large, are the most noteworthy events that took place
during this year.

27. During the archonship of Xanthippos in Athens [479/8], the Romans
[Varr. 485] appointed as consuls Quintus Fabius Silvanus <Vibulanus> and
Servius Cornelius Tricostus <Maluginensis>. At this time the Persian fleet,
except for the Phoenicians, after being worsted in the sea battle of Salamis,
lay in port at Cyme, where it spent the winter. At the beginning of summer

---

39. Oldfather 1946 (194 n. 1) correctly specifies that that "this acclaim recognized [Gel-
on's] rule as constitutional, not 'tyrannical.'"

40. Vogel's emendation of the nonsensical Greek in Diodorus' MSS: see Green 2006,
82 n. 110.

it coasted down to Samos to keep a weather eye on Ionia: the total number of vessels at Samos was over four hundred, and their job was to keep watch on the cities of the Ionians, who were suspected of anti-Persian sympathies [Hdt. 8.130].

[2] After the battle of Salamis, the Athenians were held to have been responsible for the victory, and as a result got a very high opinion of themselves. Indeed, it became clear to everyone, throughout Greece, that they meant to challenge the Lacedaemonians for the leadership at sea. This was why the Lacedaemonians, foreseeing what was liable to happen, exerted themselves to humble the Athenians' pride. Thus when a contest was proposed for the allocation of prizes for valor, through their powerful influence they saw to it that the highest award to a city was bestowed on Aegina, while the individual thus honored was Ameinias the Athenian, brother of Aeschylus the poet; for he had been the first trireme commander to ram the Persian flagship, which he in fact sank, killing the admiral. [3] When the Athenians reacted badly to this undeserved slight, the Lacedaemonians, fearing lest Themistocles, out of resentment at the outcome, might plot some great harm to them and the Hellenes generally, honored him with double the number of gifts that those awarded the prizes had received. But when Themistocles accepted these gifts, the Athenian people stripped him of his generalship and transferred the office to [Pericles' father] Xanthippus son of Ariphron.

28. When the alienation of the Athenians from the Greeks generally became public knowledge, ambassadors arrived in Athens from both the Persians and the Hellenes [Hdt. 9.141–3]. Those sent by the Persians brought a proclamation to the Athenians from Mardonius, the general, in which he declared that if they would come over to the Persian side, he would give them any land in Greece they chose, rebuild their walls and temples, and leave Athens autonomous. Those sent by the Lacedaemonians, however, urged them not to be persuaded by the *barbaroi* but rather to preserve their goodwill towards the Hellenes, who were their kin and with whom they shared a common tongue. [2] The Athenians' response to the *barbaroi* was that the Persians had neither good enough land nor sufficient gold to induce the Athenians to desert their fellow-Hellenes. To the Lacedaemonians they declared that, for their own part, they would endeavor to maintain in the future the same concern for Hellas as they had exercised in the past; and what they asked of [the Lacedaemonians] was that they, with all their allies, should come to Attica as quickly as possible, for it was all too clear that Mardonius, now that the Athenians had proclaimed their opposition to him, would march on Athens in

strength. [3] This, indeed, is what in fact happened: for Mardonius, who was waiting in Boeotia[41] with his army, at first tried to suborn certain cities in the Peloponnese by channeling funds to their chief officers; but afterwards, upon learning of the Athenian response, he became enraged and led his entire field force into Attica. [4] Besides the army left him by Xerxes, Mardonius himself had enrolled many other troops from Thrace and Macedonia and the other allied states, more than 200,000 men in all. [5] With such a vast force advancing into Attica, the Athenians sent couriers to the Lacedaemonians, asking for their help. But since the latter procrastinated, and the *barbaroi* had already entered Attica, they panicked, and once more—taking wives, children, and of their possessions only what could be quickly shifted—they abandoned their fatherland and once more sought refuge on Salamis. [6] Mardonius in his fury at them laid waste the entire countryside, leveled the city, and totally destroyed any temples that had been left standing.[42]

29. After Mardonius and his force returned to Thebes, the Greeks met in congress and voted to succor the Athenians; to march out in full strength to Plataea and fight to the death for freedom; and to make a vow to the gods that, if they should emerge victorious, the Hellenes would, on that day, celebrate a festival of freedom (*eleutheria*) and hold the games of the festival in Plataea. [2] When the Greek forces were mustered at the Isthmus, they all voted to take an oath concerning the war, designed to strengthen the concord between them, and make them nobly endure the hazards of battle. The oath went roughly as follows:

[3] "I will not value life above freedom, nor will I desert the leaders, whether living or dead; but I will bury all of the allies who have died in the fighting; and if in this war I vanquish the *barbaroi,* I will not overthrow any of the cities that engaged in the conflict, nor will I rebuild any of the burnt and demolished temples but will leave them untouched, as a memorial to future generations of the impiety of the *barbaroi.*"[43] [4] When they had sworn the

---

41. At various times Mardonius seems to have had his winter quarters in Macedonia, Thessaly (Hdt. 8.126, 133; Plut. *Arist.* 10.2), and Boeotia (D.S. 28.3; Plut. *Arist.* 10.2).

42. The second, total, destruction of Athens: Hdt. 9.13. Mardonius had entered the city ten months after its prior capture in Sept. 480, i.e., midsummer 479, and will have leveled it about a month later (after a second abortive approach to the Athenians; Hdt. 9.4–5).

43. The Oath of Plataea survives in three versions: (a) that recorded by Lycurg. *In Leocr.* 81; (b) that given here by Diodorus; and (c), most important, that on a stele from Acharnae: Rhodes-Osborne, no. 88.ii (440–449, text, translation, and commentary). Its authenticity has been much debated but cannot be disproved.

oath, they marched into Boeotia by the pass over Cithaeron, and after coming down as far as the foothills near Erythrae, they pitched camp there [Hdt. 9.19]. The leader of the Athenians was Aristeides, and the overall command was held by Pausanias, the guardian of Leonidas' son.[44]

30. On learning that the enemy forces were advancing on Boeotia, Mardonius set out from Thebes; and when he reached the Asopus River, he established his camp, which he reinforced by means of a deep ditch and surrounded with a wooden palisade. The total number of the Greeks was close to 100,000, that of the *barbaroi* about half a million. [2] The first to engage were the *barbaroi,* who sallied out against [the Greeks] at night and charged the [Greek] encampment with all the cavalry they had. The Athenians saw them coming, and forming up in close order, confronted them boldly. There ensued a hard-fought battle. [3] At length all the other Greek units routed the *barbaroi* brigaded against them; only the Megarians, who had to stand up to the cavalry commander himself and the pick of the Persian horsemen, and were hard pressed in the fighting (but did not break ranks), sent some of their men over to the Athenians and Lacedaemonians, asking for immediate reinforcements. [4] Aristeides at once dispatched the picked Athenians who acted as his personal bodyguard: these charged the *barbaroi* in close formation, rescued the Megarians from the danger threatening them, killed large numbers, including the Persian cavalry commander, and put the rest to flight [Hdt. 9.20–24].

Now that the Greeks had so brilliantly prevailed in, as it were, a qualifying round, they became optimistic about final overall victory. After this skirmish they shifted their camp from the foothills to another site, better located for such a decisive showdown [Hdt. 9.25]. [5] For on their <left> was a high hill [Pyrgos] and to their <right>, the Asopus River, while the area between was occupied by the camp, itself defended by the natural lie of the land and the protection it offered. [6] The Greeks had calculated sensibly: the restricted field contributed greatly to their victory, since the Persians' battle line could not be far extended, and in consequence, as indeed it turned out, no use could be made of the *barbaroi*'s vast numbers.[45] So Pausanias, Aristeides, and their staff,

---

44. Pausanias, son of the Agiad king Cleombrotus, and Leonidas' nephew, was regent but never king. He achieved considerable notoriety (whether deservedly or not is still debated) in the decade following Plataea (44.1–45.7). Diodorus, incidentally, does not refer to Plataea in his account of the battle, though this is the name by which it has always been known.

45. Diodorus omits all the complex maneuvers in the days prior to the final engagement: Hdt. 9.41–58; Plut. *Arist.* 15–17. Diodorus' MSS also reverse the positions of Pyrgos

emboldened by the terrain, led their forces out to battle and after assuming a formation appropriate to their circumstances, advanced against the enemy.

31. Mardonius, being thus compelled to [narrow and] deepen his battle line, disposed his troops as seemed to his best advantage, and advanced, with much shouting, to meet the Greeks. He had a bodyguard of picked soldiers, and at the head of these he charged the Lacedaemonians brigaded against him, fighting gallantly and slaying many Greeks. But the Lacedaemonians resisted stubbornly and met every challenge of battle with a will, so that the death toll among the *barbaroi* was heavy. [2] Now so long as Mardonius and his picked detachment continued to bear the brunt of the fighting, the *barbaroi* faced all dangers with a good heart; but when Mardonius, still fighting furiously, fell, and of his picked troops some were killed and others incapacitated by wounds, their courage failed them and they took to flight. [3] When the Greeks pressed them hard, the majority of the *barbaroi* sought shelter behind the wooden palisade; of the remainder, the Greeks serving with Mardonius retreated to Thebes, while all others, to a total of over 400,000, were taken charge of by Artabazus [>44.4], a man of high repute among the Persians, who retreated by the other route [Hdt. 9.66], advancing by forced marches towards Phocis.

32. Just as the *barbaroi* took these different routes in their flight, so too the mass of the Greeks was similarly divided. The Athenians, Plataeans, and Thespians took off in pursuit of those who had set out towards Thebes; the Corinthians, Sicyonians, and Phliasians, together with some others, followed after the force retreating with Artabazus; while the Lacedaemonians and the rest chased down those who had taken refuge behind the wooden palisade and laid into them with a will. [2] Meanwhile, the Thebans took in the fugitives, added them to their strength, and attacked their Athenian pursuers. A sharp battle took place under the walls, in which the Thebans fought brilliantly: not a few fell on both sides, but finally they were outfought by the Athenians, and all once more fled for refuge back inside Thebes.

[3] After this the Athenians moved off to join the Lacedaemonians and with them proceeded to assault the palisade in pursuit of those who had taken refuge in the Persian encampment. Both sides put up a tremendous struggle, the *barbaroi* resisting strongly from their fortified positions, while the Greeks battered at the wooden walls. In this desperate engagement many

Hill and the Asopus River in relation to the Athenians: I have corrected this in the text. See Green 2006, 87 n. 126.

fell wounded, and not a few met death bravely, overwhelmed by a storm of missiles. [4] The violent onset of the Greeks, however, could be halted neither by the sheer numbers of the *barbaroi* nor by the defensive palisade they had built, and all resistance was forced to yield; for the leaders of Hellas, the Lacedaemonians and the Athenians, were now vying with one another, on top of the world because of their earlier victories and with confidence in their own tried valor. [5] In the end the *barbaroi* were overcome by main force, and despite their pleas to be taken prisoner, they received no mercy. For Pausanias, the captain-general of the Hellenes, seeing how numerically superior the *barbaroi* were, was at pains to prevent any unforeseen accident due to so great a disparity: because of this he had given orders to take no prisoners, and as a result there was soon a quite incredible death toll. In the end it was only after the Greeks had butchered over 100,000 *barbaroi* that they reluctantly stopped this slaughter of their enemies.

33. Such was the outcome of this battle. When it was over, the Greeks buried their fallen, of whom there were more than 10,000. The booty they shared out proportionately to the number of their troops, after which they voted on the awards for valor. <At Aristeides' urging> they gave the award for cities to Sparta, and the individual prize to Pausanias the Lacedaemonian.[46] [Meanwhile] Artabazus, with up to 400,000 of the retreating Persians, marched through Phocis into Macedonia, taking advantage of the speediest routes, and got these troops safely back to Asia.

[2] The Greeks took a tithe of the spoils to build a golden tripod,[47] which they set up in Delphi as a token of gratitude to the god, with the following elegiac couplet inscribed on it:

> The saviors of spacious Hellas set up this offering
> having saved their cities from hateful slavery.

---

46. "At Aristeides' urging" is Post's clever emendation—accepted by both Oldfather 1946 and Haillet—of the corrupt and senseless Greek text: cf. Green 2006, 90 n. 136. On the prize-giving generally (which generated much rivalry and ill will), see Plut. *Arist.* 2–3; cf. Hdt. 9.70–71. Though all agree on Pausanias, Plutarch reveals that the Athenians balked at the award to Sparta and that the Council of the Hellenes, called on to adjudicate, gave the prize to Plataea as an acceptable *tertius gaudens*.

47. This golden tripod was mounted on an eighteen-foot bronze column of three intertwined serpents and inscribed with the names of thirty-one states, stating briefly (coil 1), "These fought in the war." The base is still in situ. The golden tripod was stolen by the Phocians during the Third Sacred War (355: 16.30.1–2). The Roman Emperor Constantine I carried the bronze column off to the Hippodrome in Constantinople, where it remains.

Epitaphs were also composed for the Lacedaemonians who died at Thermopylae [Hdt. 7.228]: this for the whole body of them in common:

> Here once against two hundred myriad there fought
> four thousand from the Peloponnese.

and this for [the Spartans] alone:

> O stranger, report to the Lacedaemonians that here
> We lie, obedient to their laws.

[3] The citizens of Athens adorned in a like fashion the tombs of those who
had fallen in the Persian War: they also then held the Funeral Games for the
first time and made a law that specially chosen speakers should deliver eulogies over those buried at the public charge.

[4] After these events Pausanias the captain-general mobilized his army
and marched to Thebes, where he demanded for punishment those men responsible for [the city's] alliance with the Persians. The Thebans were so
dumbfounded, both by the numbers of these enemies and by their reputation
as fighters, that those most responsible for their defection from the Hellenes
voluntarily agreed to be handed over, and duly received punishment at Pausanias' hands: every one of them was put to death.

34. There also took place a great battle between Greeks and Persians in Ionia, fought on the same day as the final action at Plataea; and since we propose
to describe it, we shall take up the tale of it from the beginning. [2] After the
battle of Salamis, the commanders of the naval arm, Leotychidas the Lacedaemonian and Xanthippus the Athenian, mustered the fleet off Aegina, and
after spending several days there, sailed for Delos with two hundred and fifty
triremes. While they rode at anchor there, there arrived from Samos ambassadors calling upon them to liberate the Greeks of Asia. [3] Leotychidas and his
officers consulted their captains, and when they had heard the Samians out,
they agreed to liberate the [East Greek] cities, and at once set sail from Delos.
As soon as the Persian admirals who were stationed on Samos heard about the
approach of the Greek fleet, they put out from Samos with their entire complement and made landfall at Mycale in Ionia. Seeing that their ships were in
no condition for a sea battle, they hauled them ashore and ran a wooden palisade and a deep ditch round them. Nonetheless they also summoned troops
from Sardis and other nearby cities, and rounded up in all about 100,000
men. They also laid in every other sort of handy military equipment, being
convinced that the Ionians too would defect to the enemy.

[4] Leotychidas and his men sailed in on the *barbaroi* at Mycale with his

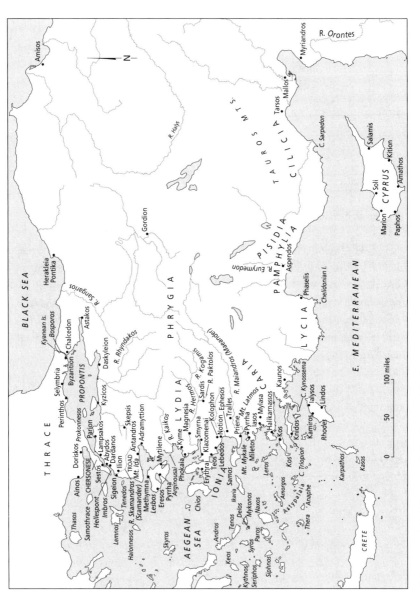

Map II.3. Asia Minor and the Eastern Mediterranean

whole fleet dressed for action, and they sent ahead a vessel carrying a herald who had the most powerful voice of anyone in the navy, and was instructed to approach the enemy and proclaim, loudly, that the Hellenes, having conquered the Persians, were now come to free the Hellenic cities of Asia [Hdt. 9.98]. [5] Leotychidas and his staff took this action in the belief that those Greeks fighting alongside the *barbaroi* would defect from the Persians, causing great confusion in the *barbaroi*'s camp; and this is just what happened. For the moment that the herald sailed up close to the ships that had been hauled ashore and made his announcement, the Persians began to mistrust the Greeks, and the Greeks began to take counsel among themselves about defecting.

35. When the Greeks [of the fleet] sensed the mood of those [ashore], they disembarked their forces. The next day, while they were making ready for combat, a rumor reached the camp that the Hellenes had defeated the Persians at Plataea. [2] At this Leotychidas and his staff summoned an assembly and encouraged their troops for battle, among other things <hinting at>⁴⁸ a Plataean victory. This they did on the assumption that it would embolden those who were going into battle. The outcome was, indeed, remarkable, for later both battles—those at Mycale and Plataea—were revealed to have taken place on the same day. [3] Thus Leotychides and his staff would appear to have not yet learned of the victory but to have made the story up themselves as deliberate propaganda, since the great distance between the two sites demonstrates the impossibility of getting a message through in time.⁴⁹ [4] Meanwhile, the Persian commanders, now thoroughly distrustful of their Greek [allies], disarmed them and gave their weapons to those on whose loyalty they could rely. They then mustered all their troops and told them that Xerxes himself with a great host [Hdt. 9.99] was coming to their aid, thus encouraging them for the coming battle.

36. When both sides had drawn up their troops in line and were advancing against each other, the Persians, reacting to the enemy's scanty numbers with scorn, raised a loud shout and charged them. [2] Now the Samians and the Milesians had all agreed beforehand to help the Greeks and were coming on ahead together at the double. When their advance brought them in view

---

48. My emendation *paradélountes* ("hinting at") for the highly inappropriate verb *parōidountes* ("parodying") of the MSS. Cf. Green 2006, 93 n. 146.

49. Leotychidas could indeed have been inventing a victory; but it is just possible that the simultaneity with Plataea was real and that news of the latter reached the Spartan and his men by means of an Aegean beacon chain.

of the Greeks, the Ionians assumed that their appearance would be cause for encouragement; in fact, it had exactly the opposite effect. [3] Leotychidas and his men thought that Xerxes had arrived from Sardis with his army and that it was they who were now coming at them. The result was panic and confusion in the ranks, with some saying that they should run for the ships and get away fast, while others argued that they should stay, hold their line, and tough it out. While all was still hubbub and disorder, the Persians came into sight, equipped in a manner calculated to inspire panic, and bore straight down on them, shouting. [4] The Greeks, thus given no time for [further] deliberation, were forced to face up to this attack by the *barbaroi*.

To begin with, both sides fought fiercely, and the battle hung in the balance, with numerous casualties on both sides. But when the Samians and Milesians made their allegiance plain, the Greeks found new strength, while the *barbaroi*, terrified, turned and fled. [5] A great slaughter then took place. The troops of Leotychidas and Xanthippus pressed hard on their beaten foes and pursued them to the camp; and once the outcome was certain, the Aeolians, as well as many other East Greeks, joined in the battle, since a passionate urge for freedom now swept through the city-states of Asia Minor. [6] In consequence, few of them gave any thought to the hostages they had given or the oaths they had taken, but along with the other Greeks began killing the *barbaroi* as they fled. In this manner, then, were the Persians defeated, and more than 40,000 of them were slain [Aug. 479]. Some of the survivors took refuge in the camp, while others retreated to Sardis. [7] When Xerxes learned of the defeat at Plataea, as well as the rout of his own troops at Mycale, he left part of his forces in Sardis to pursue hostilities against the Hellenes, while he himself, in a state of shock, set forth with the rest of his army on the long march to Ecbatana.[50]

37. Leotychidas and Xanthippus and their men now sailed back to Samos, where they made alliances with the Ionians and Aeolians, after which they tried to persuade them to abandon Asia and migrate to new homes in Europe, offering to expel those peoples who had sided with the Medes and to make them [the East Greeks] a present of their lands. [2] If they stayed in Asia, the argument ran, they would always have the enemy at their gates, with military strength far superior to their own; while their allies, being across the sea, would not be able to come to their aid in an emergency. When the Aeolians and Ionians heard these assurances, they decided to accept the Greek offer and began preparing to sail with them to Europe. [3] The Athenians,

---

50. Cf. Hdt. 9.108, where Xerxes' destination is given as Susa, the Achaemenid winter capital. Ecbatana, to the north of Susa and another royal residence, may have been an autumn way station on this occasion.

however, changed their minds and offered them contrary advice, saying they should stay where they were, since even if no other Greeks came to their assistance, the Athenians, as their kinsmen, would do so by themselves. (The conclusion they had reached was that if the Ionians were relocated by the Greeks as a whole, they would no longer consider Athens their mother-city.) This was why the Ionians changed their minds and chose to remain in Asia.

[4] Somewhat later than these events, circumstances brought it about that the forces of the Greeks were divided: the Lacedaemonians sailed back to Laconia, while the Athenians, together with the Ionians and the islanders, set out for Sestos. [5] As soon as Xanthippus, as general, made landfall there, he assaulted the city, took it, and put in a garrison. He then dismissed the allies, and with his citizen-militia returned to Athens [Hdt. 9.114–121].

[6] This, then, was the end of the so-called Median [Persian] War, which had lasted two years. Among the authors [describing it] is Herodotus, who, beginning at a point before the Trojan War, composed in nine books an account of just about all public events that took place in the inhabited world, bringing his account to a close with the battle between the Greeks and the Persians at Mycale, and the siege of Sestos.

[7] In Italy the Romans fought a campaign against the Volscians and defeated them in battle, with heavy casualties. Spurius Cassius, who had been consul the previous year and was thought to be aiming at a tyranny, was found guilty and executed.

Such, then, were the events that took place during this year.

38. In Athens Timosthenes was archon [478/7], and in Rome Caeso Fabius [Vibulanus] and Lucius Aemilius Mamercus succeeded [Varr. 484] to the consulship. During their time in office, the island of Sicily enjoyed almost continuous peace, now that the Carthaginians had finally been humbled, and Gelon's equitable rule over the Sicilian Greeks was bringing their cities a highly stable regime as well as an abundance of essential goods. [2] Now the Syracusans had, by [sumptuary] law, abolished extravagant funerals and banned the customary expenses incurred on behalf of the deceased, including in this decree even <totally neglected burial practices>.[51] King Gelon, through his desire to encourage the public's goodwill in all matters, applied the law relating to burials impartially in his own case. [3] When he fell ill [with dropsy] and his life was despaired of, he handed over the monarchy to Hieron, the eldest of his brothers, and in the matter of his obsequies gave orders that the letter of the law was to be strictly observed. Consequently, when he died his

---

51. Text uncertain through corruption: see Green 2006, 96 n. 157.

successor as king held his funeral in precise accordance with his instructions. [4] His body was laid to rest on his wife's estate, in the building known by the name of Nine Towers, famous for the massive solidity of its construction. The entire population accompanied his cortege from the city, though the site was two hundred *stadioi* [some twenty-five miles] distant. [5] Here Gelon was buried, and a fine tomb built for him at public expense, and civic honors granted him of the sort proper for heroes; later, however, his monument was torn down by the Carthaginians during a campaign against Syracuse [396: >14.63.3], while Agathocles[52] out of envy demolished the towers. Yet neither the hostility of the Carthaginians nor the mean-spiritedness of Agathocles nor any other cause has ever been able to deprive Gelon of his renown. [6] The just testimony of history has preserved his fame unblemished, proclaiming it worldwide for all eternity. It is indeed both just and advantageous for any society that, of those who have held office, the mean should bear the weight of history's outrage, whereas the generous should be immortalized in memory; for in this way above all, it will be seen, many men of later generations will be motivated to work for the common benefit of mankind.[53]

[7] Gelon was king for a period of seven years [485–478], while Hieron, his brother and successor in power, reigned over the Syracusans for eleven years and eight months [478–467].

39. In Greece the Athenians, after the victory at Plataea, conveyed their women and children back to Athens from Troezen and Salamis and at once set about fortifying the city, busying themselves with every possible precaution that might contribute to their greater security. [2] The Lacedaemonians, however, seeing that the Athenians had acquired a great reputation through the activities of their navy, eyed their increasing power with suspicion, and resolved to stop them from rebuilding their city walls. [3] They therefore at once sent ambassadors to Athens, who were to counsel them against fortifying their city at this time, ostensibly because to do so would not be to the general advantage of the Greeks: should Xerxes, they argued, return with a still larger field force, he would have walled cities handy outside the Peloponnese, from which he could make forays and easily subjugate them all. When their advice was ignored, the ambassadors approached the builders and ordered them to stop work at once.

---

52. Agathocles (361–289) was tyrant of Syracuse from 316: Diodorus deals with him in Books 19–20.

53. History as embodying a series of educative moral exempla is a recurrent leitmotif of Diodorus'. Cf. above, 3.1, and below, 46.1 (apropos Pausanias); also 1.4–2.8, 14.1.1–3, 15.88.1, and elsewhere.

[4] The Athenians were at a loss as to what they should do; but Themistocles, who at the time enjoyed the greatest prestige among them, advised them
to do nothing, pointing out that if they resorted to force, the Lacedaemonians
and Peloponnesians could easily mobilize against them and prevent them
from completing their fortification of the city. [5] But he informed the Council, confidentially, that he and some others would go on a mission to Sparta
to explain this business of the wall-building to the Lacedaemonians; and he
instructed the archons, when envoys should reach Athens from Lacedaemon,
to detain them until he himself returned from there, and meanwhile to set all
hands to work on fortifying the city. In this way, he explained to them, they
would succeed in their endeavor.

40. The Athenians agreed to this proposal, and, while Themistocles together with his fellow-envoys set off for Sparta, they set about building the
walls with enormous enthusiasm, sparing neither houses nor tombs [for mate-
rial]. Children and women joined in the work, as indeed did every noncitizen
and slave, with no lack of zeal all round. [2] Thus the work advanced at
astonishing speed, due to the multitude of laborers and the enthusiasm they
all brought to their task. Themistocles was summoned by the authorities [in
Sparta] and admonished regarding the building of the walls; but he denied
any such construction was going on, and advised them not to listen to baseless
rumors but rather to send reliable envoys to Athens, from whom they would
learn the truth of the matter. As a surety for them he offered himself and those
who had accompanied him on his mission. [3] The Lacedaemonians agreed
to Themistocles' proposal, put him and his fellow-envoys under guard, and
dispatched to Athens their most distinguished citizens to look into anything
that they felt called for investigation. But some time had now passed, and the
Athenians were well advanced with their work on the walls. Thus, when the
Lacedaemonian ambassadors reached Athens and began to denounce their
actions and threaten them with violent reprisals, the Athenians arrested them,
saying they would release them [only] when the Spartans released Themistocles and his party. [4] In this way the Lacedaemonians were outmaneuvered
and forced to let the Athenian envoys go in order to get their own ones back.
Themistocles, having by this ingenious trick built up his country's defenses
quickly and without risk, won a high reputation among his fellow-citizens.[54]

54. For the rebuilding of Athens' city walls, the Spartans' objections to this, and Themistocles' diplomatic role in deceiving them, cf. Thuc. 1.89.3–93.2. Stretches of the The-
mistoclean wall have been found (and confirm the emergency cannibalization of existing
material), but no sure trace of the pre-479 circuit has yet surfaced. Spartan distrust of
Themistocles (and subsequently of Athens' imperial aspirations) dates from this episode.

[5] At the same time as these events were taking place, the Romans fought a war against the Aequi and the citizens of Tusculum. They brought the Aequi to battle, defeated them, and killed large numbers of the enemy, after which they besieged and captured Tusculum and occupied the city of the Aequi.

41. After the end of the year, the archon in Athens was Adeimantus [477/6], while in Rome Marcus Fabius <Vibul>anus and Lucius Valerius <Volusi Potitus>[55] were elected [Varr. 483] as consuls. During their term, Themistocles, on account of his strategic skill and sharp-wittedness, was [still] in high repute not only among his fellow-citizens but throughout Greece.[56] [2] As a result, he became puffed up by his own fame and embarked on many other larger projects, aimed at the enhancement of his country's increasing power. For example, the port known as Piraeus was not at that time a harbor at all; instead, the Athenians were utilizing as their roadstead the limited space provided by Phaleron Bay. Themistocles therefore got the idea of converting Piraeus into a harbor, since it would need only a little remodeling to turn it into the best and largest harbor of any in Greece [Thuc. 1.93.3–8].[57] [3] He hoped, too, that with the addition of this facility, the city would be able to compete for the leadership at sea, since at that time the Athenians possessed the largest number of triremes, and from a long succession of sea battles had also acquired experience and prestige as experts in naval warfare. [4] In addition, he figured that they would be able to count on the Ionians through ties of kinship, and through them would get to free the other Greeks of Asia, who because of this benefaction would likewise turn in goodwill towards the Athenians; and that then all the islanders, astounded by the size of their naval arm, would promptly align themselves with those who could bring them both the greatest trouble and the greatest advantages. [5] For the Lacedaemonians, he saw, well organized though their land forces might be, lacked all natural aptitude for combat at sea.

42. After thinking these matters through, he decided not to make any open declaration of his plan, knowing for sure that the Lacedaemonians would try

---

55. Here and elsewhere throughout this text, names of Roman officials have been restored, supplemented, or emended in accordance with Broughton.

56. At the Olympic Games of 476 (Plut. *Them.* 17.2; Paus. 8.50.3; Ael. *VH* 13.43) no one had eyes for anyone else. Yet, in fact, he was clearly already persona non grata with the Spartans, and there are signs that his enemies at home had begun to ease him from power.

57. This plan, initiated during Themistocles' archonship (493/2), was fully developed only after Salamis, when Athens' vastly enlarged fleet and commercial expansion necessitated the development of a major protected harbor.

to prevent it. He therefore announced to his fellow-citizens in Assembly that there were certain large concerns, of advantage to the city, that he wanted to introduce and regarding which he had advice for them. To discuss them openly, however, was not in the public interest: they should rather implement them through the agency of a few individuals. He therefore asked the *demos* to choose two men in whom they had complete confidence and authorize them to act in this matter. [2] The majority agreed, and the *demos* chose as the two men Aristeides and Xanthippos, whom they picked not only for excellence of character but also because they saw both as active competitors with Themistocles in the pursuit of public renown and leadership, and for this reason liable to oppose him. [3] So these men were privately informed about his plan by Themistocles and then declared to the *demos* that what Themistocles had told them was indeed important, of advantage to the city, and feasible.[58]

[4] The *demos*—which, while admiring the man, also suspected that he might be entertaining such large and weighty schemes with the idea of setting himself up in a tyranny—demanded that he state openly what it was he had decided. But he repeated that it was not in the public interest that his intentions should be openly discussed. [5] At this people were all the more admiring of his cleverness and intellectual stature and bade him reveal his plans to the Council in secret session, with the assurance that if that body determined what he told them to be both feasible and advantageous, then their advice would be for the implementation of his proposal. [6] As a result, when the Council heard all the details and determined that Themistocles' recommendations were both feasible and advantageous, the *demos* promptly endorsed the Council's findings, and he was granted the authority to do whatever it was he wanted. Every man left the Assembly filled with admiration for the man's high ability, as well as with elated expectations concerning the outcome of his plan.

43. Having thus obtained authority to act, together with every kind of ready assistance in his undertaking, Themistocles once more thought up a way to outmaneuver the Lacedaemonians, knowing full well that just as they had attempted to block the fortification of the city, so they were sure to try, in the same way, to disrupt the Athenians' plans for undertaking the construction of the harbor. [2] He therefore decided to send ambassadors to the

58. If this secret plan of Themistocles is historical, it contained a second, and more notorious, proposal: not only the development of Piraeus but also a recommendation to burn the Spartan fleet, then at Pagasae (Plut. *Them.* 20.1–2; *Arist.* 22.2), a suggestion instantly, and firmly, vetoed.

Lacedaemonians, to make them see how it furthered Greece's common interests to possess a first-class harbor as defense against the new expedition that the Persians were certain to mount. Having in this manner taken the edge off the Spartan urge to interfere, he applied himself personally to the task, and since everyone was only too eager to cooperate, the work was speedily accomplished, and the harbor ready before anyone expected. [3] He also persuaded the *demos* every year to construct twenty triremes as additions to the existing fleet and to make resident aliens and craftsmen tax free, the object being to bring crowds of immigrants into the city from every quarter, and thus provide manpower for a greater number of skilled occupations. Both these acts he regarded as vital to the building up of the naval arm. These, then, were the matters with which the Athenians were occupied.

44. The Lacedaemonians appointed Pausanias, the commanding general at Plataea, as their admiral of the fleet and instructed him to free all Greek cities that were still guarded by permanent garrisons of *barbaroi*.[59] [2] He therefore took fifty triremes from the Peloponnese and sent to Athens for thirty more, under the command of Aristeides. He then sailed first of all to Cyprus, where he freed those cities that still had Persian garrisons [3] and after that to the Hellespont. Here he captured Byzantium, which had been held by the Persians. Of the other *barbaroi* there, he killed some and expelled the rest, thus liberating the city; but many high-ranking Persians whom he captured in Byzantium itself he handed over to Gongylus of Eretria to guard. Now ostensibly he was to hold these men pending future punishment, but in fact his business was to get them back safe to Xerxes, since he [Pausanias] had concluded a secret treaty of friendship with the Great King and was going to marry Xerxes' daughter, with the intention of betraying the Greeks. [4] The intermediary in this business was the general Artabazus, who was secretly furnishing Pausanias with large sums of money for the purpose of suborning Greeks in key positions.[60]

Pausanias, however, was exposed and punished in the following manner.

---

59. As he does later, at even greater length, for Themistocles (54.1–59.4), Diodorus here, clearly influenced by the Thucydidean excursus on both men (1.128.1–138.6), writes his own account of Pausanias entirely under the archon year 477/6, as a kind of extended footnote. Much of this whole episode (including Thucydides' dating of so much to Pausanias' first sojourn in Byzantium) is still fiercely debated.

60. Pausanias' supposed Medism, the account of which follows here, has often been seen as a frame-up, his real offense being his supposed favoring of the helots. It is also possible that the Athenians and Ionians used his highhandedness (of which complaints were lodged with Sparta) as a lever to undermine Spartan leadership. But the whole truth remains irretrievable.

[5] Because he aspired to emulate the luxurious Persian lifestyle, and behaved like a despot to his subordinates, everyone resented him, in particular any of the Greeks who had been appointed to some [junior] command. [6] There was, then, a great deal of gossip in the army, among both ethnic and civic groups, highly critical of Pausanias' harsh discipline. Certain Peloponnesians actually deserted him and sailed back home, from where they sent envoys [to Sparta] with a formal bill of indictment against him. Aristeides the Athenian shrewdly took advantage of this opportunity to win over various cities during official discussions, using his personal influence to bring them into the Athenian alliance. Yet the Athenians benefited even more from a stroke of pure luck, as a result of the following circumstances.

45. Pausanias had arranged that the couriers who carried correspondence from him to the Great King should not return, and thus be in a position to betray his secrets. They were, therefore, being done away with by those to whom they delivered the letters, which was why none of them ever returned safely. [2] One of these couriers, putting two and two together from their nonappearance, opened the letters and found that his guess concerning the elimination of their bearers was indeed the truth. He therefore turned them over to the ephors as evidence. [3] They, however, were suspicious because the letters had come to them already opened, and they demanded more, and more convincing, proof. The courier then offered to confront them with Pausanias acknowledging his actions in person. [4] He therefore traveled to Taenarum and seated himself as a suppliant at the shrine of Poseidon. He also set up a double-roomed tent, in which he concealed the ephors and certain other Spartans. When Pausanias approached him and enquired the reason for his being a suppliant, the man blamed Pausanias himself, inasmuch as the latter had included in the letter directions for his execution. [5] Pausanias then apologized and asked forgiveness for past mistakes, going so far as to beg the man to keep the incident secret and promising him lavish gifts. They then parted.

The ephors and those with them, despite having discovered the whole truth of the matter, at that time kept quiet and took no action. Later, however, when the Lacedaemonians were, with the ephors' assistance, investigating the matter, Pausanias was forewarned and, anticipating them, took refuge in the shrine of Athena of the Brazen House. [6] The Lacedaemonians were in a quandary as to whether, now he was a suppliant, they should punish him. The story goes that Pausanias' mother came out to the shrine but neither said nor did anything except to pick up a brick and put it at the entrance, after which she went back home; [7] at which point the Lacedaemonians, in compliance with the mother's verdict, proceeded to wall up the entrance, and in this way forced Pausanias to end his life through starvation [?471/0]. Now though the body of the deceased was handed over to his kin for burial, divine displeasure still manifested itself at this violation of the sanctity of suppliants: [8] for when the Lacedaemonians were consulting the oracle at Delphi about some quite different matters, the god gave them an oracular response bidding them return her suppliant to the goddess. [9] The Spartans regarded this sacred injunction as impracticable, and for some while were thus at a loss, being unable to carry out the order the god had given them. Resolving, however, to do what they could, they had two bronze statues of Pausanias made and set these up in Athena's shrine.

46. Since all through our history we have regularly augmented the high repute of good men with the eulogies we pronounce over them, and at the deaths of base persons have similarly uttered the appropriate reproofs, we shall not let Pausanias' vileness and treachery pass uncondemned. [2] Who, indeed, would not be astounded at the folly of this man? By his victory at Plataea, and through the performance of many other highly praised deeds, he became the benefactor of Greece. Yet he not only failed to maintain the esteem in which he was held but through his passion for Persian wealth and luxury brought shame on his existing reputation. [3] Puffed up by his successes, he came to loathe his Laconian upbringing and to ape the licentiousness and luxury of the Persians, though he least of all had cause to emulate the customs of the *barbaroi,* since he had not learned about them at second hand but had made trial of them in fact and in person, and knew well how much more his ancestral way of life inclined towards high achievement than did the luxury of the Persians.[61]

[4] It was, indeed, through his own vileness that he not only got the punishment he deserved but was responsible for his countrymen losing their supremacy at sea. By way of contrast, the diplomacy of Aristeides in his dealings with the allies— amongst other virtues, his amiability towards his subordinates— attracted much attention and led everyone, as though driven by the same impulse, to incline towards the Athenian cause. [5] Because of this they no longer paid any heed to the leaders sent from Sparta, but in their admiration for Aristeides eagerly took his word over everything, thus ensuring that he was assigned the supreme command at sea without needing to fight for it.[62]

---

61. The question of Pausanias' guilt or innocence remains ambiguous and is probably insoluble. All our evidence (including that of Thucydides) gives off the unmistakable smell of *parti pris* propaganda.

62. Diodorus now gives his version of the (still much debated) foundation of the breakaway so-called Delian League under Athens' leadership, in 478/7, according to Arist. *Ath. Pol.* 23.5; doubtless the process extended over several years.

47. Aristeides at once counseled the allies, who were meeting in general assembly, to designate Delos as [the location for] their common treasury and to deposit there all the revenues they collected; also, against [the cost of] the war that they anticipated being renewed by the Persians, to levy a tax on all the cities according to their means, with the total collected amounting to <4>60 talents. [2] When he himself was appointed as assessor of the various sums to be levied, he calculated the division [of responsibilities] so accurately and fairly that every one of the cities approved it. Consequently, since he was regarded as having achieved an impossibility, he gained a very high reputation for justice, and on account of his surpassing excellence in this area he became known as "the Just." [3] Thus at one and the same time the villainy of Pausanias deprived his countrymen of supremacy at sea, while Aristeides' all-round excellence enabled Athens to win the leadership hitherto denied her.[63]

These, then, were the events that took place during this year.

48. During the archonship of Phaedon in Athens [476/5], the 76th Olympiad was celebrated, in which Scamandrius of Mytilene won the *stadion,* while in Rome the consuls [Varr. 481] were Caeso Fabius [Vibulanus] and Spurius Furius <Fusus>.[64] [2] During their period of office, Leotychidas, the Lacedaemonian king, died after a reign of twenty-two years. His successor was Archidamus, who reigned for forty-two years.[65] There also died Anaxilas, the *tyrannos* of Rhegium and Zancle, after holding power for eighteen years; he was succeeded in his tyranny by Micythus [>66.1–4], who was entrusted with the office on the understanding that he would hand it over [in due

---

63. Delos was chosen as occupying a central point in the Aegean; it was also an international Ionian religious center. The exact annual amount of the tax imposed is still debated. Comparison with the (very ill preserved) tribute lists suggests that the actual sum collected was appreciably less than 460 talents. Diodorus' MSS put the figure at 560, probably a scribal slip for 460 (vouched for by Thuc. 1.96.2 and Plut. *Arist.* 24.3): the higher figure is certainly wrong.

64. Diodorus has lost the consuls for 482, Q. Fabius Vibulanus and C. Iulius Iullus, and in consequence is now, and through ch. 88, six, rather than seven, years ahead of the Varronian system.

65. Leotychidas II was exiled in 476/5; he did not die until 469/8, in Tegea. This has occasioned confusion. His grandson Archidamus actually died in 427/6, i.e., 42 years after Leotychidas' death. But Diodorus records Archidamus' death (12.35.4) in 434/3, i.e., 42 years after his grandfather's exile. He also, however, refers to Archidamus' activities between 434/3 and 427/6 (12.42.6, 47.1, 52.1). The archon for 476/5 was Phaedon; that for 469/8, Apsephion. But evidence exists for a second or alternative archon in 469/8: Phaedon or Phaeon (Haillet, 82 n. 2), and this may have compounded Diodorus' confusion.

course] to the sons of the deceased, who were still under age.[66] [3] Hieron, king of the Syracusans after the death of his brother Gelon, seeing the popularity of his brother Polyzelus among the Syracusans, and convinced he was simply waiting to usurp the kingship, very much wanted to get him out of the way; meanwhile, by enrolling foreign troops and surrounding himself with a foreign bodyguard, he reckoned he could safely hold on to the throne. [4] So, when the Sybarites, who were being besieged by the Crotoniates [>12.10.1], asked for his help, he enrolled large numbers of troops for the campaign and put his brother Polyzelus in command of them, on the assumption that he would be killed by the Crotoniates. [5] When Polyzelus, suspecting this, refused to undertake the campaign, his brother was furious with him; and when he fled for protection to Theron, the tyrant of Acragas, Hieron began preparations for a war against Theron.

[6] Some time after these events, it happened that Theron's son Thrasydaeus, the governor of Himera, was using undue severity in the exercise of his office, to a point at which the Himerans had become totally alienated from him. [7] They turned down the idea of going to his father and formally accusing him, in the belief that they would not get an impartial hearing; instead, they sent ambassadors to Hieron, who were to present their case against Thrasydaeus, and [at the same time] offer to make Hieron a present of Himera, and to join him in his attack on Theron. [8] Hieron, however, had already decided to enter into peaceful relations with Theron, and so he betrayed the Himerans, briefing Theron on their secret plans. After Theron had investigated this plot and found the charge to be true, he resolved his differences with Hieron and saw to it that Polyzelus regained [his brother's] goodwill as before. He then arrested the Himeran opposition leaders—there were a good many of these—and put them all to death.

49. Hieron removed the inhabitants of Naxos and Catana from their cities and replaced them with settlers of his own, comprising two lots of 5,000 each brought in from the Peloponnese and from Syracuse. He changed Catana's name to Aetna and commandeered not only this city's territory but much land adjacent to it, which he parceled out in holdings for all 10,000 settlers. [2] His object in so doing was twofold. He wanted to have solid support avail-

---

66. Anaxilas held power in Rhegium (modern Reggio) from 494. He also repopulated Zancle in Sicily, renaming it Messene (modern Messina). In the Carthaginian campaign of 480 he sided with his father-in-law Terillus of Himera and the Carthaginians against Syracuse and her allies (Hdt. 7.165), but later made his peace with Hieron, marrying his daughter.

able for any emergency, but he also hoped to receive heroic honors from this newly founded city of 10,000 inhabitants [>76.3]. The Naxians and Catanians whom he had uprooted from their native soil he transferred to Leontini, with instructions that they should make new homes in that city alongside the local population. [3] After the slaughter of the Himerans, Theron realized that the city now needed new settlers, and he brought in a very mixed crowd, granting citizen status not only to Dorians but to anyone else who applied. [4] These people got together as a citizen body and lived peacefully for fifty-eight years; but then the city was conquered and demolished by the Carthaginians [409/8: >13.61–62] and has remained deserted to this day.

50. When Dromoclides held the archonship in Athens [475/4], the Romans elected as consuls [Varr. 480] Marcus Fabius [Vibulanus] and Gnaeus Manlius [Cincinnatus]. During these officials' term, the Lacedaemonians, having without good cause lost their supremacy at sea, took that loss very hard; as a result they resented those Greeks who had broken away from them, and kept threatening them with appropriate retribution. [2] Indeed, at a meeting of the Gerousia[67] they considered declaring war on Athens over this matter of naval hegemony. [3] In the same way, when the general Assembly was convened, all the younger men and a majority of the rest showed eagerness to recover this supremacy: if they succeeded, they thought, they would enjoy great wealth, Sparta as a whole would be made greater and more powerful, and the estates of private citizens would enjoy a great rise in prosperity. [4] They also kept recalling a certain ancient oracle, in which the god told them to watch out lest they find themselves with a "lame leadership" [>64.2]: this oracle, they said, referred specifically to nothing other than the present, since their rule would without a doubt be lame if of their two supremacies they lost one.

[5] Since almost the entire citizen body strongly approved of this argument, and the Gerousia was in session to debate it, no one expected that anybody would dare to suggest something different. [6] But a certain member of the Gerousia, one Hetoemaridas, a descendant of Heracles, whose outstanding excellence of character earned him high esteem among his fellow-citizens, undertook this course. They should, he counseled them, leave the Athenians in possession of their leadership, since it was not (he asserted) in Sparta's best interests to dispute the rule of the sea with her. This unexpected proposal he had no trouble in supporting with effective arguments, so that, contrary

---

67. The Spartan Council of Elders, an advisory body consisting of twenty-eight nobly born members over the age of sixty, plus the two kings.

to general expectations, he won over both the Gerousia and the people.
[7] Thus, in the end the Lacedaemonians determined that what Hetoemaridas proposed was to their advantage and gave up this urge they had to go
to war with Athens. [8] The Athenians themselves at first expected to have a
great war with the Lacedaemonians for the supremacy at sea, and as a result
were building more triremes, raising substantial funds, and treating their allies reasonably; but when they heard the Lacedaemonians' decision, they were
freed from their fear of war and devoted all their energies to the enhancement
of their city's prestige and power.

51. When Acestorides was archon in Athens [474/3], in Rome Kaeso Fabius
[Vibulanus] and Titus Verginius [Tricostus Rutilus] succeeded [Varr. 479] to
the consulship. During their period of office, Hieron, king of the Syracusans,
was approached by ambassadors from Cumae in Italy, soliciting his aid in the
war being waged against them by the Tyrrhenians, at that time in control of
the sea, and dispatched an adequate number of triremes to their aid. [2] The
commanders of this squadron sailed to Cumae, where they joined forces with
the local inhabitants and fought a naval campaign against the Tyrrhenians,
destroying many of their ships and finally defeating them in a great sea battle.
Having thus humbled the Tyrrhenians and freed the men of Cumae from
their fears, they sailed back home to Syracuse.

52. When Menon was archon in Athens [473/2], the Romans elected as
consuls [Varr. 478] Lucius Aemilius Mamercus and Gaius †Cornelius Len-
tulus†. In Italy war broke out between the Tarantines and the Iapygians.
[2] Over a period of years these peoples had been quarreling over some land
on their borders, with skirmishes and raids into each other's territory. Since
the dispute only grew worse with time, and deaths had become frequent,
they finally plunged into an all-out conflict. [3] The Iapygians not only mobilized their own forces but also brought in an allied contingent from their
neighbors, managing in this way to raise a total of over 20,000 men. The
Tarantines, on learning the size of the army gathered against them, likewise
mobilized their citizen body, augmenting them with large numbers of their
allies the Rhegians. [4] A hard-fought battle took place, with heavy casualties
on both sides, but in the end the Iapygians won. The losers in their flight
split into two groups, the one retreating to Taras, the other seeking refuge in
Rhegium. The Iapygians in similar fashion also divided. [5] Those pursuing
the Tarantines—the latter having only a short start—killed large numbers of
them, but those on the heels of the Rhegians were so enthusiastic that they

forced their way into Rhegium[68] along with the fugitives and made themselves masters of the city [Hdt. 7.170].

53. The following year [472/1] in Athens, the archon was Chares; in Rome those elected as consuls [Varr. 477] were Titus M<ene>nius [Agrippae Lanatus] and Gaius Horatius <Pulvillus>; and the 77th Olympiad, in which Dandes the Argive won the *stadion,* was celebrated by the Eleians. It was during this period that in Sicily Theron, the ruler of Acragas, died after a reign of sixteen years and was succeeded by his son Thrasydaeus. [2] Now Theron, whose rule had been fair and unoppressive, was held in high esteem by the Acragantines during his lifetime and received heroic honors after his death; but his son, even while Theron still lived, was given to violence and murder, and after his death ruled the country in a lawless and tyrannical manner. [3] The result was that he quickly lost the loyalty of his subjects and had a miserable existence, universally hated and the target of continual plots; and indeed his life very soon came to a disastrous end well suited to his lawless nature. For after his father Theron's death, by hiring numerous mercenaries and mobilizing the citizen-militia of both Acragas and Himera, he raised a total of over 20,000 cavalry and infantry. [4] Because his intention was to use these troops against the Syracusans, King Hieron got together a very considerable force and himself marched on Acragas. A hard-fought battle took place, in which—since here Greeks were matched against Greeks—the casualties were particularly heavy. [5] In this fight the Syracusans prevailed, their dead numbering up to two thousand, whereas the other side lost over four. After suffering this humiliation, Thrasydaeus was driven out of office and fled to the city known as "Nisaean" Megara, where he was arraigned, condemned, and put to death [471/0].[69] The Acragantines, after restoring their democracy, sent ambassadors to Hieron and obtained a peace settlement [467/6].

[6] In Italy war broke out between Rome and Veii, and a great battle took place near the place called Cremera.[70] The Romans got the worst of it, and large numbers of them fell, including (as some historians have it) the three

---

68. If this is true, it has to be reckoned the most enthusiastic pursuit in all ancient history, since Rhegium lay well over two hundred miles to the south.

69. "Nisaean" Megara, so called because of its port of Nisaea on the Saronic Gulf, is given its full title by Diodorus to distinguish it from Megara Hyblaea in eastern Sicily.

70. Diodorus' six-year advance on Varronian chronology shows here: the battle of the Cremera (river, not place: today the Fossa di Valca, joining the Tiber about five miles outside Rome) was traditionally fought in 477, not 471.

hundred Fabii, who being all of the same *gens* shared an identical family name.

These, then, were the events taking place in the course of this year.

54. When Praxiergus was archon in Athens [471/0], the Romans elected as consuls [Varr. 476] Aulus Verginius Tricostus [Rutilus] and Gaius [?] Servilius Structus. During their term, the Eleians, who had been dwelling in a number of small townships, united to form the one city-state called Elis. [2] The Lacedaemonians, seeing that Sparta (because of the treacherous activities of their general Pausanias) was suffering humiliation, whereas the Athenians were well thought of since none of *their* citizens had been convicted of treason, were desperate to involve Athens in similar unsavory charges. [3] So, since Themistocles was very well thought of by the Athenians and enjoyed a high reputation for integrity, they accused him of treason, claiming that he had been a great friend of Pausanias and that together they had planned to betray Greece to Xerxes.[71] [4] They also had discussions with Themistocles' enemies, urging them to bring charges against him and supplying them with money. When Pausanias decided to betray the Greeks, they said, he revealed his private plan to Themistocles and invited him to join in the undertaking. Though Themistocles did not accept the offer, neither did he judge himself obliged to accuse a man who was his friend. [5] Be that as it may, a formal indictment was now brought against Themistocles, though at the time he was acquitted of any treasonable activities. After being thus cleared, he remained very highly thought of by the Athenians, since his fellow-citizens loved him dearly because of his achievements. Later, however, those who feared his powerful influence, as well as others who were jealous of his renown, forgot about the benefits he had brought the state and worked zealously to shrink his power and humble his high opinion of himself.[72]

---

71. Diodorus, like Thucydides (1.135–138), now devotes an excursus (54.3–59.3) to the exile and final years of Themistocles: this, though retained under the archon year of 471/0 (which is when the sequence of events described began) extends, as is Diodorus' custom (cf. 59.4 for his own admission on this score), over a lengthy period, indeed until 459/8, the year of Themistocles' death. Compare his earlier (44.1–46.4) treatment of Pausanias. Readers are warned that the chronology in particular (including that adopted here) is still highly uncertain.

72. Though Themistocles was out of office almost immediately after the defeat of Persia, his general (as opposed to his political) popularity held good at least until 477/6, when he produced Phrynichos' *Phoenician Women* and was a star figure at the Olympic Games (Plut. *Them.* 17.2).

55. So first they banished Themistocles from Athens [?471/0], using against him that device called "ostracism," which was established by law in Athens after the dissolution of the tyranny of the Peisistratids and worked as follows. [2] Each citizen would write on a potsherd [*ostrakon*] the name of the man who seemed to him most in a position to subvert the democracy; and he whose name figured on the largest number of *ostraka* was obliged to go into exile from his fatherland for a <ten>-year period.[73] [3] The Athenians would appear to have made this law not to punish evildoers but rather to humble by means of exile the arrogance of the overambitious. Themistocles, then, after being ostracized in the aforementioned manner, went as an exile from his own country to Argos. [4] When the Lacedaemonians learned of these events, it seemed to them that fate had vouchsafed them the ideal opportunity to attack Themistocles. They therefore once again sent ambassadors to Athens, to charge Themistocles with complicity in the treason of Pausanias. Since his misdeeds were the common concern of all Hellas, the ambassadors emphasized, Themistocles should not be tried privately by the Athenians but before the general congress of the Hellenes, which was customarily due to meet [in Sparta] at about that time.[74]

[5] Themistocles himself, seeing that the Lacedaemonians were eager to humiliate and defame the Athenian state, while the Athenians wanted to clear themselves of the charge that had been thus leveled against them, calculated that he would indeed be handed over to the general congress. [6] This body, as he well knew, rendered its verdicts not according to the dictates of justice but rather out of favoritism to the Lacedaemonians: this conclusion he based on a number of episodes, in particular the way the judgment had gone in the matter of the Athenians and the <Aeginetans>.[75] On that occasion, indeed, those in charge of the voting revealed so grudging an attitude to the Athenians that, even though they had provided more triremes than all the other participants in the battle combined, they made them out to be in no respect superior to the rest of the Greeks. [7] These, then, were the reasons Themistocles came to distrust the delegates to the congress. What was more, it was from Themistocles' own defense speech at his earlier [?472/1] arraignment in Athens that

---

73. D.S.'s MSS, uniquely, make the period of ostracism last five years rather than ten. For possible explanations, see Green 2006, 116 n. 206.

74. The sole evidence for such a trial being held (in absentia) is Nep. *Them.* 8.3; though the verdict went against Themistocles, the penalty was not (as is generally assumed) death, but exile.

75. D.S.'s MSS read "Argives," which cannot be right: Argos remained neutral during the invasion. Eichstädt's emendation to "Aeginetans" is convincing: cf. 27.2.

the Lacedaemonians had drawn the basis for their subsequent indictment. [8] In the course of his defense, Themistocles had acknowledged the receipt of letters from Pausanias, urging him to become a party to Pausanias' own treasonable activities, and used this as his strongest piece of evidence to establish that Pausanias would not have needed to urge him, had he not refused an earlier invitation.

56. It was for these reasons, as stated earlier,[76] that he fled [?470/69] from Argos to Admetus, the king of the Molossians, and taking refuge at the king's hearth became his suppliant.[77] The king at first gave him a friendly reception, bade him be of good cheer, and in general undertook to guarantee his security. [2] The Lacedaemonians, however, then sent to Admetus an embassy composed of the most notable Spartan citizens, who demanded the surrender of Themistocles for punishment and branded him as the betrayer and destroyer of all Hellas. To this they added the threat that, should Admetus not hand him over, they and all the Hellenes would make war on him. At this point the king—scared by their threats, yet full of compassion for his suppliant and anxious to avoid the shame he would incur by surrendering him—persuaded Themistocles to make a speedy departure unseen by the Lacedaemonians and gave him a large sum in gold as journey-money during his flight. [3] So Themistocles, being hunted from every quarter, accepted the gold and fled the land of the Molossians by night, with all possible assistance from the king in furthering his escape. Finding two young men, Lyncestians by birth, who were engaged in trade and for that reason well acquainted with the roads, he used them as guides on his journey. [4] By traveling only at night, he gave the Lacedaemonians the slip, and through the goodwill of the young men and the trouble they went to on his behalf, he made his way to Asia. There he had a personal friend, Lysitheides by name, much looked up to because of his reputation and wealth, and it was with him that Themistocles now sought refuge.[78] [5] Lysitheides happened to be a friend of Xerxes the

---

76. Diodorus in fact nowhere earlier discusses these reasons. He also omits Themistocles' initial flight to Corcyra (Thuc. 1.136.1 with schol.; Plut. *Them.* 24.1). It was when Spartan pressure scared the Corcyraeans that he moved on to the Molossian kingdom of Epirus.

77. Thuc. 1.136.2–137.1; Plut. *Them.* 24.1–3; and Nep. *Them.* 8.4–6 all tell the story of how Themistocles, either on his own initiative or with the encouragement of the king's wife Phthia, took Admetus' young child with him to the hearth when he made his act of supplication. How long Themistocles stayed on Corcyra, and then with Admetus, is uncertain. By 469/8 he was certainly on the move again.

78. Themistocles is unlikely to have reached Asia later than 468: it could well have been

Great King, and during Xerxes' passage [through Asia Minor] had entertained the entire Persian expeditionary force. Consequently, since he both enjoyed this close familiarity with Xerxes and at the same time out of compassion wanted to save Themistocles, he promised the latter that he would do all he could to further his cause. [6] However, when Themistocles asked that Lysitheides bring him to Xerxes, at first the latter refused, making it plain to him that he would suffer retribution for his previous anti-Persian activities; but later, after coming to see the possible advantages, he agreed, and—against all odds—got him safely into Persia. [7] This was because of a custom among the Persians that anyone bringing a concubine to the Great King transported her in a covered wagon, and of those who encountered it, none made difficulties about its passage or insisted on inspecting the passenger. So it came about that Lysitheides availed himself of this facility to carry out his project. [8] After fitting out the wagon and adorning it with expensive hangings, he put Themistocles in it and got him all the way through in complete safety [Plut. *Them.* 26.3–4]. He then approached the Great King, and after some guarded discussion, finally received guarantees from the King that he would do Themistocles no harm. Lysitheides then brought him into the King's presence, and Xerxes gave him leave to speak. When he was persuaded that Themistocles had done him no wrong, the King absolved him from the [threat of] punishment.

57. But just as it seemed that, against all odds, he had been rescued by his old enemy, he once more fell into even greater danger, for the following reason. Xerxes had a full sister named Mandane, daughter of that Darius who had slaughtered the Magians,[79] and she was held in high regard among the Persians. [2] This woman had been bereft of her sons on the occasion of Themistocles' victory over the Persian fleet in the sea battle off Salamis and took the loss of her children very hard. Because of the magnitude of her misfortune, she was the object of considerable public pity. [3] When she learned of Themistocles' presence, she went to the palace arrayed in mourning, and with

---

earlier. Artaxerxes succeeded towards the end of 465; Xerxes had been assassinated that August. Sources are divided as to which of them Themistocles approached: he certainly spent time in Asia Minor first, protected by powerful friends (cf. Plut. *Them.* 26.1–3). Possibly he made a deal with Xerxes but was forced to renegotiate his position after the change of regime.

79. For the supposed Magian usurpation, and its overthrow by a group of seven Persian noblemen led by Darius, who then (522/1) ascended the Achaemenid throne, see Hdt. 3.61–88.

tears begged her brother to exact retribution from him. When he took no notice of her, she went the rounds of the Persian nobles with her petition and in a general way incited the people at large to seek vengeance on Themistocles. [4] When the mob ran to the palace and with much shouting demanded his surrender for punishment, the King answered them that he would form a panel of judges from the noblest Persians and that their verdict would be carried out. [5] This decision met with general approval; and since ample time was allowed to prepare for the trial, Themistocles used it to master the Persian language. He then conducted his defense in Persian and was acquitted of the charges brought against him.[80] [6] The King was delighted by the acquittal and honored Themistocles with substantial gifts. He gave him in marriage a Persian lady of high birth and outstanding beauty, who was also highly praised for her virtues. He [also provided] a multitude of domestic slaves for his service, as well as drinking cups of every kind and all other household goods appropriate for a pleasurable and luxurious existence. [7] The King likewise made him a present of three cities well suited to his sustenance and pleasure: Magnesia on the Maeander River, which had the most grain of all the cities in Asia, for bread; Myous for relish, since its offshore waters teemed with fish; and Lampsakos, with its numerous rich vineyards, for wine.

58. So Themistocles was now freed of the fear that had threatened him on the Greek side. Equally improbably exiled by those to whom he had brought the greatest benefits, and rewarded by those who had suffered worst at his hands, he spent the rest of his life in the above-mentioned cities, amply supplied with everything that makes for a good life.

After his death he was given a fine funeral in Magnesia and a memorial that is still standing to this day. [2] Some writers state that when Xerxes conceived the desire to launch a second invasion of Greece, he invited Themistocles to be his commander-in-chief. Themistocles agreed, and received from the King a sworn guarantee that he would not march against the Greeks without Themistocles. [3] So a bull was sacrificed, and the oaths taken. Then Themistocles filled a cup with its blood, drank it down, and at once died. Xerxes as a result is supposed to have given up his plan; and thus Themistocles, by the death he chose, left behind the best possible argument that in all matters touching the Hellenes he had acted as a good citizen.[81]

---

80. No other source reports this trial, and it is generally rejected as dramatic invention (e.g., in the strongest terms, by Frost, 193; cf. Haillet, 160 n. 3).

81. The year 459/8 is generally accepted as the date of Themistocles' death, but the claim that he committed suicide by drinking bull's blood (not in fact lethal and in some

[4] We are now confronted with the death of a very great Greek, about whom disagreement still continues. Was it because he had wronged both his fatherland and the Hellenes at large that he sought asylum with the Persians? Or was it, on the contrary, that his own city and the rest of Hellas, despite the great benefits he brought them, showed him no gratitude but rather, most unjustly, exposed their benefactor to the gravest perils? [5] If anyone examines this man's character and achievements closely, without prejudice, it will be found that in both respects Themistocles stands head and shoulders above all those of whom we have record. It follows that one well might be astounded at the Athenians' readiness to deprive themselves of a man endowed with such natural brilliance.

59. Who else, while Sparta held supreme power, and the Spartan Eurybiades was in command of the fleet, could by his individual efforts have stripped Sparta of that proud glory? What other man do we find in the annals of history who by a single act raised himself above all other leaders, his city above all other Greek states, and the Greeks over the *barbaroi*? During whose term as general (*strategos*) have resources ever been slimmer or imminent danger greater? [2] Who else, confronted with the whole might of Asia and with his city evacuated, faced the enemy and won? Who else in peacetime increased the strength of his fatherland with such achievements as his? Who, when a vast war overtook the state, saw it through to safety, and by one single ruse, that involving the bridge [<19.5–6], reduced the size of the enemy forces by half, so that it fell easy victim to the Greeks? [3] As a result—when we consider the magnitude of his achievements and, examining them individually, find that his own city dishonored this man, whereas it was by his deeds that the city itself achieved its high position—then we may plausibly infer that the city with the highest reputation of all for wisdom and tolerance treated him most harshly.

[4] Though we may have digressed too long on this matter of Themistocles' great worth, we thought it not proper that we should leave that worth unrecorded.

At the same as these events, in Italy Micythus [66.1–4], whose sway extended over Rhegium and Zancle, founded the city of Pyxus.

60. While Demotion was archon in Athens [470/69], the Romans elected as consuls [Varr. 475] Publius Valerius P<op>licola and Gaius Nautius Rufus.

---

places a diet staple), current already in the 420s (Aristoph. *Kn.* 83–84 with schol.), is a legend: according to Thucydides (who knew the story), he in fact died of an illness (1.138.4).

During their term of office, the Athenians chose as general Cimon the son of Miltiades, entrusted him with a strong force, and dispatched him to the coast of Asia [Minor], to render aid to the cities in alliance with them and to liberate those still occupied by Persian garrisons. [2] Cimon picked up the flotilla stationed at Byzantium, sailed to the city known as Eion, which was under Persian control, and captured it. He then took by siege [the island of] Scyros, of which the inhabitants were Pelasgians and Dolopians, installed a colony with an Athenian as official "founder" (*ktistes*), and divided up the land into cleruchs' allotments [?470]. [3] After this, having it in mind to embark on greater enterprises, he sailed to Piraeus, where he took on more triremes and organized supplies on a generous scale. At that point he put to sea with two hundred triremes; but afterwards, what with requisitions from the Ionians and everyone else, he brought his overall total up to three hundred. [4] So he sailed with this entire fleet to Caria [?468/7]. Those cities on the coast that had been colonized from Greece he at once persuaded to revolt from the Persians. Those, however, with bilingual populations and resident Persian garrisons he dealt with by force, laying siege to them. After thus bringing over the cities of Caria, he did the same with those in Lycia, again by persuasion. [5] Also, by acquiring extra ships from these new allies as they were enrolled, he increased the size of his fleet yet further.

The Persians drew on their own peoples for their land forces, but their navy they assembled from Phoenicia and Cyprus and Cilicia: the commander-in-chief of all Persian armaments was Tithraustes, a bastard son of Xerxes. [6] When Cimon learned that the Persian fleet was lying off Cyprus, he sailed against the *barbaroi* and engaged them in a naval action, with two hundred and fifty vessels against the enemy's three hundred and forty. A fierce battle ensued, in which both sides acquitted themselves with distinction; but ultimately the Athenians were victorious, destroying large numbers of the enemy's ships and capturing more than a hundred, together with their crews. [7] The remainder got away to Cyprus, where their crews went ashore and took off for the interior; the ships themselves, being emptied of defenders, fell into the hands of the enemy.

61. After this [?466] Cimon, not content even with so substantial a victory, led his entire fleet against the Persian land force, which was then in camp by the Eurymedon River. Having a notion to outwit the *barbaroi* by a stratagem, he embarked the pick of his troops on the captured Persian vessels, giving them tiaras to wear and in all other respects dressing them up as Persians. [2] The *barbaroi* were taken in by the Persian vessels and accoutrements even when the fleet had come close inshore, and therefore, assuming that these

triremes were their own, they greeted the Athenians as friends. It was already dark when Cimon landed his troops, and the *barbaroi* welcomed them with open arms. This enabled Cimon to charge straight into their encampment, [3] causing considerable noise and confusion among the Persians. Cimon's troops slaughtered every man in their path, including Pherendates, the Persians' deputy commander and a nephew of the Great King, whom they seized in his pavilion. Of the rest, they killed some and seriously wounded others: because of the unexpectedness of the attack, they forced every last man of them into headlong flight. By and large the Persians were in such a state of panic and bewilderment that most of them had no idea who it was attacking them. [4] It never occurred to them that the strong force coming against them could be Greek; indeed, they were convinced that the Greeks had no land army at all. They assumed rather that it must be the Pisidians who were responsible for this hostile incursion, since they shared a frontier and were embroiled in continual disputes with them. Because of this they figured that the enemy attack was coming from inland and so made for the ships, assuming that these were on their side. [5] The night, being dark and moonless, simply served to increase their bewilderment: not a soul could see the true state of affairs. [6] Because of the confusion in the ranks of the *barbaroi,* a great slaughter took place. At this point Cimon—who had given his troops prior orders to come back at the double when he showed them a flaming torch as signal and marker—now raised this signal beside the ships, worried lest the wide dispersion of his men, and the possibility that they might rush off in pursuit of plunder, should produce some unlooked-for setback. [7] The soldiers, however, all abandoned their plundering and duly assembled by the lit torch. They then withdrew to the ships. Next day they set up a trophy, after which they sailed back to Cyprus, having won two outstanding victories, one on land, the other at sea. Never again since has history recorded such great and momentous actions on the same day[82] by a force that engaged both ashore and afloat.

62. Cimon's great successes, achieved through his personal bravery and strategic skill, meant that his fame got noised abroad not only among his own countrymen but throughout the rest of the Greek world; for he had captured three hundred and forty ships, over 20,000 men, and a very considerable sum of money. [2] The Persians, however, after suffering these substantial reverses,

---

82. A nice case of symbolic synchronicity (24.1 and note) being defeated by geography: the minimum distance from Cyprus to the Eurymedon is about 130 miles, and so Cimon and his fleet cannot conceivably have made the voyage in less than 8–9 hours, let alone have fought two engagements on the same day.

built yet more triremes, in even greater numbers, through their fear at the growing power of the Athenians. Indeed, from this time on the Athenian *polis* kept building up its power more and more, being in possession of an abundance of wealth and having acquired a very high reputation for bravery and military skill. [3] The Athenian *demos* dedicated a tithe of the booty to the god and inscribed the following epigraph on the dedication:

> From the day when first the sea divided Europe from Asia
> and brash Ares won a hold on the cities of men,
> never yet among earth-dwelling mortals was there such a
> deed accomplished at once on land, by sea.
> These men on Cyprus wrought many Medes' destruction,
> taking at sea a hundred Phoenician ships
> crammed full of warriors, and greatly did Asia mourn them,
> struck down with both hands by the might of war.[83]

63. Such, then, were the events that took place during this year.

When Phae<d>on [<48 and note] was archon in Athens [469/8], in Rome Lucius Furius Med<ulli>nus and <A.> Manilius V<ul>so succeeded [Varr. 474] to the consulship. During their term of office, a great and unlooked-for disaster befell the Lacedaemonians: major earthquakes took place in Sparta, so that houses collapsed from their foundations and more than 20,000 Lacedaemonians were killed.[84] [2] Since the disintegration of their city, with houses collapsing into rubble, went on nonstop for a considerable period, many were pinned by the falling walls and so perished, while the earthquake damaged no small amount of household property. [3] This evil afflicting them they suffered as though it was the handiwork of some avenging divinity—though they also faced other dangers from human enemies, for the following reasons. [4] The helots and Messenians, although nursing enmity towards the Lacedaemonians, had hitherto remained quiet, through fear of Sparta's preeminence and power; but when they perceived that the greater part of them had

---

83. The god thus honored was Delphic Apollo: the tithe paid for a bronze palm tree on which stood a Palladium, a gilt statue of armed Athena. The epigraph is generally attributed to Simonides.

84. Generally dated to 464/3 on the basis of Paus. 4.24.5–6, citing the archon year; but the evidence, including Diodorus' plural, suggests that in fact there may have been at least two earthquakes during this period, one in 469/8, the other in 464/3. Seismologically this is by no means unlikely. The numerous casualties had a serious effect on Spartan manpower. That both helots and Messenians should take advantage of the chaos produced by two major earthquakes is hardly surprising; there is no need to choose between them.

perished in the earthquake, their attitude to the few survivors became one of contempt. They therefore banded together and jointly waged war against the Lacedaemonians [469/8]. [5] The Lacedaemonian king Archidamus, by his personal foresight, both saw to his countrymen's safety at the time of the earthquake and fought nobly against the insurgents during the war [that followed]. [6] When his city was paralyzed by the intensity of the seismic shock, he was the first Spartan to grab his armor and hasten from the capital into the countryside, while calling on the other citizens to follow his example. [7] The Spartans obeyed him, and by so doing those who survived [the first shock] were saved. It was they whom King Archidamus rallied into a defense force and made ready to fight the rebels.

64. When the Messenians joined forces with the helots, they at first hurried to attack Sparta, figuring that they would have no trouble capturing it through the city's dearth of defenders. However, when they heard that the survivors were drawn up [under arms] with King Archidamus [at their head], and stood ready to fight for their fatherland, the rebels abandoned this plan and instead occupied a stronghold [Mt. Ithome] in Messenia, from which they made regular sorties to overrun Laconia. [2] The Spartans were driven to solicit aid from the Athenians, who sent them an expeditionary force; they also collected troops from the rest of their allies and thus got themselves on an equal footing with the enemy. Thus to begin with, they had the advantage over them; but later [?463/2], when a suspicion arose that the Athenians intended to defect to the Messenians, the Spartans repudiated Athens as their ally, saying that the other allies they had offered them sufficient support for the conflict ahead. [3] The Athenians, though regarding this act as an affront, at the time simply withdrew. Afterwards, however, being already on unfriendly terms with the Lacedaemonians, they were all the more inclined, [because of this incident] to fan the flames of hatred. As a result they took [the rebuff] as the beginning of the estrangement between them. Later the two states quarreled and, by launching into a series of major wars, filled all Hellas with vast misfortunes. We shall, however, write of these matters severally in their proper context [>12.38–13.107]. [4] At the time the Lacedaemonians made an expedition with their allies against Ithome and laid siege to it.[85] Meanwhile, the helots as a whole now revolted from the Lacedaemonians and allied themselves with the Messenians. The fortunes of war favored first one

85. In 463/2, by the general consensus of modern scholars. Diodorus (who here moves to and fro in time with more than his usual flexibility) makes it clear that the expedition, in any case, took place before the dismissal of the Athenians reported in 64.2.

side, then the other: for ten long years [?468–458] they continually attacked and counterattacked, without any final decision being reached.

65. After this, Theagenides was archon in Athens [468/7], while in Rome the consuls who took office [Varr. 473] were Lucius Aemilius Mamercus and <Vopisc>us Iulius Iullus, and the 78th Olympiad was held, in which Parmenides of Poseidonia won the *stadion*. During this period, war broke out between the Argives and the Mycenaeans, for the following reasons. [2] The Mycenaeans, on account of their country's ancient high repute, would not subordinate themselves to the Argives like the other cities throughout the Argolid, but took an independent line and ignored Argive authority. They also had a running dispute with them about the sacred precinct of Hera, as well as claiming that it was they who should by rights organize the Nemean Games.[86] Furthermore, when the Argives voted not to fight with the Lacedaemonians at Thermopylae unless they were allowed to share the command, the Mycenaeans, alone of those domiciled in the Argolid, fought at the Lacedaemonians' side. [3] The long and short of it was that the Argives regarded the Mycenaeans with suspicion and were worried lest any increase of strength on their part might lead them, relying on their city's ancient prestige, to challenge the Argives for the leadership. For these reasons, then, they were at loggerheads. The Argives had from of old always striven to promote their own city, and at this point they figured they had a fine opportunity, seeing that the Lacedaemonians had been weakened and could not come to the Mycenaeans' assistance. Accordingly, they put together a sizable force, from both Argos and the cities allied with her, and marched against the Mycenaeans. After defeating them in battle and driving them back inside their walls, they laid siege to the city. [4] For a while the Mycenaeans energetically stood off the besiegers; but later on, as they began to get the worst of it in the war, and the Lacedaemonians were unable to relieve them on account of their own wars and the disastrous impact of the earthquake, and since they had no other allies, they were overpowered through lack of external support. [5] The Argives sold the Mycenaeans into slavery, dedicated a tenth part of them to the god, and demolished Mycenae itself. So this city, so fortunate in ancient times, able to boast of great

---

86. The famous Heraeum, or sanctuary of Hera, stood on an ancient Bronze Age site about midway between Argos and Mycenae, and served as a common shrine for the whole Argolid (Strab. 8.6.10, C.372). The Nemean Games, first celebrated in 573, had been administered by Cleonae, a town located inside the territory of the Heraeum. From 460 (probably as a result of this dispute) the Argives took over control of the Games (Paus. 2.15.2).

heroes and with notable achievements to its credit, came to the disastrous end described above, and has remained uninhabited to this day.

These, then, were the events that took place during this year.

66. When Lysistratus was archon in Athens [467/6], the Romans elected as consuls [Varr. 472] Lucius Pinarius Mamer<c>inus [Rufus] and Publius Furius [Medullinus] <Fusus>. During their term of office, Hieron, king of the Syracusans, summoned to Syracuse the sons of Anaxilas, who had been tyrant of Zancle. Bestowing rich gifts upon them, he reminded them of the benefactions that their father had received from Gelon and counseled them, now they had come of age, to demand a reckoning from their guardian Micythus [<48.2] and assume power themselves. [2] So, when they returned to Rhegium, they asked their guardian for an accounting of his stewardship. Micythus, being an honest man, assembled the friends of the boys' father, and made so scrupulous an accounting that everyone present was amazed at his righteousness and good faith; and the boys, now regretting their action, besought Micythus to reassume authority and carry out the business of government with all the power and rank that their father had enjoyed. [3] Micythus, however, would not agree. Instead, after effecting a meticulous transfer of power, he loaded all his personal property aboard a ship and sailed away from Rhegium, accompanied by the good wishes of the populace. When he reached Greece, he spent the rest of his life in Tegea in Arcadia, the object of general esteem. [4] Hieron, the king of the Syracusans, died in Catana and received heroic honors, as having been the founder of the city. He had ruled for eleven years, and he left the kingdom to his brother Thrasybulus, who reigned over the Syracusans for one year only.

67. When Lysanius was archon in Athens [466/5], the Romans elected as consuls [Varr. 471] Appius Claudius [Crassinus Inregillensis Sabinus] and Titus Quinctius Capitolinus [Barbatus]. During their term of office, Thrasybulus, king of the Syracusans, lost his throne. Since we are describing this episode in detail, we need to go back a little in time and narrate the whole story in clear detail from the beginning.

[2] Gelon son of Deinomenes, a man who far excelled all others in courage and generalship, outfought and defeated the *barbaroi* of Carthage in a great battle, as has been narrated above [<21–22]. Now since he treated with moderation all those whom he vanquished and in general behaved with humanity to all his near neighbors, his reputation among the Sicilian Greeks stood very high. [3] Being, then, loved universally on account of his mild rule, he continued to enjoy a peaceful life until he passed away. But when Hieron,

the next oldest brother, inherited the kingdom, his manner of rule over his subjects was very different, [4] he being avaricious, violent, and, in sum, of a character wholly opposed to honesty or nobility.[87] As a result, many were eager to revolt but restrained themselves on account of Gelon's reputation and his benevolence to all Sicilian Greeks. [5] But after Hieron's death, his brother Thrasybulus succeeded to the throne, and in the matter of wickedness he outdid his predecessor. A man not merely violent but murderous by temperament, he unjustly executed many citizens and forced not a few into exile through false accusations, impounding their property for the benefit of the royal treasury. Since, by and large, those whom he wronged detested him as much as he did them, he hired a large number of foreign mercenaries, thus setting up an opposition force with which to counter the citizen-militia. [6] Indeed, since he continually exacerbated the hatred of the citizens by the numerous outrages he perpetrated on them (including not a few murders), he finally drove his victims to rebellion. The Syracusans, then, chose citizens of action to be their leaders and to a man eagerly set about the overthrow of the tyranny. Once these leaders had organized them, they clung with tenacity to the pursuit of freedom. [7] When Thrasybulus saw that the whole city was on the warpath against him, he at first tried to check the revolt by diplomacy; but when he realized that the momentum of the Syracusans' [uprising] was unstoppable, he mustered all his allies, including those colonists whom Hieron had settled in Catana, as well as a vast number of mercenaries, raising in all something like 15,000 men. [8] He then seized the quarter of the city known as Achradina, together with the Island [of Ortygia], which was fortified, and from these bases waged war against the rebels.

68. The Syracusans began by occupying the quarter called <Tyche>,[88] and from this base sent out ambassadors to Gela and Acragas and Selinus, as well as to Himera and the Sicel cities of the interior, asking them to come quickly and join with them in liberating Syracuse. [2] All responded with a will and lost no time in dispatching aid. Some sent cavalry and infantry detachments, others warships fully equipped for battle, so that in a very short time a considerable force had been put together to help the Syracusans. As a result of

---

87. Diodorus is clearly not impressed by Hieron's very considerable record as an enlightened patron of the arts, whose guests included Pindar, Bacchylides, Simonides, Xenophanes of Colophon, and Aeschylus, or indeed by his chariot victories at the Olympian and Pythian Games (Paus. 6.12.1, 8.42.9; cf. Pind. *Ol.* 1, *Pyth.* 1).

88. Correction of the meaningless *Itykên* of Diodorus' MSS: for the topographical problems see Green 2006, 135–136 n. 259.

this, the Syracusans manned their fleet and brought their land force to battle stations, thus demonstrating that they were ready and willing to pursue the struggle to its end both on land and at sea. [3] Thrasybulus, being abandoned by his allies, had to base his hopes on the mercenaries. All he held was Achradina and the Island: the rest of the city was controlled by the Syracusans. He then led his fleet out against the enemy, and after being worsted in a sea battle, and losing numerous triremes, retreated to the Island with those who remained. [4] In a like manner, he sallied out from Achradina with his land force and fought an engagement in the suburbs, which he lost. After suffering heavy losses, he was forced to withdraw into Achradina. Finally, he abandoned his claim on the tyranny, negotiated a deal with the Syracusans, and having come to terms with them, withdrew under truce to [Epizephyrian] Locri. [5] The Syracusans, after freeing their city in this manner, gave the mercenaries their leave to withdraw from Syracuse, and then freed those other cities that either were ruled by tyrants or had garrisons, and restored democratic government in them.[89] [6] From now on Syracuse had peace and greatly increased prosperity, preserving its democracy for almost sixty years, until the tyranny of Dionysius [>13.91–96]. [7] Thrasybulus, who had inherited an excellently established kingdom, lost it in a shameful manner through his own wickedness, and after fleeing to Locri lived out his days there as a private citizen.

[8] Simultaneous with these events, in Rome for the first time there were now elected [Varr. 471] four [urban] tribunes: Gaius Sic<ci>us, Lucius Numitorius, Marcus Duillius, and Spurius [I]cilius.

69. When this year had run its course, Lysitheus became archon in Athens [465/4], while in Rome the consuls elected [Varr. 470] were Lucius Valerius [Volusi Potitus] and Titus Aemilius Mamercus. During their term, in Asia Artabanus, a Hyrcanian by race, a man of the highest authority in King Xerxes' court and the commander of the palace guard, decided to eliminate Xerxes and transfer the royal power to himself. He made the eunuch Mithridates privy to his plot: this person, besides being the King's chamberlain and enjoying his absolute trust, was also Artabanus' kinsman as well as his friend, and therefore lent himself to the scheme. [2] Artabanus was brought by him at night into the [King's] bedchamber and killed Xerxes [4–8 Aug. 465]. He

---

89. This process was both lengthy and convulsive, as Diodorus himself makes very clear in subsequent chapters (72–73, 76, 78, 86, 88, 91–92). But Thrasybulus' fall did in fact bring down the whole carefully constructed political edifice of the Deinomenid dynasty. For democracy in Syracuse between 466 and 406, see Robinson.

then moved against the King's sons. These were three in number: the eldest, Darius, and Artaxerxes were both resident in the palace, but the third, Hystaspes, was abroad just then, in charge of the Bactrian satrapy. [3] So Artabanus came to Artaxerxes while it was still dark and told him that his brother Darius had murdered his father and meant to seize the throne for himself. [4] He advised Artaxerxes, therefore, before Darius could consolidate his power, to look to it that he did not, through mere passive indifference, suffer enslavement: let him rather take vengeance on his father's killer and himself become King. He also promised to bring him the royal guard as accomplices to this end. [5] Artaxerxes was convinced, and at once, with the royal guard's cooperation, assassinated his brother Darius. At this point Artabanus, seeing how well his plan was going, summoned his own sons to his side and told them that now was the moment to win the throne. He then struck Artaxerxes a blow with his sword. [6] Artaxerxes, however, though wounded, was in no way incapacitated by this assault: he defended himself vigorously against Artabanus and struck him a shrewd blow that killed him. Thus Artaxerxes survived against odds, avenged his father's murder, and succeeded to the Persian throne. Xerxes, then, died in the aforesaid manner, having reigned over the Persians for more than twenty years [486–425], and was followed by Artaxerxes [II Mnemon], who ruled for forty [late 465–425/4].[90]

70. When Archidemides was archon in Athens [464/3], the Romans elected as consuls [Varr. 469] Aulus Verginius [Caeliomontanus] and Titus <Numi>cius [Priscus], and the 79th Olympiad was held, in which Xenophon the Corinthian won the *stadion.* During their term, the Thasians revolted from the Athenians through a disagreement about certain mines: but the Athenians reduced them by siege and forcibly brought them back under their control [463]. [2] Similarly, when the Aeginetans rebelled,[91] the Athenians put Aegina under siege with the object of reducing them to servitude; for this *polis,* having fought numerous successful sea battles, was full of arrogant self-confidence, besides being well supplied with cash reserves and triremes. Thus, generally speaking, it was at permanent odds with the Athenians. [3] The latter therefore made an expedition against [the island], laid waste its territory,

90. The name Artaxerxes proved popular after Artaxerxes II Mnemon's long and successful reign: his successor Ochos also adopted it—as, with less success, the satrap Bessos also did after murdering Darius III (15.93.1).
91. "Rebelled" (*apostantas*) is an error: Aegina was independent (as Diodorus well knows: 78.3–4, where he treats this episode in chronological context) until Athens' attack (initiated in 458) by the summer of 457 reduced the island to subject-ally status, with a thirty-talent tribute assessment.

and besieged [the city of] Aegina, making every effort to take it by storm; for it was generally true that, since their current great gains in power, the Athenians no longer treated the allies equitably, as they had done earlier, but were subjecting them to a rule as harsh as it was arrogant. [4] In consequence, most of the allies, unable to tolerate their severity, were discussing the idea of revolt with one another; while some of them, in defiance of the general congress [of the League], were acting as though they were independent [Thuc. 1.98–99].

[5] Simultaneously with these events [?466/5: >12.68.1], the Athenians, as masters of the sea, sent out 10,000 colonists, recruited in part from their own citizen body and in part from the allies, to Amphipolis. They parceled out the land in cleruchies and for a while kept the Thracians in subjection; but afterwards [?464/3], when they penetrated deeper into Thrace, those thus invading the country were wiped out to the last man [at Drabescus] by a people called the Edones.

71. When Tlepolemus was archon in Athens [463/2], the Romans elected as consuls [Varr. 468] Titus Quinctius [Capitolinus Barbatus] and Quintus Servilius Structus [Priscus]. During their term, Artaxerxes, the Great King of Persia, who had recently [late 465] regained the throne [<69.5–6], first of all—after punishing those involved in the assassination of his father—reordered the government of the realm to his own advantage. [2] Of the satraps then in office he dismissed those personally hostile to him and replaced them with friends of his chosen for their proven competence. He also turned his attention to the revenues and to military preparations generally; and since his administration of the kingdom as a whole was, by and large, equitable, he was held in high esteem by the Persians.

[3] But when the Egyptians got wind of Xerxes' death, with the whole business of the attempt on the throne, and the resultant confusion throughout the Persian realm, they decided to make a bid for their freedom. So they promptly raised an army and revolted from the Persians, expelling those Persians stationed in Egypt to collect tribute [?fall 464], and setting up their own king, one Inaros by name.[92] [4] Inaros began by enlisting troops from among the native inhabitants, but later also gathered mercenaries from a variety of

---

92. Egypt had long been resentful of Persian control ever since the conquest by Cambyses in 525 (Hdt. 3.1–45). An earlier attempt at secession (486–5) had been put down by Xerxes after the death of Darius (Hdt. 7.1.3, 7.5.1, 7.7.1). As the son of Psammetichus, Inaros clearly presented himself as a national (Saïte) pharaoh. He must, however, have known that Persia would eventually act against him: the winter of 463/2 and the spring of 462, as is clear from Diodorus and Thuc. 1.104, were spent in recruiting troops and making diplomatic approaches to various potential foreign allies.

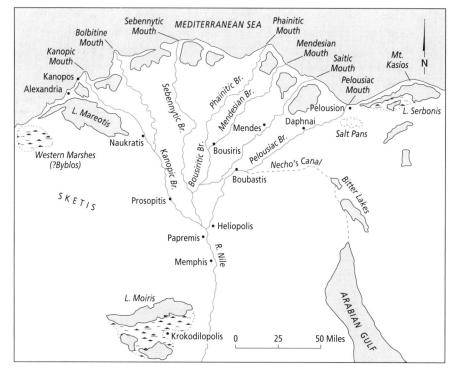

Map 11.4. The Egyptian Delta

countries, and thus built up a very sizable army He also dispatched ambassadors to the Athenians to discuss the matter of an alliance, promising them
that if they would [help] liberate the Egyptians, he would open his kingdom
to them and offer them in return benefits far greater than their service to him.
[5] The Athenians decided that it would be to their advantage to cut the
Persians down to size as far as they could and to use the Egyptians as a handy
bulwark against the random vicissitudes of fortune. They therefore voted to
come to the Egyptians' aid with a fleet of three hundred triremes.[93] [6] So the

93. We are nowhere told what so vast a force was supposed to be doing in the eastern
Mediterranean. The obvious answer would seem to be protecting the Egyptian and Le-
vantine trade routes against potential Persian aggression. Can they have all been diverted
to Egypt? It seems highly unlikely. Ctesias (F14b [36] Lenfant), for once a minimalist, puts
the size of the Athenian squadron there at forty ships only, and this is both realistic and
attractive. Thucydides' figure of two hundred triremes (1.104.2) would perhaps be reasonable for a fleet patrolling the eastern Mediterranean (Diodorus' figure of 300 is most likely
a mere slip for 200).

Athenians, with great enthusiasm, set about the preparation of this expedition. When Artaxerxes learned of the Egyptians' rebellion and their preparations for war, he figured that he would need to outstrip the Egyptians in the size of his forces. He therefore at once began to enlist troops from all the satrapies, lay down ships, and busy himself with every other sort of preparation.

Such were the events of this year in Asia and Egypt.

72. In Sicily, no sooner had the Syracusan tyranny been abolished [<68.4–6], and every city on the island liberated [466/5], than Sicily as a whole began moving very quickly towards an increase in general prosperity. The Sicilian Greeks were now at peace, and the land they cultivated was rich. The abundance of their produce soon enabled them to increase their holdings, so that they filled the countryside with servants and cattle and other manifestations of prosperity, accumulating vast revenues, while at the same time spending nothing on the wars to which they had previously grown accustomed. [2] Later, however, they once more plunged into wars and civil strife for the following reasons. Having overthrown the tyranny of Thrasybulus, [the Syracusans] convened an assembly. After debate concerning the [implementation of] their own democracy, they voted with one accord to put up a colossal statue of Zeus the Liberator [*Eleutherios*] and, on the day on which they had overthrown the tyrant and freed their native city, to celebrate an annual Festival of Liberation [*Eleutheria*] with sacrifices and high-class games, at which they would slaughter four hundred and fifty bulls in honor of the gods and use them to furnish meat for the citizens' public feast.[94] [3] All the offices of state they allotted to those who were citizens by birth: the aliens enfranchised in Gelon's time they did not consider for this honor, either because they deemed them unworthy or else because they distrusted them as men who, being acclimatized to tyranny and, indeed, as former veterans of the tyrant, might well attempt a revolution. This in fact was precisely what happened: for Gelon had put more than 10,000 foreign mercenaries on the citizen rolls, and at the time of which we are speaking, more than 7,000 of them were still left.

73. These men much resented being thus excluded from the dignity of office, and with one accord revolted from the Syracusans. They then seized two quarters of the city, Achradina and the Island, both of which possessed their own excellent fortifications. [2] The Syracusans, being thus once more

---

94. Diodorus' text suggests unanimity on all else but disagreement over the nature of the proposed democracy: Syracuse's subsequent history makes this very plausible. The aliens were in all probability Campanian mercenaries: La Genière, 24–36.

plunged into disorder, [nevertheless] held the rest of the city, and the quarter facing towards Epipolae they walled off, thus achieving a high level of security for themselves; for by so doing they at once easily cut off the rebels' access to the countryside and very soon had them short of provisions. [3] Now though these foreigners were fewer in number than the Syracusans, in military experience they far exceeded them, so when attacks and isolated skirmishes took place at various points throughout the city, the foreigners invariably came off best in such encounters. Since they were cut off from the countryside, however, they lacked supplies and went short of food.

Such were the events during this period in Sicily.

74. When Conon was archon in Athens [462/1], in Rome the consulship was held [Varr. 467] by Quintus Fabius Vibulanus and Tiberius Aemilius Mamercus. During their term, Artaxerxes, the Great King of Persia, appointed as commanding general for the campaign against the Egyptians Darius' son Achaemenes, who was also his own uncle. He handed over to him a force of over 300,000 troops, inclusive of both cavalry and infantry, with orders to crush the Egyptians utterly. [2] On reaching Egypt, Achaemenes encamped near the Nile and rested his troops after their long march. He then made preparations for battle [? late 462]. The Egyptians, however, who had been assembling an army from Libya and Egypt itself, were still awaiting the allied contingent from Athens. [3] The Athenians finally made landfall in Egypt with two hundred ships and drew up their battle line alongside the Egyptians against the Persians. A fierce struggle ensued. For a while, the Persians had the better of it because of their superior numbers, but later the Athenians went on the attack and routed the forces opposed to them, killing a good number. The rest of the *barbaroi* thereupon turned and fled. [4] Considerable slaughter took place during the retreat, until finally, after losing the greater part of their army, the Persians sought refuge in the so-called White Fort. The Athenians, who had secured victory by their own courageous actions, pursued the *barbaroi* as far as this stronghold and had no qualms about laying siege to it.[95]

[5] When Artaxerxes heard about the defeat of his troops, his first thought was to dispatch some of his friends, with large sums of cash, to Lacedaemon, with a request that the Lacedaemonians should make war on the Athenians, supposing that thus those Athenians who were winning in Egypt would surely

---

95. The Athenian squadron (or, more probably, a detachment of it, perhaps Ctesias' forty vessels) sailed up the Nile (Thuc. 1.104.2), probably by the Canopic or the Mendesian branch, to the White Fort, which was in Memphis itself.

sail back to Athens to rescue their homeland. [6] The Lacedaemonians, however, neither took the money nor paid the slightest attention to the Persians'
proposal [but see Thuc. 1.109.1–2]. So Artaxerxes, giving up any hope of
getting aid from them, set about raising a new force of his own. As joint commanders of it he appointed Artabazus [<44.3] and Megabyzus, men highly
distinguished for skill and valor [>12.3.2], and sent them off to campaign
against the Egyptians.

75. When Euthippus was archon in Athens [461/0], the Romans elected
[Varr. 466] as consuls Quintus Servilius [Priscus] and Spurius Postumius Al-
binus [Regillensis]. During their term, in Asia Artabazus and Megabyzus,
who had been sent out to prosecute the war against the Egyptians, took the
road from Persia [? July 461] with more than 300,000 cavalry and infantry.
[2] When they reached Cilicia and Phoenicia [? Sept. 461], they rested their
land forces after the march and sent orders to the Cypriots and Phoenicians
and Cilicians to provide ships for them. Three hundred triremes were supplied [? spring 460], which they then manned with their finest fighting marines, providing also arms, missiles, and everything else of use in naval warfare. [3] So these men were busy with their preparations and spent nearly the
whole year [461/0] training their troops and inuring them all to the business
of warfare. [4] Meanwhile, the Athenians in Egypt were [still] laying siege to
the troops that had fled for refuge to the White Fort near Memphis; but these
Persians mounted a vigorous defense, so that the Athenians failed to storm the
stronghold and continued to besiege it for the rest of the year.

76. In Sicily, the Syracusans were still fighting their rebellious foreign
[mercenaries]. They made continual assaults on both Achradina and the Island [Ortygia], and also defeated the rebels in a sea battle, but on land proved
unable to dislodge them from the city because of the excellent fortifications
protecting these two strongholds. [2] Later, however, when an open engagement took place outside the city—in which both sides fought vigorously,
and both suffered not a few casualties—final victory went to the Syracusans.
After the battle they bestowed the crown of valor on the picked force of six
hundred men who were responsible for the victory and presented each one of
them with a *mina* of silver.[96] [3] Simultaneously with these events, Ducetius,

---

96. This "picked force of six hundred men" may well have been mercenaries themselves,
who were bribed to change sides: one *mina* = 100 drachmas, i.e., ⅟₆₀th of a talent, and 10
talents was an extraordinarily heavy outlay, given that even the best mercenaries seldom
asked more than 2–3 drachmas per diem.

the native Sicel leader,[97] who bore a grudge against the inhabitants of Catana for robbing the Sicels of their land, led a force against them. Now it happened that the Syracusans had also mounted an expedition against Catana; so they and the Sicels shared out the land between them in allotments, and together made war on those settlers who had been sent out by Hieron as ruler [of Syracuse]. The Catanians fought back but were defeated in a series of battles and driven out of Catana, subsequently taking possession of what is now Aetna but formerly was known as Inessa. Thus, after many years the original inhabitants of Catana recovered their native city [<49.1–2].

[4] After these events, [other] groups who had been expropriated from their own cities during Hieron's reign, finding themselves now with support in the struggle, returned to their several homelands and drove out those who had unjustly seized the property of others. Among them were the inhabitants of Gela, Acragas, and Himera. [5] In a similar manner, the Rhegians and Zanclians together expelled the sons of Anaxilas who were then ruling them [<66.1–3] and liberated their native cities. Somewhat later the Geloans, who had been the original settlers of Camarina, divided up that city's territory into allotments. Virtually all the cities, in their eagerness to put an end to these wars, with one accord agreed to come to terms with their resident bodies of foreign [mercenaries]. They then took back the exiles and returned the cities to [the descendants of] their original settlers. All those foreigners who, at the behest of former tyrannical rulers, had been left in possession of cities not their own, they gave leave to remove all their personal property and to settle in Messenia.[98] [6] Thus the civil strife and anarchy that had plagued the Sicilian cities were brought to a close; and the cities themselves, after extirpating such alien forms of government as had been introduced, almost all shared out their separate territories in the shape of allotments for the entire citizen body [>16.83].

77. When Phrasiclides was archon in Athens [460/59], the 80th Olympiad was held, in which the *stadion* was won by Toryllas of Thessaly, and the Romans elected [Varr. 465] as consuls Quintus Fabius [Vibulanus] and Ti-

---

97. This is the first mention of the remarkable Sicel nationalist, for whom Diodorus is our sole ancient source and whose name was still being invoked in Sicily in the late 1940s in connection with his modern epigonos Salvatore Giuliano.

98. Messenia was still in revolt against Sparta; thus the deportees, almost all experienced mercenaries, must have been welcomed by Sparta as a useful instrument in helping to put down the insurrection, and granted land-tenure in return for their services, acting thereafter as, among other things, rural slave-masters.

tus Quinctius Capitolinus [Barbatus]. During their term, in Asia the Persian generals who had marched across country to Cilicia fitted out three hundred ships, equipping them fully for armed combat. They then took their land force and advanced through Syria and Phoenicia, and thus, with the fleet hugging the coast alongside the army, reached Memphis in Egypt [? fall 460]. [2] Their first act was to break the siege of the White Fort, [their arrival] having dumbfounded the Egyptians and Athenians; subsequently, however [? from spring 459], they implemented a more cautious policy, refusing any head-on encounters and doing their utmost to end the war by means of various stratagems.[99] Thus, since the Athenian fleet was moored at the island known as Prosopitis, they dug canals [? spring 457] to divert the river that flowed past both sides of this island, thus making the island an island no longer. [3] When the ships were in this way suddenly stranded on dry land, the Egyptians panicked, abandoned the Athenians, and cut a deal with the Persians.[100] The Athenians, now bereft of allies and seeing that their ships had been rendered useless, set fire to them to stop their falling into the hands of the enemy. They then, no whit perturbed by the serious situation they were in, encouraged one another to do nothing unworthy of their triumphant past struggles. [4] So, their fighting spirit surpassing in valiance those who died for Hellas at Thermopylae, they stood there prepared to fight it out to the death with the enemy. However, Artabazus and Megabyzus, the Persian generals, observing the enemy's courageous determination, and reckoning that they could not wipe out men such as these without losing vast numbers of their own, made a truce with the Athenians, which would allow them to pull out of Egypt without let or hindrance. [5] So the Athenians, having secured their safety by virtue of their own fighting spirit, departed from Egypt, and marching by way of Libya and Cyrene finally, against all expectation, came safely home [? 457/6].

---

99. If we allow most of the 459 campaigning season for the various activities to which Diodorus alludes, we can place the beginning of the Prosopitis siege around October 459, and its end (18 months later; Thuc. 1.109.4) in April or May 457. Allow two months for the digging of the canal and diversion of the Nile, and we have June 457 (when the Nile would be at its lowest ebb) for the final reduction of the Greek expeditionary force. This time scheme covers six campaigning seasons (462–457), agreeing with Thucydides' estimate (1.110.1) of six years. For arguments against the usual dating (460–454), see Green 2006, 149–152 nn. 301–302.

100. Ctesias (F14b [38] Lenfant) claims that the Greeks, as well as Inaros and his men, came to terms with Megabyzus. Diodorus' suspect rhetoric about Thermopylae—whether his own or his source's—does seem designed to mask some kind of less than heroic deal with the Persians. Inaros was later (after five years, says Ctesias [F14b (39) Lenfant], betrayed and impaled [Thuc. 1.110.3]).

[6] Simultaneously with these events [actually 462/1: Arist. *Ath. Pol.* 25.1–2], in Athens, Ephialtes son of Sophonides—a demagogue who had sharpened public hostility to the Areopagus Council—persuaded the *demos* to vote for a reduction in the Council's powers, thus annulling many famous ancestral traditions.[101] He did not, however, escape unscathed after undertaking such lawless actions but was assassinated one night [460/59], it never being clear afterwards just how his death came about.

78. When this year had run its course, in Athens the archon was Philocles [459/8], while in Rome Aulus Postumius [Albus] Reg<illensis> and Spurius Furius Med<ulli>nus [Fusus] succeeded [Varr. 464] to the consulship. During their term, war broke out between Athens and an alliance of Corinth and Epidaurus: the Athenians marched against the latter and, after a sharp engagement, were victorious. [2] They then with a large fleet put in at a port called Halieis, disembarked in the Peloponnese, and killed not a few of the enemy. But the Peloponnesians rallied, assembled a sizable force, and joined battle with the Athenians off the [island] called Cecryphaleia. Here once more the Athenians were victorious [459].[102] [3] After these successes [? summer 458], seeing that the Aeginetans not only had a high opinion of themselves because of their past achievements but were also hostile to Athens, [the Athenians] determined to subjugate them by force [4] and therefore sent out a strong fleet against them [<70.2–3]. The Aeginetans, who had great experience in (and a great reputation for) fighting at sea, were not disturbed by the Athenians' superiority [in numbers]. Since they possessed a sufficient number of triremes, and had besides laid down some new ones, they met the Athenians in a naval engagement but were crushingly defeated, with the loss of seventy vessels [? fall 458].[103] Their confidence broken by the magnitude of this disaster, they

---

101. Our sources agree in treating this move as a radical democratic attack on Athenian conservatism, of which the ancient Areopagus Council was a leading symbol: see Arist. *Ath. Pol.* 25, 27.1, 35.2; Plut. *Per.* 7.5–6, 9.3–4, *Mor.* 812D, *Cim.* 10.7–8, 15.1–2. The only serious power left the Areopagus was jurisdiction in certain murder trials.

102. These encounters marked the beginning of the so-called First Peloponnesian War. Athens had recently broken off her alliance with Sparta (thus repudiating Cimon's pro-Laconian policy) and made treaties with Thessaly and Sparta's Peloponnesian arch rival Argos (Thuc. 1.102.4, 2.22.3; Paus. 1.29.9, 4.24.7). A Spartan attack on Argos had been repulsed at Oenoë (Paus. 12.15.1, 10.10.4), and the Spartans had apparently seized Halieis (Hdt. 7.137.2).

103. See Thuc. 1.105.2, 108.4. After the naval defeat the Athenians besieged the island, which fell in the summer of 357, shortly after the battles of Tanagra and Oenophyta (81–83.1).

were forced to join Athens' league [? summer 457] and pay her tribute. This was accomplished for the Athenians by their general Leocrates, who spent nine months all told fighting the Aeginetans.

[5] Simultaneously with these events, in Sicily Ducetius, the king[104] of the Sicels, scion of a famous family and at the time enjoying considerable influence, founded the city of Menaenum and shared out the territory around it between the settlers. He also campaigned against the notable city of Morgantina and reduced it, thus winning high renown among his Sicel fellow-countrymen.

79. When the year drew to a close, in Athens <Habr>on[105] was archon [458/7], while in Rome Publius Servilius <Priscus> and Lucius Aebutius <Helva> succeeded [Varr. 463] to the consulship. During their term, a dispute arose between Corinth and Megara over some frontier land, and the two cities went to war. [2] To begin with, they kept raiding each other's territories and skirmishing in small groups; but as their differences grew more acute, the Megarians, who continually kept getting the worst of it and as a result were now scared of the Corinthians, contracted an alliance with Athens [Thuc. 1.103.4].[106] [3] This made the cities once more of equal strength for the contest; and so when the Corinthians, accompanied by some other Peloponnesians, marched into the Megarid [spring 458] with a strong force, the Athenians sent a task force to the aid of the Megarians, led by Myronides,[107] a man much admired for his valor. A long, hard-fought battle took place, in which each side matched the other in deeds of bravery, but in the end the Athenians won and slew many of the enemy. [4] A few days later, another

---

104. Ducetius is described as "king" (*basileus*) of the Sicels only here: elsewhere (76.3, 88.6, 91.1) he is referred to simply as the "leader" or "commander" of a union or federation (*synteleia*) of Sicel communities.

105. Corrected from "Biōn" in Diodorus' MSS on the basis of epigraphical evidence: Green 2006, 154 n. 312.

106. This quarrel about boundaries makes more sense when we realize that Megara's two ports of Nisaea and Pegae offered the only alternative to Corinth's at Cenchreae and Lechaeum for a controlled passage between the Saronic and Corinthian Gulfs. Athens baited her offer of alliance to Megara with the fortification of both ports and the construction of Long Walls from Nisaea to Megara. So long as this alliance existed, Athens could bypass Corinth, patrol the Gulf of Corinth, and keep her vital trade route to Sicily open without serious opposition from the Peloponnesian bloc.

107. Myronides was in command of a scratch force consisting of "the oldest and youngest," i.e., those over fifty and under twenty, Athens' Home Guard. Myronides himself, son of Callias (81.4), had been a young ambassador and commander in 479 (Plut. *Cim.* 10.8, 20.1) and was thus now in his early sixties (Green 2006, 155 n. 315).

fierce battle took place at the place called Cimolia, where once again the Athenians were victorious.

The Phocians went to war with the Dorians, these being the ancestors of the Lacedaemonians, who dwell in the three cities of Cytinium, Boeum, and Erineum, situated below the hill known as Parnassus. [5] To begin with, they overcame the Dorians by force and occupied their cities; but subsequently the Lacedaemonians, because of their kinship, sent out Nicomedes son of Cleomenes to help the Dorians, with 1,500 Lacedaemonians and 10,000 men from other parts of the Peloponnese. [6] Nicomedes, then the guardian of King Pleistoanax, who was still a child, brought this large force to the Dorians' aid and, after thrashing the Phocians and recovering the cities, made peace [winter 458/7] between the warring parties.

80. When the Athenians learned that the Lacedaemonians had wound up the war against the Phocians and were about to return home, they decided to strike at them while they were on the march [early spring 457]. They therefore set out [at once], taking Argive and Thessalian contingents with them, and occupied the passes about Mt. Geraneia, intending to fall upon [the Lacedaemonians] with fifty ships and 14,000 men. [2] But the Lacedaemonians, being forewarned of the Athenians' intentions, changed their route, marching to Tanagra in Boeotia. The Athenians also made their way to Boeotia, and the two sides confronted each other in a fierce battle [spring 457]. Even though during the fighting the Thessalians defected to the Lacedaemonians, the Athenians and the Argives battled on no less determinedly, and not a few fell on both sides before darkness broke off the engagement. [3] Later, when a large supply convoy was being brought to the Athenians from Attica, the Thessalians decided to attack it, taking their evening meal early and intercepting the convoy at night. [4] The Athenian guards on the convoy thought the Thessalians were still on their side and therefore received them as friends, so that numerous skirmishes of various kinds took place over the supplies. To begin with, the Thessalians, being welcomed by the enemy out of ignorance, proceeded to slay anyone they encountered, and being a disciplined group tangling with men thrown into complete confusion, inflicted heavy casualties. [5] When the Athenians in camp learned of the Thessalian attack, however, they charged up at the double, routed the Thessalians straight off, and slaughtered large numbers of them. [6] The Lacedaemonians, in battle array, now came to the rescue of the Thessalians, so that a pitched battle ensued between all the various forces, with such fierce rivalry that on both sides the death toll was heavy. The fight finally ended in a draw, with both the Lacedaemonians and the Athenians claiming victory. Since night then intervened with the

victory still in dispute, however, they exchanged embassies and concluded a four months' truce.

81. When this year had run its course, in Athens Mnesitheides became archon [457/6], while in Rome the consuls elected [Varr. 462] were Lucius Lucretius [Tricipitinus] and Titus Veturius [Geminus] Cicurinus. During their term, the Thebans, humiliated because of the alliance they had struck up with Xerxes [<33.4], were looking for some way by which they could recover their ancient influence and prestige. [2] Thus, since the Boeotians generally now despised the Thebans and no longer paid heed to them, the latter appealed to the Lacedaemonians to assist them in gaining for their city supreme control over the whole of Boeotia. In return for this favor, they offered to wage war single-handed against the Athenians, thus making it unnecessary for the Spartans to go on taking troops beyond the limits of the Peloponnese. [3] The Lacedaemonians, figuring that this proposal was to their advantage, and in the belief that a stronger Thebes would be a counterbalance to the [increasing power] of Athens, <agreed>.[108] So, since they then [early spring 457] had a large force in readiness near Tanagra, they strengthened the circuit wall around Thebes and forced the cities of Boeotia to submit themselves to Theban overlordship.

[4] The Athenians, however, being anxious to cut short this project of the Lacedaemonians, mustered a large force and chose as its general Myronides son of Callias. Myronides enrolled the necessary number of citizens and gave them his orders, stating the day on which he intended to set out from the city. [5] When the deadline came, and some of the soldiers failed to show up on the appointed day, he mustered those who had reported and with them advanced into Boeotia. Some of his officers and friends said he ought to wait for the laggards; but Myronides, who was a shrewd man as well as a forceful general, said he would not do so, explaining that those who chose to be late for departure would also prove ignoble and cowardly in battle, and thus would not face up to the perils of war in defense of their fatherland either, whereas those who presented themselves in all readiness on the appointed day clearly would not desert their post during the war. And indeed so it turned out: the force he led was few in numbers, but the bravest of the brave, so that when he matched them in Boeotia against a far larger army he outfought and defeated his opponents [Thuc. 1.108.2–3].

---

108. I agree with Oldfather 1946, against Haillet, that a main verb is missing here in the Greek text, and agreement was clearly what was in the air.

82. This action seems to me in no way to fall short of those other engagements fought by the Athenians in earlier times; for the victory at Marathon and the overcoming of the Persians at Plataea and all the other famous achievements of the Athenians in no respect outshine this victory won by Myronides over the Boeotians. [2] For of those [earlier battles] some were against the *barbaroi,* while others were finished off with the help of allies; but this engagement was won by the Athenians alone, in pitched battle, fighting against the best of the Hellenes— [3] since for firmness against odds and in all the ordeals of warfare, the Boeotians are reputed second to none. At any rate, it remains true that in a later age, at Leuctra [371: >15.55–56] and Mantinea [362: >15.84–88], the Thebans stood alone against all the Lacedaemonians and their allies, winning the highest reputation for courage and unexpectedly emerging as the leaders of all Hellas. [4] Yet although this battle [of Oenophyta] has become famous, no writer has given an account either of the way it was fought or of the positioning of the troops [that took part in it]. Thus Myronides, after defeating the Boeotians in so famous an engagement, became a rival to the most legendary commanders before his time, men such as Themistocles, Miltiades, and Cimon. [5] After this victory [Sept. 457], Myronides took Tanagra by siege, demolished its walls, and then made his way right through Boeotia, cutting [down trees and vines] and laying [the land] waste. The spoils he divided among his soldiers, lavishing abundant booty on them all.

83. The Boeotians, infuriated by the ravaging of their territory, joined up to the last man, and when they were fully mustered put a large army in the field. A battle was fought at Oenophyta in Boeotia,[109] and since both sides withstood the shock of conflict with a courageous spirit, they went on fighting all day. But the Athenians, with a great effort, [finally] put the Boeotians to flight, and Myronides became master of every city in Boeotia except Thebes.[110] [2] After this he took his troops out of Boeotia and marched against the

---

109. If the battle described in 81.4–6 and 82.4–5 is that of Oenophyta, how are we to explain this second, immediately juxtaposed, account of it, apparently motivated by Boeotian resentment of Athenian activities consequent on the first? Plato (*Menex.* 242B) places Oenophyta three, rather than sixty-two (Thuc. 1.108.2), days after Tanagra. This striking, and precise, chronological discrepancy between the two accounts suggests that there were actually two engagements fought at or near Oenophyta, one about two months after the other (Green 2006, 160–161 n. 333).

110. This incursion in fact marked the beginning of Athens' brief "land empire," an aggressive move in line with Ephialtes' gutting of the Areopagus Council's authority (77.6), the ostracism of Cimon (Plut. *Cim.* 17), and Pericles' rise to power as spokesman for the "naval radicals."

so-called Opuntian Locrians. These he overcame at their first encounter, and after taking hostages from them, he struck into Parnasia. [3] He dealt with the Phocians in much the same way as he had with the Locrians, overpowering them and then taking hostages. Next, he marched into Thessaly, criticizing [the Thessalians] for their earlier treachery, and ordering them to receive back their exiles. When the Pharsalians refused to admit him, he laid siege to their city. [4] However, since he proved unable to take the city by storm, and the Pharsalians held out for a long time under siege, for the moment he abandoned his designs on Thessaly and returned to Athens [? summer 456]. This was how Myronides, by performing a series of notable deeds in a short space of time, gained so widely bruited a reputation among his fellow-citizens.

Such, then, were the events of this year.

84. When Callias was archon in Athens [456/5], the Eleians held the 81st Olympiad, in which Polymnastus the Cyrenaean won the *stadion;* and in Rome Servius Sulpicius [Camerinus Cornutus] and Publius Volumnius Am<i>ntinus [Gallus] succeeded [Varr. 461] to the consulship. [2] During their term, Tolmides, who was in command of [Athens'] naval forces and Myronides' rival for both valor and reputation [>12.6.2], was eager to accomplish some noteworthy achievement. [3] At that time no one to date had ever ravaged Laconia: he therefore urged that the *demos* [vote to] raid the territory of the Spartans, guaranteeing that, with a thousand hoplites aboard his triremes, he and they would lay waste Laconia and diminish Spartan prestige. [4] The Athenians approved his proposition. Now he secretly wanted to take a larger hoplite force with him and therefore employed the following subterfuge. The citizens supposed he would draft for his expedition those young men who were in their prime and at the peak of their physical strength. Tolmides, however, was determined to take on campaign with him considerably more than the thousand men he had been allotted. He therefore approached every youth of exceptional physical strength, with the information that he was going to draft him. But, he said, it would look better for him to join as a volunteer rather than appear to be serving under compulsion because of the draft. [5] By employing this argument he persuaded over 3,000 to sign up as volunteers. When he saw that there were no more taking any interest, he then drafted the thousand agreed upon from those who were left.

[6] As soon as all other preparations for the expedition were complete, he put to sea, with fifty triremes and 4,000 hoplites. He made [his initial] landfall at Meth<ana> in Laconia and captured this stronghold. When the Lacedaemonians came to recover it, he withdrew again and coasted round [the Peloponnese] to Gythium, a Lacedaemonian seaport. This city too he

reduced, setting fire to the Lacedaemonians' dockyards and laying waste the countryside around. [7] From here he put out to sea and sailed to Zacynthus <from [a base on]> Cephallenia.[111] He took this island, after which he won over all the cities on Cephallenia itself, and then sailed on up to the mainland opposite and put in at Naupactus. This city too he took straight off and settled with those Messenians of note who had been freed under truce by the Lacedaemonians. [8] Around the same time [458/7] the Lacedaemonians had finally, after a prolonged war [<63–64], overcome both the Messenians and the helots: the Messenians, as stated above, they let depart from Ithome under truce, but those of the helots who had been responsible for the revolt they punished, and the rest they enslaved.

85. When Sosistratus was archon in Athens [455/4], the Romans elected as consuls [Varr. 460] Publius Valerius [Volusi] P<op>licola and Gaius Cl<au>dius Inri>gill<ensi>s [Sabinus]. During their term, Tolmides was occupied in Boeotia, and the Athenians elected as general Pericles son of Xanthippus, a man of good family,[112] and sent him out to attack the Peloponnese with fifty triremes and a thousand hoplites. [2] After laying waste much of the Peloponnese, he sailed across to Acarnania and brought over [to Athens] all the cities there <except for> Oeniadae. Thus, in the course of this year the Athenians won control of a great number of cities and acquired a high reputation for manly courage and strategic skill.[113]

86. When Ariston was archon in Athens [454/3], the Romans elected as consuls [Varr. 459] Quintus Fabius Vibulanus and Lucius Cornelius [Malugi-

---

111. "Methana" is a necessary correction for "Methone" of the MSS, which is on the wrong side of the Peloponnese and not even in Laconia. I insert *ek* ("from") before "Cephallenia" (genitive case in the Greek), since Zacynthus was not known to be subject to ("of," possessive) Cephallenia, and the construction is in any case extremely awkward: Green 2006, 163–164 nn. 340–341.

112. Pericles' father Xanthippus, a distinguished Persian War politician and general (27.1, 3; 34.1; 37.1, 5; 42.2) was married to Agariste, niece of the Alcmaeonid reformer Cleisthenes. Pericles himself first emerges as *choregos* (financial producer) for Aeschylus' play *The Persians* in 472; he prosecuted Cimon in 463/2, and the following year was associated with Ephialtes in the attack on the Areopagus (77.6).

113. By 455/4 Athens had become virtual master of the Gulf of Corinth, as well as the Saronic Gulf, through her alliance with Megara and reduction of Aegina. She had completed the construction of the Long Walls linking Athens and Piraeus (Thuc. 1.108.3). Her powerful fleet meanwhile—not significantly weakened by the setback in Egypt, be it noted—had used the Delian League (and its tribute) to turn the Aegean into a forerunner of Rome's *mare nostrum,* an economically profitable private lake.

nensis] Uritinus. During their term, Cimon of Athens negotiated a five-year truce between the Athenians and the Peloponnesians.[114]

[2] In Sicily [<76.8, 78.5] the Egestans and Lilybaeans went to war <against the Selinuntines>[115] over the territory adjacent to the Mazarus River. A fierce battle took place between them, with heavy casualties on both sides, but this did not diminish their rivalry. [3] Now, after the admissions to citizenship that had taken place in so many communities, together with the reallotment of land, it followed—since many had been added to the citizen rolls in a disorganized and random fashion—that the condition of the cities was less than healthy, so that they were once more lapsing into civil strife and anarchy. It was above all in Syracuse that this evil had taken hold. [4] The responsibility lay with one Tyndarides, a fellow brimful of effrontery and presumption, who began by acquiring numerous followers from among the poor. These he armed and drilled and thus created a personal bodyguard for himself, ready to set up a tyranny. At this point, however, since it was plain that he was reaching out after supreme power, he was brought to trial and condemned to death. [5] While he was being escorted to prison, however, the followers for whom he had done so much charged in a body and laid violent hands on those escorting him. The city was in an uproar, but at this point the most responsible citizens got together, seized the revolutionaries, and did away with them, together with Tyndarides. Since such occurrences were now of frequent occurrence, and many bold fellows had their minds set on a tyranny [Thuc. 6.38.2–3], the [Syracusan] *demos* was induced to copy the Athenians and to pass a law very like that which the latter had established in regard to ostracism [<55.1–2].

87. Among the Athenians each citizen had to inscribe a potsherd (*ostrakon*) with the name of the person he considered best able to set up a tyranny over his fellow-citizens. Among the Syracusans, however, the name of the most powerful citizen had to be written on an olive leaf (*petalon*), and when the leaves were counted, whoever got the largest number went into exile for a five-year period. [2] In this way they supposed they would humble the ar-

114. The chronology and nature (even the existence) of this truce are much debated. Cimon was still in ostracized exile (unless he returned in 457, after five rather than the usual ten years, Plut. *Per.* 10.3–4). It is just possible that an unofficial truce was negotiated by the still technically ostracized—but usefully philo-Laconian—Cimon in 454/3, to be ratified officially in 451 on the completion of his ten-year sentence and his restoration to civic privileges; this would explain the chronology, but it remains highly speculative.

115. The addition is by Wentker (59–60), on the convincing grounds that Egesta and Lilybaeum were not (as generally supposed) fighting each other but in joint defense against Selinus. Cf. Green 2006, 166 n. 353.

rogance of the most powerful men in their respective cities, since the general objective they sought was not to punish them for breaking any law but rather to curb such men's influence and self-aggrandizement. The Athenians called this type of legislation "ostracism" from its mode of implementation, while the Syracusan name for it was "petalism." [3] This law remained on the books in Athens for a long time;[116] but in Syracuse it was very soon repealed, for the following reasons. [4] With those at the top being exiled, the most responsible citizens—men who by reason of their personal integrity were in a position to bring about many constitutional reforms—were no longer involving themselves in public affairs, through their fear of this law: instead, they led strictly private lives, busy with the improvement of their personal fortunes and inclining towards luxury. It was, by contrast, the most unprincipled and presumptuous citizens who were now devoting themselves to public affairs and turning the masses towards anarchy and revolution. [5] As a result, with civil strife once more on the rise, and the commons beginning to air grievances, the city relapsed into a state of acute and virtually continuous anarchy. A whole crowd of demagogues and informers was springing up, while the young were all busy practicing the clever tricks of public speaking: in a word, people were, in large numbers, discarding their traditional serious upbringing in favor of mean and trivial pursuits. Prolonged peace was promoting private wealth, but there was scant concern for concord or principled behavior. For these reasons, the Syracusans changed their minds and repealed the petalism law after using it for only a short period.

Such, then, was the course of affairs in Sicily at this time.

88. When Lysicrates was archon in Athens [453/2], in Rome there were elected as consuls [Varr. 458] Gaius Nautius Rutilus and Lucius Minucius [Esquilinus] <Augurinus>. During their term, Pericles, the Athenian general, went ashore in the Peloponnese and laid waste the territory of the Sicyonians [<85.1–2]. [2] The Sicyonians thereupon sallied out against him in full force, and a battle took place. Pericles was victorious, killed many fugitives, and chased the rest into their city, which he then besieged. He made assaults on the walls but was unable to take the city; and when, on top of this, the Lacedaemonians sent help to the besieged, he withdrew from Sicyon and made landfall in Acarnania. Here he overran the Oeniadians' territory, picked up a

---

116. For about seventy years (488–417/6), counting from its first known use, or just under a century if we date it back to Cleisthenes' legislation between 508 and 500 (Arist. *Ath. Pol.* 22). Its discontinuation is associated with the removal of Hyperbolus, its last victim (Thuc. 8.73; Plut. *Nic.* 11.3–4).

mass of booty, and then left Acarnania, again by sea. [3] Next, he proceeded to the [Thracian] Chersonese and shared out this territory in settlers' allotments among one thousand [Athenian] citizens. Simultaneously with these events, Tolmides, the other general, crossed over into Euboea, parceling out both it and the territory of the Naxians among a second group of one thousand citizens.[117]

[4] In Sicily, since Tyrrhenian [Etruscan] pirates were active at sea, the Syracusans chose Phaÿllus as admiral and sent him to Tyrrhenia. He sailed at first to the island called Aethaleia [Elba] and laid it waste, but then secretly took money from the Tyrrhenians and sailed back to Sicily without having accomplished anything worthy of note. [5] The Syracusans condemned him as a traitor and exiled him; they then picked another commander, Apelles, and dispatched him against the Tyrrhenians with sixty triremes. He overran the Tyrrhenian coastal area and then crossed over to Cyrnus [Corsica], which the Tyrrhenians at this time held. After ravaging the greater part of the island and reducing Aethaleia, he returned to Syracuse with a large number of captives and no small amount of other booty. [6] After this, Ducetius, the Sicel leader, united all those cities that were of the same [i.e., Sicel] ethnic origin, Hybla excepted, into a single common federation. He was a man of action and, as such, always hankering after revolution: this was how he came to muster a sizable army from the Sicel federation and remove Menae, his native city, [from its site], relocating it in the plain. Also near the precinct of the so-called Palici he founded a notable city, which he named Palice after these deities.

89. Since we have made mention of these gods, we should not fail to put on record both the antiquity and the incredible nature of their shrine, and, generally speaking, the uniqueness as a phenomenon of "The Craters," as they are called. According to mythic tradition, this precinct surpasses all others in antiquity and the degree to which it inspires reverence, and tradition records numerous marvels associated with it. [2] To begin with, the actual craters are not at all imposing in size, yet they hurl skywards extraordinary jets of water from untold depths, much as cauldrons heated from below by a banked-up fire throw up boiling water. [3] The water thus thrown up has the appearance of being boiling hot, but this is not known for certain, since no one dares to touch it; for the awe engendered by these gushers is so great

117. The "settlers' allotments" that Diodorus mentions here are, as his Greek reveals, what were known as "cleruchies" (*klêrouchiai*), i.e., settlements where the occupants retained their Athenian citizenship and privileges, acting in effect as imperial colonists. Cf. Green 2006, 169–170 n. 364.

that the phenomenon is thought to be due to some divine compulsion. [4] For the water smells overpoweringly of sulphur, while the chasm emits a loud and terrifying roar; and more amazing still, the water neither spills over nor subsides but maintains a power and energy in its jet that raises it to a quite astonishing height. [5] Since this precinct is pervaded by so numinous an atmosphere, the most binding of oaths are sworn to there, and divine retribution instantly overtakes any who perjure themselves: some, indeed, have lost their sight before they pass out of the precinct. [6] Moreover, the sense of divine awe is so great here that when litigants are under pressure from some person of greater influence, they seek adjudication on the basis of preliminary depositions sworn to in the name of these deities. This precinct has also for some while now been regarded as a sanctuary and has provided much help to slaves unlucky enough to have fallen into the clutches of uncivilized masters; [7] for their masters have no authority to forcibly remove those who have sought refuge at the shrine, and they remain there, safe from harm, until the owners win their consent through guarantees of humane treatment and give pledges, secured by oaths, to honor their agreement. Only then can they take them away. [8] Nor is there any record of anyone who had given their servants such a guarantee ever breaking it, so strongly does the awe felt for these deities keep those who have sworn the oath in good faith with their slaves. The precinct itself is located on level ground fitting for a god, and it has been adorned with an adequate number of colonnades and other resting places. On this topic, then, let what has been set down here suffice, and we shall now resume our narrative at the point where we left it.

90. When Ducetius had founded Palice and walled it strongly around, he shared out the nearby territory in allotments. On account of the richness of the soil and the large number of settlers, it came about that this city achieved a rapid growth. [2] After a brief period of prosperity, however, it was torn down and has remained uninhabited to this day: concerning which matter we shall provide a detailed account under the appropriate year.[118]

[3] Affairs in Sicily, then, were such as we have described.

---

118. There is no further reference to Palice as such in Diodorus' surviving text and fragments. It is possible, however, that this foundation is to be identified with Trinacie—the otherwise unknown city, the Masada-like defense of which, together with its utter destruction by Syracuse in 440, is graphically described by Diodorus at 12.29.1–4. Palice may have been renamed Trinacie to give the Sicel movement more national appeal: the expansion of Ducetius' activities into western Sicily (91.1) would be an appropriate moment for the change.

In Italy, fifty-eight years after the destruction of Sybaris by the Crotoniates [510: >12.9–10], a certain Thessalian collected the surviving Sybarites and refounded their city on its site between two rivers, the Sybaris and the Crathis; [4] and since they had rich farmland, they quickly built up their fortunes. But when they had possessed the city for six years, they were once again driven out of Sybaris, concerning which matter we shall attempt a detailed account in the following book [>12.9–11.3].

[The year 452/1 = Olymp. 82.1 is missing in all surviving MSS.]

91. When Antidotus was archon in Athens [451/0], the Romans elected as consuls [Varr. 457] †Lucius Postumius† and Marcus Horatius [Pulvillus].[119] During their term, Ducetius, who had the leadership of the Sicels, captured the city of Aetna [<76.3] after treacherously murdering its leader. He then marched with his army into Acragantine territory and besieged Motyon, which was garrisoned from Acragas. When the Acragantines and Syracusans came to the aid of the city, Ducetius brought them to battle, defeated them both, and chased them out of their camps.[120] [2] With winter now coming on, they returned each to their own homes. The Syracusans arraigned their general Bolcon—who was responsible for the defeat and indeed incurred suspicion of having secretly made a deal with Ducetius—found him guilty of treason, and put him to death. At the beginning of summer [450] they appointed a replacement, assigning him a strong force, with a commission to eliminate Ducetius. [3] He thereupon set out with his army and came upon Ducetius when he was encamped near Nomae. A major pitched battle took place, in which many fell on both sides, and the Syracusans barely succeeded in overcoming the Sicels. But then they put them to flight and killed many of them as they fled. The bulk of the survivors reached safety in the various strongholds of the Sicels, but a few chose rather to share the hopes of Ducetius. [4] At the same time as these events, the Acragantines stormed the stronghold of Motyon, which was held by Sicels supporting Ducetius. They then joined forces with the already victorious Syracusans, and the two groups

119. There has been serious confusion on Diodorus' part here, caused, as so often, by a misreading of his Roman consular sources. M. Horatius Pulvillus and Q. Minucius Esquilinus were consuls for 457. Thus the six-year chronological gap between Diodorus' (correct) Athenian archons and his (misdated) Roman consuls now increases from six years to seven. The extra year would be accounted for by the omission of the 452/1 archon year.

120. This move into western Sicily marked a radical departure from Ducetius' previous activities, which had all been concentrated on creating and consolidating a federation of the Sicel communities located in the mountainous region northwest of Syracuse.

now set up camp together. Ducetius had been totally crushed by this defeat: some of his soldiers were defecting, others actively plotting against him, and he was in utter despair.

92. Finally, seeing that his remaining friends were going to lay hands on him, he stole a march on them by slipping away and riding to Syracuse at night. While it was still dark, he came into the Syracusan marketplace, seated himself at the altars, and became a suppliant of the city, surrendering both his person and the territory of which he was master to the Syracusans. [2] This unlooked-for event brought the populace streaming into the marketplace, and the magistrates summoned [a meeting of] the assembly and put before them the question of what action should be taken concerning Ducetius. [3] Some of the habitual rabble-rousers argued that he should be punished as an enemy and suffer the appropriate penalty for his misdeeds. The more responsible older citizens, however, came forward and insisted that they needs must safeguard a suppliant, thus paying due heed both to Fortune and to [the risk of] divine retribution. They had to consider not what punishment Ducetius deserved but rather what action was fitting for the Syracusans to take: since to kill one who had fallen out of Fortune's favor was improper, whereas to maintain a pious attitude towards both gods and suppliants was a proof of public magnanimity. [4] At this the *demos* cried out as with one voice that they should spare the suppliant. The Syracusans accordingly freed Ducetius from [any liability for] punishment and sent him away to Corinth, ordering him to remain there permanently, and furnishing him with an adequate living allowance.[121]

[5] Since we have arrived at the year before the Athenian expedition to Cyprus under Cimon's leadership, we now, in accordance with the plan outlined at the beginning of this book, bring it to a close.

---

121. For Ducetius' return to Sicily, foundation of Cale Acte, and death, see 12.8.1–13 and 29.1.

BOOK 12: 450–415 B.C.E.

1. One might well feel at a loss when pausing to consider the anomaly inherent in human existence: namely, that of those things deemed good not one is found bestowed on mankind in its entirety, while among evils there is none so absolute that it lacks some advantageous element. We can find demonstrations [of this principle] by considering past events, especially those of major importance.[1] [2] For example, the expedition made against Hellas by Xerxes, the Great King of Persia, occasioned the greatest fear among the Greeks on account of the vastness of his forces, since it was for the issue of freedom or slavery that they would be fighting; and since the Greek cities of Asia [Minor] had already been enslaved, it was universally assumed that those of [mainland] Greece would suffer a like fate. [3] But—against all expectation—the war came to a wholly unforeseen end, so that the inhabitants of Hellas not only were freed from the dangers they had faced but also won themselves high fame; and every Hellenic city was filled with such abundance of wealth that all men were amazed at this total reversal of fortune. [4] From this time forward for the next fifty years, indeed, Greece made huge advances in prosperity. During this period, financial plenty meant that the arts flourished as never before, and the record indicates that it was then that the greatest artists lived, including the sculptor Pheidias.[2] There were likewise great advances in education: philosophy and oratory were prized throughout Greece, but above all by the Athe-

---

1. As Casevitz 1972 remarks (93), this preamble reads as though it was designed as a preface to both Books 11 and 12, and it is possible that originally Book 11 did have such a preface, which is here partially recapitulated.

2. Pheidias son of Charmides (*fl.* c. 470 to c. 425), best known for a series of gigantic statues: the forty-foot chryselephantine Athena in the Parthenon; the bronze Athena Promachus, her spear tip supposedly visible from Sunium; an even more colossal Zeus at Olympia. He also (Plut. *Per.* 13) served as director-general of Pericles' building projects on the Acropolis. Prosecuted in 438 for alleged embezzlement of gold and ivory, Pheidias fled to Olympia, where his workshop has been found.

nians. [5] {This was because the philosophers included Socrates, Plato, and Aristotle, with their schools, while Pericles, as well as Isocrates and his students, were numbered among the orators.}[3] There were, too, men who have become famous as generals: Miltiades, Themistocles, Aristeides, Cimon, Myronides, and more besides, concerning whom it would take too long to write.[4]

2. The Athenians in particular had risen so high in prowess and renown that their name had become familiar throughout almost the whole of the inhabited world. To such a degree did they consolidate their supremacy that alone, with no help from the Lacedaemonians or [others in] the Peloponnese, they outfought vast Persian forces both on land and at sea, humbling the far-famed Persian leadership to such an extent that they compelled them, by treaty, to liberate all the cities of Asia. [2] But concerning these matters we have given a fuller and more particular account in two books, this [>4.1−6] and the preceding one [<11.60−61]: we shall turn now to immediate events, after first determining the chronological limits appropriate for this section. [3] In the previous book, starting from Xerxes' campaign, we dealt with the affairs of nations down to the year preceding the Athenians' expedition to Cyprus under Cimon's command; in the present one we shall begin with this Athenian campaign against Cyprus and continue as far as the war that the Athenians voted to conduct against the Syracusans.[5]

3. When Euthydemus was archon in Athens [450/49], the Romans elected [? Varr. 457] as consuls Lucius Quinctius Cincinnatus and Marcus Fabius Vibulanus.[6] During their term, the Athenians—who had been fighting the

---

3. In a period supposedly restricted to the Pentekontaetia (479−431), the philosophers and orators here listed all belong to the late 5th and the 4th centuries. Since Diodorus is both well aware of the correct dates for those incorrectly listed (Socrates [14.37.7], Plato [15.7.1], Isocrates and Aristotle [15.76.4]) and also reveals a striking distaste, precisely, for philosophers (2.29.5−6, 9.9, 10.7.2−3) and for rhetoricians or orators (1.76, 9.26.3, 20.1−2.2), it is a reasonable guess that the first sentence in §5 is an interpolation, by some ancient *littérateur* with a shaky sense of dates.

4. Here, as Casevitz 1972 (94) correctly notes, the generals mentioned all in effect belong to Book 11 rather than to Book 12. The list, interestingly, does not include Tolmides (11.84.1−8, 85.1, 88.3, and cf. 12.6.1−2).

5. I.e., the Sicilian Expedition of 415.

6. Diodorus is the sole source for the consular college here listed. At this point the chronological gap between archons (correctly dated) and consuls is seven years. Diodorus' reading of "Euthydemus" as the archon's name is generally emended to "Euthynus"; but see R. S. Stroud, *The Athenian Empire on Stone* (Athens 2006), 16−17 with n. 10, for powerful arguments that "Euthydemus" is in fact correct.

Persians on behalf of the Egyptians, and had lost their entire flotilla at the island known as Prosopitis [<11.77.2–3]—after a brief interval once more decided to go to war with the Persians, [this time] on behalf of the Greeks in Asia Minor. They fitted out a fleet of two hundred triremes and chose as their general Cimon son of Miltiades, with orders to sail to Cyprus and campaign against the Persians. [2] Cimon took the fleet, which had been provided with first-class crews and ample supplies, and sailed for Cyprus.[7] At that point the generals in command of the Persian forces were Artabazus and Megabyzus [<11.77.4]. Artabazus, the commander-in-chief, was based on Cyprus, with three hundred triremes, while Megabyzus was encamped in Cilicia at the head of a land army numbering 300,000. [3] Cimon now reached Cyprus and established control of the sea: he laid siege to Citium and Marium and reduced them both, treating the vanquished with humane consideration. After this, when triremes from Cilicia and Phoenicia were on course for the island, Cimon put out to sea, forced an engagement [spring 449], sank many of these ships, captured a hundred along with their crews, and chased the rest all the way to Phoenicia. [4] Those Persians with ships that had survived fled to the coastal area where Megabyzus was encamped with the land forces, and they went ashore there. The Athenians sailed in, disembarked their troops, and joined battle. During this engagement, Anaxicrates, the deputy commander, after a brilliant fight, ended his life heroically. The rest gained the upper hand in the battle, and after killing large numbers, returned to the ships. The Athenians thereupon sailed back to Cyprus.[8]

Such were the events in the first year of this war.

4. When Pedieus was archon in Athens [449/8], the Romans elected as consuls [Varr. 456] Marcus Valerius [Maximus] Lactuc<in>us and Spurius Verginius Tricostus [Caeliomontanus]. During their term, the Athenian general Cimon, who now enjoyed supremacy at sea, set about subduing the cities of Cyprus. Since Salamis was garrisoned by a large Persian guard, and packed

---

7. Athens' desperate search for grain and timber was surely the prime reason for action so far afield, and the only one justifying the huge outlay involved; it also more than explains the collateral interest in Egypt, then as later one of the great natural breadbaskets of the Mediterranean. Diodorus does not mention that a flotilla sixty strong was detached from the main force to aid Amyrtaeus (Thuc. 1.112.3 and Plut. *Cim.* 18.4), the rebel Egyptian leader in the western marshes, just as the earlier expedition had supported Amyrtaeus' predecessor Inaros (11.71.3–4).

8. This engagement effectively broke the back of Persian naval dominance in the eastern Mediterranean and was largely responsible for the subsequent diplomatic standoff (below, 12.4.4–6).

with every kind of weapon and missile, as well as grain and all other essential supplies, he came to the conclusion that his most advantageous course would be to reduce it by siege. [2] This, he figured, was the easiest way for him to become master of the entire island and also to put the Persians at a complete loss: they would be unable, with Athens controlling the seas, to relieve the Salaminians, and this abandonment of an ally would make them the target of scorn. In brief, were all Cyprus to be forcibly reduced, the [issue of the] entire war would be decided. This, indeed, is exactly what happened. [3] The Athenians set about the siege of Salamis and launched daily assaults on its walls; but the troops in the city, being well supplied with missiles and other gear, easily stood them off. [4] Nevertheless, King Artaxerxes, after learning of the various setbacks on Cyprus, took counsel with his Friends concerning the war and judged it advantageous[9] to make peace with the Greeks.[10] He therefore furnished both his satraps and the commanders on Cyprus with the conditions, in writing, on which they could come to terms. [5] As a result, Artabazus and Megabyzus sent ambassadors to Athens to discuss a settlement. The Athenians listened favorably to their proposals and responded by dispatching ambassadors plenipotentiary, under Callias son of Hipponicus.[11] A peace treaty was then concluded between the Athenians (and their allies) and the Persians, the main terms of which are as follows: "All the Greek cities in Asia [Minor] are to be subject to their own laws. No Persian satrap is to come nearer than a three days' journey to the coast. No Persian warship is to enter the waters between Phaselis and Cyaneae. Provided the Great King's

---

9. It is seldom pointed out just how advantageous the eventual terms were to Persia: she resumed de facto control of Cyprus, and the threat to Egypt was likewise removed. Whether the peace looked glorious or not in the hindsight of the 4th century, to many contemporary Athenians it must have seemed a sad comedown from the triumphs of 480/79.

10. The Peace of Callias is one of the most hotly debated problems in all Greek history. Basically, the question is this: Was such a formal peace ever in fact concluded, and, if it was, did it take place (a) c. 466, under Xerxes, with a renewal in 449 (cf. *Suda* s.v. Callias), after—as I would argue—an initial rejection by Artaxerxes on his accession, probably in 464/3 (cf. 12.61.1 and 12.71.2); or (b) in 449 for the first time? For a full conspectus of the evidence, a masterly summary of the problem as such, the history of its scholarship, and the arguments favoring (b), see Meiggs, 129–151, 487–495. The case for (a)—with which I am in substantial agreement—has been argued, with exemplary common sense, by Badian, 1–72. Though there are still some dissenting voices, at least the existence of the treaty is now widely accepted.

11. Callias (c. 520–c. 440), an immensely wealthy aristocrat and seasoned diplomat, turns up at Susa leading a delegation to the Great King about 464 (Hdt. 7.151) and as a negotiator of the Thirty Years' Peace with Sparta (ch. 7).

generals observe these conditions, the Athenians shall not move troops into any territory under the King's jurisdiction." [6] Once the treaty had been solemnized, the Athenians—after winning a brilliant victory and securing most notable peace terms—withdrew their forces from Cyprus. As ill luck would have it, however, Cimon succumbed to an illness [? late summer 449] while still stationed on the island.

5. When Philiscus was archon in Athens [448/7], the Romans elected as consuls [Varr. 455] Titus Romilius Vaticanus and Gaius Veturius Cic<urin>us, and the Eleians held the 83rd Olympiad, in which Crison of Himera won the *stadion.* [2] During their term, the Megarians revolted from the Athenians, sent ambassadors to the Lacedaemonians, and made an alliance with them. In annoyance at this, the Athenians sent troops into Megarian territory, and by plundering the holdings got possession of much booty. When [the Megarians] emerged from Megara to defend their territory, a battle took place. The Athenians were victorious and pursued the Megarians back within their fortifications.[12]

6. When Timarchides was archon in Athens [447/6], the Romans elected as consuls [Varr. 454] Spurius Tarpeius [Montanus Capitolinus] and Aulus A{s}ter<n>ius [Varus] Fontin<ali>s. During their term, the Lacedaemonians invaded Attica and laid waste a considerable amount of territory: then, after besieging certain of the fortresses, they returned to the Peloponnese. Meanwhile, Tolmides, the Athenian general, took Chaeroneia. [2] But the Boeotians regrouped their forces and ambushed Tolmides' troops, and a hard-fought battle took place at Coroneia [spring 446], during which Tolmides fell fighting, and of the other Athenians, those who were not cut down were taken alive.[13] This major disaster meant that the Athenians (if they hoped to

12. Athens' attitude to her "subject-allies" undoubtedly toughened now, and setbacks abroad made her tougher still. The "tightening up" was, first and foremost, an increasingly ruthless extraction of tribute. This suggests an urgent need for increased income on Athens' part. Why? The collapse of her Cimonian Cypro-Egyptian policy, combined with a grain famine in 445, suggests one answer. Until an alternative safe source not only of grain but also of the timber crucial for Athens' imperial fleet was found and secured, these commodities had to be sought on the open market (e.g., South Russia, where gold was the preferred mode of payment) and came very expensive. Athens' increased interest in the West, culminating in the ill-fated Sicilian expedition of 415–413, can be seen as a logical consequence of this dilemma.

13. Athenian casualties were heavy, including Alcibiades' father Cleinias (thus leaving the boy as a ward of Pericles). On this occasion Athens was lucky to negotiate the evacu-

recover their prisoners) were forced to let all the cities of Boeotia choose their own form of government.

7. When Callimachus was archon in Athens [446/5], the Romans chose as consuls [Varr. 453] Sextus Quincti<li>us <and P. Curiatius Fistus> Trigeminus. During their term, since the Athenians had lost prestige throughout Greece because of the defeat they suffered at Coroneia in Boeotia, numerous cities now defected from them. Since the inhabitants of Euboea were leading figures in this revolt [Thuc. 1.114; Plut. *Per.* 22.1–2], Pericles (who had been elected general) led a major expeditionary force against Euboea. He stormed the city of Hestiaia and deported its citizen body; the other cities he scared back into submission to Athenian authority [? July 446].

A thirty-year treaty [>26.2, 28.4] was made [between Athens and Sparta], negotiated and confirmed by Callias and Chares.[14]

8. In Sicily, a war broke out between Syracuse and Acragas for the following reasons. The Syracusans had overcome Ducetius, the Sicel leader, and when he became a suppliant, absolved him from all charges, designating Corinth henceforth as his place of residence [<11.91.2–4]. [2] But after a short stay in Corinth, he broke the agreement, and—his excuse being that he had been instructed, by a divine oracle, to settle the Sicilian site of Calê Actê—sailed back to the island with a group of colonists. (Some of the Sicels were also involved, amongst whom was Archonidas, the ruler of Herbita.) [3] So it came about that the Acragantines—partly out of envy of the Syracusans and partly because (they charged) the Syracusans had freed Ducetius, their common enemy, without consulting them—declared war on Syracuse. [4] The cities of Greek Sicily were divided, some lining up with Syracuse, others with Acragas: thus both sides put sizable armies into the field. Great rivalry was evident between the various cities when they encamped facing one another on either side of the Himera River. A pitched battle was fought, in which the

---

ation of Boeotia after her defeat (Thuc. 1.113.3–4). A year later, the occupying force in Megara was not so fortunate: it was massacred (Thuc. 1.114.1).

14. This peace in fact lasted only fourteen years (Thuc. 2.2.1). The five-year truce of (?) 451 (11.86.1) had run out, and Athens badly needed relief from external, in particular Peloponnesian, pressure. The degree of her need can be gauged from the ceding of Pegae and Nisaea, Megara's ports on the Corinthian and Saronic Gulfs (Thuc. 1.115.1). The long walls Athens had built linking Nisaea to Megara formed part of an alternative Isthmus crossing to that dominated by Corinth: this explains why regaining control of Megara became increasingly important to Athens in the decades that followed, emerging as a major cause of hostilities by 431.

Syracusans were victorious and killed over a thousand Acragantines. After the battle the Acragantines sent an embassy to negotiate terms, and the Syracusans made peace with them.

9. Events in Sicily, then, were as described above. In Italy the foundation of the city of Thourioi came about in the following circumstances.[15] When at an earlier period [c. 719/8] the Greeks had founded Sybaris as an Italian city, because of the richness of the soil it had achieved rapid growth. [2] Since it lay between two rivers, the Crathis and the Sybaris (from which it got its name), its inhabitants, by exploiting this extensive and richly productive region, acquired very considerable wealth. Further, their practice of granting citizenship to numerous [applicants] swelled their numbers to such an extent that they were reputed to be the largest city in Italy: their population so outstripped the rest that they had 300,000 citizens.

There now [510/9] emerged among them a popular leader called Telys, who, by bringing charges against the most important men in the city, persuaded the Sybarites to exile their five hundred richest citizens and impound their property for public use. [3] These exiles went to Croton, where they sought sanctuary at the altars in the marketplace. Telys then sent ambassadors to the Crotoniates, with the message that they should either surrender the exiles or prepare themselves for war. [4] An assembly was thereupon convened, with the agenda of discussing whether to hand over their suppliants to the Sybarites, or face a war with a more powerful opponent. Neither council nor *demos* could decide this issue. At first, because of [the threat of] war, public opinion inclined towards surrendering the suppliants. Subsequently, however, when Pythagoras the philosopher[16] advised them to ensure the suppliants' safety, they reversed their opinion and prepared to face war on those grounds. [5] The Sybarites thereupon marched against them with 300,000 men, against whom the Crotoniates mustered 100,000, under the command of Milo the athlete, who through his unrivaled physical strength was the first to rout those ranged against him. [6] This man, a six-time Olympic champion, whose courage matched his bodily power, is said to have gone into battle wearing his Olympic wreaths and rigged out in the manner of Heracles with

---

15. Chs. 9–19 form a lengthy excursus on the foundation of Thurii and the code of laws allegedly drafted for that city by Charondas, together with a note (chs. 20–21) on another South Italian lawgiver, Zaleucus of Epizephyrian Locri.

16. Then about seventy years old (Diog. Laert. 8.44), with another decade still to live. He is credited with drafting a constitution for Croton, and the government of the city was apparently an oligarchy controlled by his followers (Diog. Laert. 8.3).

lionskin and club. He was, indeed, responsible for [Croton's] victory and earned the wondering admiration of his fellow-citizens in consequence.

10. The Crotoniates in their fury refused to take any prisoners but killed all who fell into their hands during the rout, so that the larger part of the Sybarites perished. They then sacked the city itself and reduced it to a mere wasteland [but cf. 11.48.4]. [2] Fifty-eight years later [452/1], Thessalians helped refound the city, but a little while later, in the Athenian archonship of Callimachus [446/5], they were driven out by Crotoniates, in the period now under discussion, five years after the second foundation [<11.90.3]. [3] A little later, the city was transferred to a new site and was given a new name. Its founders were Lampon and Xenocritus, and the circumstances were as follows.

The Sybarites thus evicted for the second time from their homeland sent ambassadors to Greece, to the Lacedaemonians and Athenians, asking for their help in getting back there and inviting them to participate in the settlement [445/4]. [4] The Lacedaemonians ignored them, but the Athenians agreed to take part in the venture. They therefore manned ten ships and dispatched them to the Sybarites under the command of [the seers] Lampon and Xenocritus; they also sent a proclamation round the cities of the Peloponnese, throwing open this colonizing enterprise to anyone who cared to participate in it. [5] Volunteers were numerous. An oracular response was received from Apollo, telling them to found a city in the place where they would be

Drinking water in measure but eating bread without measure.[17]

So they sailed for Italy, and when they reached Sybaris, proceeded to search for the place in which the god had commanded them to settle. [6] Not far from Sybaris they found a spring called Thuria, fitted with a bronze waterpipe of the sort known to locals as a *medimnos*. Concluding that this must be the spot indicated by the god, they walled it around, founded their city there, and named it Thurion after the spring. [7] They divided the city lengthwise into

----

17. This declaredly "Panhellenic" foundation was Athenian in origin and to a great extent in constitution. What with the collapse of Cimon's Cypro-Egyptian policy, the exactly contemporary 445 famine in Attica—relieved only by a shipment of grain from the rebel pharaoh in the western marshes—and the mass of colonies/cleruchies being sent out to Imbros, Chalcis, Eretria, Erythrae, Colophon, the Chersonese, and elsewhere, a clear indication (Kagan 1969, 157, and cf. Plut. *Per.* 11.5) of "the need to rid Athens of excess population," it is hard to believe that the motives for this reaching out to one of the naturally richest sites in the West did not include the chance of securing desperately needed grain and timber. Apollo was right: "eating bread without measure" was precisely what it was all about.

four with avenues named respectively Heracleia, Aphrodisia, Olympias, and Dionysias; breadthwise they divided it by means of three avenues, naming these Heroa, Thuria, and Thurina. <· · ·> When these narrow alleys[18] were filled up, it was evident that, as regards housing, the city had been admirably planned.

11. The Thurians, however, lived peaceably together for a short time only [? late summer 445: >22.1], after which acute civil dissension broke out between them—and not without reason. The former Sybarites were assigning the most prestigious offices to themselves, and the unimportant ones to those who had been enrolled as citizens later. They were also of the opinion that, among women citizens, their wives should take precedence when sacrifices were made to the gods, while later arrivals should yield place to them. What was more, the land adjacent to the city they were parceling out into holdings for themselves, while the outlying tracts went to the newcomers.[19] [2] When dissension arose for these causes as stated, the citizens who had been added to the rolls later, being both more numerous and more powerful, massacred virtually all the original Sybarites and settled the city by themselves. Since their territory was extensive as well as fertile, they brought in [444/3] numerous settlers from Greece, assigning them their own part of the city and allotting them land holdings on an equal basis. [3] Those who stayed on soon acquired great wealth. They established friendly relationships with the Crotoniates and in general practiced good government. Under the democratic system that they set up, they divided the citizens into ten tribes, giving each one a name from the various peoples that composed them. Three consisted of people from the Peloponnese: these tribes they named the Arcadian, the Achaean, and the Eleian. A like number, formed from racially linked groups dwelling outside [the Peloponnese], they named the Boeotian, the Amphictyonian, and the Dorian; while the remaining four, made up from other peoples, became the Ionian, the Athenian, the Euboean, and the Nesiotic tribes. They also chose as their lawgiver the best of all citizens that were highly esteemed for

---

18. There is a clear lacuna in Diodorus' MSS: a reference to alleys (probably as surviving from the old or rebuilt site: Thurii overlapped with Sybaris) has dropped out of the text. For a discussion of editorial suggestions here, see Lapini. I accept Vogel's text, except that I read *tas oikias* of the MSS rather than Wesseling's *tais oikiais*.

19. In a city open to constant attack, it was the frontiersmen of the outer territories who both bore the brunt of all raids and were called upon to defend the more privileged central holdings. The Athenians, who understood all this very well, had no intention of being treated as second-class citizens by the losers they had come to help.

learning: Charondas.[20] [4] This was the man who, after making a study of all legislations, picked out the best elements in them, which he then embodied in his own laws. But he also worked out and formulated many ideas of his own, and these it will not be irrelevant to put on record here, for the better instruction of our readers.[21]

12. First, there is the decree he instituted regarding such men as brought in a stepmother to be in charge of their existing children: these, by way of penalty, he banned from serving as counselors for their fatherland, in the belief that anyone who planned badly with regard to his own children would be an equally poor counselor to the state. His argument was that those whose first marriages had been successful should remain content with their good fortune, whereas those who had made unfortunate marriages, and then repeated their mistake, must be regarded as senseless. [2] Those found guilty of *sykophantia*,[22] he decreed, should, when they went out, wear a tamarisk wreath, so as to make clear to all their fellow-citizens that they had won first prize for base conduct. In consequence, certain persons who had been condemned on this charge, unable to bear such great humiliation, voluntarily removed themselves from the company of the living. When this happened, all who had regularly practiced *sykophantia* were banished from the city; and the government, rid of this plague, thenceforth enjoyed a happy existence. [3] Charondas also

---

20. The Ionian Charondas of Catana and the Achaean Zaleucus of Epizephyrian Locri (12.20–21) were the earliest known Greek lawgivers. Charondas made laws not only for Catana but for other Chalcidic cities on the coasts of Sicily and South Italy. His *floruit*, like that of Zaleucus, was most probably in the 7th century BCE, and in any case he was dead by the end of the 6th. Thus, he cannot have legislated directly for Thurii; nor indeed (though this is most often assumed) does Diodorus specifically claim that he did. Diogenes Laertius (9.50) cites Heraclides Ponticus' treatise *On Laws* for Protagoras (one of Thurii's early colonists) having been the city's lawgiver, and this is highly plausible. Others (Athen. 11.508a; *Suda* s.v. Zaleucus) attribute Thurii's laws to Zaleucus, and since he supposedly made them for Sybaris, this too is likely. If we say that Protagoras largely used Charondas but also borrowed items from Zaleucus for what seemed best suited to a Panhellenic colony, we will probably be not too far from the truth.

21. How far, if at all, the various "laws" that follow reflect early colonial legislation, and how far any genuine matter in them has been overlaid with later anecdotage and moralizing apothegms, is impossible, for lack of evidence, to disentangle.

22. There is no one adequate English translation of *sykophantia*—least of all "sycophancy," which carries a very different meaning from the ancient Greek (and particularly Athenian) activity. The most notorious function of the *sykophantes* was as an informer, the equivalent of the later Roman *delator*.

wrote an unparalleled law on the keeping of bad company, something that all other lawgivers had overlooked. His assumption was that good men, through friendship and habitual intercourse with those of base character, sometimes have their own morals corrupted: that badness, like some pestilent disease, invades the life of mankind, infecting the souls even of the best. For steep is the downward path to the worse, offering an easy journey. This, [he concluded,] was why many men of average character become ensnared by factitious pleasures and end up stuck with really abominable habits. Wanting, therefore, to banish this source of corruption, the lawgiver banned all friendship and intimate association with base persons, provided actions at law against the keeping of bad company and by means of stringent penalties, discouraged those about to commit such errors. [4] He also framed another law of greater merit even than this one and similarly overlooked by previous lawgivers. This laid down that all the sons of citizens should learn to read and write and that the state should be responsible for paying teachers' salaries. His assumption here was that the poor, who could not afford such fees from their own resources, would [otherwise] be debarred from the most honorable pursuits.

13. Indeed, this lawgiver ranked literacy above every other kind of learning, and was right to do so: for this is what enables the bulk—and the most valuable part—of human affairs to be carried out: voting, letter writing, the engrossment of laws and covenants, and all other things that most contribute to the proper regulation of life. [2] Who could sufficiently praise the acquisition of letters? It is by this alone that the dead survive in the memory of the living or that people in places widely separated one from the other communicate, even with those at the greatest distance from them, by means of the written word, just as though they were close by. Also, as regards wartime treaties between peoples or monarchs, the firmest guarantee that such agreements will hold good is the certainty provided by a written text. In sum, this is what alone preserves the most satisfying pronouncements of wise men and the oracles of the gods, not to mention philosophy and all educational knowledge, and is forever handing them on to generation after generation down the ages. [3] Thus, while we must acknowledge that nature is the cause of life, we must also agree that the good life is brought about by an upbringing grounded in literacy. It was, then, to right the wrong done the illiterate (in thus depriving them of certain enormous benefits) that [Charondas] by his legislation judged them deserving of public concern and expenditure; [4] and whereas earlier legislators had decreed that private individuals, when sick, should enjoy medical services at the expense of the state, he went far beyond what they did,

since they [merely] thought bodies worth healing, while he offered care to souls burdened through lack of education. Indeed, while we must pray that we never stand in need of those [other] physicians, we most heartily desire that all our time may be spent among such teachers of knowledge.

14. Both the earlier laws here mentioned have received witness from many poets in verse: that on keeping bad company as follows:

> The man who loves the company of the base
> I never question, well aware that he
> is just like those whose comradeship he seeks.[23]
> The law regarding stepmothers produced this:
> The lawgiver Charondas, men say, in one
> of his decrees, among much else, declares:
> The man who on his children foists a stepmother
> should rank as nought and share in no debate
> among his fellows, having himself dragged in
> this foreign plague to damn his own affairs.
> If you were lucky the first time you wed
> (he says) don't press your luck; and if you weren't,
> trying a second time proves you insane.[24]

It is certainly true that anyone who makes the same mistake twice may justly be regarded as a fool. [2] Philemon too, the comic playwright, writing about habitual seafarers, says:

> That law stirs wonder in me—not when a man
> sets out by sea the first time, but the second.[25]

In the same way, one might assert that one is not amazed by a man's marrying but only if he marries twice: for it is preferable to expose oneself twice to the sea than to a woman. [3] The greatest and most terrible domestic dissensions are those that pit children against their fathers because of a stepmother,

---

23. Euripedes., *Phoenix* fr. 812 Nauck. The passage is quoted at considerably greater length by Aeschines in his speech against Timarchos (1.152). The lines immediately preceding those given by Diodorus declare: "So I, like any man of common wisdom, / figure the truth by looking into a man's / nature, the character of his daily life. . . ."

24. Fragment of an unidentified late comic poet: fr. adesp. 110 Kock.

25. Philemon, c. 365–?262 (23.6.1), was a poet of the New Comedy and Menander's main rival.

something that occasions the portrayal on the tragic stage of countless such lawless acts.

15. Charondas wrote yet another law that deserves our endorsement: the one dealing with the guardianship of orphans. On the surface this law would appear, when first examined, to have no exceptional or particularly praiseworthy feature; but when looked at again, and subjected to close scrutiny, it reveals zealous study and high merit. [2] Now what he wrote was that the property of orphans should be managed by the next of kin on the father's side, but that the orphans themselves should be brought up by their relatives on the mother's side. Now at first sight this law reveals no wise or exceptional content; but on examining it more deeply, one finds it justly worthy of praise. For when one looks for the reason why he entrusted the property of orphans to one group, but their upbringing to another, the lawgiver's outstanding ingenuity becomes apparent: [3] for the relatives on the mother's side, having no claim on the distribution of the orphans' inheritance, will not make plots against them; while the close kin on the father's side are in no position to hatch such plots, since they are not entrusted with their physical protection. Moreover, since, if the orphans die of an illness or some other accidental hazard, the estate reverts to them, they will manage that estate with more than usual care, since they treat as [already] their own expectations that are in fact dependent upon the whims of Fortune.

16. He also drafted a law aimed at those who deserted their post in wartime or flatly refused to take up arms at all in defense of their fatherland. Whereas other legislators had stipulated death as the punishment for such men, Charondas decreed that they should sit in the marketplace for three days dressed as women. [2] Now, this law is both more humane than its equivalent elsewhere, and also, because of the extreme humiliation it inflicts, tends subconsciously to deter those similarly inclined from cowardly behavior; for death is preferable to suffering so great an indignity in one's native city. At the same time he did not do away with the offenders but saved them for the military needs of the state, his belief being that the punishment meted out for their disgraceful offense would make them determined to vindicate themselves, and by fresh deeds of valor wipe out their past shame. [3] It was through the stringency of the laws he enacted that this lawgiver ensured their maintenance. For instance, he prescribed obedience to the law whatever the circumstances, even if it had been fundamentally ill drafted; at the same time he allowed for redrafting should the need arise. [4] His argument was this: to be overruled by a lawgiver

was reasonable, but [to be overruled] by a private citizen was wholly out of place, even should this be to one's advantage. He [had in mind] those who serve up in court the excuses and devious tricks of lawbreakers rather than the actual letter of the law; and it was above all by this means that he stopped them from using their innovative quibbles to undermine the paramount authority of the laws. [5] This was why, when one of those who had advanced such arguments was haranguing the jurors about the [proper] way to punish lawbreakers, he told them they must save either the law or the man.

17. What has been described as the most improbable legislation by Charondas, however, is that to do with his revision of the legal code. Remarking that in most cities the sheer number of efforts to revise the laws both debased established legislation and encouraged civil dissension in the masses, he drafted a decree that was both personal and quite extraordinary. [2] His ruling was that anyone wishing to amend a law should put his neck in a noose when advancing his proposed revision, and so remain until the *demos* returned a verdict on it. If the assembly accepted the amendment, the proposer would be released; but if his proposal was voted down, he was to be hanged on the spot. [3] With such legislation in force regarding revision of the laws, subsequent lawmakers were held back by fear, and not one of them dared to utter a word on the subject. Indeed, from that day to this, only three men in Thurii are related as having, on account of certain compelling circumstances, presented themselves before the council in charge of revision.[26]

[4] In the first case, there was a law that if a man put someone's eye out, he himself should lose an eye by way of reprisal.[27] Now a certain one-eyed man had had that eye destroyed and thereby lost his sight entirely. He therefore argued that the offender, by forfeiting only one eye in return, had paid less than a fair penalty, since he who blinded a fellow-citizen, and paid only the penalty prescribed by law, would not have suffered a comparable loss. To be fair, and to make the punishment equitable, anyone who robbed a one-eyed man of sight should have *both* his eyes put out.[28] [5] Thus the one-eyed man, who had become extremely embittered, had the courage to raise in the assembly the matter of his personal loss, and while lamenting to his fellow-citizens over the mishap he had suffered, also proposed to the commons a revision

---

26. The text of this final clause is uncertain: see Green 2006, 203–204 n. 78.

27. The concept of retaliation (the *lex talionis* in Roman law) is one of the oldest and most widespread legal principles in European and Near East history.

28. An identical story is recounted by Demosthenes (24.139–141) but attributed to the Locrians. Cf. Arist. *Rhet.* 1365b 17; Ael. *VH* 13.24 (specifically attributed to Zaleucus).

of the law, winding up by putting his neck in a noose. He got his proposal carried, had the law as it stood revoked and the amendment confirmed, and also escaped death by hanging.

18. The second law to be revised was one giving a wife the right to divorce her husband and [thereafter] marry whomsoever she pleased. A husband who was well advanced in years had a younger wife who had left him. This man proposed before the Thurians a rider amending the law, to the effect that a woman who left her husband might indeed marry whomsoever she pleased— provided that he was no younger than his predecessor; and similarly, that if a man put away his wife, he could not then marry a woman younger than the wife he had divorced. [2] This petitioner likewise had his proposal carried, got the earlier law set aside, and escaped the risk of being hanged; while his wife, thus prevented from moving in with a younger man, remarried the husband she had left.

[3] The third law to be revised, one that also features in Solon's legislation, was the one concerning heiresses. Charondas decreed that the next of kin be legally required to marry an heiress and that an heiress similarly be required to marry her closest relative, who then had either to marry her or, in the case of an indigent heiress, pay five hundred drachmas into an account for her dowry.[29] [4] A certain orphaned heiress, of good family but wholly without means of support, and because of her poverty unable to marry, sought remedy from the *demos,* weeping as she laid before them the hopeless and despised nature of her position. She then went on to describe her proposed amendment to the law, that instead of the five hundred drachmas payment, it should state that the next of kin *must* marry the heiress assigned to him by law. The *demos* out of pity voted for the amendment; and thus, while the orphan escaped hanging, the next of kin (who was wealthy) was compelled to marry a penniless heiress who brought him no dowry.

19. It remains for us to speak of Charondas' death, concerning which a most peculiar and unlooked-for accident befell him. When he left town for the country, he had armed himself with a dagger as a defense against highwaymen. On his return he found the assembly in session and the populace greatly upset, and being curious as to the cause of dissension, went in. [2] Now he had once passed a law that no one should enter the assembly carrying a weapon,

---

29. The term "heiress" for *epiklēros* is unavoidable but misleading: the property did not come to her absolutely (or, indeed, to the man she married) but was simply held by her in trust until her son was of an age to inherit.

and it had slipped his mind on this occasion that himself had a dirk strapped to his waist. He thus offered certain of his enemies a fine opportunity to bring a charge against him. But when one of them said, "You've revoked your own law," he replied, "No, by God, I shall maintain it," and with that drew his dirk and killed himself. Certain writers, however, attribute this act to Diocles, the lawgiver of the Syracusans [>13.33.2, 13.35.1–5].

[3] Now that we have expatiated at sufficient length on matters concerning Charondas the lawgiver, we would like to add a brief discussion of another lawgiver, Zaleucus, since these men chose very similar ways of life and were in fact born in neighboring cities.

20. Zaleucus was by birth a Locrian from Italy, a man of good family and much esteemed for his education, having been a student of Pythagoras the philosopher.[30] Since he enjoyed a high reputation in his native city, he was chosen as lawmaker and proceeded to hand down, from scratch, a completely new code of laws, beginning with the heavenly deities. [2] For right at the beginning, in the general preamble to his legislation, he stated that the inhabitants of the city must, first and foremost, by reason as by faith, believe that the gods do indeed exist; that intelligent contemplation of the heavens, and the ordering and pattern thereof, should leave them with the conviction that these creations are the result neither of chance nor of human labor; that they should [therefore] revere the gods as the cause of all that is fine and good in human existence; and that they should keep the soul clean of all evil, on the grounds that the gods take no joy in the sacrifices or costly outlay of the wicked but rather in the just and decent practices of good men. [3] After thus in his preamble summoning the citizen body to follow piety and justice, he tacked on a further requirement, that they should treat none of their fellows as an irreconcilable enemy but should assume, when enmity came between them, that matters would come back eventually to resolution and a renewal of friendship; and that anyone who acted otherwise should be regarded by his fellows as being of a wild and uncivilized temperament. He also exhorted the officers of state not to be aggressive or over-proud, and not to make judgments on the basis of friendship or enmity. Further, among his various ordinances were many that he himself formulated, with outstanding wisdom.

21. For instance, where all other societies imposed financial penalties on erring wives, he found a most artful device whereby to curb their licentious-

---

30. Zaleucus' *floruit* was about the middle of the 7th century: it is thus impossible that he could have been a student of Pythagoras.

ness, through the following laws that he drafted. A free woman could not be escorted abroad by more than one female attendant—unless she was drunk. Nor could she leave the city at night—except to commit adultery; nor could she wear gold jewelry or a purple-bordered dress—unless she was a courtesan. A husband, similarly, could not wear a gilded ring or an outer garment in the Milesian style—unless set on whoring or adultery. [2] As a result, by imposing a sense of shame in lieu of the old penalties, he had no trouble in steering [citizens] away from damaging luxury and licentious practices; for no one wanted to become a laughingstock among the other citizens by openly admitting to such shameful and self-indulgent habits. [3] He wrote excellent laws on many other vexed aspects of life, including contracts; but it would take too long to recount these, and they are not germane to the plan of this history. We shall therefore resume our narrative at the point where we left it.

22. When Lysimachides was archon in Athens [445/4], the Romans elected as consuls [Varr. 452] Titus Menenius [Lanatus] and Publius Sestius Capitolinus [Vaticanus]. During their term, the Sybarites, fleeing from the perils of civil dissension [<11.2], settled on the Traïs River. They remained there for some while, but later [c. 356/5: >16.15.1–2] they were driven out by the Bruttii and done away with. [2] In Greece the Athenians, having recovered Euboea and expropriated the Hestiaeans from their city [446: <12.7], now sent out to it a colony of their own, consisting of a thousand citizens, under Pericles' command, parceling out both city and surrounding countryside into settlers' holdings.

23. When Praxiteles was archon in Athens [444/3], the 84th Olympiad was held, in which Crison of Himera won the *stadion;* and in Rome ten men were elected as legislators: <App.> Cl<au>dius [Crassus] <Inrigill<ensi>s [Sabinus], Titus <Ge>nucius <Augurinus>, Spurius Veturius [Crassus Cicurinus], Gaius Iulius [Iullus], <Ser.?> Sulpicius [Camerinus], Publius Sestius [Vibi Capito>, [T.] Rom<ili>us [Rocus Vaticanus], Spurius Postumius <Albus> [Regillensis]. These were the men who tabulated the laws.[31] [2] During their term, the Thurians and the Tarantines were continually at war, raiding and laying waste each other's territory by land and sea [>36.4]. Though they engaged in numerous minor battles and skirmishes, they achieved no action worthy of note.

---

31. This first appointment of the Decemviri took place in 451. Though Diodorus (correctly) speaks of ten names, only eight appear here: A. Manlius Vulso and P. Curiatius Fistus Trigeminus are missing.

24. When Lysanias was archon in Athens [443/2], the Romans again chose ten men as legislators: Appius Cl<au>dius [Crassus Inregillensis Sabinus], Marcus Cornelius [Maluginensis], Lucius Minucius [Esquilinus Augurinus], Gaius [?] Sergius [Esquilinus], Quintus P<oetel>ius [Libo Visolus], Manius Rabuleius, and Spurius †Veturius† [Oppius Cornicen].³² [2] These men proved unable to complete their appointed task.³³ One of them [Appius Claudius], out of lust for a maiden who was of good character but penniless, at first tried to seduce her by bribery, and then, when she would not submit to his advances, sent a public informer [his *cliens* M. Claudius] round to her house, with orders to bring about her enslavement. [3] When the informer declared that she was indeed his slave, and brought her before the magistrate [Appius Claudius himself], the latter then formally entered the charge against her of being a slave. After hearing the accuser's case, he handed over the girl, at which point the informer took possession of "his slave" and carried her off. [4] The girl's father [L. Verginius, a centurion], who had been present, and took it very hard that no one would listen to him, happened to pass by a butcher's shop, where he grabbed the cleaver left lying on the block and proceeded—in his determination that she should not suffer ravishment—to strike his daughter a blow with it that killed her. He then hurried out of the city to the military encampment then located on Mt. Algidus. [5] There he made an appeal to the troops, weeping as he reported the calamity that had befallen him, and aroused their pity and strong sympathy. They sallied forth in a body to bring aid to the unfortunate and charged into Rome at night, fully armed, occupying the hill known as the Aventine.³⁴

25. When dawn broke, and the soldiers' hatred of the crime that had been committed became manifest, the ten legislators, in support of their fellow-magistrate, mustered a strong body of young men, intending to settle the issue by armed combat. The intense contention thus aroused led the more responsible citizens (who foresaw just how dangerous this situation might be-

32. Again, Diodorus' list comes up short: only seven names appear on it. Missing (Liv. 3.36.3–37.8, Dion. Hal. *AR* 10.59.1–60.6) are Q. Fabius Vibulanus, T. Antonius Merenda, and K. Duillius [? Longus].

33. I.e., the compilation and setting down of the first Roman written legal code, the so-called Law of the Twelve Tables. There is general agreement that the first ten of these *tabulae* were drafted by the 451 committee. Over the last two, opinions differ. Cicero (*Rep.* 2.63) attributes them to the Decemviri of 450, whereas Diodorus (26.1) has them added by the consuls of 449, L. Valerius Potitus and M. Horatius Barbatus.

34. This act became known as the Second Secession of the Plebs. For the earlier secession (also to the Aventine), see Liv. 2.32.3.

come) to broker an agreement between the two sides, earnestly begging them to give over their dissension and not to risk overwhelming their fatherland with so serious a crisis. [2] All were finally persuaded, and they reached an agreement with one another. Ten tribunes were to be elected, with the greatest authority among all the officers of state, and these were to act as guardians of civic freedom.[35] Of the annually elected consuls, one should be chosen from the patricians, and one, invariably, from the plebeians, the people being empowered to appoint both from the plebeians [should they so desire].[36] [3] They did this in their determination to lessen the overall superiority of the patricians, since these men, because of their blue blood and the prestige conferred on them by their ancestry, were virtual masters of the city. The agreement also contained a clause stating that when the tribunes had served their year in office, they must ensure that a like number were appointed in their place: failure to do so would mean their being burned alive. Further, if the tribunes could not reach agreement among themselves, they were responsible for ensuring that the mediator between them was free to act without let or hindrance. This, then, was the resolution of the civil strife in Rome.

26. When Diphilus was archon in Athens [442/1], the Romans elected [Varr. 449] as consuls <M.> Horatius [Barbatus] and Lucius Valerius <Potitus>.[37] During their term, in Rome, since the codification of the laws was still unfinished on account of civil strife, the consuls completed it. Now of the so-called Twelve Tables, ten had been finished, and the consuls drafted the remaining two. With the legislation they had embarked on now complete, the consuls engraved it upon twelve bronze plaques, which they nailed to the rostra then located in front of the senate house. The brief and concise manner in which this legislation was drafted has continued to excite admiration down to our own times.

[2] During the period covered by these events, the majority of nations in the inhabited world remained quiet, since just about all of them were at peace. The Persians had two treaties with the Greeks, the first being with the Athenians and their allies. By this treaty the Greek cities of Asia [Minor] were to be

---

35. The office of tribune in fact went back some way: Diodorus himself (11.68.8) records the appointment of four in 471/0. It is not the existence of tribunes that is at issue here but their increasing number.

36. Diodorus anticipates the reservation of one consulship to the plebeians by almost a century: the proposal of the tribunes C. Licinius and L. Sextius (367/6; Liv. 6.42) was ratified by a plebiscite and became regular only in 342.

37. These were the men primarily responsible for the abrogation of the Decemvirate and the reconciliation of the patrician and plebeian orders.

subject to their own laws [<12.4.4–6]. They also concluded a later [411] pact with the Lacedaemonians, and this contained a clause stating the exact opposite, that is, that the Greek cities of Asia [Minor] were to be subject to the Persians [Thuc. 8.58]. There was likewise peace between the various Greek states, now that the Athenians and the Lacedaemonians had agreed on a thirty-year truce [<ch. 7]. [3] In Sicily too peace prevailed, since the Carthaginians had made a treaty with Gelon [480/79: <11.26.1–3], the Sicilian Greek cities had of their own volition ceded the hegemony to Syracuse [<11.72.1–2], and the Acragantines, after their defeat at the Himera River [<446/5: <12.8.1–4], had come to terms with the Syracusans. [4] Things were quiet among the Italian and Celtic peoples, as well as in Iberia, and throughout just about all the rest of the inhabited world. Consequently, during this period no military action worthy of mention took place, and universal peace prevailed; while festivals, games, sacrificial feast days in honor of the gods, and all other elements that go to make a happy life flourished everywhere.

27. When Timocles was archon in Athens [441/0], the Romans elected as consuls [Varr. 448] Lar{inu}s Herminius [Coritinesanus] and Titus <V>er<g>inius <Tricostus Caeliomontanus>. During their term, the Samians went to war with Miletus over a dispute concerning Priene. Perceiving that the Athenians were inclining favorably towards Miletus,[38] they revolted from Athens. The Athenians, who had elected Pericles as general, thereupon dispatched him with forty triremes against the Samians. [2] He made landfall on Samos, forced his way into the city, and took it over. He then set up a democracy, fined the Samians eighty talents, and took the same number of young men as hostages. Having thus taken care of everything in a few days, he returned to Athens [late July 441].

[3] Samos was, however, [soon] split by civil dissension, with one group backing the democracy and another in favor of aristocratic rule, so that the city was in utter disorder. Those who opposed the democracy crossed over to Asia and traveled to Sardis, to seek help from the Persian satrap [of Lydia], Pissuthnes. Pissuthnes gave them seven hundred soldiers, hoping thus to gain control of the island. The Samians sailed back home at night, taking the troops that had been given them, and—through the assistance of certain citizens—got into the city unobserved. They made themselves masters of Samos without

---

38. Samos clearly was after territorial expansion on the mainland opposite at the expense of a weakened Miletus. At the same time, it was inevitable that Pericles' enemies would accuse him of favoring Miletus because his mistress Aspasia was a Milesian. Canard this may be, but the relationship can only have encouraged the decision he took on other grounds.

any difficulty and deported from the city all who opposed them. Next, they went to Lemnos and surreptitiously rescued the hostages [? fall 441]. Then, after taking every precaution to safeguard Samos, they openly declared themselves enemies of the Athenians.[39] [4] The Athenians again chose Pericles as general and sent him off against the Samians with sixty ships [early spring 440]. He promptly [? late Apr.] fought a sea battle against seventy Samian triremes and beat them. Then, after calling up twenty-five vessels as reinforcements from Chios and Mytilene, he and they laid joint siege to Samos. After a few days, however, Pericles, leaving part of his force for the siege, put out to sea to intercept the Phoenician squadron that the Persians had sent to relieve Samos.

28. The Samians, convinced that Pericles' departure had given them an ideal opportunity to attack the ships that remained, sailed out against them, won the engagement, and were very full of themselves in consequence. [2] When Pericles heard about the defeat of his forces, however, he at once turned back and assembled a powerful fleet, being determined to crush the enemy squadrons once and for all. The Athenians hastened to send him sixty triremes [fall 440], and the Chians and Mytilenaeans, thirty. With this enlarged armament, Pericles resumed the siege by both land and sea, making continuous assaults. [3] He also utilized siege engines, being the first to employ the so-called rams and tortoises, which Artemon of Clazomenae built for him. Thus, by prosecuting the siege energetically and [finally] breaching the walls with his siege engines, he became master of Samos [winter 440/39]. After punishing those responsible [for the revolt], he dunned the Samians for the cost of the siege, assessing the figure at <one thousand> two hundred talents.[40] [4] He also impounded their fleet and demolished their city walls. This done, he returned to Athens.

The thirty-year truce between the Athenians and the Lacedaemonians was still firmly in place up to this point.

Such were the events that took place during this year.

29. When Morychides was archon in Athens [440/39], the Romans elected as consuls [Varr. 447] <C.> Julius [? Iullus] and Marcus Geganius [Macerinus], and the Eleians held the 85th Olympiad, in which Crison of Himera

---

39. They were now (Plut. *Per.* 25.3) "firmly resolved to vie with Athens for mastery of the sea," a determination that put a new and most dangerous Aegean-wide complexion on their rebellion.

40. Diodorus' MSS give the figure as 200 talents, which may possibly have been the annual installment: Green 2006, 220–221 n. 139.

won the *stadion* for the second time.[41] During their term, in Sicily Ducetius, the former leader of the Sicel cities, established the city [Cale Acte] of the Calactians [<8.2], and while settling numerous colonists there, [once more] made a bid for the Sicel leadership; but in the midst of this endeavor his life was cut short by illness. [2] Since Trinacie was the only Sicel city that the Syracusans had failed to make subject to them, they decided to launch an expedition against it [<11.90.2 and note]; they also had a strong suspicion that the Trinacians, as being of the same race, might lay claim to the leadership of the Sicels. This was a city that had in it many distinguished men, since it had always taken first place among the cities of the Sicels, being full of commanders who prided themselves on their warrior spirit. [3] So the Syracusans mustered all their forces, both from Syracuse itself and from the cities allied with them, and marched against Trinacie. The Trinacians had no allies, all the other [Sicel] cities being subject to the Syracusans, but nevertheless they mounted a courageous defense, holding out passionately against great odds. They slew great numbers themselves, and all died fighting heroically. [4] In like fashion, most of the older men took their own lives rather than face the humiliation to which they would be exposed after the city fell. The Syracusans, after so signally defeating men hitherto unconquered [by anyone], sold the rest of the population into slavery and completely demolished their city, sending the pick of the booty to Delphi as a thank offering to the god.

30. When Glauki<nu>s was archon in Athens [439/8], the Romans elected as consuls [Varr. 446] Titus Quinctius [Capitolinus Barbatus] and Agrippa Furius [Fusus]. During their term, the Syracusans, on account of the successes described above [<also 8.21.3–4], laid down one hundred new triremes and doubled the number of their cavalry; they also paid attention to their infantry arm and raised extra revenue in advance by imposing heavier tribute on the Sicels who had been made subject to them. These actions they took with the intention of gradually subjugating all Sicily.

[2] At the same time as these events,[42] in Greece the so-called Corinthian War had its beginning for the following reasons [Thuc. 1.24–26]. The

41. Crison of Himera had in fact already won the *stadion* twice on Diodorus' reckoning: see above, 5.1 and 23.1.

42. During the Corcyraean and Potidaean episodes, Diodorus follows a chronological schema two years higher than that deducible from the rest of our surviving evidence: e.g., he has the sea battle 31.2 in 437 rather than 435, and the engagement off Sybota in 435 rather than 433. By using two archon years (434/3 and 433/2) as fillers, and resuming his historical narrative only at ch. 37 in the archon year 432/1, he contrives to return there to the accepted date line.

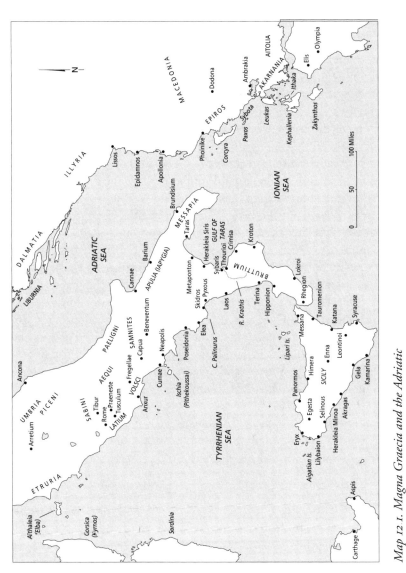

Map 12.1. Magna Graecia and the Adriatic

Epidamnians, who live on the Adriatic coast and are colonists of the Corcyraeans and Corinthians, split into warring factions, and the prevailing group exiled large numbers of their opponents. These exiles, however, united together, brought in the Illyrians on their side, and with them sailed against Epidamnus. [3] Now the barbarians had fielded a large force, with which they first laid waste the countryside, and then proceeded to besiege the city. The Epidamnians, who by themselves were no match for them in battle, sent ambassadors to Corcyra, asking the Corcyraeans, as their kinsmen, to render them aid. When Corcyra ignored this request, they dispatched an embassy to Corinth in pursuit of an alliance, declaring Corinth to be their one true mother-city, and at the same time soliciting colonists. [4] The Corinthians, out of pity for the Epidamnians—but also because they detested the Corcyraeans, since of all their colonists, only these did not send the customary sacrificial beasts to their mother-city—decided to respond to this request. They therefore sent Epidamnus colonists and also enough troops to garrison the city. [5] The Corcyraeans, in annoyance at this action, dispatched fifty triremes under one of their generals, who sailed to Epidamnus and ordered the inhabitants to take back their exiles [Thuc. 1.26.3]. They also sent ambassadors to the Corinthians, requesting that the status of the colony be determined in court, not by an act of war. When the Corinthians would not agree to their proposals, both sides decided to go to war and began fitting out substantial naval forces and rounding up allies. Thus the Corinthian War, so-called, broke out for the above-mentioned reasons.

[6] Meanwhile [Varr. 446], the Romans were at war with the Volscians: to begin with, they met only in skirmishes and minor engagements, but later [the Romans] won a major pitched battle and massacred most of their opponents.

31. When Theodorus was archon in Athens [438/7], the Romans elected as consuls [Varr. 445] Marcus Genucius [Augurinus] and Agrippa Curtius <P>hilo. During their term, in Italy, the nation of the Campani came into existence, acquiring its name from the rich soil of the plain nearby.[43]

In Asia, the kings of the Cimmerian Bosporus, the dynasty known as the Archaeanactidae, [had] ruled for forty-two years [480–438]; and the successor to the kingdom was Spartocus, who ruled for seven years [438–433/2: >36.1].

---

43. After initial peaceful infiltration, Oscan-speaking Samnite immigrants, during the mid 5th century, took over the principal Campanian cities, including Capua (Liv. 4.37.1), and proclaimed themselves a new Italic nation, the Campani.

[2] In Greece, the Corinthians were still at war with the Corcyraeans. When both had readied their naval forces, they moved them into position for a sea battle. The Corinthians bore down on the enemy with seventy well-equipped vessels; but the Corcyraeans met them with eighty and defeated them. They then reduced Epidamnus, putting to death all prisoners they took bar the Corinthians, whom they chained and jailed [Thuc. 1.29.1–5]. [3] After this sea battle the Corinthians withdrew, in considerable disarray, to the Peloponnese, while the Corcyraeans, who were now supreme at sea in those parts, kept raiding the Corinthians' allies and laying waste their land [but see Thuc. 1.30.2–4].

32. When this year was over, the [new] archon in Athens was Euthymenes [437/6], while in Rome in lieu of consuls three military tribunes were elected [Varr. 444]: Aulus Sempronius [Atratinus], Lucius Atilius [Luscus], and Titus Quinctius [Capitolinus Barbatus].[44] During their term, the Corinthians, after being thus worsted at sea, decided to build up a more substantial fleet. [2] So after amassing large quantities of timber, and hiring shipwrights from various cities, they began with zealous enthusiasm to make ready not only triremes but also every kind of weapon and missile, and, in a word, to stockpile all the gear they needed for the war. Regarding the triremes, some they laid down new, some worn-out ones they rebuilt, and others they requisitioned from their allies. [3] Since the Corcyraeans were doing much the same thing, and were no whit less determined about it, it was clear that the war was going to intensify very considerably.[45]

While these events were in progress, the Athenians also founded a colony at Amphipolis [<11.70.5], taking some of the settlers from among their own citizens, and others from garrisons in the area [>68.1–2].

33. When Lysimachus was archon in Athens [436/5], the Romans elected as consuls [Varr. 443] Titus Quinctius [Capitolinus Barbatus] and Marcus Geganius Macerinus, and the Eleians held the 86th Olympiad, that in which Theopompus of Thessaly won the *stadion*. During their term, the Corcyraeans, on discovering the size of the forces being assembled against them, sent

44. The third military tribune was in fact T. Cloelius: they abdicated after three months due to "flaws in the auspices at their election" (Broughton, 53; cf. Liv. 4.7.2–3). T. Quinctius Capitolinus Barbatus was the interrex appointed as a result (Liv. 4.7.10).

45. Thuc. 1.31.1. Most scholars date this battle in the spring or summer of 435, so that we reach early 433 for the appeal to Athens and the subsequent battle off Sybota in the summer. Diodorus' schema places both events in 435, in the archonship of Lysimachus.

ambassadors to the Athenians soliciting their support. [2] Since the Corinthians had done the same thing, an assembly was convened, at which the *demos,*
after listening to the ambassadors [of both sides], voted to make an alliance
with Corcyra [Thuc. 1.31.2–45.3].[46] Having done so, they at once sent them
ten fully equipped triremes, with a promise to send more later if they should
have need of them. [3] The Corinthians, having failed to get an alliance with
Athens, manned ninety triremes themselves and got sixty more from their
allies. With the one hundred and fifty fully equipped warships that this gave
them, and after appointing to the command their most highly regarded generals, they set sail for Corcyra, having decided to force an immediate sea battle.
[4] When the Corcyraeans learned that the enemy fleet was not far off, they
put out against them with one hundred and twenty triremes, including those
provided by Athens. A hard-fought engagement took place [off the Sybota
Islands: Thuc. 1.46–51], in which to begin with the Corinthians had the best
of it; but later the Athenians showed up with twenty more ships, furnished in
accordance with their second agreement, and this tipped the balance in favor
of a Corcyraean victory.[47] The next day, when the Corcyraeans put out in full
strength against them, the Corinthians did not leave harbor.

34. When Antiochides was archon in Athens [435/4], the Romans elected
as consuls [Varr. 442] Marcus Fabius [Vibulanus] and Postumus Aebutius
<Helva Cornicen>. During their term [? summer 433], the Corinthians were
highly annoyed with the Athenians, since the latter had not only fought side
by side with the Corcyraeans but had been responsible for their victory in
the sea battle. [2] So, being determined to pay the Athenians back, they got
one of their own colonies, the city of Potidaea, to revolt from Athens. In like

---

46. It is fairly clear why Corcyra would wish to enlist Athens' support, and Corinth
to prevent this: the Athenian navy was by far the most powerful in the Aegean. But why
should Athens want to involve herself in this affair? The answer involved not only the
permit of essential imports but if possible the control of both them and the routes to them.
Cimon's expeditions to Cyprus and Egypt, the famine of 445, Pericles' cruise into the Black
Sea, the establishment of Amphipolis and Thurii, the treaties with Rhegium and Leontini, the eventual expeditions to Sicily: all carry a subtext involving the pursuit of grain,
timber, and precious metals. An empire without bread starves. A naval empire without
ship timber rapidly becomes a contradiction in terms. As both Thucydides (1.44.3) and
Diodorus (54.3) emphasize, Corcyra was also a key point on the coastal voyage to Sicily.
To control a trade route was no less important than controlling the source of the essential
import that traveled it.

47. Thucydides (1.50–51) makes it clear that what happened was rather an indecisive
standoff; this may explain why afterwards both sides claimed the victory (Thuc. 1.54.2).

fashion, Perdiccas, the king of Macedon,[48] who also had his differences with the Athenians, persuaded those Chalcidians who had broken with Athens to abandon their coastal cities and all settle in Olynthos. [3] When the Athenians heard about the defection of Potidaea, they sent out thirty ships with instructions to lay waste these rebels' territory and to sack their city.[49] Those thus dispatched made landfall in Macedonia according to their instructions from the *demos* and at once laid siege to Potidaea [but see Thuc. 1.59.2]. [4] When the Corinthians sent a contingent of two thousand troops to relieve the besieged, the Athenian *demos* countered with two thousand of its own. A battle took place on the isthmus near Pallene, which the Athenians won, killing more than three hundred of the enemy [Thuc. 1.62–63]. Potidaea was now completely invested [but see Thuc. 1.64.1]. [5] Simultaneously with these events, the Athenians founded that city in the Propontis known as †Letanon†.[50]

In Italy, the Romans sent settlers to Ardea and divided up the [adjacent] territory into land holdings.

35. When Crates was archon in Athens [434/3], the Romans elected as consuls [Varr. 441] <C.> Furius <Pacilus> Fusus and Manius Papirius Crassus. During their term,[51] in Italy the inhabitants of Thurii [<10–11>], who had been assembled from numerous cities, split into hostile factions over two problems: from which city should the Thurians be said to have come as settlers, and what man should properly be called their founder? [2] The Athenians asserted their right to the first privilege, since the bulk of the colony's settlers had come from Athens; but the cities of the Peloponnese, which likewise had contributed not a few of their citizens to the founding of Thurii, maintained that the entitlement of the colony should be ascribed to them. [3] Similarly with the second point: since many highly qualified men had shared

---

48. Perdiccas II of Macedon (c. 452–413/2) was an astute and shifty opportunist who survived by switching sides again and again before and during the Peloponnesian War.

49. Neither the timing nor the instructions in Diodorus (the Athenians react to a fait accompli; the instructions—slash and burn, sack—are more stringent) agree with those of Thuc. 1.58.1–59.1. Diodorus here preferred an alternative source (? Ephorus). Presumably he felt Thucydides was airbrushing Athenian brutality. His version also, interestingly, suggests that Athens was not expecting serious resistance, let alone a long siege: precisely the same expensive mistake she had made over Samos.

50. Despite numerous suggestions and emendations, the identity of this place remains quite uncertain. Cf. Green 2006, 232 n. 184.

51. Diodorus here breaks off his narrative of the Potidaean campaign, picking it up again (where he left it) at 37.1—after a two-year break marked only by two nonrelated items, the dispute over Thurii's foundation and Meton's reform of the Athenian calendar, both clearly fillers of a gap between incompatible chronologies.

in the process of colonization, and had performed numerous essential services, there was much discussion about this, since each one of them was eager to have the honor. In the end the Thurians sent to Delphi to find out just whom they should name as their city's founder. The god's oracular response was that he himself should be regarded as the founder. Once the dispute had been settled in this manner, they declared Apollo the founder of Thurii, after which the citizen body, thus freed from civil dissension, returned to their previous state of concord.

[4] In Greece, King Archidamus of the Lacedaemonians died[52] after ruling forty-two years, and Agis succeeded him, to reign for twenty-seven years.

36. When Apseudes was archon in Athens [433/2], the Romans elected as consuls [Varr. 440] Titus Menenius [Agripp. Lanatus] and Proculus Geganius Macerinus.[53] During their term, Spartocus, king of the Bosporus, died, after ruling for seven years and was succeeded by <Satyrus>,[54] who reigned for forty years.

[2] In Athens Meton son of Pausanias, who had won a high reputation as an astronomer, published what is known as his nineteen-year cycle, which he set to begin on the thirteenth day of the Athenian month Skirophorion. By the end of these nineteen years, the stars return to the positions from which they started, thus completing what we may term the circuit of a Great Year, called by some in consequence Meton's Year.[55] [3] This man would seem to have been quite extraordinarily accurate in his prediction and written forecast, since the stars do indeed accomplish their cycle and produce the consequent effects of this, in accordance with his written calculations. As a result, from

---

52. King Archidamus II actually died in 427/6, as Diodorus (who noted his activities during the first phase of the Peloponnesian War, e.g., 42.6) knew perfectly well. For a possible explanation of the error, see 11.48.2, with n. 65. His son and successor, Agis II, played a leading role in the war and died in 400.

53. We should note, during this year, Athens' renewal of treaties with Rhegium and Leontini, evidence of her steadily increasing interest in the West.

54. Here, by a scribal slip, called "Seleucus" in Diodorus' MSS. At 14.93.1 we find the correct reading.

55. On Meton, see G. J. Toomey, *OCD* 969–970. What Meton and Euctemon did, in the first instance, in 432 was to observe the summer solstice (the beginning of the solar year) as part of an attempt to measure the length of the year more accurately. The point of the nineteen-year cycle was to adjust the lunar year by intercalation, made necessary by the fact that a tropical year is longer than 12 synodic months by 0.3683 a month. Diodorus, who speaks of "stars" rather than planets, was clearly no astronomer (Oldfather 1946, 448 n. 1).

that day to this most Greeks go by the nineteen-year cycle and are not cheated of the truth in so doing.

[4] In Italy the Tarantines expropriated the inhabitants of Siris from their native city, added a number of settlers from among their own citizens, and founded the city known as Heracleia [<23.2].

37. When Pythodorus was archon in Athens [432/1], the Romans elected as consuls [Varr. 439] Titus Quinctius [Capitolinus Barbatus] and <Agrippa> Menenius [Lanatus], and the Eleians held the 87th Olympiad, in which the *stadion* was won by Sophron the Ambraciot. During their term, in Rome, Spurius Maelius was done away with while aiming for tyrannical power.[56] The Athenians, after scoring a brilliant victory at Potidaea [? June 432], sent out Phormio [? late July 432] as general to replace Callias, who had fallen in the line of battle.[57] Phormio took over command of the army and dug in for the siege; but though he made endless assaults on the city, its defenders stood him off valiantly, and the siege became a lengthy business.

[2] Thucydides the Athenian began his history at this point, it being an account of the so-called Peloponnesian War, fought by the Athenians against the Lacedaemonians. This war lasted for twenty-seven years [431–404], of which Thucydides wrote up twenty-two [>411/10], in eight (or, as others divide it, nine) books.[58]

38. When Euthydemus was archon in Athens [431/0], the Romans elected in lieu of consuls [Varr. 438] three military tribunes: Ma<m..> Aemili{an}us Mamerc<in>us, Gaius Julius [Iullus], and Lucius Quinctius. During their term, there broke out between Athenians and Lacedaemonians the Peloponnesian War, as it has been called, the longest of all wars on record; and it is both essential and appropriate for our history as planned to begin by laying out its causes.

---

56. Sp. Maelius was an equestrian, who, at a time of near-famine, bought up grain wholesale from Etruria and sold it to the plebs at giveaway prices, thus assuring himself a populist power base.

57. Thuc. 1.64.1–2. It is clear from Thucydides that the action Diodorus resumes here from 34.4, under the archon year 435/4, was in fact more or less continuous and thus to be located near the end of 433/2.

58. On Thucydides' life and work, see H. T. Wade-Gery et al., *OCD,* 3rd ed., 1516–1521, and Hornblower 1987, 1–6: both discreetly ignore evidence from the (untranslated) Marcellinus *vita.* The variant number of books cited by Diodorus (eight is today accepted as the standard number) reminds us that such formal divisions were not made by 5th-century authors themselves but imposed on their works later by Hellenistic scholars.

[2] While the Athenians were still pursuing supremacy at sea, they took the funds that had been stored as [the League's] common property on Delos, some eight thousand talents all told, transferred this sum to Athens,[59] and made Pericles responsible for its safekeeping. This man stood head and shoulders above his fellow-citizens in birth, reputation, and skill as a public speaker. Over a period of time, however, he spent a very considerable portion of these monies for his own private purposes; and when he was required to give an accounting of them, he fell ill, since he was unable to produce a balanced statement of the funds that had been entrusted to him.[60] [3] While he was thus at a loss, his nephew Alcibiades,[61] who as an orphan was being brought up in his house, showed him a way to deal with this business of accounting for monies. Seeing that his uncle was worried, he asked him the cause of his worry. Pericles said: "I've been asked for an accounting of these funds, and I'm trying to figure out how to produce a statement for the citizens." To which Alcibiades responded: "What you ought to be doing is figuring out not how to produce such a statement but how not to." [4] Pericles accepted the boy's comment and kept trying to find a way of plunging the Athenians into a major war, since he reckoned this would be the best way, what with all the confusion and distractions and fears that would occupy the city, to avoid giving a precise accounting of the funds.[62] He was further nudged towards this course by something that befell him quite by chance: here is how it came about.

---

59. This transfer is generally dated in 454, to coincide with the beginning of annual treasury tithe payments (*aparchai*) to Athena. For my arguments backdating the transfer to 463/2 or 462/1, see Green 2006, 130–131 n. 240, 139 n. 270. These 8,000 talents were added to the reserve already in the treasury, producing a maximum total (40.2, 54.3, 13.21.2; Thuc. 2.13.3) of 10,000.

60. On Pericles, see Podlecki 1998. He was regularly criticized for extravagance and asserted the Athenians' right to spend League monies how they pleased (Plut. *Per.* 12.3, 14.1–2), so his anxiety may well have been genuine, not merely anecdotal; but both here and over his covert use of large sums to bribe Sparta prior to the war (Plut. *Per.* 23.1; schol. Aristoph. *Clouds* 859), the *demos,* far from holding him to account, in fact approved his expenses without question.

61. Alcibiades (451–404), ward of Pericles, dazzling (and handsome) aristocrat, student and close friend of Socrates, lavish spender on chariot racing, backstairs imperialist politician, and chief mover (84.1) in the ill-fated Sicilian expedition. Historians tend to be seduced by his charm and fail to notice how little he actually achieved. He was, in that pregnant Texan phrase, a classic case of the rancher who is all hat and no cattle.

62. Plut. *Alcib.* 7.2 gives a simpler, more convincing, version of this anecdote, unrelated to the war. The (clearly nonsensical) idea of Pericles starting the war to get the *demos* off his back seems to derive from a piece of political vaudeville by Aristophanes in 421 (*Peace* 605–611), involving him in the case against Pheidias (see below, 40.6).

39. The statue of Athena was the creation of Pheidias, and Pericles son of Xanthippus had been appointed the supervisor [of its construction]. There were certain men, former workers with Pheidias on the project, who were [afterwards] suborned by Pericles' enemies: these now seated themselves as suppliants at the altars of the gods. When challenged regarding their unlooked-for action, they said they would show that Pheidias was in possession of a substantial proportion of the sacred funds, with the knowledge and active connivance of Pericles as supervisor. [2] So when the assembly met to discuss these matters, Pericles' enemies persuaded the *demos* to arrest Pheidias and charged Pericles himself with theft of sacred property. They also laid information against Pericles' teacher, the sophist Anaxagoras, on the grounds of his impious attitude towards the gods, and strove to ensnare Pericles too in their various slanderous accusations, envy sharpening their determination to undercut both his eminence and the high esteem in which he was held.[63]

[3] Pericles, however, well aware that while a war is being fought, people admire men of excellence because of the pressing need they have for them, whereas in peacetime they lay false information against them out of idle envy, decided it would benefit him to plunge his city into a major war. Because of its urgent need then for Pericles' intelligence and military expertise, it would ignore the charges against him; nor would it have the time or leisure to make a close scrutiny of the accounting he would offer of the monies [in his charge].

[4] Now since the Athenians had passed a vote to debar the Megarians from their markets and harbors, the latter turned for aid to the Spartans.[64] The Lacedaemonians were persuaded by the Megarians, and quite openly dispatched ambassadors—following a decision by the general council [of the Peloponnesian League]—bidding the Athenians rescind their decree against the Megarians, and threatening, should they refuse, to war against them with the help of their allies. [5] When the assembly met to consider this [threat],

---

63. On Pheidias, see n. 2 to 1.4 above. Anaxagoras of Clazomenae (500–428) had been resident in Athens for perhaps twenty years before his (alleged) trial for impiety (? 437/6), evidence for which is highly confused and contradictory. Afterwards, he left Athens for Lampsacus, where he died. Diodorus (or Ephorus) is probably right about the various charges and innuendos brought against Pericles and his circle by the conservatives being no more than nasty political fictions (Podlecki 1998, 31–34, 101–117), of the kind in favor again today.

64. For the importance of Megara's ports as an alternative link to that provided by Corinth between the Saronic and Corinthian Gulfs, see n. 14 to ch. 7. Ever since 446 Megara had been a Peloponnesian ally. The importance to Athens of controlling the city is clear: there were invasions annually until 424 and then a democratic near takeover in Athens' favor, foiled by the Spartan Brasidas (66.1–67.1).

Pericles, who as a skilled public speaker far surpassed all other citizens, persuaded the Athenians not to lift the ban, asserting that to cave in to Lacedaemonian demands against their own best interests was the beginning of slavery
[Thuc. 1.140.2–141.1]. He accordingly counseled them to bring [all their pos-
sessions] from the countryside into the city [Thuc. 2.13.2], and to battle it out
with the Spartans on the basis of their supremacy at sea [Thuc. 1.142.5–9].

40. Having thus dealt in a well-calculated manner with the issue of going
to war, Pericles proceeded to enumerate the mass of allies their city possessed,
the superiority of its naval strength, and, in addition, the vast funds that had
been transferred from Delos to Athens, consisting of tribute payments collected for the common benefit of the cities. [2] From the 10,000 talents in this
common fund, 4,000 had been spent on the construction of the Propylaea
and the siege of Potidaea, [offset by] an annual income of four hundred and
sixty talents from the payment of tribute by the allies. Apart from this, he assured them that the sacred processional vessels and booty from the Persians
were between them worth [another] five hundred talents; [3] he also drew
their attention to the mass of offerings in the various temples, as well as to fifty
talents'-worth of gold adorning the statue of Athena, so fitted as to be remov-
able. All these items, he insisted, they could, if faced with a critical emergency,
borrow from the gods and return to them in time of peace.[65] Their lives, he
reminded the citizen body, because of the lengthy peace [they had already
enjoyed], had increased greatly in prosperity.

[4] Over and above these financial reserves, he pointed out, the city had
at its disposal—not counting the allies and those garrisoning the frontier
fortresses—12,000 hoplites, while the garrisons and the resident aliens were
more than 17,000 in number, and they had three hundred triremes in commission [Thuc. 2.13.6–8]. [5] [By comparison], he emphasized, the Lacedaemonians were strapped for funds and lagged far behind the Athenians in
naval power. This detailed itemization, coupled with a rousing call to arms,
persuaded the Athenian people that they need not be bothered about the
Lacedaemonians—an end Pericles easily achieved by his oratorical skill, the
reason for his being nicknamed "the Olympian." [6] Aristophanes, the poet

---

65. The enumeration of funds derives from Thuc. 2.13.3–5. Diodorus combines into
one occasion material that in Thucydides is the subject of two separate speeches (1.140–144
and 2.13.2–9). His figures in general agree with those of Thucydides, except that he gives
the original estimate of 460 talents (as opposed to Thucydides' 600) for Athens' current
annual revenue, and he names a sum (50 talents), which Thucydides does not, for the value
of the gold on the statue of Athena.

of [Attic] Old Comedy, who was coeval with Pericles, likewise alludes to this in the following [trochaic] tetrameters:

O you band of wretched farmers, listen well and ponder my
utterances, if you want to | hear how Peace was lost to us.
Pheidias it was began it, with his scandalous default—
Pericles then, scared he might be | implicated in the mess . . .
Tossing in the tiny spark he'd kindled with the Megara vote
huffed and puffed up such a giant | warflame that its spreading smoke
left all eyes in Hellas weeping, over there and here alike [*Peace* 603–
606, 609–611].

Elsewhere [*Acharn.* 530–531] he also writes how

Pericles the Olympian
flashed lightning, thundered, stirred the pot of Hellas.[66]

And here is the poet Eupolis [in *The Demes*]:[67]

Some strange persuasion dwelt upon his lips:
Such was his charm, alone of all the speakers
he left his sting in every man who heard him.

41. These, then, were the causes of the Peloponnesian War as Ephorus described them. Now when the leading states had plunged into hostilities in this manner, the Lacedaemonians, in joint session with the [other] Peloponnesian states, voted for war against Athens. They also dispatched ambassadors to the Great King of Persia, calling upon him to join their alliance, and similarly used diplomatic approaches to persuade their allies in Sicily and Italy to help

---

66. This is the earliest (425) reference to Pericles as "Olympian." The ancient world referred the nickname either to his lofty mien and character or else (as here) to his Zeus-like thunder-and-lightning oratory; but his aristocratic avoidance of social life (Plut. *Per.* 7.4–5) must surely have been at least partly responsible. The rest of the speech (*Acharn.* 515–540) presents a second comic version of the origins of the Peloponnesian War. Once again it involves the Megarian Decree and Pericles' private motives; but otherwise (in a parody of the opening chapters of Herodotus), it lays the blame on a quarrel over prostitutes, smearing Pericles' mistress Aspasia as a high-class brothel keeper. Both versions clearly reflect the conservative opposition's violent political propaganda. How much of all this Ephorus really believed, and what other causes, if any, he listed (41.1), must remain, in the absence of his full text, an open question. In any case, Diodorus seems from now on to agree with Thucydides about the significance of Plataea.

67. Eupolis (446/5–411), Aristophanes' precocious rival in Old Comedy, was killed on active service in the Hellespont during a sea battle against the Spartans. Afterwards, the Athenian *demos* exempted established poets from frontline duty.

them out with two hundred triremes [Thuc. 2.7.1–2].[68] [2] They themselves meanwhile, together with the Peloponnesians, organized their land forces, made all other military preparations, and were the first to embark on the conflict.

It happened this way [Thuc. 2.2–6]. The city of Plataea was an independent state within Boeotia and had an alliance with the Athenians. [3] But certain of the citizens wanted to abolish this independence and therefore had private discussions with the Boeotians, offering to bring their city into the confederacy led by the Thebans and to hand Plataea over to them if they would send troops to help [in the takeover]. [4] So the Boeotians dispatched three hundred picked troops by night, and the traitors secretly admitted them within the walls and made them masters of the city. [5] The Plataeans, anxious to preserve their alliance with Athens, and at first assuming that the Thebans had come out in full force, entered into negotiations with the captors of the city and made a strong plea for a truce; but as the night went on, and they realized how few [their attackers] were, they got together and began a fierce struggle for their freedom. [6] Battle was joined in the streets, and to begin with, the Thebans, because of their fighting quality, prevailed and slew many of their opponents; but when slaves and children began throwing tiles at them from the housetops, and actually wounding them, they broke and ran. Some of them got out of the city to safety, but some others, who had taken refuge in a house, were forced to surrender. [7] When the Thebans heard what had happened from those who got away, they at once marched out at the double, in full force. Because those living out in the countryside were not expecting an attack, they were quite unprepared: many were killed, and quite a few taken alive, while the entire region was in an uproar, with much pillage.

42. The Plataeans dispatched envoys to the Thebans, demanding that they withdraw from their, the Plataeans', territory and take back their own prisoners. So when this had been agreed, the Thebans got their prisoners back [but see Thuc. 2.5.7], returned the loot they had amassed, and withdrew to Thebes. The Plataeans sent ambassadors to Athens soliciting aid, and themselves brought the bulk of their property into the city. [2] When the Athenians heard about events in Plataea, they at once sent a sizable body of troops there. These arrived with dispatch—though not ahead of the Thebans—and fetched the remaining goods in from the countryside. They then assembled the women and children, together with the riffraff, and sent them all off to Athens.

---

68. Reading Herbst's emendation in Thuc. (s' for -san, i.e., 200).

[3] The Lacedaemonians, judging that the Athenians had broken the truce,[69] raised a very considerable army from both Lacedaemon and the rest of the Peloponnesians. [4] There were allied with the Lacedaemonians at this point all those dwelling in the Peloponnese (except for the Argives, and they remained neutral); and of those outside the Peloponnese, the Megarians, the Ambraciots, the Leucadians, the Phocians, the Boeotians; and of the Locrians, the bulk of those on the [eastward], Euboean side; but of the rest [only] the Amphissans. [5] There were allied with the Athenians those occupying the coastal strip of Asia [Minor]: the Carians, Dorians, Ionians, and Hellespontines, together with all the islanders except for the inhabitants of Melos and Thera, as well as those in the Thraceward regions except for Chalcidice and Potidaea. In addition to these, there were the Messenians domiciled in Naupactus and the Corcyraeans. <Of these the Chians, Lesbians, and Corcyraeans contributed ships,> while all the rest sent ground troops. Such, then, were the allies on either side.[70]

[6] The Lacedaemonians put in hand a considerable army and entrusted the command over it to King Archidamus. He invaded Attica with this force [May/June 431], pressed home attacks on its frontier forts, and laid waste much of the countryside. The Athenians were furious at his ranging freely over their territory, and they longed to go out and fight the enemy [Thuc. 2.21.2–3]; but Pericles, who was general and supreme commander, told the young men to sit tight, promising to get the Lacedaemonians out of Attica without the risk of an engagement. [7] He thereupon manned a hundred triremes, put a strong force aboard them, with Carcinus and some others in command, and sent them to attack the Peloponnese. This force laid waste a good deal of coastal territory and captured some fortresses, which so alarmed the Lacedaemonians that they quickly recalled their army from Attica [but see Thuc. 2.23.3], thus safeguarding the states of the Peloponnese. [8] In this way Attica was rid of the enemy, and Pericles rose high in his fellow-citizens' estimation for his generalship and for toughing it out with the Lacedaemonians.

---

69. Thucydides (2.7.1) clearly, and rightly, believes it was the Thebans' attack on Plataea that broke the Thirty Years' Truce. Yet at 1.66 he argues that Corinth's earlier actions against Athens over Potidaea, *being undertaken independently of the Peloponnesian League,* did not violate the treaty; and the Spartans seem to have taken much the same line over Thebes. Thus, their claim that it was *Athens* that broke the truce by going to the aid of her ally Plataea looks disingenuous, to put it mildly.

70. Diodorus' account of the allies on either side is taken directly, and almost exactly, from Thuc. 2.9.1–6. The parallels are so clear that Wesseling (followed by Oldfather 1950) could confidently fill the lacuna in Diodorus' text at 42.5 from Thuc. 2.9.6, and I have done likewise.

43. When Apollodorus was archon in Athens [430/29], the Romans elected as consuls [Varr. 437] Marcus Geganius [Macerinus] and Lucius Sergius [Fidenas]. During their term,[71] the Athenian commander never stopped raiding and ravaging territory in the Peloponnese, and besieging their fortresses. When he was joined by fifty triremes from Corcyra, he intensified his slash-and-burn raids into Peloponnesian territory, in particular laying waste the coastal area called Acte and burning its farm buildings. [2] After this he sailed to Methone in the territory of Laconia, ravaged the countryside, and launched a succession of attacks on the city.[72] At this point the Spartan Brasidas [>62.1–5]—who though still young in years was a man of outstanding strength and bravery—seeing that Methone was in danger of being stormed, rounded up some fellow-Spartans, daringly charged and scattered the enemy cordon, killing large numbers of them, and made his way into the [beleaguered] stronghold. [3] While the city was under siege, Brasidas mounted so brilliant a defense that the Athenian efforts to capture it came to nothing, and they withdrew to their ships. For thus by his individual prowess and bravery saving Methone, Brasidas became much esteemed by his fellow-Spartans [Thuc. 2.25.2]. Further, having risen very high in his own conceit on account of this courageous episode, he frequently thereafter fought with extraordinary daring and thus acquired a great reputation for valor. [4] The Athenians meanwhile sailed round [the Peloponnese] to Elis, laid waste the countryside, and besieged Pheia, a stronghold of the Eleians.

When the Eleians came to Pheia's defense, they defeated them in battle, slew large numbers of the enemy, and took Pheia by storm. [5] But after this the Eleians mustered in full strength and fought [another] engagement with the Athenians, who were driven back to their ships. They then sailed away to Cephallenia and won over the [island's] inhabitants into their alliance; after which they set course back to Athens.

44. Subsequently, the Athenians chose as general Cleopompus and sent him out with thirty ships, his orders being to keep watch over Euboea and to

71. The events narrated by Diodorus in chs. 43–44 in fact still belong to the 431/0 archon year: see Thuc. 2.25–32.

72. Acte (the name simply means "promontory" or "peninsula") is generally referred to as being "the coastal region east of Argos" (Hornblower 1991, 281), which would suggest that the ancient sources confused Methone with the peninsula of Methana. Raiding in the area around Cythera and Gytheion (see Map, p. 10), however, would make more sense. Both Diodorus and Thucydides (2.25.1) place Methone in Laconia, though in fact it is on the southwest coast of Messenia: possibly they regarded Messenia as, in effect, Laconian territory.

conduct a campaign against the Locrians. He duly sailed, ravaged the coast of Locris, and reduced the city of Thronium by siege; when the Locrians raised a force against him, he brought them to battle near a city named Alope and defeated them. He then turned the island of Atalanta, offshore from Locris, into a fortress base for his raids against the local population. [2] The Athenians also accused the Aeginetans of collaboration with the Lacedaemonians, expropriated them from their own city, and sent out Athenian settlers to divide up their city and territory as land holdings. [3] The Lacedaemonians gave these dispossessed Aeginetans the district known as Thyreae to live in, on the grounds that the Athenians had similarly thrown open Naupactus to the refugees driven out of Messene [<11.84.7]. The Athenians also sent Pericles at the head of a field force to make war on the Megarians. He raided their territory, did much damage to the property there, and returned to Athens with large quantities of plunder [Thuc. 2.31.1–3].[73]

45. The Lacedaemonians, accompanied by the Peloponnesians and their other allies, now [spring 430] carried out their second invasion of Attica. In their march through the countryside they cut down trees, set fire to the steadings, and spread destruction through almost the entire state except for the region known as the Tetrapolis. This area they kept clear of because their forefathers [the Heraclidae] had dwelt there, sallying forth from it to defeat Eurystheus: they thought it only fair that those who had done their ancestors a favor should receive from those ancestors' descendants a fitting favor in return.[74] [2] The Athenians did not dare to meet them in a pitched battle; and being cooped up inside the walls, they were exposed to a crisis occasioned by an outbreak of plague [Thuc. 2.47.3–54.5]. Since vast crowds of every sort of person had flocked into the city, the resultant cramped living space had made them fall easy victims to diseases through breathing infected air. [3] Consequently, since they were unable to drive the enemy out of their own territory, they once more dispatched a strong fleet against the Peloponnese, with Pericles in command. He laid waste large swathes of coastal territory, plundered several cities, and thus caused the Lacedaemonians to withdraw from Attica. [4] After this the Athenians, with their countryside stripped of trees and the plague exacting a heavy death toll, became exceedingly despon-

73. It was during the subsequent winter (431/0) that Pericles delivered his famous eulogy on the battle casualties of the previous season's campaigning (Thuc. 2.34–46).

74. See D.S. 4.57.4–5. The Tetrapolis in northeast Attica consisted of the four demes of Marathon, Probalinthus, Oenoë, and Tricorythus; it was the last of these that the Heraclidae occupied.

dent; and since they regarded Pericles as the one responsible for their being at war, they vented their anger on him: they removed him from his generalship and, seizing on some trumpery excuses for a prosecution, fined him †eighty† talents.[75] [5] They then sent embassies to the Lacedaemonians proposing an end to hostilities. When not a soul responded to these approaches, however, they were forced to reelect Pericles general [? 429].

Such, then, were the events that took place during the course of this year.

46. When Epameinon was archon in Athens [429/8], the Romans elected as consuls Lucius Papirius [Crassus] and <M.> Cornelius Ma<lug>in<ensi>s [436]. During their term [? Sept. 429], in Athens, Pericles the general died, a man who for birth and wealth, as well as rhetorical and strategic expertise, far outshone the rest of the citizen body.

[2] Since the [Athenian] people were ambitious to take Potidaea [<34.3–4] by storm, they sent out Hagnon as general, with the troops that Pericles had previously commanded.[76] He made landfall at Potidaea with his entire expeditionary force, and he set everything in order for prosecuting the siege. He procured siege engines of every description, as well as a mass of arms and missiles, and grain in abundance, sufficient for the entire army. He then launched continuous daily assaults on the city over a very considerable period but was unable to take it; [3] for the besieged, through their fear of capture, put up a fierce defense, and—trusting in the unusual height of their walls—had an advantage over those attacking from the harbor, whereas plague was spreading among the besiegers and had already killed large numbers of them, thus causing a serious fall in morale throughout the camp. [4] Now Hagnon, being well aware that the Athenians had already spent more than a thousand talents on the siege and were furious with Potidaea for having been the first [city] to defect to the Lacedaemonians, was afraid to abandon the siege. In consequence he forced himself to hang on, and drove his men, beyond their strength, to keep up their attacks against the city. [5] But since these assaults, as well as the ravages of the plague, were claiming the lives of many Athenian citizens, he left part of his force to keep up the siege and [with the remainder] sailed back to Athens, having lost more than a thousand of his troops. [6] No sooner

75. The amount of the fine given by Diodorus is ridiculous and may be due to scribal error. Plutarch (*Per.* 35.4) quotes estimates ranging from 15 to 50 talents. Thucydides (2.65.3) gives no figure. The actual charge is uncertain but was most probably mismanagement of the Argolid expedition.

76. Thucydides (2.58.1) places Hagnon's disastrous forty-day expedition in the summer of 430, and the surrender of Potidaea (2.70.1–5) during the winter of 430/29.

were they gone, however, than the Potidaeans—their grain reserves all used up, and the city's inhabitants desperate—sent heralds out to the besiegers to negotiate a surrender. They were eagerly welcomed, and an armistice was concluded on the following terms: the Potidaeans were to evacuate their city en masse, taking nothing with them except one garment each for the men, and two for the women. [7] On the agreement being sworn to, all the Potidaeans, together with their wives and children, in accordance with its requirements, left their native land and journeyed to the Chalcidians of the Thraceward regions, where they settled. The Athenians meanwhile sent up to a thousand of their citizens to Potidaea as colonists and divided up both the city and its [surrounding] territory into allotments for them.

47. The Athenians now, having elected Phormio general, sent him out with twenty triremes [winter 430/29]. He sailed around the Peloponnese and took up station at Naupactus: operating from here, he secured control of the Crisaean [Corinthian] Gulf, thus stopping Lacedaemonian sea traffic in the area. The Lacedaemonians dispatched a strong force into Boeotia under King Archidamus, who encamped before Plataea. With the threat that he would otherwise lay waste their territory, Archidamus, backed by his army, demanded that the Plataeans secede from their Athenian alliance. When they ignored him, he plundered the countryside and destroyed their holdings everywhere. [2] After this he completely invested the city with a wall, hoping that by depriving the Plataeans of all the necessities of life he might force them into surrender. At the same time, he and his men never slackened their efforts, bringing up siege engines to pound at the walls and making assaults without end. However, when they found themselves unable to reduce the city by these assaults, they left an adequate guard force behind and returned to the Peloponnese.

[3] The Athenians also appointed Xenophon and Phanomachus generals and dispatched them into the Thraceward regions at the head of a thousand troops. When they reached Spartolus in Bottiaean territory, they ravaged the region, destroying the grain while it was still green. The Olynthians, however, came to the relief of the Bottiaeans, and in the resultant battle the Athenians were defeated, the death toll including both generals and the majority of their soldiers [Thuc. 2.79.1–7]. [4] At about the same time as these events, the Lacedaemonians, acceding to a request from the Ambraciots, sent an expedition into Acarnania under Cnemus, who had with him one thousand infantry and a few ships. Reinforcing these with a sufficient number of troops from the allies, he entered Acarnania and pitched camp near the city of Stratus. [5] The Acarnanians, however, assembled their forces, ambushed the enemy

with great slaughter, and forced Cnemus to withdraw his column to the city of Oeniadae.

48. About the same time [summer 429] the Athenian general Phormio, with his twenty triremes, encountered a Lacedaemonian squadron forty-seven strong and engaged them in a sea battle [Thuc. 2.83–84]. He sank the enemy's flagship, rendered many of the other vessels unseaworthy, captured twelve of them with their crews, and pursued the remainder to the coast. The Lacedaemonians, worsted against their expectations, retreated with their surviving vessels to Patrae in Achaea. This naval engagement was fought off Rhion. The Athenians erected a trophy, dedicated one vessel to Poseidon <at the narrows>,[77] and sailed back to the allied port of Naupactus. [2] The Lacedaemonians sent naval reinforcements to Patrae: these joined up with the triremes that had survived the sea battle and assembled at Rhion. A Peloponnesian land force met them at the same place and encamped close to the fleet. [3] Phormio, made arrogant by his earlier victory, now dared to attack the ships of the enemy, although they far outnumbered his. Though he sank some, he also lost a number of his own, so that the victory he won was dubious. The Athenians then sent him twenty more triremes [as reinforcements], at which the Lacedaemonians, not daring to challenge him to another engagement, sailed away to Corinth.

Such, then, were the events that took place during the course of this year.

49. When Diotimus was archon in Athens [428/7], the Romans elected [Varr. 435] as consuls Gaius Julius [? Iullus] and Proc<u>lus Verginius Tricostus, and the Eleians held the 88th Olympiad, in which the *stadion* was won by Symmachus of Messene in Sicily. [2] During their term, Cnemus the Lacedaemonian admiral, now stationed at Corinth, made up his mind to capture Piraeus.[78] News had reached him that no vessels inside the harbor there were launched ready for action, nor had any troops been assigned to guard [the port facilities]: the Athenians, it seemed, had become careless about its security, since they could not imagine anyone daring to [try and] capture the place. [3] So, starting from Megara, Cnemus launched forty triremes that had been beached there and sailed for Salamis, where he made a completely unexpected attack on the fortress known as Boudorion, towed off three ships, and then overran the entire island. [4] When the Salaminians lit beacon fires to alert

---

77. Diodorus' MSS place this trophy at the Isthmus, which contradicts Thuc. 2.84.4. Palmer's reading *porthmou* ("narrows") for *Isthmou* I find persuasive.

78. Thucydides (2.93–94) dates this raid to "the beginning of winter," 429. Though Diodorus closely follows Thucydides here, he continues to date events a year later.

those across in Attica, the Athenians, thinking that Piraeus had been taken, rushed out in great confusion to the rescue; but on learning what had really happened, they hurriedly manned a sufficient number of ships and sailed across to Salamis. [5] The Peloponnesians, thus foiled in their venture, left Salamis and sailed back home. With the enemy squadron gone, the Athenians set a more watchful guard on Salamis and stationed an adequate garrison there; they also reinforced Piraeus' defenses with booms and strong guards.

50. About the same time Sitalces, king of the [Odrysian] Thracians,[79] had come to the throne of a small country, in which, by his personal courage and insights, he nevertheless contrived to extend his authority and dominion very considerably. He governed his subjects equitably, he was a brave and strategically shrewd commander in battle, and he also paid particular attention to his state revenues. Ultimately he acquired such power that he ruled over more territory than any of his royal predecessors in Thrace. [2] The coastline of his kingdom extended from the territory of Abdera as far as the Ister [Danube] River; and from the sea into the interior the distance [to his frontier] was so great that the journey took a man traveling light thirteen days. Since he ruled over so extensive a kingdom, he took in annual revenues of more than one thousand talents. [3] While he was at war during the period under discussion, he raised from Thrace itself over 120,000 infantry and 50,000 cavalry.

We must, however, begin by laying out the causes of this war, to ensure that our subsequent account of it will be clear to our readers. Since Sitalces had signed a treaty of friendship with the Athenians, he agreed to act as their ally during their war in Thrace; and since he himself was eager to use Athenian support to reduce the Chalcidians, he made ready a very considerable army. [4] Further, being at the same time on bad terms with Perdiccas [II], king of Macedon, he decided to restore [his brother] Philip's son Amyntas to the Macedonian throne. He thus had these two good reasons that made it essential for him to muster a serious force. When all his preparations for the campaign had been satisfactorily concluded, he marched through Thrace at the head of his entire army and invaded Macedonia. [5] The Macedonians, alarmed at the vast size of his host, dared not face him in a pitched battle; instead, they transported both their grain and such property as they could

---

79. Thuc. 2.95–101, including an ethnic digression on the Thracians. In 430 the Spartans had tried, unsuccessfully, to lure Sitalces into abandoning his Athenian alliance and sending an army to help Potidaea. 51.2: His nephew and successor Seuthes married Perdiccas' sister (Thuc. 2.101.6). He himself was killed in 424 during a campaign against the Triballi, a rival Thracian people.

manage into the strongest fortresses at their disposal, where they sat tight and waited on events. [6] After putting Amyntas on the throne, the Thracians at first tried to win over the various cities by means of discussions and embassies; but as everyone ignored them, they promptly launched an assault on the nearest fortress and took it by storm. [7] After this some of the cities and fortresses voluntarily submitted to them out of fear. So after ravaging all Macedonia and laying hands on a great deal of booty, the Thracians turned their attention to the Greek cities of Chalcidice.

51. While Sitalces was occupied with these matters, the Thessalians, Achaeans, Magnesians, and all other Greeks domiciled between Macedonia and Thermopylae had joint discussions, and between them mustered a very considerable army, since they were nervous that the Thracians, with their huge forces, might invade their territory and set their native cities at risk. [2] Since the Chalcidians had done the same thing, Sitalces, aware now not only that the Greeks had raised powerful armies but that his own troops were suffering from wintry conditions, came to terms with Perdiccas, arranged a marriage between the two houses, and then withdrew his forces to Thrace.

52. At the same time as these events [May 428], the Lacedaemonians, together with their Peloponnesian allies, and under the command of King Archidamus, invaded Attica [Thuc. 3.1], destroying the grain crop while it was still green and ravaging the countryside. They then returned to their various homelands. Since the Athenians dared not meet them in the field, and were hard pressed by the plague [<45.4] and a shortage of grain, they had no great hopes for the future.
Such, then, were the events that took place during this year.

53. When Eucles was archon in Athens [427/6], the Romans elected in lieu of consuls [Varr. 434] three military tribunes: Marcus Man<l>ius [Capitolinus], Quintus Sulpicius [Camerinus] Praetextatus, and Servius Cornelius Cossus. During their term, in Sicily, the Leontines, who were colonists from Chalcis and also kin to the Athenians, came under attack from the Syracusans. Being hard-pressed in this war, and in danger of capture on account of the Syracusans' greater strength, they sent ambassadors to Athens, asking the *demos* for immediate relief and the rescue of their city from the danger to which it was presently exposed.[80] [2] The ambassadorial leader of these

---

80. They cited as reasons for Athens to support them not only their Ionian kinship but also an earlier alliance (Thuc. 3.86.3). Fragments of treaties made (or perhaps renewed)

delegates was Gorgias the rhetorician, who in skill at public speaking far surpassed all his contemporaries. He was the first man to formulate technical
rules for rhetoric, and so far outstripped all his rivals in sophistic expertise
that the fee he received [for the course] from his students was one hundred
minas. [3] So when he reached Athens and was presented before the *demos,* he
delivered a discourse to the Athenians on the subject of the alliance, and by
his innovative style of speech amazed the Athenians, a people both naturally
clever and in love with words. [4] He was the first to employ those overdone
if technically extraordinary figures of speech—constructing sentences with
antitheses, equal parts, balanced clauses, matched endings, and the like—a
practice much esteemed at the time for its exotic novelty but now regarded as
excessive and indeed, when employed too often or to surfeit, as deserving of
ridicule.[81] [5] Thus, in the end he talked the Athenians into an alliance with
the Leontines; and after collecting much praise in Athens for his rhetorical
skill, he made his way back to Leontini.

54. For a long time now the Athenians had been covetous of Sicily on account of its agricultural richness: this was why they now welcomed Gorgias'
proposal and voted to send an allied force to the relief of the Leontines,
advancing as an excuse this urgent appeal from their kinsmen, but in truth
hot to get possession of the island. [2] Indeed, not many years before, when
Corinth and Corcyra were at war, and both badly wanted the Athenians as
their allies, the *demos* chose to side with the Corcyraeans [<33.1–2], because
Corcyra was strategically sited on the sea route to Sicily [<5.2, n. 12]. [3] In
general, by attaining to supremacy at sea, and other great achievements, they
now enjoyed the support of numerous allies and had acquired powerful military resources of their own. They had also, by transferring the common fund
of the Hellenes from Delos [to Athens], taken over a massive sum in ready
cash, totaling more than 10,000 talents; and they had at their disposal great

---

between Athens and both Rhegium and Leontini in 433/2 survive: Fornara, nos. 124–125.
The Athenians agreed, Thucydides argues, (a) because they were already contemplating
the conquest of Sicily and (b) to cut off the Peloponnese from imported Sicilian grain.
Diodorus' mention of "agricultural richness" (i.e., grain and timber) as a motive goes to
the heart of the matter. Gorgias (see n. 81) had no real need of superior rhetoric to win
his case.

81. Gorgias of Leontini (? 485–c. 380), a student of Empedocles, was the foremost
sophist of his time, best known for his antithetical stylistic tricks of rhetoric. These made
a great initial impression but were soon being parodied, e.g., by Plato in the *Symposium*
(194E-197E). 100 *minas* = 10,000 drachmas. The average daily wage of an Athenian seldom
exceeded 2 drachmas.

commanders, whose generalship had been well tested in action. For all these reasons, they were confident that they would subjugate the Lacedaemonians. But when they had thus attained supremacy over the whole of Greece, they also looked forward to getting their hands on Sicily.

[4] It was for these reasons, then, that they voted to send aid to the Leontines. They dispatched twenty ships to Sicily under Laches and Charoeades: these sailed to Rhegium, where they took on twenty more vessels from the Rhegians and the rest of the Chalcidian colonists. From here they conducted various sorties. First, they overran the Lipari Islands, because the Liparareans were allied with Syracuse. Next, they sailed to [Epizephyrian] Locri and captured five Locrian vessels. After this they laid siege to the stronghold of Mylae. [5] When the Sicilian Greeks in the area came to the relief of the Mylaeans, a battle took place, which the Athenians won, killing more than a thousand and capturing not less than six hundred. Immediately after this, they stormed and occupied the stronghold.

[6] During the course of these events [winter 426/5: Thuc. 3.115.1–4] there sailed in forty [more] ships, sent out by the [Athenian] *demos* in furtherance of their determination to prosecute this war more vigorously. They were under the command of Eurymedon and Sophocles.[82] When all these triremes were assembled in one place, they added up to a very considerable fleet, eighty vessels strong. [7] With hostilities now dragging on indefinitely, however, the Leontines made diplomatic overtures to the Syracusans and reached an agreement with them [at Gela, in 424]. The Athenian triremes accordingly sailed back home. The Syracusans now granted the Leontines citizen rights en bloc and designated their city as a Syracusan stronghold.

Such were the events going on in Sicily at this time.

55. In Hellas, the Lesbians seceded from Athens:[83] their complaint being that, when they wanted to unite all the cities in the island as part of Mytilene, the Athenians vetoed the proposal. [2] They now sent ambassadors to the Lacedaemonians and entered on an alliance with them; this done, they counseled the Spartans to aim for supremacy at sea, and in furtherance of this objective, they promised to supply them with numerous triremes for the war. [3] The Lacedaemonians accepted their offer with pleasure; but while they

---

82. Not the playwright. This Sophocles (son of Sostratides), on his return to Athens in 424, was fined and exiled on a charge of taking bribes not to conquer the whole of Sicily: Thuc. 4.65.3–4.

83. Again, Diodorus dates this episode a year later than Thucydides (3.2.1), who places it in May 428.

were still occupied with the readying of the triremes, the Athenians forestalled this move by promptly manning and dispatching a force of forty triremes against Lesbos, under the command of Cleïppides. After picking up reinforcements from the allies, he sailed straight for Mytilene. [4] In the naval engagement that followed, the Mytilenaians were beaten, driven within their city, and laid under siege. The Lacedaemonians had voted support for Mytilene, and were readying a considerable fleet, but the Athenians [once again] stole a march on them by sending to Lesbos not only more ships but a thousand infantrymen. [5] Their commander, Paches son of Epic<u>rus,[84] on reaching Mytilene took over the force already there, invested the city with a ring wall, and proceeded to make nonstop assaults on it, by sea as well as land.

[6] The Lacedaemonians dispatched to Mytilene a force of forty-five triremes, with Alcidas in command. They also, together with their allies, invaded Attica, seeking out and ravaging those areas that they had previously bypassed, and then returning home. [7] The Mytilenaeans, who were hard-pressed by a shortage of food as well as the war, and in addition were divided among themselves, now agreed to surrender, and handed over the city to the besiegers [summer 427].

[8] In Athens the *demos* debated what action to take regarding Mytilene. Cleon, the populist leader [>63.4], a man of savage and violent character [Thuc. 3.36.6], whipped up public opinion, declaring that they should execute all adult males and sell the women and children into slavery [Thuc. 3.37–40]. [9] Finally, the Athenians were persuaded to vote in favor of Cleon's proposal, and [messengers] were dispatched to Mytilene to inform the general of what the *demos* had decided. [10] Just as Paches had finished reading the decree, a second one arrived, countermanding the first. Paches was delighted to learn of this change of heart on the part of the Athenians, and convening an assembly of the Mytilenaeans, he formally relieved them of the charges — and indeed of their most profound fears. The Athenians demolished the city walls of Mytilene and divided up the whole of Lesbos into colonists' land holdings [Thuc. 3.50.2], except for the territory of the Methymnaeans.

Such was the conclusion of the Lesbians' revolt against the Athenians.

56. At about the same time [late summer 427], the Lacedaemonians besieging Plataea [<47.2] walled the city all around and manned the wall with a large military guard. Though the siege was now of long duration, the Athenians had still sent the defenders no relief, so that they were both pinched

---

84. Corrected from Thuc. 3.18.3; Diodorus' MSS all call him Epiclerus, seemingly non-existent as a masculine name in Athens (perhaps because its literal meaning is "heiress"?).

for lack of food and had lost many of their citizens during the assaults. [2] In their dilemma they conferred together as to how they might be saved, and most of them were for sitting tight and doing nothing; but the rest, about two hundred in number, decided to break through the cordon by night and escape to Athens. [3] So they waited for a moonless night [winter 428/7] and then got the others to make a [diversionary] assault on the far side of the wall. Meanwhile, they ran out their scaling ladders, and when the enemy hurried round to defend the fortifications opposite, they used these ladders to get up on the wall, killed the [remaining] guards, and got away to Athens [Thuc. 3.22–24]. [4] The next day, the Lacedaemonians, infuriated by the escape of the men who had broken out of the city, launched an all-out assault on Plataea, making every effort to force the besieged into surrender. The Plataeans, their spirits crushed, sent representatives to parley[85] and surrendered themselves and their city to the enemy. [5] The Lacedaemonian commanders interrogated each Plataean individually, asking what good he had [ever] done the Lacedaemonians. When each one conceded that he had never done them any good, he was then asked if he had ever done anything to harm the Spartans; and since none of them could deny that, they condemned them all to death. [6] So they did away with the survivors, every man of them, demolished their city, and rented out their land.[86] Thus the Plataeans, who had stuck with their Athenian alliance through thick and thin, succumbed unjustly to the most appalling fate [Thuc. 3.52–68].

57. At the same time as these events, on Corcyra rancorous civil dissension and rivalry broke out, for the following reasons. During the war over Epidamnus, numerous Corcyraeans had been taken prisoner and thrown into the public jail; set them free, they now promised the Corinthians, and they would guarantee to make them a present of Corcyra. [2] The Corinthians jumped at the opportunity. The Corcyraeans then made a pretense of getting themselves ransomed and were bailed out by their *proxenoi*[87] for very substantial sums. [3] They were, however, faithful to the bargain they had struck: no sooner were they back in their homeland than they picked up all the best-known popular leaders and champions of the masses and murdered them. They then

---

85. In fact they held out, with increasing difficulty, until the summer of 427: Thuc. 3.52.1.

86. To the Thebans, for ten years: Thuc. 3.68.3–4.

87. The *proxenos* was something like a consular representative, except that he was a native of the host city rather than that of the foreign occupant: e.g., Nicias was the resident Athenian *proxenos* of Syracuse, 13.27.3.

abolished the democracy. Soon after this, however, the Athenians came to the rescue of the common people, and the Corcyraeans, their freedom recovered, were determined to punish those responsible for the revolutionary *coup*. [Knowing and] fearing the penalty, the latter sought sanctuary at the altars of the gods and made themselves suppliants of both gods and *demos*. [4] The Corcyraeans, because of their pious reverence for the gods, revoked the normal penalty in their case and instead deported them from the city. They promptly, however, embarked on a second revolution, fortified a strong position [elsewhere] on the island, and [from this base] continued to annoy the Corcyraeans.[88]

Such, then, were the events that took place during this year.

58. When Euthynes was archon in Athens [426/5], the Romans elected in lieu of consuls [Varr. 433] three military tribunes: Marcus Fabius [Vibulanus], Marcus F<ol>ius [Flaccinator], and Lucius Ser<g>ius [Fidenas]. During their term, the Athenians, having had some respite from the plague [<45.4], were once more[89] afflicted with the same misfortune. [2] Indeed, they were so badly ravaged by the disease that of their troops they lost over 4,000 infantry and four hundred cavalry; and of the rest, both free and slave, over 10,000. Now since history is anxious to find a cause for the malign effect of this disease, we needs must set the whole matter forth.

[3] Heavy downpours earlier that past winter had left the ground waterlogged; many low-lying areas had absorbed such a mass of rain that they formed swampy pools and held stagnant water much in the way that marshland does. When these pools warmed up during the summer, they turned noxious, giving off thick, foul-smelling vapors that rose up in fumes, infecting all the air around—just the same process as can be seen taking place in swamps or marshes, which have a naturally pestilential atmosphere. [4] Another factor contributing to the disease was the rottenness of the food coming in: harvests that year were sodden, and their natural quality spoiled. A third

---

88. This episode is condensed from the account by Thucydides (3.69–85), with its famous disquisition (82–83) on the nature of revolution. Diodorus' tribute to the piety of the Corcyraeans is misplaced: far from merely deporting the suppliants, they lured them out of sanctuary to stand trial and then executed them (Thuc. 3.81.2–3).

89. During the winter of 427/6, according to Thuc. 3.87.1, who once more is a year behind Diodorus. Diodorus also reserves until the second outbreak his own general discussion of the plague, though this, with its summer dating, is clearly related to the first outbreak rather than the second. Thucydides' own lengthy discussion (2.47–54), on the other hand, not only deals with the original appearance of the plague but accompanies its description.

cause of the disease turned out to be the failure of the Etesian winds to blow, since they normally cool off the worst of the summer heat. So when the heat intensified and the air grew furnacelike, people's bodies, with nothing to cool them, fell sick; [5] and all seasonal diseases were now feverish on account of the soaring temperature. It was for this reason that most of the sick threw themselves into cisterns and springs, in a desperate desire to cool their bodies. [6] Because of the severity of this disease, however, the Athenians ascribed the causes of their misfortune to divine [displeasure]. Because of this—and in accordance with the terms of a certain oracle–they purified the island of Delos, which was sacred to Apollo and was held to have been polluted by burials of the dead. [7] They therefore dug up every grave on Delos and transferred their contents to the nearby island of Rheneia; they further passed a law that neither birth nor burial should take place on Delos and reinstituted the Festival of the Delians, which had been held in the distant past but long since discontinued.[90]

59. While the Athenians were thus occupied, the Lacedaemonians, accompanied by the [other] Peloponnesians, encamped at the Isthmus, intending to conduct yet another invasion of Attica; but several severe earth tremors occurred, at which they were seized with superstitious panic and went back home. [2] In many parts of Greece the shocks were so strong that the sea flooded and destroyed some coastal cities, while in Locris it actually broke through the neck of a peninsula to create the island known today as Atalanta.[91]

[3] Contemporary with these events [summer 426: Thuc. 3.89.1, 92.1] was the colonization of Trachis by the Lacedaemonians, who renamed it Heracleia for the following reasons. [4] The Trachinians had been at war with the Oetaeans, whose territory bordered on theirs, for many years now, and [in this conflict] had lost the majority of their citizens. Since the city had become [largely] deserted, they thought fit to petition the Lacedaemonians, who were colonists from there, with a proposal that they should assume responsibility

---

90. Since Thucydides is describing symptoms, while Diodorus is looking for causes, their accounts are very different: the only items which they have in common are the purification of Delos (Thuc. 3.104) and the sick throwing themselves into cisterns (Thuc. 2.49.5), and even here Diodorus' antecedent causes differ from his predecessor's. His climatic and dietetic explanations are in the regular Hippocratic tradition.

91. Thuc. 3.87.4, 89.2, where the description makes it clear that what happened was a classic tsunami: "and it destroyed all those who could not run up to high ground ahead of it." Atalanta (89.3) is treated both here and previously (44.1) by Diodorus, as an island already; but its creation, now or earlier, in the manner described by Diodorus is very probable.

for it. The Lacedaemonians—not only on account of their kinship but also because their ancestor Heracles had in ancient times dwelt in Trachis[92]—decided to make it a major city. [5] So they and the rest of the Peloponnesians sent out four thousand settlers and welcomed any other Greeks who wished to have a share in the colony: of these volunteers there were not less than 6,000. Thus they provided Trachis with a population 10,000 strong; and after dividing the territory into holdings, they named the city Heracleia.

60. When Stratocles was archon in Athens [425/4], at Rome there were elected [Varr. 432] in lieu of consuls three military tribunes: Lucius Furius [Medullinus], Spurius <Postumius Albus>, <L.> Pinarius <Mamercinus>, {and Gaius Metellus}. During their term [summer 426: Thuc. 3.91.1], the Athenians elected Demosthenes[93] general and sent him on campaign with thirty ships and a sufficient body of troops. After reinforcing these with fifteen triremes from Corcyra, plus troops supplied by the Cephallenians, the Acarnanians, and the Messenians in Naupactus, he sailed to Leucas and laid waste the islanders' territory. He then moved across to Aetolia and raided many villages there. The Aetolians, however, gathered their forces against him, and a battle took place in which the Athenians were defeated. They thereupon withdrew to Naupactus. [2] The Aetolians were elated by their victory. Reinforced by three thousand Lacedaemonian soldiers, they set out to attack Naupactus, inhabited at that time by Messenians, but were beaten off. [3] After this they marched against a town called Molycria and took it. The Athenian general Demosthenes, however, worried that the Aetolians might also reduce Naupactus, detailed a thousand hoplites from Acarnania to go to that city's defense. [4] While he was still in Acarnania himself, he ran across an encampment of a thousand Ambraciots, brought them to battle, and virtually annihilated them. At this the men of Ambracia made a massed sortie against him, and once more Demosthenes slaughtered them almost to the last man, leaving their city all but deserted. [5] Demosthenes now decided that he should storm Ambracia, figuring that because of its lack of defenders, he would have no trouble in taking it. At this point the Acarnanians—scared that if the Athenians got control of the city, they would become tougher

---

92. Not to mention the less high-minded fact (Thuc. 3.92.4) that it was exceptionally well situated strategically for pursuing the war against Athens, by both land and sea.

93. Son of Alcisthenes (and no relation to the 4th-century orator), Demosthenes (c. 455–413) was a shrewd tactician, though given to overelaborate strategies, e.g., at Delium (69–70). Given prominence by his capture of Spartan hoplites at Sphacteria (63.3–4), he was captured and executed in Sicily by the Syracusans (13.19.2, 33.1).

neighbors than the Ambraciots—refused to follow him. [6] As a result of this disagreement, the Acarnanians broke off hostilities with the Ambraciots and concluded a hundred years' peace with them. Demosthenes, thus left high and dry by the Acarnanians, took his twenty ships and sailed back to Athens. After this great disaster that they had experienced, and out of fear of Athens, the Ambraciots requested a garrison from the Lacedaemonians.

61. Demosthenes then made an expedition to Pylos [Thuc. 4.2.4–23.2, 26.1–40.2], his objective being to fortify it as a bridgehead into the Peloponnese, for it occupies an outstandingly strong position in Messenia, four hundred *stadioi* [about forty-four miles] from Sparta. Since on this occasion he had many ships and a fair number of troops, he built a perimeter wall round Pylos in twenty days. When the Lacedaemonians heard about the fortification of Pylos, they mustered a large force, not just of infantry but of ships too. [2] Thus, when they sailed for Pylos it was with forty-five excellently equipped triremes and 12,000 troops; for they held it a disgrace that those who dared not come out to fight for Attica when its territory was being laid waste should thus fortify and occupy a stronghold in the Peloponnese. [3] So this force, commanded by Thrasymedes, pitched camp in the vicinity of Pylos, and the troops were ready and eager to storm the wall, whatever the dangers involved. The Lacedaemonians therefore moored their ships with prows facing the harbor mouth, so that they could use them to block any attempt by the enemy to force a passage in. Then, by hurling their infantry in relays at the wall, and displaying the most extraordinary competitive zeal, they brought to the engagement a rare and extraordinary fighting spirit.

[4] There is an island called Sphacteria, which stretches lengthwise across the face of the harbor and ensures calm waters inside it. Here [the Lacedaemonians] proceeded to station the best of their own and their allied troops, their motive being a desire to anticipate the Athenians in establishing control over the island, since its position was ideal for enforcing a siege. [5] Though they were engaged daily in assaults on the fortifications, and kept suffering serious wounds because of the considerable height of the wall, this did not in any way abate their fury. In consequence, since they were trying to force a heavily strengthened position, numbers of them were killed and not a few seriously wounded. [6] The Athenians, who had found a naturally strong site and occupied it well in advance and had, besides, missiles in plenty and an abundance of all essentials, kept up a vigorous defense. Their hope was, if they brought off their plan, to carry the entire war into the Peloponnese, and little by little lay waste the enemy's territory.

62. During this siege, both sides displayed unsurpassable zeal, notably the Spartans in their attacks on the walls; and while many other individuals won admiration for their brave actions, it was Brasidas [Thuc. 4.11.3–12.1][94] who achieved the highest renown. [2] The trireme captains had shrunk from running their vessels aground because of the rocky shoreline; but he, as a trireme captain himself, shouted a command to his steersman not to spare the hull but to drive her onshore at full speed. It would (he exclaimed) be a shameful business for Spartans to be prodigal of their lives in pursuit of victory yet to spare their ships' hulls and tolerate the sight of Athenians in possession of Laconian territory. [3] Finally, he forced the steersman to run their trireme aground, and as it struck, Brasidas sprang on to the ship's forward gangplank, and from there fought back the mass of Athenians who converged on him. To begin with, he slew many of these oncomers, but after a while the rain of missiles hurled at him left him with numerous wounds on the front of his body. [4] Finally, these wounds caused him to lose so much blood that he fainted: his arm dropped forward over the ship's side, so that his shield slipped off and fell into the sea, where it came into the possession of the enemy. [5] Thus the man who had piled up so many enemy dead was himself borne off his ship half-dead by his own men, after so far exceeding all others in valor that, whereas other men who cast away their shields suffer the death penalty, he for that very reason won high renown.

[6] Though the Lacedaemonians had suffered heavy losses in their endless assaults on Pylos, they held on grimly through the worst of the fighting. Indeed, one well might wonder at the paradoxical nature of Fortune and the peculiar way in which she disposed matters at Pylos, [7] seeing that Athenians, fighting from a Laconian base, were gaining the mastery over Spartans, while Lacedaemonians, forced to treat their own soil as hostile, were attacking their enemies from the sea. Champion land fighters were now in control at sea, while those who ruled the waves were standing off the enemy from a position ashore [Thuc. 4.12.3; Lévy 2001].

63. So the siege wore on, and after their victory at sea, the Athenians cut off deliveries of food to the region. Because of this, the troops stranded on the island were in danger of perishing from starvation. [2] The Lacedaemonians, concerned for their safety, sent envoys to Athens to discuss ending the war.

---

94. The Spartan general (43.2–3) who, by capturing Amphipolis before Thucydides could stop him (Thuc. 4.104.4–106.4), was responsible for the historian's exile (and got from his self-exculpatory victim a dazzling write-up for unmatchable speed and brilliance).

When they failed to reach an agreement, they asked for an exchange of prisoners, by which the Athenians would get back an equal number of their own troops now held captive; but not even to this would the Athenians agree. At this point in Athens the ambassadors observed, bluntly, that by refusing to sanction an exchange of prisoners, the Athenians were admitting that Lacedaemonians were better men than themselves.

[3] Meanwhile, the Athenians at Sphacteria, after reducing the men on the island to breaking point through lack of essential supplies, accepted their unconditional surrender. Of the troops thus giving themselves up, one hundred and twenty were Spartan [citizens], while one hundred and eighty were from their allies. [4] So these [captives] were taken back to Athens in chains by Cleon the populist leader, since at that time he had the office of general; and the *demos* voted to keep them in detention, should the Lacedaemonians agree to end the war; but to kill every last captive should they determine to continue it.[95] [5] After this they sent for the best troops from among the Messenians now settled in Naupactus, reinforced them with sufficient additions from their other allies, and made this force responsible for the garrisoning of Pylos, figuring that the Messenians—on account of the hatred they bore the Spartans—would, once they had a strong base from which to operate, show especial zeal in raiding and harrying Laconian territory.

Such were the events concerning Pylos during this period.

64. Artaxerxes [<11.69] the Great King of Persia died [? June 424] after ruling for forty years and was succeeded by Xerxes [>71.1 and n. 107], who reigned for one year [in fact less than two months].

In Italy, during the war that followed the revolt of the Aequi [? Varr. 432], the Romans, appointing Aulus Postumius [Tubertus] Dictator and Lucius Julius [Iullus] Master of Horse, [2] took a large and powerful force into the rebels' territory [Liv. 4.26–29]. They began by plundering their property; but later, when the Aequi came out against them, a battle was fought, which the Romans won, killing large numbers of the enemy, taking not a few prisoners, and getting their hands on large quantities of booty. [3] After the battle, the rebels, shattered by their defeat, made submission to the Romans. Postumius,

---

95. Diodorus omits two crucial points mentioned by Thuc. 4.30.2–4, 32–36: (i) a suggestively opportune fire removed much of the Spartans' camouflage; (ii) this facilitated a well-planned attack on the island, which, at least as much as starvation, was ultimately responsible for the surrender. Cleon had assured the Athenian *demos* that he would bring the force on the island back as prisoners in twenty days, and he did (Thuc. 4.39.3). The whole siege lasted just over ten weeks.

who was held to have conducted his campaign with distinction, celebrated the customary triumph. He is also said to have taken one quite incredible personal action: during the battle, his son, out of overeagerness, sprang forward from the station his father had assigned him, whereupon Postumius, in observance of the ancestral code, executed the boy as a rank breaker.[96]

65. When this year had run its course, in Athens the archon was Isarchus [424/3], while in Rome there were elected [Varr. 431] as consuls Titus Quinctius and Gaius Julius, and at Elis the 89th Olympiad was held, in which Symmachus [of Messene] won the *stadion* for the second time [<49.1]. During their term, the Athenians elected Nicias son of Niceratus general, supplied him with sixty triremes and 3,000 hoplites, and sent him out with a commission to raid the allies of the Lacedaemonians.[97] [2] His first target was Melos. After sailing there he laid waste the island's territory and besieged its city for a number of days, since Melos, alone among the Cyclades, was, as a Spartan colony, keeping up an alliance with the Lacedaemonians. [3] Owing to a gallant defense by the Melians, however, Nicias proved unable to take the city, and so sailed away to Oropus in Boeotia. Leaving his ships there, he and his hoplites made their way into Tanagran territory, where he met another Athenian unit, led by Hipponicus son of Callias. [4] The two contingents now united to form a single force, with which the generals advanced, laying waste the territory as they went. When the Thebans sallied out to the rescue, the Athenians brought them to battle and defeated them with heavy losses.

[5] After the battle, Hipponicus and his troops made their way back to Athens, but Nicias returned to his ships and sailed along inshore to Locris, where he laid waste the coastal territory and also received from the allies an additional forty triremes, so that in all he now had one hundred vessels. He also enlisted a substantial body of infantry, and having thus assembled an impressive armament, sailed against Corinth. [6] When he disembarked his troops, the Corinthians mustered their forces against him. The Athenians defeated them in two battles, killed large numbers of them, and set up a trophy. There perished in these engagements †about eight†[98] Athenians and

---

96. Cf. Livy (4.29.5–6), who rejects the story as spurious.

97. Thucydides (3.91.1–6) dates Nicias' activities, from Melos to Locris, in the summer of 426, and the expedition against Corinth, Crommyon, and Methana a year later (4.42–45). Diodorus, still chronologically ahead of Thucydides, not only dates them both in 424/3 but runs the two campaigns together into a single sequence.

98. Thucydides (4.44.6) puts the number, more plausibly, at "slightly under fifty." Vogel suspected a lacuna here: "forty-eight" would agree nicely with Thucydides.

over three hundred Corinthians. [7] Nicias then sailed to Crommyon, laid waste its territory, and captured its stronghold, immediately after which he struck camp and moved on to <Methana>, where he built a stronghold of his own. He left a garrison there for the double purpose of guarding the area and raiding the nearby countryside; he himself ravaged the coastal strip[99] and then returned to Athens.

[8] After this[100] [the Athenians] dispatched sixty ships and two thousand hoplites to Cythera, under the command of Nicias and certain other generals. He took this force to the island, launched assaults on the city, and received its surrender by agreement. He then left a garrison on the island and sailed along the coast of the Peloponnese, laying waste the adjacent countryside as he went. [9] He then stormed and captured Thyreae, which lies in border country between Laconia and the Argolid, enslaving its population and demolishing the city. There were Aeginetans living there, and these, along with Tantalos, the Spartan garrison commander, he took prisoner and removed to Athens. The Athenians fettered Tantalos and kept him in detention, together with the other captives and the Aeginetans [Thuc. 4.53–57].

66. At the same time as these events were taking place, the Megarians found themselves hard pressed through being at war not only with the Athenians but also with their own exiles. While parleys were going on between the two sides over the latter, certain citizens opposed to the exiles got in touch with the Athenian generals and offered to betray the city to them. [2] The generals, Hippocrates and Demosthenes, accepted this offer of betrayal and dispatched six hundred soldiers to the city at night. The conspirators let these Athenians in through the fortifications. When their treachery became known throughout the city, the public was divided according to individual allegiance, some wanting to side with the Athenians, others to help the Lacedaemonians. At this point, a certain man [the Athenian herald: Thuc. 4.68.3], acting on his own initiative, proclaimed that any who so desired could take up arms along with the Athenians and the Megarians. [3] As a result, since [it seemed as

---

99. Thucydides (4.95.2) identifies this Methana as the peninsula between Epidaurus and Troezen and describes Nicias' business there as walling off the peninsula's neck. Diodorus' description, with the ravaging of the coastal strip (*parathalattion*), sounds more appropriate for the Methana situated on the east coast of the Peloponnese, at the southern end of the Thyreatic plain (11.84.6), a far likelier target (and cf. §9). The situation is confused further by the necessary correction in the MSS of both authors, of "Methone"— situated far away in southwest Messenia—to "Methana."

100. In the summer of 424 (Thuc. 4.53.1): Diodorus and Thucydides are now chronologically in alignment.

though] the Lacedaemonians were about to be deserted by the Megarians, it happened that those guarding the long walls left their post and sought refuge in Nisaea, the Megarians' seaport. [4] The Athenians then dug a ditch around Nisaea and besieged it, after which they fetched skilled workers from Athens and added a ring wall. At this the Peloponnesians, terrified that they might be taken by force and put to death, agreed to surrender Nisaea to the Athenians [Thuc. 4.66–72].

Such at this juncture were the affairs of the Megarians.

67. Brasidas, after levying a reasonable force from Lacedaemon and the other Peloponnesian [states], marched on Megara. He gave the Athenians a bad scare and drove them out of Nisaea;[101] after which he liberated Megara and restored it to the Lacedaemonian alliance [Thuc. 4.70–73]. He and his army then made the long march through Thessaly and reached Dium in Macedonia. [2] From there he went on to Acanthus and made a fighting alliance with the cities of Chalcidice [late summer 424]. This city of the Acanthians was the first that he induced—by a blend of terror and amiable persuasion—to revolt from the Athenians; in the days that followed, he persuaded many more in the Thraceward regions to join the Lacedaemonian alliance [Thuc. 4.84–88]. [3] After this, Brasidas, wanting to prosecute the war more actively, called for reinforcements from Lacedaemon in his determination to put together a worthwhile army. Now the Spartans had this plan to do away with the most outstanding of the helots; so in furtherance of it they sent him a thousand who seemed especially self-opinionated, in the belief that most of them would be killed in battle. [4] They also committed another act, as violent as it was savage, by means of which they figured they would abase helot pride. They had it proclaimed that any helot who had achieved some good for Sparta should submit his claim in writing and that those who passed their scrutiny they would set free. Two thousand so applied, and they then ordered their most powerful [citizens] to murder them, each in his own home. [5] This they did through a gnawing fear that [such helots] might seize an opportunity to join the enemy and expose Sparta to mortal peril.[102] Even so, with this addition of a thousand helots to his command, as well as troops

101. According to Thucydides (4.73.4, 74.2), there was no engagement but rather a standoff, and the Athenians, having first withdrawn to Nisaea, then proceeded (rather surprisingly) to pull out altogether, of their own volition.

102. Thucydides (4.80.2–5) gives the number of helots posted to Brasidas' army as seven hundred and claims, plausibly, that Spartan fear of a helot revolt had been exacerbated by the Athenians' creation of their Messenian bridgehead at Pylos.

requisitioned from the allies, Brasidas had now got a serious fighting force together.

68. So it was now with confident trust in the bulk of his troops that Brasidas advanced [424/3] against the city of Amphipolis [Thuc. 4.102–114]. The [original] foundation of this city had been undertaken earlier by Aristagoras the Milesian, when he was on the run from Darius, the Great King of the Persians. [2] After Aristagoras' death, his settlers were dislodged by those Thracians known as the Edones; and thirty-two years later the Athenians sent out 10,000 colonists to the site. These were similarly annihilated by the Thracians at Drabescus; but after a <twenty-nine> year interval, [the Athenians] under Hagnon's leadership once more recovered the place.[103] [3] Since this city had often been fought over, Brasidas was eager to gain the mastery of it. He therefore marched against it with a considerable force and pitched camp by the [Strymon] bridge. He began by occupying the outer suburb; then next day, having thus thoroughly scared the Amphipolitans, he took over the city by an agreed surrender, anyone who so desired being free to take his property and depart.

[4] As one immediate result, he gained the allegiance of a majority of the cities in the area, of which the most notable were Oesyme and Galepsus, both colonies of the Thasians, and Myrcinus, a small town of the Edones. He also undertook the construction of a number of triremes on the Strymon River and called for more troops, from both Lacedaemon and the other allies. [5] Besides this, he had numerous suits of armor made, distributing these among the young men who possessed none, as well as laying in stores of missiles and grain and everything else. When all his preparations were made, he marched his army away from Amphipolis and pitched camp when he reached the district known as Acte. In this region there were five cities, of which some were Greek, colonized from Andros, while the others were occupied by a mob of bilingual *barbaroi*, Bisaltic in origin. [6] After getting control of these, he made an expedition against the city of Torone, a colony of the Chalcidians now held by Athens. As he found certain persons [willing to] betray the city,

---

103. This first site was established at Ennea Hodoi ("Nine Ways") in 498: Hdt. 5.126. Thucydides (4.102.2–3), like Diodorus, dates the foundation of the second colony thirty-two years after the first, i.e., in 466 (cf. schol. Aeschin. 2.31), and that of the third colony twenty-nine years after the second, i.e., in 437, a date confirmed by Diodorus (32.3) and Fornara 1983, no. 62. These dates are secure, and the reading of Diodorus' MSS here ("two" rather than "twenty-nine") is clearly wrong. Diodorus' note (11.70.5) dates the foundation of colony II in 464, but this must in fact be the date of its destruction.

he got himself [and his men] let in by night, and so won Torone without having to risk an engagement.

To such a degree, then, did Brasidas' affairs advance during the course of this year.

69. During the same period as these events [early winter 424], a pitched battle took place between the Athenians and the Boeotians at Delium in Boeotia [Thuc. 4.89–96]: it came about in the following manner. Some of the Boeotians, who were dissatisfied with their current form of government, and hot to establish democracies in their cities, held talks with the Athenian generals Hippocrates and Demosthenes concerning their own [political] agenda, and promised to turn the cities in Boeotia over to them [summer 424]. [2] This offer the Athenians accepted with alacrity [Thuc. 4.76–77]. With regard to the planning of the attack, the generals divided their forces. Demosthenes took the bulk of the army and launched an invasion into Boeotia; but on finding that the Boeotians had been alerted to the treachery [thus planned], he withdrew without accomplishing anything. Hippocrates meanwhile led the Athenians in full force against Delium, occupied the town (which is situated close to the Boeotian border, opposite the territory of Oropus), and fortified it before the Boeotians could get there. [3] Pagondas, the Boeotian commander, called up troops from every city in Boeotia and thus had a major field force with him when he reached Delium: not far short of 20,000 infantry and about 1,000 horse. [4] Though the Athenians outnumbered the Boeotians, they were not so well armed as their opponents, having set out from home suddenly and with little warning, indeed in such haste that they came ill prepared.

70. Both sides, nevertheless, moved into battle stations with high enthusiasm, and the opposing ranks were drawn up as follows. On the Boeotian side, the Thebans occupied the right wing, the men of Orchomenus the left, while the center was brigaded from the various other Boeotians [Thuc. 4.93.3–4]. Out in front of them all there was a line of fighters whom they called the "charioteers and footmen," a picked group of three hundred warriors.[104] The

---

104. The title suggests an ancient traditional corps (chariots in warfare had long been discontinued) of wealthy aristocrats: the "footman" (*parabates*) was the soldier who stood, and fought, beside the driver. It is often assumed that this was the famous Theban Sacred Band, consisting of 150 pairs of dedicated warrior-lovers, but this last, though it could have been based on the traditional grouping, seems to have been a much later creation. Cf. O'Sullivan, 383–385.

Athenians were forced to join battle while still marshaling their forces. [2] A violent conflict developed, in which to begin with the Athenian cavalry, fighting brilliantly, turned the horsemen opposing them to flight. Subsequently, however, when the infantry lines engaged, the Athenians facing the Thebans were overpowered and routed, even though the rest of them broke the other Boeotians, killed large numbers of them, and pursued them for a considerable distance. [3] But the Thebans, whose physical condition was superior, cut short their own pursuit, and falling on these Athenian pursuers, put them to flight. Having thus won a clear and manifest victory, they found themselves highly esteemed for valor. [4] Of the Athenians, some sought refuge in Oropus; others, in Delium; a number made for the sea and [the safety of] their own ships; while others again scattered haphazardly in this direction or that. By nightfall the tally of Boeotian dead was not more than five hundred, whereas the Athenians lost many times that number.[105] Indeed, had darkness not supervened, interrupting this headlong rout and thus preserving the fugitives, most of the Athenians would surely have perished. [5] Even so, the total number of those slain was so great that from the profits of the booty, the Thebans built the great colonnade (*stoa*) in their marketplace and decorated it with bronze statues; they also virtually "bronzed" their temples and other marketplace colonnades with the arms and armor from the spoils that they nailed up in them. It was, moreover, with these funds that that they instituted the Festival of the Delians.

[6] After this battle, the Boeotians assaulted Delium and took the town by storm.[106] Most of the garrison in Delium died fighting bravely, but two hundred were taken prisoner. The remainder fled to the ships and were ferried back to Attica together with the other [refugees]. Such was the disaster to which those Athenians who plotted against the Boeotians fell victim.

71. In Asia, King Xerxes died after a reign of one year or, as some record, two months [? Jul.–Aug. 424], and was succeeded on the throne by his brother Sogdianus, who reigned for seven months [> Feb. 423] and was murdered by Darius, who reigned for nineteen years [>13.108.1].[107]

---

105. Thucydides (4.101.2) puts Athenian hoplite losses at under a thousand (Hippocrates among them), "as well as a large number of light-armed troops and baggage-carriers."

106. Seventeen days later (Thuc. 4.101.1), with the aid of a flame thrower (4.100.2–4) that destroyed the city's wooden defense wall.

107. Babylonian tablets (Briant 2002, 588–589; Hornblower 1996, 207–209 with bibliography) let us date these events more closely: Darius (II) is first recorded as king in March 423. But there are problems. Ctesias (F15 §48 Lenfant) gives Xerxes (II) a 45-day reign, and Sogdianus or Secyndianus (F15 §50 Lenfant) 6 months and 15 days. These are

[2] Among writers, Antiochus of Syracuse terminated his history of Sicilian affairs in this year [i.e., with the Congress of Gela; Thuc. 4.58–65]. It took Cocalus, the king of the Sicani [cf. D.S. 4.78–79], as its starting point and was completed in nine books.[108]

72. When Ameinias was archon in Athens [423/2], the Romans elected [Varr. 430] as consuls Gaius Papirius [Crassus] and Lucius Ju<l>ius [Iullus]. During their term [Mar./Apr. 423: Thuc. 4.120.1], the occupants of Scione, scorning the Athenians because of their defeat at Delium, defected to the Lacedaemonians and delivered their city up to Brasidas, who was in command of Lacedaemonian forces in the Thraceward regions.

[2] On Lesbos, after the takeover of Mytilene by the Athenians [427: <55.6–10], numerous refugees had escaped into exile, and these for some while had been plotting a return to the island. They now banded together and seized Antandros, and from there carried on a running war with the Athenians in charge at Mytilene [spring 424: Thuc. 4.52.3–4]. [3] The Athenian *demos,* angered by this turn of events, sent an expedition against them under two generals, Aristeides and Symmachus. They sailed to Lesbos and from there, by means of repeated attacks, captured Antandros [summer 424: Thuc. 75.1–2]. Some of the exiles they killed, others they deported; then, leaving a garrison to guard the place, they sailed away again. [4] Later [fall 424] Lamachus the general sailed into the Black Sea with ten triremes and dropped anchor at Heracleia, on the Cales River. Here he lost all his ships, for torrential rains fell, and so violent a downstream current was produced that his craft were driven ashore in a rocky area and broke up.

[5] The Athenians negotiated [Mar. 423: Thuc. 4.117–119] a year-long truce with the Lacedaemonians, on the basis of each side keeping what they controlled at the time. After numerous discussions, they concluded that they should end the war and discontinue their rivalry: besides, the Lacedaemoni-

---

likelier than Diodorus' rounded figures and would fix Artaxerxes I's death in June 424. This would also fit with Thucydides (4.50), who records that (at some point fairly soon after the end of winter 425/4) envoys learn that Artaxerxes is dead, and return to Athens. But Babylonian records show Artaxerxes' reign terminating in his 41st regnal year, i.e., between Dec. 427 and Feb. 423. In other words, Sogdianus certainly, and Xerxes possibly, was not recognized in Babylon as a legitimate successor (the unlikely alternative is to treat their reigns, legitimate or not, as an elaborate Ctesianic fiction).

108. Antiochus of Syracuse (*fl.* mid 5th century) was one of the first Western Greek historians: he also wrote a one-book monograph *On Italy,* using the most plausible local traditions to reconstruct the origins of various South Italian cities, including Rhegium and Tarentum.

ans were anxious to recover the prisoners taken on Sphacteria. [6] When the truce had been solemnized on the terms outlined here, they were in agreement on all other matters, but each disputed the other's claim to Scione. So great a controversy flared up that they revoked the truce and, over the sole issue of Scione,[109] continued at war with one another.

[7] About this time the city of Mende likewise defected to the Lacedaemonians, an act that still further exacerbated the dissension over Scione. Brasidas therefore evacuated the women and children from Mende and Scione, along with their most indispensable property, and secured both cities with strong garrisons. [8] The Athenians, angered by these actions, voted to execute all adult male Scionians when they took the city, and sent out a fleet of fifty triremes against them, with Nicias and Nicostratus as commanders. [9] They sailed first to Mende and took it when certain men betrayed it to them. They then invested Scione with a ring wall, and set about besieging it, making continual assaults against [its defenses]. [10] But the garrison in Scione was a large one, with an ample stock of missiles and food and other necessities: they had no trouble in holding off the Athenians, and since they were fighting from higher ground, kept inflicting severe wounds on them.

Such, then, were the events that took place during the course of this year.

73. The following year, Alcaeus was archon in Athens [422/1], and in Rome [Varr. 429] the consuls were <Hostus> Lucretius [Tricipitinus] and Lucius Sergius Fiden<a>s. During their term, the Athenians accused the inhabitants of Delos [<58.6–7; Thuc. 3.107] of contracting a secret alliance with the Lacedaemonians, deported them from the island, and took over their city themselves. The Delians thus exiled were given the city of Adramyttium to live in by the satrap Pharnaces [Thuc. 5.1].

[2] The Athenians now elected Cleon the populist leader as general, provided him with a strong body of infantry, and sent him out to the Thraceward regions. He sailed first to Scione, where he requisitioned additional troops from among the city's besiegers, and then sailed away again and made landfall at Torone, in the knowledge that Brasidas had gone elsewhere and that the troops left in Torone were not fit for serious fighting. [3] He therefore pitched camp near Torone, besieged it both by land and by sea, and took it by storm

---

109. The issue at stake was whether Scione had revolted before (according to Brasidas) or after (Athens' version) the armistice came into force: Thucydides (4.122.1–6), who claims the defection came two days after. Even so, Athens could have called for arbitration. The vote for extirpation (*andrapodismós*: 72.8, 76.3) was moved by Cleon (Thuc. 4.122.6).

[Thuc. 5.2.3–3.6]. The women and children he sold into slavery, but those who had garrisoned the city he took prisoner and sent to Athens in chains. He then left a sufficient garrison of his own behind there, stood out to sea with his armament, and anchored on the Strymon River in Thrace. He then encamped near the city of Eïon, a little under four miles beyond Amphipolis, and made a series of assaults on the town.

74. When Cleon learned that Brasidas and his army had stationed themselves at Amphipolis, he struck camp and matched against him. Brasidas, on hearing of the enemy's approach, disposed his troops for battle and went out to meet the Athenians. A major pitched battle took place, in which both armies fought brilliantly. To begin with, the struggle was evenly balanced; but after a while, as the leaders on both sides strove to decide the issue by their own individual efforts, it was the fate of many fine warriors to be slain, while the generals themselves plunged into the forefront of the combat, bringing to it an unsurpassable rivalry in the struggle for victory. [2] Thus Brasidas, after putting up a superb fight in the course of which he slew numerous opponents, ended his life still fighting heroically; but when Cleon likewise fell in battle, both sides were thrown into confusion through lack of leadership. Finally, however, the Lacedaemonians prevailed and set up a trophy [Thuc. 5.7–10].[110] The Athenians recovered their dead under truce, buried them, and then sailed back to Athens. [3] Now when some survivors of the battle reached Lacedaemon, bringing at one and the same time the news both of Brasidas' victory and of his death, Brasidas' mother, on hearing the course of the battle described, asked how Brasidas had comported himself in the battle line. When they replied that of all the Lacedaemonians he had proved the best, the dead man's mother remarked that though her son Brasidas had courage, there were many others who excelled him.[111] [4] When this saying became known throughout the city, the ephors paid public tribute to the woman, because she had rated praise of country higher than her son's renown.

[5] After the above-mentioned battle, the Athenians voted [spring 421] to conclude a fifty-year peace treaty with the Lacedaemonians, the terms being

110. Thucydides' account of the battle is contemptuously critical of Cleon and makes it in effect a Lacedaemonian walkover. This view is generally accepted. But Thucydides had reasons of his own to denigrate the man who had been responsible for his exile, and it is possible that the battle of Amphipolis was indeed a more close-run business than tends to be assumed.

111. He was buried in Amphipolis, where he attracted a hero cult and replaced the Athenian Hagnon (68.1) as the official founder of the city (Thuc. 5.11.1). His mother's comment became famous: Plut. *Mor.* 190B, 219D; Ael. *VH* 2.19.

as follows: Prisoners of war on both sides were to be released, and each side should give back those cities captured during the course of hostilities [Thuc. 5.15–24]. Thus the Peloponnesian[112] War, after lasting for ten years up to the period under discussion, came to an end in the manner described.

75. When Aristion was archon in Athens [421/0], the Romans elected [Varr. 428] as consuls Titus Quinctius [Poenus Cincinnatus] and Aulus Cornelius Cossus. During their term, although the Peloponnesian War was barely over, further disturbances and military activities took place throughout Greece, for the following reasons. [2] Though the Athenians and Lacedaemonians had concluded and ratified their armistice together with their allies, they then proceeded, unbeknown to the other allied cities, to form an alliance [with one another].[113] By so doing they came to be suspected of having acted with a private objective, this being the enslavement of the other Greeks. [3] As a result, the most important cities engaged in a flurry of diplomatic discussions with one another, in pursuit of a common policy and general alliance against both Athens and Sparta. The four cities most committed to this course of action were also the most powerful, that is, Argos, Thebes, Corinth, and Elis. [4] [Athens and Sparta] could very plausibly be suspected of conspiring against [the rest of] Hellas, since a rider had been tacked on to the general treaty, to the effect that the Athenians and Lacedaemonians were entitled to add clauses to, or strike them from, the main text as seemed best to those [two] cities [Thuc. 5.18, clause 12 of the treaty]. Apart from this, the Athenians, by formal vote, had empowered a board of ten men to take counsel regarding "matters advantageous to the city"; and since the Lacedaemonians too had made a very similar arrangement, the ambitious greed of both states was now manifest.

[5] Numerous cities responded to the cry of "freedom for all"; and now that the Athenians were looked down on because of their disastrous showing at Delium [<69.1–70.6], while the Lacedaemonians had fallen in public esteem after their surrender on Sphacteria [<63.3–4], a large number got together and elected the city of Argos as their leader. [6] This city enjoys a high reputation on account of its achievements in ancient times: indeed, prior to

112. This initial phase of the war, up to the peace of 421 (known, from its chief Athenian negotiator, as the Peace of Nicias, Thuc. 5.16.1), is referred to by Athenian orators (and modern historians) as the Archidamian War, Archidamus (II) being the Spartan king (469–427) who led the early invasions of Attica (42.6, 52.1–2).

113. Thuc. 5.22–23. Sparta's allies Corinth, Megara, Boeotia, Elis, and the cities of Chalcidice all, having been largely ignored in the peace treaty, in fact refused to sign it; Corinth, Elis, Mantinea, and the Chalcidic cities joined a new league under Sparta's old rival Argos, and it was in alarm at this that Sparta and Athens set up their ad hoc alliance.

the Return of the Heraclidae, almost all the most outstanding kings had come from the Argolid.[114] Furthermore, since it had enjoyed a long and unbroken spell of peace, it was in receipt of rich revenues and could draw on vast reserves of both wealth and manpower. [7] The Argives, on the assumption that they were to be entrusted with overall leadership, selected one thousand of their younger citizens, the criteria being wealth and physical fitness. These men (whom they freed from all other obligatory service) were then maintained at public expense and put through a nonstop program of training and exercise. As a result of their subsidized support and rigorous training, the youths in question quickly became established as athletes—but athletes whose specialty was war [>80.2].

76. The Lacedaemonians, when they saw the Peloponnese thus uniting against them, and in the foreknowledge of just how serious a war could come about as a result, began to shore up their leadership by every means at their disposal. To begin with, they freed the one thousand helots who had campaigned with Brasidas in Thrace. Next, there were the Spartans who had been taken prisoner on Sphacteria and had lost their civic rights for having caused Sparta public humiliation: these had their civic rights restored to them [Thuc. 5.34.1–2]. [2] In furtherance of this policy, men were encouraged, by a system of official commendations and honors issued during the course of the war, to eclipse in the struggles that still lay ahead their own previous deeds of valor. Towards their allies [the Lacedaemonians] now behaved more equitably, conciliating even the most ill disposed of them with various kindnesses. [3] The Athenians, on the contrary, determined to terrorize all those they suspected of defection, put on display a public example in their punishment of the inhabitants of Scione: after forcing their surrender [summer 421], they executed all adult males, sold the women and children into slavery [but see 72.4], and turned over the island[115] to the Plataeans to live in, since the latter's expulsion from their native city [<42.1–2] had been on the Athenians' account.

[4] About the same time in Italy, the Campanians made an expedition against Cyme with a large army, defeated the Cymaeans in battle, and slaugh-

114. See D.S. 4.57–58. The exiled (Dorian) descendants of Heracles were traditionally believed to have returned to, and conquered, the Peloponnese at the end of the 12th century BCE, dividing Messenia, Argos, and Lacedaemon between them. The myth may reflect in part a genuine Dorian infiltration but certainly served as authorization for the various Dorian states in the historical period. The Atreid dynasty of Mycenae, including Agamemnon and Menelaus, came from the Argolid.

115. Scione (on the Pallene peninsula) is in fact linked to the mainland, like Methana in the Argolid or Monemvasia on the southeast coast of the Peloponnese.

tered most of the forces opposed to them. They then set about besieging the city, made a number of assaults against it, and finally took it by storm. They then looted it, sold the survivors into slavery, and designated a corresponding number of their own citizens to go there as settlers [Livy 4.44.12].

77. When Astyphilus was archon in Athens [420/19], the Romans elected as consuls Lucius Quinctius [Cincinnatus] and Aulus Sempronius [Atratinus],[116] and the Eleians held the 90th Olympiad, in which Hyperbius of Syracuse won the *stadion.* During their term,[117] the Athenians, in accordance with a certain oracle, restored Delos to its original inhabitants, and so the Delians who had been living in Adramyttium [<73.1] returned to their native land. [2] Since the Athenians had not returned Pylos to the Lacedaemonians, these two cities were once more in dispute and hostile towards each other. When the Argive *demos* became aware of this, they prevailed upon the Athenians to agree to a treaty of friendship with Argos [summer 420].[118] [3] As the disagreement intensified, the Lacedaemonians persuaded the Corinthians to abandon their common league [<75.2–3 and n. 113] and make an alliance with them. Such, then, was the situation in the Peloponnese that this lack of stability and absence of leadership had brought about.

[4] In the regions outside [the Peloponnese], the Aenianians, Dolopians, and Malians came to an agreement among themselves and took a strong expeditionary force against Heracleia in Trachis [winter 420/19: Thuc. 5.51]. The Heracleians came out to fight them, and a fierce battle took place, in which the inhabitants of Heracleia got the worst of it, suffering heavy casualties and retreating within their walls. They accordingly sent for help from the Boeotians. Thebes sent them one thousand picked hoplites, and with these they stood off their attackers.

[5] Simultaneously with these events,[119] the Olynthians marched against the city of Mecyberna, then garrisoned by the Athenians, expelled the garrison, and took over the city themselves.

---

116. Diodorus agrees with Liv. 4.30.4 for the consuls of Varr. 428 (matched to archon year 421/0) and Varr. 427 (below, 78.1; Liv. 4.30.12, matched to archon year 419/8). For archon year 420/19, however, he lists as consuls men who were in fact military tribunes three years later (81.1). From archon year 419/8 he is thus eight, rather than seven, years ahead of the Varronian system.

117. In the summer of 421, according to Thuc. 5.32.1: Diodorus is here once more running a year ahead.

118. For the diplomacy leading up to this treaty (in which Alcibiades played a leading part) and the terms of the treaty itself, see Thuc. 5.43.1–47.12.

119. In the winter of 421/0, according to Thuc. 5.39.1: see n. 116 above.

78. When Archias was archon in Athens [419/8], the Romans elected [Varr. 427] as consuls Lucius Papirius Mugil<l>anus and Gaius Servilius Structus [Ahala]. During their term [July 419], the Argives, on the excuse (as they charged) that the Lacedaemonians were not providing †Pythian† Apollo with his proper sacrifices, declared war on them,[120] at precisely the same time as the Athenian general Alcibiades entered Argive territory at the head of an army. [2] The Argives took over this force and marched on Troezen, a city allied to the Lacedaemonians, plundering the countryside and burning farms. They then returned home. The Lacedaemonians, outraged by these lawless acts committed against Troezen, decided to go to war with Argos. They therefore mustered an army and made King Agis its commander. [3] He took this force, marched against the Argives, and laid waste their territory. Then he brought his army into the area adjacent to the city and challenged the enemy to a battle. [4] The Argives, who had reinforced their numbers with 3,000 troops from Elis and not many less from Mantinea, now emerged from the city at the head of their combined forces. When a pitched battle was on the point of taking place, however, the generals from each side held a parley and agreed to a four months' truce [Thuc. 5.60.1–2]. [5] When the armies returned home with nothing accomplished, both cities were angry with their generals for concluding such a truce. The Argives, indeed, began to hurl stones at their commanders and made as though to kill them. It was only with great reluctance, and after much imploring, that their lives were finally spared; and even so, their houses were demolished and their property impounded. [6] The Lacedaemonians were moving to punish Agis, but when he promised to make amends for his error by worthy actions, they grudgingly excused him. For the future, however, they chose ten of their shrewdest men to act as his advisers and instructed him to do nothing without first consulting them.

79. After this the Athenians sent out to Argos, by sea, one thousand picked hoplites and two hundred cavalry, under the command of Laches and Nicostratus. Alcibiades accompanied them, though in a private capacity, because of his friendship with the Eleians and Mantineans. When they all met together in council, they agreed to let the truce go hang and concentrate all their energies on the war. [2] Each general therefore addressed his own men, urging them to welcome the conflict; and when all responded with enthusiasm, they set up camp outside the city. They agreed to march first of all against

120. Thuc. 5.53 has Argos declaring war not on the Lacedaemonians but (more plausibly) on Epidaurus. Most scholars are agreed that the actual shrine involved was that of Apollo Pythiaeus at Asine.

Orchomenus in Arcadia. So after arriving in Arcadia, they set about besieging Orchomenus and made daily assaults on its walls. [3] Having reduced Orchomenus, they moved on to the vicinity of Tegea, with the intention of besieging it as well. When the men of Tegea sent an urgent appeal for aid to the Lacedaemonians, the Spartans mustered all their own troops and their allies as well and made for Mantinea, figuring that once Mantinea came under attack, the siege of Tegea would be abandoned. [4] The Mantineans rounded up their allies and marched out in full strength to face the Lacedaemonians [Thuc. 5.66–73]. A fierce battle ensued, in which those one thousand Argive picked troops, with their superb training for combat, were the first to rout their opponents and made a great slaughter of them during the pursuit. [5] The Lacedaemonians, however, after themselves putting to flight other units of the [enemy] forces and inflicting heavy casualties on them, turned back to deal with [these elite troops] and surrounded them, with the intention of wiping them out to the last man. [6] Now this picked body, though in numbers far inferior, nevertheless remained preeminent as regards feats of bravery: even so, the Lacedaemonian king was foremost in the fight, held firm against odds, and meant to have slain them all, being determined to fulfill the promise he made to his fellow-citizens, and by one great deed to right the low esteem in which he had come to be held. However, he was not allowed to carry out his chosen plan. Pharax the Spartan, who was one of his advisers and most highly esteemed of any man in Sparta, ordered him to leave an escape route for these crack Argive troops, rather than, by going head to head against men who had given up any hope of survival, to get experience of the kind of bravery engendered by despair. [7] Agis, then, was compelled, in accordance with the instructions recently given him, to leave these men an escape route as Pharax had advised.[121] So the [Argive] thousand were let through in the manner described, and got to safety, while the Lacedaemonians, after winning this major victory and setting up a trophy, went back home.

80. When this year had come to its close, in Athens the archon was Antiphon [418/7] and in Rome in lieu of consuls four military tribunes were elected [Varr. 426]: Gaius Furius [Pacilus Fusus], Titus Quinctius [Poenus Cincinnatus], Marcus Poatumius [Albinus Regillensis], and Aulus Cornelius

121. Thucydides does not mention this action by Pharax, but he does report the Lacedaemonians, together with a thousand Argives, as overthrowing the democracy at Argos and setting up a pro-Spartan oligarchy (? Oct. 418: 5.81.2). This is clearly the same action as that Diodorus describes (without mention of Spartan involvement) at 80.2–3 and hints at collusion during the battle of Mantinea. Cf. Plut. *Alcib.* 15.2.

[Cossus]. During their term, the Argives and the Lacedaemonians, after diplomatic exchanges, concluded a peace treaty and made an alliance [Thuc. 5.76–79]. [2] In consequence, the Mantineans, having lost the support of the Argives, had no option but to submit themselves to the Lacedaemonians. About the same time, in Argos, the elite Thousand, the cream of the entire citizen body, agreed amongst themselves to abolish the democracy and establish an aristocracy from their own ranks. [3] Now because of their wealth and courageous exploits, they stood out among their fellow-citizens and thus could count on widespread support. They therefore began by arresting the regular populist leaders and executing them. Having thus terrorized the rest of the citizen body, they revoked the existing laws and proceeded to take the direction of public affairs into their own hands. They maintained this regime for eight months, after which the people united against them, and they were overthrown [summer 417: Thuc. 5.82.2–5]. With their execution the people recovered democratic government.

[4] Another upheaval in Greece involved the Phocians, who, having quarreled with the Locrians [421: Thuc. 5.32.2], settled the issue by their own valor in a pitched battle, gaining the victory and killing more than a thousand Locrians.

[5] The Athenians, led by Nicias, captured two cities, Cythera and Nisaea; they also reduced Melos by siege, butchered all adult males, and sold the women and children into slavery.[122]

[6] Such were the activities of the Greeks during this period. In Italy, the occupants of Fideni, when ambassadors from Rome arrived in their city, put them to death on trumpery excuses. [7] The Romans, infuriated by this action, voted for war. They mustered a strong force, choosing as Dictator †Anius† Aemilius [Mamercinus], and to assist him, in accordance with custom, Aulus Cornelius as Master of Horse. [8] When Aemilius had completed his preparations for war, he set out with his army against Fideni. When the Fidenates ranged their forces against his, a fierce and drawn-out battle ensued. Losses on both sides were heavy, and the issue remained undecided.[123]

---

122. Diodorus here confuses Nicias' earlier campaign (which he has already described) against Melos (65.2–3), Cythera (65.8), and Nisaea (66.3–4) with his subsequent notorious siege and *andrapodismós* of Melos in 416 (13.30.6; Thuc. 5.116.3–4).

123. This episode took place in 437 (Liv. 4.17–20), and Diodorus reports the consuls for that year correctly (43.1). The Dictator's praenomen was Mamercus, not †Anius†, and the Master of Horse was L. Quinctius Cincinnatus, not Aulus Cornelius [Cossus]. The last named was in fact a tribune and cavalryman who distinguished himself in the battle (Liv. 4.19.1–6). His presence also explains why Diodorus reports the occasion under Varr. 426, since some sources date his exploit to that year (Broughton, 59).

81. When Euphemus was archon in Athens [417/6], in Rome there were elected [Varr. 425] in lieu of consuls the following as military tribunes: Lucius Furius [Medullinus], Lucius <Quinctius> [Cincinnatus], and Aulus Sempronius [Atratinus]. During their term [winter 417/6], the Lacedaemonians and their allies made an expedition into the Argolid. They captured the stronghold of Hysiae, slaughtered its occupants, and demolished its fortress; then, when they ascertained that the Argives had extended their long walls as far as the sea, they marched thither, pulled down the recently constructed walls, and made their way back home.

[2] The Athenians elected Alcibiades general, gave him twenty ships, and instructed him to assist the Argives in stabilizing their government, affairs continuing in confusion there due to many [300: Thuc. 5.84.1] supporters of the aristocracy still being around. [3] Alcibiades on arrival [summer 416] consulted with the advocates of a democracy; he then weeded out those Argives who were reputed to be the most committed supporters of the Lacedaemonian cause and deported them from the city. After thus helping to firmly establish the democratic regime, he sailed back to Athens.

[4] Near the end of this year[124] the Lacedaemonians invaded the Argolid with a strong force and laid waste much of the countryside. They also settled the refugees from Argos at Orneae, fortifying it as a stronghold in Argive territory and leaving a strong garrison there, with orders to harass the Argives. [5] But when the Lacedaemonians had withdrawn from the Argolid, the Athenians sent out to the Argives a relief force of forty triremes and 1,200 hoplites; the Argives and the Athenians together then marched on Orneae and took the city by storm. Some of the garrison and refugees they put to death, while others they merely deported from the city.

Such were the events that took place during the fifteenth year of the Peloponnesian War.

82. In the sixteenth year [of that war], among the Athenians the archon was Arimnestus [416/5], and in Rome in lieu of consuls four military tribunes were elected [Varr. 424]: Titus [?] Claudius [Crassus], Spurius Nautius [Rutilus], Lucius Se<rg>ius [Fidenas], and Sextus Julius [Iullus]. During their term, in Elis, the 91st Olympiad was held, that in which Exaenetus of Acragas won the *stadion* [>13.34.1, 82.7]. [2] The Byzantines and men of Chalcedon, taking [a contingent of] Thracians along with them, invaded Bithynia in vast numbers, devastated the countryside, and reduced many of the smaller towns. Their conduct was marked by quite exceptional savagery: of the nu-

---

124. A year later, in the winter of 416/5, according to Thuc. 6.7.1–2.

merous prisoners they took, they slaughtered every last one, men, women, and children alike.

[3] About the same time, in Sicily, the Egestans and Selinuntines went to war over a territorial dispute, involving a river that divided the lands of the disputants [Thuc. 6.6.2]. [4] The Selinuntines crossed this stream and at first forcibly seized the river frontage. Later they also cut off for themselves a large portion of the adjacent territory, with no regard for the injured parties. [5] The Egestans, angered by this, at first attempted to persuade them by argument not to trespass in this manner on another city's territory; but as no one paid them the slightest attention, they came out in force against those occupying the territory, threw them all off their fields, and took over the land themselves. [6] Since the dispute between these two cities had now become serious, both sides mustered troops and were all for settling the issue by armed force. They therefore lined up in battle order and a hard-fought battle took place, in which the Selinuntines slaughtered not a few Egestans and emerged victorious. [7] So the Egestans, after being thus worsted, and lacking the strength to make a fight of it unaided, first attempted to talk Acragas and Syracuse into an alliance with them. When this gambit failed, they sent ambassadors to solicit aid from Carthage. Since the Carthaginians ignored them, they cast around for an overseas alliance; and here chance came to their aid.

83. Now the Leontines had been expropriated from their city and territory by the Syracusans and relocated elsewhere. These exiles now got together and decided to once more make allies of the Athenians, as being their kin. [2] They then discussed this proposition with the peoples who were on their side, and after reaching an agreement, they sent a joint embassy to the Athenians, soliciting aid for these wrongs done them and offering to help Athens settle affairs in Sicily. [3] So when the ambassadors reached Athens, the Leontines emphasized their kinship and earlier alliance [with the Athenians], while the Egestans promised a large cash contribution towards [the expenses of] the war, also undertaking to fight as [Athens'] ally against Syracuse.[125] The Athenians then voted to send some of their most distinguished men to investigate the situation on the island generally and at Egesta in particular. [4] When these men arrived in Egesta, they were shown a vast sum of money: this had in fact been borrowed, partly from local individuals, partly from neighboring

---

125. Thuc. 6.6.2–3 has an embassy composed solely of Egestans, with the envoys making Leontini's points as well as their own. Plut. *Nic.* 12.1 agrees with Diodorus. The "cash contribution" (despite the deceptive trick about Egesta's wealth) existed: sixty talents (a month's pay for sixty ships) was provided (Thuc. 6.8.1).

peoples, to create a deceptive impression [Thuc. 6.46.3–5]. [5] So the ambassadors returned and reported on the affluence of the Egestans, and the *demos* met to debate the issue. When the council's motion concerning an expedition to Sicily was introduced, Nicias the son of Niceratus,[126] a man with a high reputation for integrity among his fellow-citizens, advised against such an expedition [Thuc. 6.8.4–14]. [6] It was, he argued, out of the question for them at one and the same time to carry on a war against the Lacedaemonians and to send a major expeditionary force overseas; and so long as they remained incapable of winning supremacy over the Greeks, it was a vain hope to suppose that they would be able to subjugate the largest island in the inhabited world. Even the Carthaginians, whose domain was far-reaching and who had fought many campaigns to try and win Sicily, had never been able to gain control of the island: so how could the Athenians, whose military reserves were far inferior to those of Carthage, possibly turn this most powerful of all islands into spear-won territory?[127]

84. After he had expatiated on these and many other matters germane to the proposal under consideration, Alcibiades, chief advocate of the opposite view and the Athenian most in the public eye [<38.3 and n. 61], persuaded the *demos* to choose to go to war [Thuc. 6.16–18], he being the most skilled public speaker in Athens at that time and famous by reason of his breeding, wealth, and military expertise. [2] So the *demos* at once made ready an imposing fleet, taking thirty triremes from their allies and fitting out one hundred of their own. [3] When they had equipped these vessels with all the gear appropriate for active service, they enrolled up to 5,000 hoplites, and elected three generals, Alcibiades, Lamachus, and Nicias, to the high command [Thuc. 6.25–26].

[4] The Athenians, then, were occupied with these matters. For ourselves, since we have now reached the beginning of the war between the Athenians and the Syracusans, we shall, in accordance with the program laid out at the beginning [of this book], deal with subsequent events in the book immediately following.

---

126. Nicias (c. 470–413): conservative politician, cautious general, wealthy slave-owner, much satirized by comedians for his indecisiveness and superstition. According to Thuc. 6.8.2, the initial motion to send a small expedition of sixty ships was actually passed at one meeting, and it was not until a second, supplementary assembly, held five days later, that the debate between Nicias and Alcibiades took place.

127. This powerful argument is not referred to by Thucydides.

BOOK 13: 415–405 B.C.E.

1. If we were composing a work in the common historical manner, we should probably discuss certain topics in each preface at whatever length was suitable, and through these achieve continuity with the narrative that follows; and indeed, were we covering a limited period in our text, we would have the leisure to enjoy the harvest such prefaces yield.[1] [2] However, since we undertook in a few books not only to write (as best we could) a narrative of events but also to cover a period of more than eleven hundred years, we have no option but to forego such lengthy preambles and come straight to the narrative itself. Let it suffice, then, by way of introduction, to say that in the previous six books we followed the course of events from the matter of Troy to the war voted by decree of the Athenians against the Syracusans—a period, taken from Troy's capture to the Syracusan expedition, covering seven hundred and sixty-eight years [1184–415]. [3] In the present book, as we cover the period immediately following, we shall begin with the expedition against Syracuse and conclude [but see 114.3] with the beginning of the second war fought by the Carthaginians against Dionysius the *tyrannos* of Syracuse.

2. When Chabrias was archon in Athens [415/4], the Romans elected [Varr. 418][2] in lieu of consuls three military tribunes: Lucius Sergius [Fidenas], Marcus Papirius [Mugillanus], and <C.> Servilius [Axilla]. During their term, the Athenians, having voted for war against Syracuse [Apr. 415], fitted out a fleet,

---

1. Perhaps an implied criticism of the 4th-century historian Ephorus, who was famous for his elegantly discursive style (Polyb. 12.28.10) and prefaced each book with a general introduction (16.76.5), which, of course, for the most part Diodorus does himself. This is no reason for assuming (as has sometimes been the case) that Diodorus' are necessarily spurious.

2. Diodorus or his source, for whatever reason, completely omits the consular colleges of 423–419 inclusive. Thus, from 415 his archon year is only three years ahead of the Varronian system.

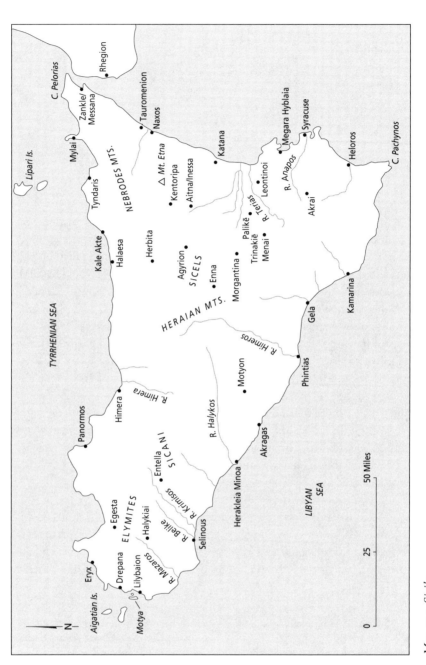

Map 13.1. Sicily

requisitioned funds, and with great enthusiasm set about making all necessary preparations for the expedition. The three generals they elected, Alcibiades, Nicias, and Lamachus, were given full, independent authority over all matters pertaining to the campaign [Thuc. 6.26.2; Plut. *Nic.* 12.3–4, *Alcib.* 18.2]. [2] Among the citizen body, those of ample means were eager to find favor with the public in its enthusiasms: some fitted out triremes at their own expense, while others undertook to supply funds for the military commissariat [Thuc. 6.31]. Many of Athens' populists, both citizens and aliens, as well as volunteers from the allies, approached the generals independently and insisted on enlisting as soldiers. To such a degree were they all airborne in their expectations, and looking forward to carving up Sicily into colonists' land holdings.

[3] When the expedition was already fitted out, the numerous herms scattered throughout the city came to be mutilated in one and the same night [June 415]. The *demos* was convinced that this act had been perpetrated not by casual vandals but rather by persons of high station and repute and with the aim of overthrowing the democracy. In its repugnance for the offense it instituted a search for the offenders, offering substantial rewards to anyone who would lay information against them. [4] A certain private individual [Diocleides: Andoc. 1.37–66] then presented himself before the Council and said he had seen some men, amongst whom was Alcibiades, entering the house of a resident alien (*metic*)[3] about midnight on the first day of the new moon. On being questioned by the Council as to how he recognized their faces at night, he said he had seen them by the light of the moon. Having thus refuted himself, he was disregarded as a liar, and no one else could discover any trace of [those responsible for] the crime.[4]

---

3. Diodorus deals only with the mutilation of the herms, not with the related case of the profanation of the Mysteries by parody in private houses. The two charges were confused at the time, probably deliberately, since Alcibiades may have been guilty of the second but was certainly innocent of the first. Thus, Diodorus here mistakenly introduces evidence relating to the Mysteries (entry to the house of a resident alien, Pulytion, Andoc. 1.12) into an account of the defacement of the herms.

4. Herms were square pillars topped with the head of Hermes and ithyphallic. For the mutilation, see Thuc. 6.27–29, 53, 60–61; Plut. *Alcib.* 18–21, *Nic.* 13.2; and Andoc. 1, *On the Mysteries,* Maidment, 325–481; cf. Gagarin & MacDowell 1998. The true motive for the vandalism seems to have been to create a bad enough omen (Hermes was the god of travelers) to stop the fleet from sailing. This would suggest that those responsible were the kind of rich conservatives who sympathized with Nicias. Granted immunity, Andocides claimed that just such a group, the political club (*hetaireia*) to which he belonged, was responsible. This is likely to be the truth, but scholars disagree over every detail of the episode. See Kagan 1981, 192–209, and Furley 1996 for useful discussions.

[5] One hundred and forty triremes were fitted out, besides a vast number of merchantmen and horse transports and vessels to carry grain and other stores. There were hoplites and slingers, also cavalry (including some from the allies), to a total of 7,000, not counting the crews [Thuc. 6.43–44.1].[5] [6] At this point, then, the generals met in secret session with the Council to discuss what policy they should adopt regarding Sicilian affairs, should they conquer the island. They agreed on the enslavement of the Selinuntines and Syracusans but decided that the other inhabitants should merely be made subject to individual assessments of tribute, to be delivered annually to Athens.[6]

3. The next day the generals, together with their troops, went down to Piraeus, accompanied by the entire population of the city, a mingled throng of citizens and aliens, with everybody seeing off their own relatives and friends [Thuc. 6.30–32.2]. [2] The entire harbor was full of anchored triremes, with the figureheads on their prows and the gleam of armor embellishing their appearance. All around the waterfront was a mass of incense burners and silver mixing bowls, from which people were pouring libations with golden cups, honoring the gods and praying for success to attend the expedition. [3] When they put out from Piraeus, they circumnavigated the Peloponnese and made landfall at Corcyra, their orders being to wait there and pick up local allied contingents. When they had a full muster, they crossed the Ionian Strait on course for the tip of Iapygia and from that point hugged the coast of Italy. [4] The Tarantines would not admit them, and they also sailed on past Metapontum and Heracleia; but they did put in at Thurii, where they were welcomed with every kind of hospitable consideration. Thence they sailed to Croton, where the citizens granted them a market, and from there they coasted on past the temple of Lacinian Hera and rounded the so-called promontory of the Dioscuri. [5] After this they continued past Scylletium and Locri and anchored off shore from Rhegium. When they tried to argue the Rhegians into an alliance, however, the latter temporized by saying they would consult with the other Greek cities of Italy [Thuc. 6.44.1–4].

---

5. Forty of Diodorus' triremes were in fact troop transports. Thuc. 6.43 ad fin. also specifies that cavalry was limited to a single horse transport with thirty mounts: shortage of cavalry (6.5) was to become one of the expedition's fatal weaknesses.

6. Diodorus is the only source to mention this conference, and his evidence is generally ignored. But the idea (as Alcibiades made clear in his speech; Thuc. 6.18.4) was very much in the air, and planning ahead in confidence how to act in the event of complete success is not wholly implausible.

4. When the Syracusans heard that the Athenian expeditionary force had reached the straits [of Messina], they appointed three generals with full, independent powers, Hermocrates, Sicanus, and Heraclides.[7] These not only enlisted troops but sent embassies to all the cities of Sicily, begging them to share in preserving their common freedom and pointing out that the Athenians, while claiming to be making war on Syracuse, had as their true goal the subjugation of the entire island. [2] The Acragantines and Naxians said they would side with the Athenians. The men of Camarina and Messene agreed to keep the peace, but put off to a later date their response regarding an alliance. The inhabitants of Himera, Selinus, Gela, and Catana,[8] however, all promised to join Syracuse in her struggle. The cities of the Sicels, which were inclined on balance to favor Syracuse,[9] nevertheless remained uncommitted, waiting on the outcome of events.

[3] When the Egestans refused to contribute more than thirty talents, the Athenian generals, after [vainly] remonstrating with them, put out with their whole host from Rhegium, and sailed over to Naxos in Sicily, where they were given a friendly welcome by the inhabitants. From there they coasted to Catana. [4] The Catanaeans would not admit their troops into the city, but they allowed the Athenian generals to enter and called a meeting of the assembly, at which the Athenians put their case for an alliance. [5] But while Alcibiades was haranguing them, some soldiers broke down a postern gate and burst into the city [Thuc. 6.51.1–2]. It was because of this that Catana was forced to join in the war against Syracuse.

5. While these events were going on, those in Athens whose hatred of Alcibiades was based on personal enmity now had, in the mutilation of the statues, a fine excuse to attack him. Accordingly, they charged him in public speeches with having made a conspiracy against the democracy [Plut. *Alcib.* 20.3]. Their accusations got some support from an incident that had taken

---

7. Thucydides (6.73) and Plutarch (*Nic.* 16.5) date these appointments (made on Hermocrates' recommendation) later that summer, as a result of the first inconclusive Athenian attack on Syracuse (Thuc. 6.69–71).

8. Though many of the Sicilian cities exhibited a certain fence-sitting flexibility in their alliances or neutrality during the Athenian invasion, Catana in fact remained loyal to Athens throughout (Thuc. 2.57.11, 74.1, 98.1; 7.13.3, 60.1, 85.4). Thucydides makes it clear (6.51.1–2) that the episode of the broken postern gate (3.5) simply drove the pro-Syracusans out of town, not that Catana as a whole was kept subservient by *force majeure*.

9. Not so, according to Thucydides, who repeatedly notes their tendency to side with the Athenians: 6.65.2, 88.3–6, 98.1, 103.2; 7.32.2, 67.11, 77.6, 80.5.

place in Argos [Thuc. 6.61.3], where certain private friends of his had hatched a plot to overthrow the existing democracy but had all been put to death by the citizen body. [2] So the *demos,* convinced by these accusations, and whipped up into a fine frenzy by the demagogues, dispatched the vessel called the *Salaminia* to Sicily, carrying orders instructing Alcibiades to return with all speed to face trial. When this vessel reached Catana, and Alcibiades heard from the envoys what the *demos* had decreed, he took those others accused with him aboard his own trireme and put to sea in the company of the *Salaminia.* [3] On arrival at Thurii, however, Alcibiades—either because he had, in fact, been involved in the act of impiety or simply through alarm at the seriousness of his position—made a clean getaway, along with the rest of those charged. The party that had come over aboard the *Salaminia* at first went searching for Alcibiades and his companions; but when they failed to find him, they sailed back to Athens and reported to the *demos* what had happened [Thuc. 6.61.4–7]. [4] The Athenians accordingly turned over the names of Alcibiades and his fellow-fugitives to the judiciary, and a court duly condemned them to death in absentia [Plut. *Alcib.* 22.3–4]. Alcibiades meanwhile [Sept. 415] took ship from Italy to the Peloponnese and fled to Sparta, where he kept inciting the Lacedaemonians to attack Athens.

6. The generals in Sicily sailed on to Egesta with the Athenian expeditionary force and took Hyccara, a small Sicel town, the booty from which yielded them one hundred talents. After also collecting their thirty talents from Egesta, they sailed back to Catana. [2] Now they had a plan to capture, at no risk to themselves, the Syracusan position on the Great Harbor [Thuc. 6.64.2–71]. In furtherance of this they sent a certain Catanaean—loyal to them but also trusted by the Syracusan generals—with instructions to inform the leadership in Syracuse that certain Catanaeans had formed a group with the intention of suddenly seizing a large number of Athenians (who had got in the habit of spending nights in the city away from their arms) and of setting fire to the ships in the harbor. To aid in bringing off this plan, and to ensure that nothing went wrong, he was to ask the generals to show up with their troops. [3] The Catanaean approached the Syracusan leaders and pitched them the above story. They were convinced by it, set the night on which they would come out, and sent the man back to Catana.

[4] When the appointed night came [Oct. 415], the Syracusans brought their ground forces to Catana. Meanwhile, the Athenians, operating in complete silence, sailed into the Great Harbor, occupied the Olympieum, seized the territory adjacent to it, and constructed a camp. [5] When the Syracusan generals perceived how they had been duped, they returned with all speed

and proceeded to attack the Athenian camp. The enemy emerged to face them, and a battle took place, in which the Athenians killed four hundred [Thuc. 6.71.1 says 260] of their opponents, overpowered the Syracusans, and put them to flight. [6] The Athenian generals, noting the enemy's superiority in cavalry, and being anxious to get themselves better prepared for besieging the city, now sailed back to Catana. They dispatched men to Athens [winter 415/4] with letters addressed to the *demos,* in which they asked them to send cavalry and cash [Thuc. 6.74.2], in the conviction that the siege of Syracuse would be a long, drawn-out affair. The Athenians voted to send to Sicily three hundred talents and some [7.3] of their cavalry.

[7] While these events were taking place, Diagoras,[10] known as "The Atheist," was charged with impiety, and in fear of the *demos* fled from Attica; and the Athenians proclaimed that whoever slew Diagoras would receive a talent of silver.

[8] In Italy, the Romans, who were at war with the Aequi, took Labici by siege [Liv. 4.47.1–6].

These, then, were the events that took place during this year.

7. When Tisander was archon in Athens [414/3], the Romans elected [Varr. 417] in lieu of consuls four military tribunes: Publius Lucretius [Hosti Tricipitinus], Gaius Servilius [Axilla], Agrippa Menenius [Agripp. Lanatus], and Spurius Veturius [Crassus Cicurinus]. During their term [winter 415/4], the Syracusans dispatched ambassadors to Corinth and Lacedaemon [Thuc. 6.73.2], calling on them to come to their relief and not to look idly on while they faced complete and utter disaster. [2] With Alcibiades backing their appeal, the Lacedaemonians voted [Thuc. 6.93.1–2] to send aid to Syracuse and selected Gylippus[11] as general. The Corinthians set preparations in hand for a number of triremes, but at that point they dispatched an advance party of two vessels only, under Pythes, to accompany Gylippus. [3] In Catana, the Athenian generals Nicias and Lamachus, after two hundred and fifty cavalry and three hundred talents of silver had reached them from Athens, embarked their forces [? Apr. 414] and sailed for Syracuse. Putting in at night, they slipped past the Syracusans unnoticed and occupied [the heights of] Epipolae. When

---

10. Diagoras of Melos, lyric poet: his "atheism" appears to have involved mockery of the Eleusinian Mysteries, the same charge as that brought against Alcibiades and others.

11. The son of Cleandridas (106.10), adviser to King Pleistoanax in 446/5, who went into exile at Thurii after being charged with advising the acceptance of a bribe from Pericles to withdraw the Spartan army from Attica. Thus disgraced by his father's conduct, Gylippus urgently needed to prove himself: a psychologically shrewd appointment.

the Syracusans discovered this, they hastened to the rescue but were chased back into the city with the loss of three hundred of their troops.

[4] After this the Athenians received three hundred horsemen from Egesta, and two hundred and fifty more from the Sicels, so that they now had assembled a cavalry force eight hundred strong. They then, after building a fort at Labdalum, began to wall off the city of Syracuse, to the great consternation of its inhabitants. [5] They therefore made a sally from the city and attempted to hinder those building the wall, but in the ensuing cavalry skirmish, they suffered heavy casualties and were routed. The Athenians with a part of their force now occupied the position above the harbor, and by fortifying that part of it known as "The Hamlet" (*Polichne:* Thuc. 7.4.6), they blocked off the temple of Zeus and indeed were now investing Syracuse from both sides. [6] With these various setbacks to the Syracusans, the inhabitants of the city were in low spirits; but when they heard that Gylippus had landed at Himera and was recruiting troops, they took heart once more. [7] Gylippus in fact had put in there with four triremes (which he hauled up on shore), had talked the Himerans into an alliance with Syracuse, and was now acquiring recruits not only from them but also from Gela, Selinus, and the Sicans. By these means he got together a force of 3,000 infantry and 200 cavalry, which he then took through the interior to Syracuse [Thuc. 7.1.1–5].

8. A few days later Gylippus, along with the Syracusans, led out his force against the Athenians. A hard-fought battle took place, in which heavy casualties were suffered on both sides; and though the Athenian general Lamachus fell fighting,[12] final victory went to Athens. [2] After the battle was over, thirteen triremes arrived from Corinth: Gylippus took their crews, and with a force made up from them and the Syracusans, assaulted the enemy camp, and pressed home his attack on Epipolae. When the Athenians made a sally, the Syracusans joined battle with them, slaughtered them in large numbers, and emerged victorious, after which they demolished the [Athenian] wall for the entire length of Epipolae. Upon this the Athenians abandoned their position on Epipolae altogether and transferred their entire force to the other camp.

[3] After these events, the Syracusans dispatched ambassadors to Corinth and Lacedaemon to solicit support. The Corinthians, along with the Boeotians and Sicyonians, sent them one thousand men, and the Spartans, six hundred. [4] Gylippus meanwhile traveled around the various cities in Sicily

---

12. Both Thuc. 6.101.6 and Plut. *Nic.* 18.3 place Lamachus' death in an earlier skirmish, before Gylippus' arrival.

and persuaded many [groups] to ally themselves [with Syracuse]. After collecting 3,000 soldiers from the Himerans and Sicans, he marched them back across country; and when the Athenians got wind of their approach, they made an attack and slaughtered half of them. The remainder, however, got safely to Syracuse.

[5] With the arrival of their allies, the Syracusans conceived a desire to try their hand at naval warfare too: they therefore launched their existing ships and fitted out others, giving them their trials in the small harbor. [6] Nicias, the Athenian general, sent dispatches to Athens [Thuc. 7.8.1–3, 10–16.1] in which he made it clear that numerous allies had now joined the Syracusans, while the latter had manned a considerable number of ships with the intention of fighting at sea. He was therefore asking them for the speedy dispatch of triremes and funds, as well as generals who could share the responsibilities of the campaign with him. With Lamachus dead and Alcibiades a deserter, he was the only commander left, and a sick man at that.[13] [7] The Athenians, about the time of the winter solstice [414/3], ordered ten ships to Sicily, as well as a general, Eurymedon, and a hundred and forty talents of silver; they also set about the preparations for the dispatch of a full-sized fleet in the spring. To this end they began requisitioning troops from their allies everywhere and also amassing funds.

[8] In the Peloponnese the Lacedaemonians, at Alcibiades' urging, broke their solemn truce with the Athenians [Thuc. 7.18], and so this [Peloponnesian] war continued for another †twelve† years.[14]

9. When this year drew to a close, Cleocritus was archon in Athens [413/2], and in Rome [Varr. 416] in lieu of consuls there were four military tribunes: Aulus Sempronius [Atratinus], Marcus Papirius [Mugillanus], Quintus Fabius [Vibulanus], and Spurius Nautius [Rutilus]. [2] During their term [early spring 413], the Lacedaemonians, together with their allies, invaded Attica, their leaders being [King] Agis and Alcibiades the Athenian.[15] They captured the stronghold of Deceleia and made it a fortress for [raids on] Attica, which

---

13. He was suffering from acute nephritis: Thuc. 7.15.1.

14. If the war had lasted 18 years by 414 (Thuc. 7.18.4), and was to total 27 years in all, it had 10, not 12, further years to run. I suspect that at some point Diodorus' MS tradition converted *deka* (10) into *dōdeka* (12).

15. Only Diodorus puts Alcibiades in the field with Agis. Both Thucydides (6.91.6) and Plutarch (*Alcib.* 23.3) agree that he suggested the occupation of Deceleia; but Plutarch (*Alcib.* 23.7–8) has him getting Agis' wife Timaea pregnant while Agis was absent on campaign. *Caveat lector.*

was how this stage of hostilities came to be known as the Deceleian War
[Thuc. 7.19.1–2]. The Athenians sent out thirty triremes to patrol Laconian
waters under the command of Charicles and voted a force of eighty triremes
and 5,000 hoplites for the Sicilian campaign [Thuc. 7.20.1–2].

[3] The Syracusans, being set now on a sea battle [spring 413], manned
eighty triremes and sailed against the enemy [Thuc. 7.21–24]. The Athenians
put out against them with sixty ships, and so fierce an engagement ensued
that all the Athenians in the forts came crowding down to the sea, some simply from a desire to watch the battle, others hoping to be of assistance to the
fugitives in the event of a reverse. [4] The Syracusan generals, however, having
anticipated the actual course of events, had dispatched their troops in the city
against these Athenian strongholds, which were crammed with cash, naval
stores, and every other sort of gear. In the process of capturing these—which
were guarded by far too few troops, even with the help of those who came up
from the sea—they slaughtered the defendants wholesale. [5] The uproar that
now arose around the forts and the camp made the Athenians engaged in the
sea battle turn tail in alarm and flee towards the one fort that was still holding
out. The Syracusans pursued them in wild disorder, but the Athenians—
unable to seek refuge ashore because the Syracusans now controlled two of the
forts—were forced to put about and renew the battle at sea. [6] Now since
the Syracusans had broken their line and become scattered in the course of
the pursuit, [the Athenians], by making a massed attack, sank eleven [enemy
ships] and pursued the rest as far as the Island [of Ortygia]. After the battle
was over, both sides set up a trophy, the Athenians for the sea fight, and the
Syracusans for their achievements on land.

10. The sea battle having ended thus, the Athenians—on learning that the
armada under Demosthenes [<12.69.1–2] would arrive within a few days—
decided to risk no further action until these reinforcements were there with
them. The Syracusans, however, wanted just the opposite: a final and decisive showdown before Demosthenes and his expeditionary force showed up.
They therefore continued to sail out daily and persist in their battle against
the Athenian fleet. [2] Also, when Ariston the Corinthian steersman advised
them to redesign the prows of their vessels, making them both shorter and
lower, the Syracusans did as he suggested, and because of this had a considerable advantage in subsequent engagements [Thuc. 7.36.1–6]. [3] Since Attic
triremes had prows that were both higher and less solid, it followed that in
ramming they did damage [only] above the waterline, with no great harm to
the enemy. These Syracusan vessels, on the other hand, with their reinforced

and lowered prow structures, would frequently, when they came to ram, sink Athenian triremes at first impact.

[4] For days on end the Syracusans continued to assault the enemy camp by both land and sea, but since the Athenians stayed put, their efforts got nowhere. After a while, however, some trireme captains, unable to stand the contempt of the Syracusans, put out against the enemy in the Great Harbor, and this led to a sea battle involving all the triremes. [5] Those of the Athenians were fast sailers, and their crews had the edge in naval experience and the skill of their steersmen; yet their superiority in these matters proved useless here, since the engagement was being fought in a restricted space. The Syracusans pressed home their attack at close quarters and gave the enemy no chance to maneuver; by pelting [the marines] on deck with javelins and [sling-] stones, they drove them off the prows; and simply by ramming many of the vessels they encountered, and then boarding them, they set up land battles on the ships. [6] Hard-pressed on all sides, the Athenians broke and fled. During their pursuit, the Syracusans sank seven triremes and put a number more out of action [Thuc. 7.40.5–41.4].

11. But just when Syracusan hopes had been raised high by their defeat of the enemy both on land and at sea, Eurymedon and Demosthenes arrived from Athens [summer 413] with their huge armada, including allied troops that they had picked up en route from the Thurians and Messapians. [2] They brought with them more than eighty triremes and 5,000 troops (not counting the crews of the ships) and were accompanied by a fleet of merchantmen loaded with siege engines and other equipment. Because of all this, the Syracusans' hopes were dashed yet again, since they thought that to match the enemy's resources would no longer be any easy matter for them [Thuc. 7.42.1–2; Plut. *Nic.* 21.1–2].

[3] Demosthenes persuaded his fellow-commanders that they must assault [and capture] Epipolae, since otherwise it would be impossible to wall off the city. He himself took a force of 10,000 hoplites and as many more light-armed troops and carried out a night attack [Thuc. 7.42.3–45.2]. Since this move had not been anticipated, they overran some guard posts, broke through the defenses on Epipolae, and demolished a stretch of the wall. [4] But the Syracusans hurriedly converged on this scene from all directions, and Hermocrates also came to the rescue with his elite unit, so that the Athenians were forced out again, and because of the darkness and their unfamiliarity with the terrain scattered here, there, and everywhere. [5] The Syracusans and their allies pursued them, killing 2,500, wounding a good number, and capturing arms and

armor galore. [6] After the battle, the Syracusans sent one of their generals, Sicanus, with twelve triremes, on a round of visits to the other cities, both to notify the allies of this victory and to solicit their support [Thuc. 7.46].

12. The Athenians, what with this deterioration in their affairs, and an outbreak of pestilence in camp due to the marshy nature of the surrounding terrain, held a meeting to discuss how best they could cope with the situation. [2] Demosthenes' opinion was that they should sail back to Athens as soon as possible: to risk their lives fighting the Lacedaemonians in defense of their native city, he said, was preferable to sitting there in Sicily and getting nothing useful done. Nicias, however, argued that they should not abandon the siege in this disgraceful way, seeing that they still had triremes, troops, and money in abundance. What was more, if they were to make peace with Syracuse and sail back home without an authorizing vote from the Athenian *demos,* they would be courting danger from those who habitually brought spurious charges against generals [Plut. *Nic.* 22].

[3] Of those others in attendance, some supported Demosthenes' plan for pulling out by sea, but others expressed the same opinion as Nicias: the result was that they reached no clear-cut decision and remained inactive [Thuc. 7.48 – 49]. [4] Allied support now came in to Syracuse from the Sicels and Selinuntines and from Gela, as well as from Himera and Camarina: this encouraged the Syracusans but left the Athenians in considerable alarm. The epidemic, too, was spreading at a great rate: many of the soldiers were dying, and all were sorry that they had not started the voyage home long before. [5] Thus, with the other ranks in an uproar, and everyone wild to board the ships, Nicias was forced to yield on the issue of the return home. Since the generals were now all of the same mind, the soldiers began assembling their gear, loading up the triremes and raising the yardarms; and the generals issued an order to the troops in general that, when the signal was given, no one in camp should miss the call, since any latecomer would be left behind. [6] But the night before the morning on which they were to sail [27 Aug. 413], the moon was eclipsed. Because of this, Nicias, who was superstitious by nature, and also cautious on account of the epidemic in camp, sent for the soothsayers. When these pronounced it necessary to postpone departure for the customary three days, even Demosthenes and his supporters were compelled to give in, out of pious respect for the divine.[16]

---

16. Thuc. 7.50.4 and Plut. *Nic.* 23.6 agree that the seers prescribed waiting not three, but twenty-seven days, i.e., a full lunar cycle. Nicias was notoriously superstitious (Thuc.

13. When the Syracusans found out from some deserters the reason the departure had been delayed, they manned all their triremes (to a total of seventy-four), led out their ground forces, and assaulted the enemy by both land and sea. [2] The Athenians manned eighty-six triremes: they gave command of the right wing to their general Eurymedon, opposing whom was the Syracusan general Agatharchus; Euthydemus was assigned to the other wing, and against him was posted the Syracusan commander Sicanus; the command of the Athenian center went to Menander, and that of the Syracusan, to Pythes the Corinthian. [3] Since the Athenians were committing a larger number of triremes to the engagement, their line extended further; but this, which they thought would give them an advantage, in fact was not the least part of their undoing. Eurymedon, in an attempt to outflank his opponents' wing, became separated from his own battle line. The Syracusans came about to face him, and he was cut off and chivvied into the bay known as Dascon, which was in their possession. [4] Being thus driven into a narrow area, he was forced to jump ship, and once ashore was dealt a mortal wound by some person and so ended his life; seven of his ships were destroyed in this area.

[5] The conflict had now become general throughout both fleets [Thuc. 7.52.1–54]. When word spread that the general had been killed and some ships destroyed, at first only those vessels nearest to the ones lost put about; but later—with the Syracusans pressing them hard, and fighting more boldly on account of the success they had scored—the whole Athenian line was overwhelmed and put to flight. [6] Since the pursuit was towards the shallow part of the harbor, not a few of the triremes ran aground among the shoals. At this, Sicanus the Syracusan general quickly had a merchantman loaded with firewood, pine torches, and pitch, and set fire to the vessels now rolling helplessly in the shallows. [7] But no sooner were they alight than the Athenians quenched the flames and then, finding no other road to safety, conducted a vigorous defense from their ships against [the enemy's] headlong assault. Also, the land forces now came to their relief along the beach on which their ships had run aground. [8] Since they all stoutly withstood the attack, on land the Syracusans were repulsed; but at sea they came out ahead and sailed back to the city. Syracusan casualties were few, but the Athenians lost not less than 2,000 men, as well as eighteen triremes.

7.50.4; Plut. *Nic.* 4.1). Yet the nature of a lunar eclipse was known, and nothing better demonstrates the appalling power of belief than that commander and men alike chose to sit inactive by a pestilential swamp and wait while their chance of retreat, by sea or land, was systematically cut off.

14. The Syracusans now reckoned that, far from their city being in critical danger any longer, the contest had become one for the capture of camp and enemy together [Thuc. 7.56.1, 59.2–3]. They accordingly closed off the harbor mouth by the construction of a boom. [2] They anchored a number of various craft—skiffs, triremes, merchantmen—linking them with iron chains and running a bridge of spars from hull to hull: this work they completed in three days. [3] The Athenians, seeing the roads to safety being closed off all around them, decided to man all their triremes, put their best fighting troops aboard them, and thus—by the sheer numbers of their ships, and the plain desperation of men fighting for their very survival—strike terror into the Syracusans [Thuc. 7.60.1–4; Plut. *Nic.* 24.3–4]. [4] They therefore manned no less than one hundred and fifteen triremes with commissioned officers and the cream of the entire expeditionary force, posting the troops that were left ashore along the beach. The Syracusans stationed their ground troops in front of the city, and manned seventy-four triremes, these being escorted by young free-born boys in dinghies, who though under military age were nevertheless joining in the fight alongside their fathers. [5] The walls around the harbor and every vantage point overlooking it were packed with spectators. Women, young girls, and those precluded by age from war service were all, in an agony of uncertainty, preparing to watch the battle that would decide the final outcome of the entire war.

15. At this point the Athenian general Nicias, after surveying the ships and calculating the sheer magnitude of the conflict [now imminent], would not remain at his command post ashore but left the ground forces, boarded a launch, and sailed along the [battle line of] the Athenian triremes. Addressing each captain by name and reaching out his hands, he besought them all, now if ever, to hold fast to the sole hope left them: for on the valor of those about to engage in this sea battle hung the survival of every man of them and of their fatherland. [2] Those who were fathers of children he bade remember their sons; those born of famous fathers he urged not to bring shame on the great deeds of their ancestors; those whom the *demos* had honored he encouraged to show themselves worthy of their decorations; all of them he begged to keep in mind the trophies at Salamis and not to besmirch the widespread renown of their fatherland or submit themselves like slaves to the Syracusans [Thuc. 7.61–68].

[3] After Nicias had delivered this exhortation, he returned to his own station. Those aboard the ships raised the paean, advanced, and set about breaking through the boom before the enemy could get to them. But the Syracusans hurriedly put to sea, got their triremes in battle formation, and

engaged the enemy, forcing them to turn back from the boom and fight it out. [4] As the triremes began to back water—some towards the shoreline, others into the middle of the harbor, others again in the direction of the city walls—they very soon all became separated from one another, and once they were clear of the barrier, the whole harbor became dotted with small clusters of ships in combat. [5] From then on, both sides became engaged in a life-and-death struggle for victory. The Athenians, taking courage from the size of their fleet, and seeing no other hope of survival, fought savagely, displaying a noble readiness to face death in battle; the Syracusans, who had parents and children as eyewitnesses of their struggle, strove in emulation with one another, each wanting victory for the fatherland through his own individual efforts.

16. Thus many, when their own vessel had been incapacitated by attack and they were stranded in the midst of their enemies, would get on to the prows of those enemies' ships. Some, by throwing grappling irons [i.e., to lock deck to deck], forced their adversaries to fight a land battle on water. [2] Frequently, those whose own ships had been broken up would jump aboard their opponents' triremes, and—by killing some and tossing others overboard—proceed to take them over. In a word, from throughout the harbor there came the noise of ship ramming ship, and the cries of desperate combatants perishing on either side. [3] For when a ship was isolated by several triremes, and struck from every quarter by their bronze-sheathed rams, the water would cascade in, and the vessel would be swallowed up [by the sea], crew and all. Some, when their ships went down, managed to swim clear; but these would then be shot by archers or speared to death. [4] The helmsmen, as they watched the confused course of the battle—with noisy disorder everywhere, and very often a number of ships converging on a single one—had no idea what signals to give, since the same commands were not appropriate for every circumstance. In any case, because of the rain of missiles, it was impossible for rowers to keep their eyes on those giving them their orders; [5] nor, indeed, could anyone hear any of the commands, what with the stoving in of hulls and the snapping off of oarblades, not to mention the shouting of those in combat on the ships and the supporting cheers from their friends ashore. [6] The beach was occupied, for all its length, partly by Athenian troops and partly by the Syracusans, so that at times those fighting close inshore got help from the soldiers lined up along the strand. [7] The spectators on the walls would burst out into [cheers and] victory songs whenever they saw their own side winning, but greet reverses with groans and tears and appeals to the gods. Indeed, on occasion it happened that some Syracusan triremes

would be destroyed close to the walls, and their crews butchered before the eyes of their own kin, so that parents would witness the violent end of their children, or sisters and wives the piteous fate of husbands and brothers.

17. For a long time, despite the heavy death toll, there was no end to the fighting, since not even the hardest pressed would dare to seek refuge ashore. The Athenians would ask those shrinking from battle and turning landwards if they supposed they could sail overland to Athens, while the Syracusan ground troops would quiz any bringing their vessels inshore as to why, when *they* were eager to serve aboard the triremes, they'd refused them, if now they were betraying their fatherland anyway? Was that the reason for blocking the harbor mouth, they enquired, so that after stopping the enemy getting out, they'd [have a good excuse for] fleeing to the beach themselves? Since it was the fate of all men to die, what finer death could they embrace than one met for the sake of their country, which they were now so shamefully abandoning, even though it was a witness to their struggle? [2] When the soldiers ashore cast such reproaches in the teeth of those retreating towards them, those seeking refuge on the beaches would turn back, even though their ships were disabled and they themselves weighed down by their wounds. [3] But when the Athenians fighting near the city were overcome and turned to flight, those next in line began to give way, and little by little all of them joined the rout. [4] At this the Syracusans, with whooping and shouting, began to pursue their ships to land, while such Athenians as had not lost their lives out on the water, on reaching the shallows jumped ship and sought safety with the land forces. [5] The harbor was brimming with arms and naval wreckage, since of the Attic fleet sixty vessels had been lost, while of the Syracusan eight had been totally destroyed, and sixteen seriously damaged. The Syracusans hauled ashore as many of their triremes as they could, collected the bodies of those who had died, both citizens and allies, and honored them with a public funeral [Thuc. 7.69.4–72.1; Plut. *Nic.* 25.1–3].[17]

18. The Athenians flocked to the tents of their commanders, begging the generals to take thought not for the ships but for their personal safety. Demosthenes, then, argued that, since the barrier had been broken, they should at once man the triremes: if they made an unexpected attack, he was sure that

---

17. Diodorus' account of this battle contains vivid details not recorded elsewhere. These may be no more than rhetorical embellishment, but there is a strong possibility that they ultimately derive from the Syracusan historian Philistus, an eyewitness (Plut. *Nic.* 19.5).

they would easily attain their goal. [2] Nicias, however, counseled[18] that they should abandon the ships and retreat through the interior to the cities that were allied with them. This suggestion met with general agreement. They therefore burned some of the ships and made ready for the retreat.

[3] When it became clear that they were going to set out during the night, Hermocrates advised the Syracusans to march out their entire force under cover of darkness and occupy all the roads ahead of them. [4] The generals, however, rejected this suggestion, since many of their soldiers were wounded, and all of them were physically exhausted after the battle. Hermocrates therefore sent a detachment of cavalry to the Athenian camp, with the information that the Syracusans had already dispatched [forces] in advance to secure the roads and the most important positions. [5] It was already dark when the horsemen carried out their mission, so that the Athenians, thinking it was friends from Leontini who had brought the news out of kindly concern for them, were not a little disconcerted by it and postponed their departure: had they not been tricked in this fashion, they would have gotten clean away [Thuc. 7.73.1–4]. [6] It was not in fact until dawn was breaking that the Syracusans sent out detachments to forestall the Athenians by occupying the narrow passes along the various routes. Meanwhile, the Athenian generals divided their troops into two separate bodies, put the pack animals and the sick in the middle, stationed those fit to fight in the van and the rear, and then set out for Catana,[19] with Demosthenes leading one corps, and Nicias the other.

19. The Syracusans took the [Athenians'] fifty abandoned ships in tow and brought them back to the city. They then disembarked all their own trireme crews, armed them, and set out after the Athenians with their entire armament, harassing them and hampering their advance. [2] For three days they kept up this close pursuit, and by riding herd on them from all sides, prevented them from taking the direct route towards their ally Catana, forcing them instead to backtrack through the Helorine plain. At the Assinarus River they surrounded them, killed 18,000, and took 7,000 prisoners, including the generals Demosthenes and Nicias: the remainder were seized as booty by individual soldiers. [3] Since their escape routes in every direction had been cut, the Athenians were forced to surrender themselves and their arms to the

<hr/>

18. In Thucydides' version (7.72.3–4), Nicias agrees with Demosthenes but is faced by a mass refusal to man the triremes, and sanctions the retreat by land only as a last resort.

19. Directly contradicted by Thuc. 7.80.2 but almost certainly correct. For topographical details of the final march (virtually eliminated in Diodorus' account), Thuc. 7.78.2–87.6 should be read with Green 1971, 315–343 and Kagan 1981, 339–353.

enemy. This done, the Syracusans set up two trophies, to each of which they nailed a general's arms [Plut. *Nic.* 27.6]. Then they returned to the city.

[4] At this juncture the entire community offered sacrifice to the gods; and the next day the assembly met to consider how they should deal with their captives. A certain Diocles, the most prominent of the populist leaders, gave it as his opinion that they should put the Athenian generals to death after torture, while the other prisoners should, for the present, all be consigned to the stone quarries; in due course, however, those who had joined the Athenian alliance should be sold as spoils of war, while the Athenians themselves should be put to hard prison labor, on a [daily] ration of two *kotylae* [about 1 pint] of barley meal. [6] When this motion had been read, Hermocrates came forward and tried to make a speech arguing that to use a victory with humanity was better than the victory itself [Plut. *Nic.* 28.2]; [6] but the *demos* shouted him down and would not let him finish his address. At this a man named Nicolaüs, who had lost two sons in the war, climbed up to the platform, supported by house slaves on account of his age. When people saw him, they stopped shouting, in the belief that he would denounce the prisoners. With silence thus obtained, the old man began his speech.[20]

20. "Of this war's misfortunes, men of Syracuse, I have had no small share. I was the father of two sons and sent them out to join the struggle for our fatherland; but what I got back in their stead was a message informing me of their death. [2] Every day, as I vainly seek their familiar presence and remind myself that they are no more, I deem them blessed, yet pity my own condition, since I regard myself as the most wretched man alive. [3] They spent on the preservation of their fatherland that death owed to nature [by us all], and in so doing bequeathed us their deathless renown; whereas I, bereft at my own life's furthest extremity of those who were to care for my old age, suffer grief doubly, since it is not only my own flesh and blood whose absence I lament but their valor. [4] The more noble their death, the rarer and more precious the memory of themselves they have left us. Thus I have good cause to hate the Athenians, since it is because of them that I am guided here, as you see, not by my own sons but by servants. [5] Men of Syracuse, if it was clear to me that this present debate was simply about the Athenians, I might well have

---

20. Though this speech, and its rebuttal by Gylippus (28–32) are no more to be taken as accurate reports of what was actually said than those of Thucydides, it is reasonable to suppose that some such public debate did take place, that Nicolaüs was as real a person as Gylippus, and that the historian Philistus recorded their exchange, having almost certainly witnessed it (Plut. *Nic.* 19.5).

dealt harshly with them, by reason both of our country's common misfortunes and of my own private loss. But other factors are involved: apart from the pity that is misfortune's due, the issue concerns what may best benefit our community, not to mention the good name of the Syracusan people, which will [thus] be exposed to the judgment of all mankind. I shall therefore devote my attention exclusively to the question of expediency.

21. "The Athenian people have been visited with a punishment worthy of their own folly: in the first instance from the gods, and then from us, as the ones whom they had wronged. [2] That divinity should involve in unlooked-for calamities those who embark on an unjust war, and do not temper their high station with humanity, is indeed a [great] good. [3] Who, indeed, could have expected that the Athenians, after removing ten thousand talents [<12.38.2] from Delos to Athens, and sending out to Sicily two hundred triremes and over forty thousand fighting men, would ever succumb to disasters on such a scale? From the gigantic force they fitted out not one ship, not one man has returned home, so that there is not even a survivor left to bring them the news of this disaster [but see Thuc. 8.1.1]. [4] You are well aware, men of Syracuse, that the arrogant incur hatred from both gods and men: bow before Fortune, then, and in no way exceed conduct befitting a mortal. What virtue lies in murdering your fallen opponent? What glory subsists in visiting revenge on him? He who maintains an immutably savage front in the face of human misfortunes also misconstrues the common weakness of mankind; [5] for there is no mortal clever enough to outmuscle Fortune, who by her nature delights in human suffering and works such sharp changes in human prosperity.

"Some perhaps may say, 'They did wrong, and we are entitled to impose a punishment on them.' [6] But have you not already taken a far harsher vengeance on the Athenian people? Do you not find the punishment meted out to the captives adequate? They have surrendered themselves and their arms, trusting in the civilized attitude of their conquerors; it is not proper that we should now cheat them of such humane treatment. [7] Those who maintained their enmity towards us unaltered until the end died fighting; but those who delivered themselves into our hands have changed from enemies into suppliants.[21] Men who in battle deliver their persons into the hands

---

21. Though the rule was frequently disregarded, troops that surrendered were generally regarded as suppliants (29.3–4) and thus entitled to humane treatment: Diodorus (30.18.2), perhaps drawing on Polybius, refers to this among other conventions of warfare.

of their opponents do so with the hope of saving their lives. But if such trust is rewarded with so extreme a punishment, then even though its victims will endure their misfortune, its enforcers would get a name for harshness. [8] Those with pretensions to leadership, men of Syracuse, need to spend less time improving their military standing, and more showing themselves reasonable in their attitudes.

22. "The subjugated watch for their opportunity to retaliate, out of hatred, against those who use fear to repress them; whereas humane leaders they regard with constant affection and thus invariably help to strengthen their authority. What was it destroyed the empire of the Medes but brutality to those weaker than themselves? [2] When the Persians revolted from them, most of the other [subject] nations joined in the attack. How did Cyrus[22] rise from private individual to become monarch of all Asia? By his civilized behavior towards those he conquered. When he captured King Croesus, for instance, far from treating him unjustly, he conferred positive benefits upon him; and he dealt in much the same way with the rest of the kings and peoples [under his rule]. [3] The result was that after his merciful generosity became everywhere known, all those dwelling in Asia vied with one another to be the first to join the king's alliance.

[4] "But why speak of things remote in both place and time? In our own city, not all that long ago, Gelon, starting as a private citizen, became leader of all Sicily [<11.38.5–6]. The cities willingly acknowledged his authority, since the man's moderation, taken in conjunction with his sympathy for the unfortunate, proved generally attractive. [5] Since from that time on our city has asseverated its claim to leadership in Sicily, let us not besmirch the good name of our ancestors nor show ourselves brutish and implacable in the face of human misfortune. It is not fitting to give envy the opportunity to say of us that we are making unworthy use of our good fortune: best is to have those who will both share our grief when Fortune turns against us and also delight in our successes. [6] Advantages won by force of arms are often determined by chance and opportunity; but continuing moderation amid success is a peculiar sign of good character in the prosperous. So do not begrudge our country the opportunity for worldwide acclaim after excelling the Athenians not just in combat but also in humanity. [7] They, who take pride in their superiority to all others when it comes to the exercise of mercy, will manifestly

---

22. For Cyrus the Great (c. 580–530), and especially his conquest of Croesus, see Briant, ch. 1, and Kuhrt, 656–661, before venturing on to Book 1 of Herodotus.

then have received every consideration consonant with our civilized attitude; and as the first to raise an altar to Compassion,[23] they will find that same quality here in Syracuse. [8] From these considerations it will be clear to all that they met with a well-merited defeat and that we deserved our success—if, that is, they strove to wrong the kind of men who treated even their enemies with generosity, whereas we defeated the kind of men who ventured to plot aggression against those who spare compassion for even their worst enemies. Thus the Athenians would not only incur condemnation from all other nations but would also condemn themselves for having undertaken to wrong such men.

23. "Men of Syracuse, it is an excellent thing to make the first move in establishing a friendship, and by showing the unfortunate some compassion, to heal existing differences.

Goodwill towards friends must be kept eternally alive, whereas hatred for opponents should be allowed to perish, since thus it will happen that allies will multiply but enemies will decrease in number. [2] To nurse a quarrel eternally, and bequeath it to one's children's children, is neither generous nor prudent, since sometimes those who appear more powerful become, through a sudden turn of Fortune, weaker than their former subjects. [3] One testament to this is the war that has just ended: the men who came here to besiege us, and through their superior strength walled off our city, have now, as you see, through a change in Fortune become our captives. It is, then, an excellent thing to display lenience amidst the misfortunes of others, since we thus secure a ready fund of compassion from everyone should some human ill befall us. Countless indeed are the unforeseeable occurrences that life contains—civil insurrections, brigandage, wars, situations in which it is no easy matter for a mere mortal to stay out of danger. [4] Thus, if we cut off all compassion for the vanquished, we shall be establishing for future ages a bitter ruling against ourselves. It will be impossible for those who have used others ruthlessly ever to expect civilized treatment themselves; or for those guilty of such outrageous acts ever to be dealt with generously; or indeed for those who have—in violation of Greek custom—murdered so many fellow-[Greeks]

---

23. This altar, in the agora, was seen by the 2nd-century CE travel writer Pausanias (1.17.1), who also commented on the Athenian pietistic tendency to erect other such altars to abstractions. Athens' tradition as a refuge for the oppressed went back a long way (see, e.g., Soph. *OC* 260–263) and may have originally been based on the tradition that, alone of Mycenaean strongholds, Athens held out uncaptured at the onset of the Dark Age (c. 1100–800).

to appeal, when upset by life's reversals, to the common usages of mankind. [5] What Greek ever presumed that those who surrender themselves out of trust in the civilized attitude of their conquerors deserve unremitting punishment? Who has ever rated compassion as a lesser force than savagery, or prudence lesser than headstrong impulsiveness?

24. "We all extend ourselves to the uttermost against our foes in the battle line but go easy on those who have yielded to us: we wear down the aggression of the one but show pity for the misfortune of the other. Our fighting spirit is cut off short whenever a former enemy—now by a change of Fortune become a suppliant—stands ready to endure whatever suffering his conquerors may see fit to impose on him. [2] It is my impression that the spirits of civilized men are especially susceptible to compassion because of that common bond of sympathy inherent in our nature. During the Peloponnesian War the Athenians blockaded numerous Lacedaemonians on the island of Sphacteria and took them prisoner [<12.63.4]; yet they released them to the Spartans for ransom. [3] The Lacedaemonians too, after capturing many of the Athenians and their allies, dealt with them in much the same way. Both acted well in so doing; for hatred between Greeks should not outlast the moment of victory, nor retribution, the subjection of one's opponents. [4] To take that further step, and revenge oneself on a conquered foe who is appealing to the decency of his conqueror, is no longer a matter of punishing one's enemy but, far more, of offending against human weakness. [5] Against hard-heartedness such as this one might cite the sayings of wise men in past ages: *Man, be not proud,* and *Know thyself,* and *See how Fortune is mistress of all.*[24] What object did the ancestors of all the Hellenes have in prescribing that the trophies marking victories in wars should be built not of stone but from any wood handy? [6] Was it not to ensure that such memorials of enmity, being soon perishable, would swiftly disappear? In short, if you seek to perpetuate this quarrel for all time, be aware that you are disparaging human weakness: for a moment's decision, a minute shift in Fortune's balance, often humbles the arrogant.

25. "If, as is likely, you cease hostilities, what better opportunity will you ever find than the one now at hand to make your humane attitude to the

---

24. *Know thyself* was one of the Delphic maxims. Warnings against overreaching pride were a staple of Attic literature, especially drama: the specimen here cited forms part of an iambic trimeter: cf. Demosthenes (21.62), who, like Diodorus, cites a similar metrical aphorism in a prose passage. The notion of Fortune (*Tyche*) as all-powerful (29.4–6) emerges from the 4th century onwards in Middle and New Comedy.

prostrate a starting point for friendship? Do not suppose, either, that the Athenian people have become completely debilitated as a result of their Sicilian catastrophe, seeing that they control virtually all the islands of Greece, not to mention their hegemony over the coastal regions of both Europe and Asia. [2] On one previous occasion, indeed, when they had lost three hundred triremes, with their crews [<11.74–77], they still forced the Great King (despite his having to all appearances got the better of them) to accept the most ignominious treaty [<12.4.4–6]; and again, soon after Xerxes had leveled their city, they defeated him also, and secured the leadership of all Hellas [<11.19.4–6, 36.6–7]. [3] Their city, indeed, has a clever knack of achieving its most substantial advances in power concurrently with its greatest mishaps and of never formulating a humble policy. It would be no bad thing, therefore, to spare our Athenian prisoners and afterwards to have Athens as our ally instead of intensifying their resentment of us. [4] By putting these men to death, we shall merely be satisfying our passions; whereas if we keep them in detention, we shall earn their gratitude for treating them well and win universal approbation into the bargain.

26. "'Yes, but there *are* Greeks who have butchered their prisoners' [>30.6]. What of it? If such an act wins them praise, let us nevertheless rather imitate those who are more careful of their reputation; and if we are the first to find fault with them, let us not then ourselves commit the same crimes as they have openly confessed to. [2] As long as those who have entrusted their persons to our good faith suffer no irreversible penalty, it is the Athenian *demos* that will, quite rightly, continue to attract universal condemnation; but if word gets out that—in defiance of the common principles governing mankind—we have deprived these captives of their sworn protection, the world's accusations will then turn against us. Indeed, if the reputation of any city properly merits our respect, and our gratitude for benefactions to mankind, that city is Athens. [3] It was the Athenians who first introduced the Greeks to cultivated grain: though they had it as a gift from the gods for their own use, they made it available to all at need.[25] They it was also who discovered laws, by means of which the life of mankind advanced from a savage and unregulated state to that of a civilized and law-abiding society. They likewise were the first to spare the lives of those who sought refuge with them and by so doing ensured that their laws regarding suppliants would come into force worldwide. Since

---

25. Ironically, at 5.4.3–5, Diodorus lists the Athenians as the first to receive the gift of wheat from Demeter after the Sicilians.

they pioneered these laws, it would be unseemly to deprive them [of their protection].

"Thus far, then, to you all; but there are some among you in particular whom I shall now remind of the essentials of humane behavior.

27. "Those of you who have lived in that city, and had your share of the oratorical and educational training offered there, extend your compassion now to men who offer their native city as a school to the whole of mankind; and do you, all of you who have taken part in those most sacred Mysteries, now save those who initiated you—some as an expression of gratitude for favors already received; others, who look ahead to such, to ensure that anger does not rob you of that expectation? [2] Besides, what place is there to which foreigners may turn for a liberal education once Athens has been destroyed? Hatred for their offense will be ephemeral; but many and great are their accomplishments that should evoke goodwill.

"Further, quite apart from concern for [Athens as] a city, an investigation of individual prisoners might well find some deserving of compassion. The allies, for instance, being forcibly subject to the authority of their masters, joined the expedition under duress. [3] Thus, though it may be just to exact retribution from persons who offended by conscious choice, it would surely be fitting to regard as worthy of forgiveness those who err against their will. [In this connection] what can I say of Nicias, who from the very beginning proposed a policy in the best interests of Syracuse, who was the only man to oppose the Sicilian expedition, and who has always looked after the interests of Syracusans resident in Athens, serving indeed as their *proxenos*? [<12.57.2 and n. 87] [4] It would indeed be out of place for Nicias, who publicly espoused our cause in Athens, to be punished—getting no mercy in return for his goodwill towards us, but rather suffering implacable punishment on account of his public service to his country—while Alcibiades, who was instrumental in getting war declared against Syracuse, should escape punishment both from us and from the Athenians—and yet the man who is agreed to be the most humane Athenian of them all should not even meet with common compassion! [5] For my part, then, when I contemplate the change his life has undergone, I pity his lot. Previously, being one of the most distinguished of all Hellenes and in high repute because of his gentlemanly character, he was regarded as fortunate, and much admired, throughout the Greek world. [6] But now, hands tied behind him, in a filthy-looking tunic, he has experienced the miseries of captivity, as though Fortune wanted to demonstrate, in the life of this man, the full extent of her powers. The prosperity she gives we must needs bear with proper humanity and not display barbarous savagery in our dealings with those of our own race."

28. With these words Nicolaüs concluded his public address, in the course of which he had won the sympathy of his listeners. Gylippus the Laconian [<8.1–2], however, who still nursed an implacable hatred of Athenians, now mounted the speakers' platform and made this the opening theme of his speech.

[2] "I am greatly surprised, men of Syracuse, to see you, regarding matters in which you have endured such sufferings in truth and deed, so quickly talked around by mere words. To stave off ruin and desolation, you made your stand against the men who came bent on the destruction of your country. But if you now relax your ardor, what need for us, who have been in no way wronged, to exert ourselves? [3] I beg you, men of Syracuse, in the name of the gods, to pardon me for setting out my case bluntly: but being a Spartan, I have a Spartan's way of speaking. First, then, one might ask how Nicolaüs can tell you to pity the Athenians, who have rendered his old age so piteous through childlessness? How can he come before this assembly in mourning attire and declare with tears that you should show compassion to the murderers of his own children? [4] Anyone who forgets his nearest and dearest once they are dead, and chooses instead to save the lives of his deadliest enemies, is no longer a reasonably balanced individual. Tell me, how many of you assembled here had to mourn sons killed in the course of the war?" A good number of his listeners responded noisily, at which point Gylippus, cutting them short, exclaimed: [5] "Do you see these men, [Nicolaüs], whose outcry proclaims their misfortune? And how many of you seek in vain for brothers or kinsmen or friends you have lost?" At this a far greater number answered him. [6] Gylippus then went on: "Do you observe the great numbers of those who are suffering because of the Athenians? All of them, though they had done the Athenians no wrong, were deprived of their nearest flesh and blood, and the hatred they feel for the Athenians must surely match the love they bore their own kin.

29. "Men of Syracuse, how can it not be out of place if those who perished chose death voluntarily for your sake, and yet you do not on their behalf exact retribution even from your bitterest enemies? Or that while you praise those who laid down their lives for the sake of our common freedom, you regard it as more important to safeguard their murderers' lives than their own honor? [2] You passed a vote to adorn the tombs of the deceased at public expense;

yet what finer decoration will you find than the punishment of their slayers? Unless, by Zeus, you want to leave behind living trophies of the departed by enrolling them as citizens! [3] Oh, but they have changed their title: they are now enemies no longer, but *suppliants*. On what basis would this charitable concession have been granted them? Those who originally established the traditions concerning these matters laid down pity as the proper response to misfortune, but prescribed punishment in the case of wrongdoing dictated by plain wickedness. [4] So, in which category are we to put these prisoners? Among the unfortunate? But what Fortune was it compelled them, un-wronged and unprovoked, to make war on Syracuse, to throw away the peace that is cherished by all and appear here bent on the destruction of your city? [5] Therefore, let those who deliberately chose an unjust war bear its grim consequences with steadfast heart; and do not allow such men—who, had they triumphed, would have treated you with implacable savagery—now that they have failed of their purpose, to beg off from punishment by exploiting the generous compassion that greets an act of supplication. [6] If they stand convicted of having stumbled into their catastrophic setbacks through wick-edness and greed, let them not blame Fortune, nor summon up the word 'supplication' to their aid. That is reserved, in this world, for those who, while pure in heart, have suffered the inequities of Fortune. [7] But these men, whose lives are full of wrongdoing, have left themselves no place to which they can turn for pity and refuge.

30. "Is there any utterly shameful action they have not planned, any really horrible crime they have not perpetrated? It is a peculiar quality of greedy overreaching not to be satisfied with one's own good fortune but to covet what is distant and the property of others, which is precisely what these men did. Though they were the most prosperous of all the Hellenes, they bore their good fortune as though it were an irksome burden. Thus they con-ceived this passion for Sicily, sundered though it was from them by so great a stretch of sea: they dreamed of selling the inhabitants into slavery, of par-celing out the island in holdings for their own colonists. [2] It is an appall-ing thing to start a war without having suffered any prior wrong, yet this is what they did. Previously they had been your friends—and then, suddenly and without warning, they laid siege to Syracuse with this vast armada of theirs. [3] Arrogant men typically anticipate Fortune by decreeing punish-ments for [opponents] as yet unconquered: this also they did not fail to do. Indeed, before they ever invaded Sicily, they ratified a decree to sell the Syra-cusans and Selinuntines into slavery and to subject the rest [of the island's inhabitants] to tribute. When there coexist in the same men greedy ambition,

arrogance, and a taste for devious intrigue, who in his right mind would show them pity? [4] How, pray, did the Athenians treat the citizens of Mytilene? Once they had conquered them—even though the Mytilenaeans wished them no harm but merely sought their own freedom—they voted to butcher all men in the city [<12.55.8–10]: a most savage and barbarous act. [5] This crime, moreover, they committed against fellow-Greeks, against allies, against men who had frequently been their benefactors. So let them not now complain if, after acting in such a manner against others, they meet with much the same punishment themselves. It is, after all, only fair for someone attainted by a law he laid down for others to suffer in silence. [6] And what about the Melians [<12.80.5], whom they reduced by siege, afterwards killing all adult males? Not to mention the Scioneans [<12.76.3], whom—despite being their kinsmen—they subjected to the same fate as the Melians? Here we have two peoples who, after thus becoming the victims of Attic fury, were not left even with enough mourners to give the dead formal burial. [7] It was not Scythians who did such things, either, but the people who vaunt themselves as being preeminent in their humanity—yet by their decrees utterly annihilated these cities. Consider, then, how they would have acted had it been Syracuse that they sacked: men who deal so brutally with their own kin would have found a still heavier punishment for those with whom they had no such ties.

31. "Thus there is no just store of compassion laid up for them: any that might have existed for their own misfortunes they themselves have destroyed. Where can these men find a meritorious refuge? With the gods, whom they chose to strip of their ancestral honors? With humankind, whom they have approached only to enslave? Will they appeal to Demeter and Corê and their Mysteries after devastating their own holy island? [2] 'Yes, but it's not the Athenian people as a whole who are to blame—only Alcibiades, who proposed this expedition.' In fact, we shall find that, by and large, advisers hew very close to the wishes of their audience, so that in fact it is the voter who suggests to the speaker an argument germane to his own purpose. An orator is not the master of the many: quite the reverse. It is the *demos* that, by adopting excellent resolutions, accustoms the orator likewise to advocate what is best. [3] But if we pardon those guilty of irremediable crimes when they lay the responsibility on their advisers, what an easy and obvious defense we are offering to the wicked! Quite simply, nothing could be more unjust than the notion that, whereas in the case of benefactions it is not the advisers but the people who get the recipients' thanks, as regards injustices the blame should be passed on to the speakers.

[4] "Yet some have strayed so far from rational argument as to assert that

it is Alcibiades, who stands beyond the reach of our authority, who should be punished, whereas those prisoners now being brought to their well-merited deserts we should release, thus making it clear to all that the Syracusan people nurse no righteous wrath against wrongdoers. [5] But if it is really true that responsibility for the war lies with those who advocated it, let the masses blame the speakers for the upshot of their deception; but you will then be justified in seeking retribution from those same masses in respect of the wrongs that you suffered. In short, if [the Athenians] did what they did in clear knowledge that these were criminal acts, then on the basis of their intention they deserve punishment. Even if they began the war on a mere random impulse, not even so should they get off free: they must learn not to get in the habit of casual behavior in matters affecting the lives of others. It is in no way just that Athenian ignorance should bring destruction to Syracusans nor that in a case in which the act is irremediable, any kind of defense should be left open for the perpetrators.

32. "'Well, yes, but Nicias came out in public on the side of the Syracusans and was the only person who counseled against going to war.' What took place over there we know only by report, but what was done here we witnessed for ourselves. [2] He who spoke against the expedition there was its commander-in-chief here, while the staunch defender of Syracusans in debate also invested your city; and when Demosthenes and all the rest wanted to raise the siege, it was the man with so civilized and humane an attitude to you who alone compelled them to stay and continue the campaign. It is therefore my verdict that you should not attach greater importance to words than to deeds, to facts reported rather than to those actually experienced, to things unseen as against what has been seen by all.

[3] "'Well, yes, but it's a good thing not to make our enmity everlasting.' Fine: after the criminals have been punished, if you so decide, you can resolve your enmity in an appropriate manner. But it is not right that those who, after winning, treat their captives as slaves should, when vanquished, receive sympathy, as though they had done nothing wrong. Moreover, even though they are released from any obligation to make amends for their misdeeds, by means of specious arguments they will keep that friendship in mind only so long as it is to their advantage. [4] I will not stress the fact, also, that if you act thus, you will be doing an injustice to many, not least the Lacedaemonians, who for your benefit both renewed the war over there and sent you allied aid here—especially since they might well have decided to uphold the peace and look on while Sicily was being devastated. [5] It follows that if you release the prisoners and establish friendly relations [with Athens], those who

joined your alliance will regard you as traitors. Further, though you have it in your power to humble our common enemy, by freeing so great a number of soldiers you will render that enemy strong once more. Personally, I could never believe that the Athenians, having once got themselves involved in so deep-rooted an enmity, would maintain a friendship of this sort firm and unbroken: while they are still weak they will put on a show of goodwill, but when they are fully recovered, they will carry through their original resolve to completion. [6] I therefore, in the name of Zeus and all the gods, adjure you not to save the lives of your enemies, not to leave your allies in the lurch, not once again to put your country at risk. Men of Syracuse, if you let these men go, and trouble comes of it, it is you who will leave yourselves with not even the shreds of a decent defense."

33. After this speech from the Laconian, the majority had a change of heart and ratified Diocles' proposal [<19.4]. As a result, the generals and the allies were executed at once, while the Athenians were removed to the stone quarries.[26] Later, those of them who had had a higher education were spirited away by members of the younger generation[27] and so survived; but just about all the rest ended their lives in pitiable fashion while still suffering the indignities of their place of imprisonment [Thuc. 7.87.1–4; Plut. *Nic.* 29.1–3].

[2] After the termination of hostilities, Diocles revised the Syracusan law code [>35.1–5 and nn. 30–31], and a most strange reversal of fortune befell him as a result. He proved inflexible in the setting of penalties and very harsh in the punishment of offenders: among other laws he drafted one stating that if a man turned up in the marketplace carrying a weapon, the penalty was death, with no concession made for ignorance or any other [mitigating] circumstance. [3] So, at a time when enemies had been reported abroad in the countryside, he set out wearing a sword; but then sudden dissension

---

26. Thucydides (7.86.2) and Plutarch (*Nic.* 28.2) state that Gylippus argued for sparing the Athenian generals' lives so that he might enjoy the kudos of parading them in Sparta. (Diocles also in fact recommended selling off the allies rather than executing them: 19.4.) In any case, the Syracusans lost no time in executing them, partly at least since Nicias had been in contact with a pro-Athenian group in the city (Thuc. 7.86.4), and it was feared that he might reveal embarrassing information about this, particularly if interrogated under torture.

27. This probably refers to the famous tradition that the Syracusans had such a passion for the plays of Euripides (who appealed above all to the younger generation) that they offered special treatment to anyone who could recall verbatim passages from his dialogue or sing one of his choruses (Plut. *Nic.* 29). This was remarkable testimony to the continued dominance in the late 5th century of an oral over a written culture.

and uproar arose in the marketplace, and without thinking he hurried there, his sword still at his side. When some private citizen noticed this and remarked that he was breaking his own laws, he cried out: "Not so, by God: I shall maintain them still," and with that drew his sword and killed himself [<12.19.1–2].

Such, then, were the events that took place during the course of this year.

34. When Callias was archon in Athens [412/11], the Romans elected in lieu of consuls [Varr. 415] four military tribunes: Publius Cornelius [Cossus], <C. Valerius Volusi Potitus Volusus, Q. Quinctius Cicinnatus>, and Gaius [?] Fabius Vibulanus; and in Elis the 92nd Olympiad was held, in which Exaenetus of Acragas won the *stadion.* During their term, it came about that, after the collapse of the Athenians in Sicily, their pretensions to leadership were treated with contempt: [2] Chios, Samos, Byzantium, and many [more] of their allies at once [412/11] defected to the Lacedaemonians.[28] In consequence, the *demos,* in pessimistic mood, voluntarily abandoned their democracy [? May 411] and chose a body of four hundred to whom they turned over the day-to-day government of the state;[29] and the leaders of the oligarchy, after constructing a good number of triremes, sent forty of them to sea, with generals, [3] though these last were bitterly divided amongst themselves. They sailed to Oropus, however, where the enemy's triremes were moored, and in the battle that took place the Lacedaemonians were victorious, capturing twenty-two of their vessels [>36.2].

[4] Now that the Syracusans had brought their war with Athens to a close, they gave an honorable share of the booty to those Lacedaemonians

---

28. The Chians revolted now (Thuc. 8.14.2), largely at the instigation of Alcibiades. Byzantium (according to Thucydides: 8.80.2–3) did not do so until 411. In Samos a pro-Spartan oligarchic group briefly seized power but was quickly overcome by the *demos* (*IG* I³ 96.3–6; Thuc. 8.63.3): by the following year (38.3; Thuc. 8.25.1) the Athenian fleet had Samos as its base, and the island remained staunchly pro-Athenian until the end of the Peloponnesian War.

29. Seldom can Diodorus' weakness for ruthless compression at historically inappropriate moments have shown itself to worse effect than in his handling of the oligarchic revolution of the Four Hundred at Athens. Those interested should look at the full accounts of Arist. *Ath. Pol.* 29–33 (whose version of a voluntary change Diodorus is following) and Thuc. 8.65–70 (for whom the takeover was a conspiratorial coup). For background, see Hornblower 1991, 174–181 (short but punchy) and the detailed account in Kagan 1987, chs. 5–10 (pp. 106–273). The Four Hundred were overthrown after four months; the compromise government of the Five Thousand survived until July 410. Cf. also the more controversial account in Munn, 127–152.

who had fought in their alliance under the command of Gylippus; and they sent back with them to Lacedaemon [summer 412], as allies in the campaign there against the Athenians, a force of thirty-five triremes under the command of their most prominent citizen, Hermocrates [Thuc. 8.26.1]. [5] They themselves gathered up the spoils that fell to their lot as a result of the war, adorned their temples with offerings and captured arms, and honored with fitting gifts those soldiers who had distinguished themselves in combat. [6] It was now that Diocles—the populist leader who, of all such, had most influence among them—persuaded the *demos* to introduce a change of government, with state business in the hands of officials chosen by lot, and legislators appointed to organize the political structure and draft new laws on their own initiative.[30]

35. The Syracusans accordingly chose lawgivers from among their most intellectually distinguished citizens, the most manifestly outstanding of all being Diocles himself. Indeed, he so far surpassed his colleagues in understanding and reputation that though the drafting of this new legislation was a task they carried out together, the final code came to be known as "The Laws of Diocles."[31] [2] Not only did the Syracusans respect this man while he was alive, but after his death they accorded him heroic honors and built a temple [commemorating him] at public expense: the same one as was later demolished by Dionysius during the construction of the [new] city fortifications. Diocles was held in equally high regard among the other Sicilian Greeks: [3] indeed, many cities throughout the island went on using his laws until such time as all the Sicilian Greeks were granted Roman citizenship. Further legislation was enacted for the Syracusans by Cephalus in the time of Timoleon [c. 342: >16.82.6–7] and by Polydorus during King Hiero's reign [c. 271–216]; yet neither of these did they call a lawgiver but rather a "commentator on the lawgiver," since the original laws, being written in archaic idiom, were regarded as hard to understand. [4] His legislation is clearly the fruit of deep reflection. He reveals himself as implacably hostile to wrongdoers by

---

30. What Diocles also, and most importantly, did we know from Arist. *Pol.* 1304a 27: he and his colleagues changed the regime from a *politeia* (which operated with a limited franchise based on status and income) to a *demokratia* (full suffrage for all adult male citizens).

31. Diodorus both in what follows and at 33.2–3 confuses the radical Syracusan politician and reformer Diocles of 412 with a much earlier lawgiver of the same name (probably a Corinthian), whose statutes were composed in archaic language and who was the subject of the heroic Syracusan honors mentioned here.

setting harsher penalties against all offenders than any other legislator; as just, in that the penalty for each man is fixed, more than was done by any predecessor, according to his deserts; as both practical and greatly experienced, from his belief that every charge or dispute, be it public or private, merits a fixed penalty. He is also concise in his style and leaves his readers with much room for reflection. [5] Moreover, the curious circumstances of his death testify to his integrity and austerity of spirit. I have been impelled to set out these matters in some detail since most writers have devoted comparatively little space to him.

36. When the Athenians learned that their expeditionary force in Sicily had been annihilated, they took the sheer magnitude of the disaster very hard. Yet they did not on that account give up their passionate ambition for supremacy but rather began building more ships and securing funds to let them go on striving to be top power until all hope was spent. [2] They chose four hundred men whom they invested with independent authority to manage the conduct of the war, on the assumption that in such circumstances an oligarchy was better suited to this purpose than a democracy. [3] Events, however, did not turn out according to their prediction, and the Four Hundred ran the war far worse [than their predecessors]. They did send forty triremes to sea [? late summer 411], but they put in command two generals who were at loggerheads with one another; and though, with Athenian affairs at such a low point, the crisis called for complete unanimity, these generals persisted in their feuding. [4] In the end they did sail to Oropus, woefully unprepared, and fought a sea battle against Peloponnesian forces. They made a clumsy start in this engagement and made a very poor showing when it came to close combat, losing twenty-two ships and only barely getting the rest across to the safety of Eretria.[32]

[5] After these events had taken place, the Athenians' allies, because of the disasters in Sicily and the bad relations between the commanders, went over to the Lacedaemonians. Moreover, since Darius [II Ochus], the King of Persia, had an alliance with the Lacedaemonians,[33] Pharnabazus, who was

---

32. This passage and 34.2–3 are perhaps alternative versions of a final draft. The importance of Oropus, especially with Deceleia in Spartan hands (9.2; Thuc. 7.27–28), was that provisions could be routed through it from Euboea to Athens (Thuc. 7.28.1). But in Feb./Mar. 411 (Thuc. 8.60.1) the Boeotians captured Oropus (cf. 34.3). The failed effort by the 400 to retake it (Thuc. 8.94–95.5) was followed very soon (Thuc. 8.95.7) by the loss of Euboea; Eretria (apart from a fort held by Athens) had already gone over to Sparta.

33. There were three successive Persian treaties with the Lacedaemonians: (1) in summer 412, "with the King and Tissaphernes," Thuc. 8.18.1–3; (2) in the winter of 412/11, "with

military commander of the regions bordering on the sea, provided them with funds; he also sent [to Phoenicia] for the three hundred triremes that were being supplied by that country, intending [>37.4–5] to dispatch them to the Lacedaemonians by way of support.³⁴

37. Since such damaging reverses had befallen the Athenians simultaneously, everyone had taken it for granted that the war was over: no one expected that Athens could continue to withstand setbacks of this nature, for however short a period. But events did not turn out in a way that agreed with most people's assumptions. On the contrary, due to the superior quality of the combatants, the entire situation underwent a radical change. This is how it came about.

[2] Alcibiades, now a fugitive from Athens [<9.2], had for some time been on the Lacedaemonian side and had done them great service in the war; for he was a highly skilled speaker, far ahead of all other citizens in daring, and in birth and wealth first among the Athenians. [3] Now, since he longed to win a return to his native city, he contrived in every way he could to do the Athenians useful favors, in particular on those critical occasions when they seemed to be losing all along the line. [4] He enjoyed a friendly relationship with Darius' satrap <Tissaphernes>;³⁵ and when he saw that <Tissaphernes> intended to send three hundred ships to join the Lacedaemonian alliance, he dissuaded him from this project, making him see that it was not to the Great King's advantage to give the Lacedaemonians overmuch power, since that would not benefit the Persians. It would be better policy to remain unaligned with either side while they continued evenly matched and to encourage them to persist in their differences as long as possible [Plut. *Alcib.* 26.6–7; cf. Thuc. 8.87]. [5] As a result <Tissaphernes>, convinced that Alcibiades' advice was good, sent the fleet back to Phoenicia. So, on this occasion [Alcibiades] deprived the Lacedaemonians of a huge allied force; and some time later, when he had secured his return home and held a military command [408: >68.2 69.3], he defeated the Lacedaemonians in many battles and once more completely

---

King Darius and the King's sons and Tissaphernes," Thuc. 8.37.1–5; and (3) in late March 411 (?), "with Tissaphernes, Hieramenes and the sons of Pharnaces concerning the King's affairs," Thuc. 8.58.1–4, each a little more detailed than its predecessor.

34. He and Tissaphernes were serious rivals (Thuc. 8.6.1–2). Whether the Phoenician fleet of 300 warships actually existed is open to question. Thucydides (8.87.3; cf. Plut. *Alcib.* 25.3) reports 147 of them getting as far as Aspendus but no further. They certainly never reached the Aegean: Briant, 592–595.

35. From Thuc. 8.45–46 (and cf. Plut. *Alcib.* 24–25) it is clear that the satrap whom Alcibiades cultivated in this connection was not Pharnabazus, as in Diodorus' MSS, but Tissaphernes: I have emended the text accordingly.

restored the fallen fortunes of the Athenians. [6] But we will go into these matters more closely at the appropriate time, to avoid any unnatural anticipation of events in our narrative.

38. When the year had run its course, the archon in Athens was Theopompus [411/10], and the Romans elected [Varr. 414] in lieu of consuls four military tribunes: <P.> Postumius [Albinus Regillensis], <Cn.> Cornelius [Cossus], <L.> Valerius [Potitus], and <Q.> Fabius [Vibulanus]. About this time [c. Sept. 411] the Athenians ended the oligarchy of the Four Hundred and reconstituted the government from those who were <hoplites> [Arist. *Ath. Pol.* 33–34.1; Thuc. 8.97.1–3].[36] [2] The person who introduced all these [changes] was Theramenes,[37] a man of orderly lifestyle and with the reputation of excelling all the rest in intelligence of judgment. He was the sole advocate of bringing back Alcibiades, through whom the Athenians achieved their recovery; and since he sponsored many other measures for his country's good, he enjoyed no small degree of public esteem.

[3] These events, however, took place at a slightly later date. To carry on the war, the Athenians now appointed as generals Thrasyllus and Thrasybulus [Thuc. 8.76.2], who assembled the fleet at Samos and trained the troops in naval battle drill, making them carry out daily exercises. [4] Mindarus, the Lacedaemonian admiral, had for some while been holding station off Miletus, waiting for the aid from <Tissaphernes>; on hearing that those three hundred triremes had sailed in from Phoenicia he was full of high hopes, convinced that with so huge an armada he could destroy Athens' supremacy. [5] A little later, however, he found out from various people that [Tissaphernes] had been talked round by Alcibiades and had sent the fleet back to Phoenicia. He therefore abandoned the hopes he had had of <Tissaphernes> and proceeded

36. Reading Krueger's emendation *hoplitōn* ("hoplites," "infantrymen") for *politōn* ("citizens") of the MSS. This change was precipitated (as Diodorus does not make clear) by the defeat at Oropus (Thuc. 8.96–97.1): see above, 36.4 and n. 32. Nor was Theramenes the only person to vote for Alcibiades' recall: Thuc. 8.97.3. The supposed "government of the Five Thousand" was theoretically kept in place as a sop to the oligarchs until full democracy could be restored in 410.

37. Theramenes son of Hagnon (Pericles' friend and the founder in 437 of Amphipolis [12.68.1]) was an adroit politician known as "The Buskin" (a boot that could be worn on either foot) for his skill in switching allegiances (101.1–7). Having helped establish the Four Hundred, he soon took against their totalitarian habits and played a leading part in their overthrow. After distinguished service in the Aegean (49.3–51.8, 66.3–67.7), he opposed the establishment of the Thirty (14.3.6–7), was elected one of them (14.4.1), and was then executed for speaking out against them (14.4.5–5.5).

to act on his own. After fitting out both the ships sent him from the Peloponnese and those supplied from abroad by his allies, he dispatched Dorieus with thirteen ships to Rhodes, having learned that a revolution was being plotted there. [6] He himself took all the remaining vessels, eighty-three in number, and sailed for the Hellespont, since he had found out that the Athenian fleet was stationed at Samos [Thuc. 8.99]. [7] As soon as the Athenian commanders spotted them sailing by, they put out against them with sixty ships. But when the Lacedaemonians put in at Chios, the Athenians decided to sail on and requisition triremes from their allies on Lesbos, to avoid the risk of being outnumbered by the enemy fleet.

39. While they were thus occupied, the Lacedaemonian admiral Mindarus set out by night with his entire fleet and made with all speed for the Hellespont, arriving on the second day at Sigeium. When the Athenians [at Sestos] found they had been thus overtaken, they decided not to wait for all the triremes from their allies, but when only three had joined them, they went in pursuit of the Lacedaemonians. [2] On reaching Sigeium, they found the fleet had already left, except for three ships left behind, which they promptly captured. After this they sailed over to Elaeus and began to make preparations for a sea battle. [3] The Lacedaemonians, observing the enemy thus readying themselves for combat, likewise spent five days conducting trials and exercising their rowers. They then drew up their fleet, eighty-eight vessels strong, in battle formation, taking up a position on the Asian side [of the Hellespont]. The Athenians—fewer in number but better trained—faced them from the European side [Thuc. 8.104–105]. [4] The Lacedaemonians posted the Syracusans under Hermocrates on their right wing; the Peloponnesians themselves made up the left wing, with Mindarus as commander. On the Athenian side, Thrasyllus commanded the right wing and Thrasybulus, the left.[38] At first, both sides vied determinedly for a position in which they would not have the current against them. [5] Because of this they kept circling each other for a long time, attempting to block off the narrows and jockeying for an advantageous station; this was because the engagement took place between Sestos and Abydos, with the result that the current in the narrows handicapped [the combatants] to no small degree. This, however, was where the Athenian steersmen, with their far greater experience, helped substantially to bring victory about.

---

38. Thuc. 8.104.3 reverses these commands, with Thrasybulus on the right wing and Thrasyllus on the left.

40. Though the Peloponnesians held the advantage in the number of their ships and the fighting spirit of their marines, the professional skill of the Athenian steersmen rendered that advantage ineffectual. Whenever the Peloponnesian vessels charged swiftly en masse with the intention of ramming, [the steersmen] would maneuver their own ships so cleverly that [their opponents] could make contact with them at no other spot, but were forced to meet them head-on, ram against ram. [2] As a result of this, Mindarus, seeing that the rams, for all their striking power, were achieving nothing, ordered his ships to engage in small groups or individually. But this tactic likewise failed to neutralize the skill of the Athenian steersmen: neatly slipping by the oncoming rams of the [enemy] vessels, they then swung in at an angle and seriously damaged large numbers of them. [3] Both sides were in hot competition, so that they fought the engagement not only by means of ramming tactics but also by grappling ship to ship and slugging it out between marines. Though they were hindered by the force of the current from achieving any consistent success, they continued the battle for a considerable time, neither side being able to gain the victory. [4] While the issue was thus in the balance, there appeared, rounding a promontory, twenty-five ships dispatched to the Athenians from their allies.[39] The Peloponnesians, in some alarm, retreated towards Abydos, with the Athenians hard on their heels in hot pursuit.

[5] This was the end of the sea battle [summer 411]: the Athenians captured eight ships from the Chians; five from the Corinthians; two from the Ambraciots; and one each from the Syracusans, the Pellenians, and the Leucadians, while themselves losing five vessels, all of which, as it happened, were sunk. [6] Afterwards, Thrasybulus and his crew set up a trophy on that headland where the memorial of Hecuba stands and sent messengers to Athens with news of the victory [Thuc. 8.106.3–5].[40] They then put to sea with the entire fleet and

---

39. Thucydides' report has no mention of this opportune arrival of Athenian reinforcements, which does not necessarily mean that they were an invention (? stimulated by Alcibiades' similar intervention at Abydos: 46.2). The value of Diodorus' accounts of the sea battles during this period is that (like Aeschylus' description of Salamis in *The Persians*) they give a quarterdeck glimpse of the action rather than a strategic overview (Kagan 1987, 222). Polybius (12.25.1) concedes to Ephorus (whom, Diodorus cites in this context, 41.3) some skill in descriptions of naval warfare, and Diodorus' versions of the battles of Cynossema, Abydos (45.7–46.6), and Cyzicus (49.5–51.7) very probably draw on Ephorus' *Histories,* as well as the Oxyrhynchus Historian.

40. The battle of Cynossema ("The Bitch's Tomb," i.e., Hecuba's, in myth thus metamorphosed after the fall of Troy) was of huge importance for Athens, already cut off from imports via Euboea: had it been lost, the Athenians had no reserves to build another fleet and would quickly have been forced to surrender.

made for Cyzicus, since before the sea battle that city had defected to Darius'
general Pharnabazus and Clearchus, the Lacedaemonian commander. Finding
it unfortified, they easily attained their objective, and after extracting a cash
payment from the inhabitants, they sailed back to Sestos [Thuc. 8.107.1–2].

41. After his defeat the Lacedaemonian admiral Mindarus retreated to
Abydos, where he repaired those of his ships that had suffered damage. He
also sent Epicles the Spartan to the triremes located in Euboea, with orders
to fetch them over post haste. [2] When Epicles got there, he assembled the
ships, fifty in all, and hurriedly put to sea. But off Mt. Athos so huge a storm
arose that every ship went down, and of their crews only twelve men survived.
[3] These facts are set out on a dedication which, as Ephorus tells us, stands in
the temple at Coroneia and carries the following inscription:

> These from fifty vessels, escaping death
> brought their bodies ashore by Athos' reefs—
> twelve only; all others the sea's great gulf destroyed
> with their ships, hit by fearful gales.

[4] At about the same time, Alcibiades, in command of thirteen triremes,
reached the fleet stationed at Samos [Thuc. 8.108.1]. Those there had already
heard about his persuading <Tissaphernes> not to send the three hundred
[Phoenician] triremes as reinforcements for the Lacedaemonians. [5] Since he
got a friendly reception on Samos, he initiated discussions about the matter
of his return home, with many promises about how he could be of service to
his country. He also defended his own previous conduct, shedding many tears
over his personal misfortunes, in that he had been compelled by his enemies
to demonstrate his valor at the expense of his native city.[41]

42. Since the troops enthusiastically welcomed what he said, and reported it
all back to Athens, the *demos* voted to dismiss the charges outstanding against
him and to let him participate in the command. Observation of the practical
effects of his daring, coupled with his renown among the Greeks, led them
to assume, with probability, that if he joined them this would be no small
factor in the recovery of their position. [2] What was more, Theramenes—a
leading figure in the government of the day, who, if anyone, was seen as a

---

41. In Thucydides' account (8.81.1–82.1), this episode takes place earlier in the summer of 411, before the battle of Cynossema. Despite his endorsement by the democrats at
Samos, and latterly by the *demos* in Athens, Alcibiades shrewdly preferred to rack up some
victories before returning home (Plut. *Alcib.* 27.1).

man of good sense—advised the *demos* to recall Alcibiades. When news of these matters reached Samos, Alcibiades added nine ships to his own thirteen and took them to Halicarnassus. After getting a cash payment from that city, [3] he proceeded to sack Meropis [Cos] and then returned to Samos with a great deal of booty [Thuc. 8.108.1–2]. Since the accumulated spoils were so large, he divided the proceeds between the troops on Samos and his own men, thus very quickly ensuring that those who enjoyed his bounty would be well disposed towards him.

[4] About the same time, the citizens of Antandros, who were controlled by a garrison, sent to the Lacedaemonians asking for troops, with whose help they threw out their guards, thus making Antandros a free city. The reason they got help from the Lacedaemonians is that the latter were furious with <Tissaphernes> for sending the three hundred ships back to Phoenicia [Thuc. 8.108.3–5].

[5] Of the [historical] writers, Thucydides ended his history [during this year], having covered a period of twenty-two years in eight—or, as some divide it, nine—books: both Xenophon and Theopompus begin at the point where Thucydides leaves off. Xenophon covers a period of forty-eight years, while Theopompus deals with a seventeen-year segment of Greek history, bringing his narrative to a close, in twelve books, with the sea battle off Cnidos.[42]

[6] These, then, were the events that took place in Greece and Asia [Minor]. The Romans were at war with the Aequi and invaded their territory with a large force; after completely investing the city of Bolae, they reduced it by siege [415/4: Liv. 4.49.7–9].

43. When the events of this year had reached their conclusion, Glaucippus was archon in Athens [410/09], and in Rome the consuls elected [Varr. 413] were Marcus Cornelius [Cossus] and Lucius Furius [Medullinus]. About this time, in Sicily, the Egestans, who had become allies of the Athenians against Syracuse, had fallen into a state of acute panic once the war was over, since they anticipated (what seemed very probable) having to make retribution to the Sicilian Greeks for the wrongs committed against them. [2] Since the Selinuntines were at war with them over a territorial dispute, they voluntarily

---

42. Thucydides' unfinished text breaks off in mid-passage at 8.109, in the middle of Tissaphernes' response to the actions of the Antandrians. Xenophon's *Hellenica* takes over (leaving a gap of several months) and continues the narrative until the battle of Mantinea in 362 (15.85.1–88.4). Theopompus of Chios (378/7–c. 320), rhetorician and historian, likewise wrote a *Hellenica* but in greater detail (now lost), concluding in 394 with Conon's defeat of the Spartans (14.83.4–7) and the end of Sparta's postwar hegemony.

withdrew from the land in question, out of concern lest the Syracusans should use this excuse to join in the war on the side of Selinus, with the consequent risk of Egesta being utterly destroyed.[43] [3] The Selinuntines, however, then proceeded to cut themselves a large slice of adjacent land quite separate from the area in dispute; and at this point the Egestans dispatched ambassadors to Carthage, soliciting aid and placing their city in Carthaginian hands. [4] When those sent on this task arrived, and informed the council of the instructions their *demos* had given them, the Carthaginians were faced with a very real dilemma. While they were eager to acquire a city so advantageously placed for them, at the same time they stood in fear of the Syracusans, having just seen how they had annihilated Athens' expeditionary forces.[44] [5] However, when <Hannibal,> their most distinguished citizen, also <advised them>[45] to take over this city, they told the ambassadors in reply that they would come to their assistance; and to direct this undertaking, in case it should necessitate war, they appointed as general Hannibal himself, at the time their constitutional sovereign. He was the grandson of that Hamilcar who warred against Gelon and died at Himera [<11.21–22], and the son of Gescon, who because of his father's defeat had gone into exile and ended his days in Selinus [>59.5].

[6] Hannibal, being by nature a hater of Greeks, and at the same time eager to redeem the dishonors incurred by his ancestors, was zealous to achieve on his own something of value to his country. Seeing, then, that the Selinuntines were not satisfied by the cession of the disputed territory, he, together with the Egestans, sent ambassadors to the Syracusans, referring the decision in

---

43. The Egestans were not Greek but Elymian, and had always maintained close ties with their Phoenician neighbors. Thucydides (6.2.3), Strabo (13.1.53, C.608), and others give them a Trojan background. This is clearly mythical. Hellanicus (cited by Dion. Hal. *AR* 1.22) claims they were driven from South Italy by the Oenotrians, and recent work on graffiti and inscriptions confirms their Italian (possibly Ligurian) origin. Their differences with Selinus were centuries old· see, e.g., D.S. 5.9.2–3.

44. Carthage had remained carefully neutral at the time of the Athenian expedition, refusing solicitations from both Egesta (416: 12.82.7) and Athens (Thuc. 6.88.6). Egesta's renewed request in 410 created a problem for her. Do nothing, and Selinus (the ally of Syracuse) would eliminate Egesta and encourage Syracuse to attack Carthage's other allies in western Sicily. Move in, and there was a real danger of becoming embroiled in a dangerous war with Sicily's Greek states, perhaps even with those of South Italy. Athens' recent disastrous venture was fresh in everyone's mind. Yet (as the Athenians too had seen) the rewards of success promised to be considerable: for Carthage, the effective dominance of almost the entire western Mediterranean.

45. Lacunas in the Greek text plausibly filled by Vogel 1893 and Reiske, accepted by Oldfather 1950, 238 n. 1.

this matter to them. Though he claimed ostensibly to be seeing that justice was done, in actual fact he acted in the belief that when the Selinuntines refused to accept arbitration, the Syracusans would not join their alliance. [7] But since the Selinuntines too dispatched ambassadors who not only turned down the offer of arbitration but made lengthy speeches in reply to the ambassadors from Carthage and Egesta, in the end the Syracusans decided to vote to preserve both their alliance with Selinus and their peaceful relations with Carthage.[46]

44. After the return of their ambassadors, the Carthaginians sent over to the Egestans five thousand Libyans and eight hundred Campanians. [2] These [mercenaries] had been hired by the [Sicilian] Chalcidians for the Athenians in their war against Syracuse. After the [Athenian] defeat, they sailed back, but found no one to pay their wages. Now [summer 410] the Carthaginians bought horses for them all, advanced them substantial sums, and forwarded them to Egesta.

[3] The Selinuntines at this time were enjoying considerable success, with a heavily populated city, and regarded the Egestans with some contempt. At first—since they had a far better army—they raided the territory immediately beyond their frontier in battle order; but afterwards, scorning their opponents, they scattered all over the countryside. [4] The Egestan generals watched and waited and then attacked them, reinforced by the Carthaginians and Campanians. Since their onset was unexpected, they routed the Selinuntines without difficulty, killing about a thousand of their soldiers and capturing all their loot. After this battle, both sides at once dispatched ambassadors in search of aid, the Selinuntines to Syracuse and the Egestans to Carthage. [5] Both of these offered alliance, and in this way the Carthaginian War had its beginning. The Carthaginians, anticipating the extent of this war, made their general Hannibal responsible for determining the size of their forces and in every matter gave him more than willing assistance. [6] During the summer and the following winter [410/09], Hannibal signed up numerous mercenaries from Iberia, besides enlisting not a few from among the citizens; he also traveled through Libya, selecting the strongest men from every city, and began fitting out ships, with the intention of ferrying his forces across early [Apr. 409] that spring.

This, then, was the situation in Sicily.

---

46. Thus releasing Carthage to support Egesta against Selinus, a city with which (unlike Syracuse) the Carthaginians were not bound by any peace treaty.

45. In Greece Dorieus the Rhodian, the admiral in command of the triremes from Italy, once he had put down the disturbance on Rhodes, set sail for the Hellespont [Nov. 411].[47] He was eager to join Mindarus, who had stationed himself at Abydos and was collecting from every quarter ships belonging to the Peloponnesian alliance. [2] When Dorieus was already near Sigeium in the Troad, the Athenians at Sestos, having heard about his progress along the coast, put out against him with their entire fleet, some seventy-four ships in all [Xen. *Hell.* 1.1.2–8]. [3] For a while Dorieus held course, having no notion what was happening; but when he perceived the size of the [Athenian] fleet, he took fright, and seeing no other way of escape, sought refuge at Dardanos. [4] He disembarked his troops, took over the city garrison, and speedily fetched in a massive supply of missiles. He then divided his forces, stationing part on the prows [of the ships], and part in well-chosen positions ashore. [5] The Athenians came sailing in at full tilt and set about hauling the ships off; and since they outflanked and outnumbered their opponents all around, they [soon] began to wear them down. [6] As soon as the Peloponnesian admiral Mindarus heard about this, he at once put out to sea from Abydos with his entire fleet and set course for the Dardanian promontory, bringing eighty-four vessels to reinforce those under Dorieus. The ground forces of Pharnabazus were also in the vicinity, as support for the Lacedaemonians.

[7] When the two fleets approached each other, both sides ranged their triremes in battle order: Mindarus, with ninety-seven ships, posted the Syracusans on his left wing, while he himself commanded the right; on the Athenian side, Thrasybulus commanded the right wing and Thrasyllus, the other. [8] After they had disposed their forces in this manner, the commanders raised the signal for battle, and their trumpeters, at the one command, began to sound the attack; and since the rowers evinced no lack of enthusiasm, while the steersmen handled their helms most skillfully, the struggle that ensued was breathtaking. [9] Whenever the triremes surged forward to ram, then the steersmen, at just the right instant, would turn their ships at the precise angle to force a head-on collision. [10] Thus the marines, seeing their vessels borne broadside on towards the enemy's triremes, would be in high alarm and despair for their lives; but then, when the steersmen, through their seasoned

---

47. Dorieus, an aristocratic exile (c. 425) from his native Rhodes (Xen. *Hell.* 1.5.19), became a citizen of Thurii (12.9.1–10.7) and joined the Spartans during the Ionian-Decelean War with ten triremes (Thuc. 8.35.1). The "disturbance on Rhodes" (38.5) was an attempted democratic counterrevolution against Rhodes' secession from Athens (in which Dorieus had most likely been involved). His chief fame was as a pancratiast (see n. 10 to 14.5.7) who had notched up an impressive number of victories (Paus. 6.7.1–7).

expertise, would foil the attack, they would once more become cheerful and optimistic.

46. Nor did those men who had been posted on the decks fail to convert their eagerness into action. Some, from long range, shot arrow after arrow, until soon the air was full of missiles; others, every time they moved in close, would throw their javelins, aiming either at the defending marines or else at the steersmen themselves. Whenever ships collided, they would keep up the fight with their spears and then, at the moment of impact, would jump aboard the enemy's triremes and engage in hand-to-hand combat with swords. [2] At every setback the victors would start whooping and yelling, while the other side would be shouting as they charged to the rescue, so that over the entire battle scene a huge, confused uproar prevailed.

For a long time the battle hung in the balance because of the high degree of rivalry animating both sides; but somewhat later [towards evening: Plut. *Alcib.* 27.2–4] Alcibiades unexpectedly showed up from Samos with twenty ships, happening to be on a voyage to the Hellespont. [3] While these vessels were still far off, each side, hoping that it was for them that reinforcements had come, were buoyed up in their hopes and fought with even greater passion and daring. When the squadron drew close, however, no signal was displayed for the Lacedaemonians; instead, Alcibiades ran up a red ensign from his own ship for the Athenians, this being the signal he and they had arranged beforehand.[48] At this the Lacedaemonians, in some alarm, turned and fled; and the Athenians, elated by their advantage, pressed on in pursuit of the retreating vessels. [4] They quickly captured ten of them; but after this a storm and strong winds arose, which greatly hampered them in their pursuit. With the waves running so high, ships would not answer their helms, and ramming proved impracticable, since the [target] vessels were receding at the moment of impact. [5] The Lacedaemonians finally got to shore and took refuge with the land forces of Pharnabazus.[49] The Athenians at first tried to drag [their opponents'] vessels out to sea and fought savagely to this end; but they were

48. It would be clear from this alone that Alcibiades' welcome appearance during the Battle of Abydos was in fact far from fortuitous, and at Plut. *Alcib.* 27.2 we learn that he was acting on intelligence received; but he obviously showed up at the exact critical moment, and this could hardly have been planned.

49. Xenophon (*Hell.* 1.1.6) provides the vivid detail of Pharnabazus riding his horse out into the sea to encourage his troops. This also should remind us, yet again (cf., e.g., 36.5 and n. 34), that the Hellespontine satraps had no navies of their own but only the unreliable support of Phoenician or Egyptian squadrons.

cut up by Persian troops and so withdrew to Sestos. [6] This was because Pharnabazus, in his desire to rebut the charges the Lacedaemonians were making against him, attacked the Athenians with more than ordinary violence. At the same time, regarding the three hundred ships sent back to Phoenicia [<38.4–5], he informed them that he had done this on learning that the kings of Arabia and Egypt were hatching plots together against that country.

47. After the sea battle had ended in this manner, the Athenians, it being already dark, sailed off to Sestos; but when day dawned, they came back to pick up their wrecks and set up a second trophy beside the first one. [2] About the first watch of the night, Mindarus made for Abydos: here he repaired his damaged vessels and sent a request to the Lacedaemonians for both naval and infantry support, since he planned, while the fleet was being got ready, and with the help of Pharnabazus, to lay siege to such cities as were allied with the Athenians.

[3] The citizens of Chalcis, together with most of the other inhabitants of Euboea, had revolted from Athens, and because of this were extremely worried that, as islanders, they might be reduced by the Athenians, who had control of the seas. They therefore invited the Boeotians to join them in spanning the Euripus with a causeway, thus linking Euboea to Boeotia. [4] The Boeotians agreed, it being to their advantage too that Euboea should remain an island for all others but become mainland for them. All the cities then embarked energetically, vying one with another, on the building of this mole, since it was not only all citizens who were required to turn out but also the resident foreigners. Thus, by reason of the great number who presented themselves for work, the undertaking was very soon completed. [5] On the Euboean side the mole was lined up in the direction of Chalcis, and in Boeotia towards Aulis, since it was here that the gap was narrowest. As it happened, there had always been a tidal current at that point, with the sea regularly reversing its flow; and now the force of the current became greatly intensified, since the sea was forced into an excessively narrow channel, with clear passage left for one vessel only. They also built high towers at the end of each arm [of the mole] and set up wooden bridges across the channel.[50]

[6] Theramenes, who had been sent out by the Athenians with thirty ships,

50. In antiquity the Euripus was c. 200 ft. across (Strab. 9.2.2, C.400); it has since been widened somewhat and generally (for reasons Diodorus makes clear) bridged rather than causewayed. It was only in 1962 (as older travelers will recall) that the charming 19th-century iron swing-bridge was modernized. What Diodorus describes is something like a miniature version of Tower Bridge on the Thames in London. The wooden bridges (prob-

at first endeavored to hinder those engaged on these works, but since the mole-builders were protected by a strong military guard, he gave up that idea and instead set course for the islands. [7] Being anxious to afford both [Athenian] citizens and their allies relief from the levies they paid, he went ravaging enemy territory and amassed considerable spoils. He also went around the cities of the allies and extracted cash payments from any persons in them promoting revolution. [8] When he touched at Paros, he found an oligarchy [established] in the city: he thereupon restored freedom to the people, and on those who been involved with the oligarchy, he imposed heavy fines.[51]

48. About this same time it so happened that violent civil dissension, with some butchery, took place on Corcyra. Several reasons have been alleged for this, but above all the rancorous mutual hatred that existed between its inhabitants.[52] [2] Never in any other city did so great a slaughter of citizens occur, nor sharper strife and contentiousness leading to such destruction. Before this particular conflict, indeed, the number of those killed by their own fellows had already, it would seem, reached about 1,500, and every one of them was a prominent citizen. [3] Despite these previous misfortunes, however, Fortune laid yet another calamity on them, by once more heightening the differences that divided them. The Corcyraeans of the highest rank, being bent on introducing an oligarchy, were in sympathy with the Lacedaemonian cause, whereas the radical masses were all for an Athenian alliance. [4] Indeed, the peoples now struggling for the leadership embraced quite different principles: the Lacedaemonians made the most prominent citizens in the cities allied to them responsible for the conduct of public affairs, whereas the Athenians established democracies in such cities. [5] The Corcyraeans, then, seeing their most powerful citizens in the mood to hand their city over to the Lacedaemonians, sent word to the Athenians requesting a body of troops as a protective garrison. [6] Conon, the Athenian general, sailed to Corcyra and left there six hundred of the Messenians from Naupactus; he himself coasted on with

---

ably bascules) spanned the narrow central channel and could be raised from the towers, by rope or counterbalance, to let traffic through.

51. It is clear from this paragraph (a) that those "promoting revolution" (*neōterizontas*) were doing so on behalf of the oligarchs and (b) that though the Five Thousand were still the official government of Athens, Theramenes and those who thought like him were busy laying the ground for a return to full democracy.

52. The most notorious instance of this had occurred in 428/7 and forms the basis of Thucydides' disquisition on civil war (3.70–83). Diodorus is our sole source for the later outbreak.

his ships and anchored close to the precinct of Hera. [7] The six hundred, together with the [local] populists, made a sudden attack on the Lacedaemonians' supporters when the market had filled up, arresting some, killing others, and driving more than a thousand into exile. They also freed the slaves and enfranchised the resident aliens, as a countermeasure against the numbers and influence of those who had fled the country. [8] The latter had sought refuge on the mainland opposite; and after a few days, certain persons in the city who supported the exiles' cause took over the marketplace, recalled the exiles, and launched an all-out struggle to settle this matter once and for all. When darkness fell and the fighting broke off, they came to an agreement with each other, abandoned their cutthroat rivalry, and thenceforward shared their native city as a single people.

Such was the conclusion of the massacre on Corcyra.

49. King Archelaus of Macedon, finding that the citizens of Pydna would not submit to his authority, brought up a strong force and put their city under siege. He received assistance also from Theramenes, with his fleet; but after the siege had gone on for some while, the latter sailed on to Thrace to join Thrasybulus, the commander-in-chief of the entire expeditionary force. [2] Archelaus now continued the siege of Pydna with increased determination, and when he finally reduced the city, removed it some twenty *stadioi* [between two and three miles] inland.

Winter now being nearly over,[53] Mindarus began assembling his triremes from all quarters, including many from the Peloponnese as well as from other allies. When the Athenian generals in Sestos discovered the size of the fleet being put together by the enemy, they were highly worried by the possibility of an attack in strength that might capture their ships. [3] They therefore hauled down the vessels they had ashore at Sestos, cruised round the Chersonese, and dropped anchor at Cardia. From here they sent triremes to Thrasybulus and Theramenes in Thrace, requesting them to bring their fleet there as speedily as possible; they also summoned Alcibiades from Lesbos[54] with such ships

53. By Diodorus' reckoning, the winter of 410/09, but in fact that of 411/10: as often during this period, Diodorus is a year ahead of events when dealing with events in Greece and Asia Minor. The battle of Abydos, like that of Cynossema, was fought in 411; that of Cyzicus (49.2–51) took place in March or April of 410, still in Theopompus' archon year.

54. Diodorus' account completely ignores the fact that Alcibiades, after Abydos, had gone to Tissaphernes, hoping to ingratiate himself further; but that Tissaphernes—whom the Spartans (encouraged by his rival Pharnabazus) had been calumniating to the Great

as he had. The entire armada thus converged on one spot, the commanders being eager for a finally decisive engagement [Xen. *Hell.* 1.1.11–18; Plut. *Alcib.* 28.1–6].[55]

[4] Meanwhile, Mindarus, the Lacedaemonian admiral, sailed to Cyzicus, put his entire force ashore, and invested the city. Pharnabazus also appeared there with a large army, and the two of them together laid siege to Cyzicus and took it by storm [Xen. *Hell.* 1.1.14].

[5] The Athenian generals took the decision to sail to Cyzicus, stood out to sea with their entire fleet, and sailed round the Chersonese [into the Hellespont]. Their first landfall was at Eleus; but after that they were careful to sail past Abydos at night, to avoid revealing the great number of their ships to the enemy. [6] When they reached Proconnesus, they bivouacked there for the night; next day they disembarked the troops they had transported on Cyzicene territory, with orders to Chaereas, their commander, to lead his army against the city.

50. The generals meanwhile divided the fleet into three squadrons, of which Alcibiades commanded one; Theramenes, another; and Thrasybulus, the third. Alcibiades and his squadron sailed well ahead of the others, with the intention of provoking the Lacedaemonians into a battle, while Theramenes and Thrasybulus planned to [outflank and] encircle the enemy and cut off their retreat to the city once they had sailed out. [2] Mindarus, seeing only the twenty ships of Alcibiades bearing down on him, and knowing nothing of the rest, regarded them with contempt and boldly set out against them from the city with a fleet eighty strong. When he got close to Alcibiades' squadron, the Athenians, as they had been instructed, feigned flight, and the Peloponnesians, in great excitement, followed hard after them, convinced they were winning. [3] But when Alcibiades had drawn them on a good way further from the city, he gave the signal, and instantly, at one and the same time, his own triremes went about to confront the enemy, and Theramenes and Thrasyb-

King, inter alia blaming him for Athens' dangerous naval recovery in the Hellespont—far from welcoming the charming but notorious turncoat, unceremoniously jailed him at Sardis. A month later, Alcibiades either escaped or bribed his way out and fled to Lesbos via Clazomenae; but his vaunted "influence" with Tissaphernes was now exposed as, at best, obsolete. See Plut. *Alcib.* 27.4–28.1; Xen. *Hell.* 1.1.9–10.

55. On the battle of Cyzicus, Diodorus' account has come, rightly, to be seen as the most convincing. It, and other minor references agreeing with it (e.g., Front. 2.5.54 and Polyaen. 1.40.9) almost certainly derive from the Oxyrhynchus Historian. Xenophon's account differs in essential details and seems designed throughout to glorify Alcibiades, who in fact was Thrasybulus' subordinate (50.7).

ulus sailed towards the city and cut off the Lacedaemonians' line of retreat.
[4] Mindarus and his officers, now aware of the great size of the enemy fleet,
and realizing that they had been outgeneraled, became considerably alarmed.
In the end, with Athenians appearing from all directions, and the Peloponnesians' way back to the city already barred, Mindarus was forced to seek refuge ashore at the place known as Cleri, which was where Pharnabazus and his
army were stationed. [5] Alcibiades pursued him energetically, sank some of his
ships, and disabled and captured others; most of them had been moored along
the shore, and these he seized, throwing out grappling irons on to them and
attempting by means of these to drag them clear of land. [6] When the ground
forces from ashore came to the aid of the Peloponnesians, a great slaughter took
place: the Athenians, because of the edge they held, were fighting with greater
daring than was prudent, while the Peloponnesians had a great advantage in
numbers, since Pharnabazus' army was backing up the Lacedaemonians and
fighting from the land, which gave its position greater security. [7] Thrasybulus, seeing these ground troops assisting the enemy, disembarked the rest of his
own marines, with the intention of providing relief for Alcibiades; he also sent
word to Theramenes to link up with Chaereas and his infantry and come with
all speed, to continue the fight on land.

51. While the Athenians were thus occupied, Mindarus the Lacedaemonian commander was engaged in a struggle with Alcibiades for the ships that
were being dragged off, and dispatched Clearchus the Spartan with part of
the Peloponnesian contingent, as well as the mercenary corps from Pharnabazus' army, against the troops under Thrasybulus. [2] Thrasybulus, with
the marines and archers, at first put up a vigorous defense against the enemy;
but though he inflicted heavy casualties on them, he saw not a few of his own
men fall as well. However, just when the mercenaries serving Pharnabazus
had the Athenians encircled, and were crowding in on them from all sides,
Theramenes showed up, bringing both his own troops and Chaereas' infantry. [3] Though Thrasybulus' troops were exhausted and had given up hope of
rescue, their spirits suddenly soared once more with the arrival of such powerful reinforcements. [4] A long and hard-fought battle ensued. First, Pharnabazus' mercenaries began to retreat, so that the continuity of their battle line
was broken; and finally, the Peloponnesians left behind with Clearchus, after
both inflicting and suffering heavy casualties, were forced out.
[5] Once these were overcome, Theramenes and his men hurried to relieve Alcibiades' embattled troops. Even when their forces were combined,
however, Mindarus did not let Theramenes' attack trouble him. He simply
divided the Peloponnesians and used half of them to hold this advance; with

the remaining half, which he commanded in person, he drew up his battle line against Alcibiades' troops, adjuring each of his own soldiers not to bring Sparta's renown into disrepute—and in an infantry battle, at that. [6] He put up a heroic struggle for the ships, fighting in the very forefront of the battle, but though he slew many of his opponents, in the end he was cut down by Alcibiades' men as he contended honorably for his fatherland. When he fell, the Peloponnesians and all the allies flocked together and broke into panic-stricken flight. [7] The Athenians pursued their enemies for a while, but on learning that Pharnabazus was approaching at great speed with a large cavalry force, they changed direction and made for the ships. They secured the city and then set up two trophies, one for each victory: the first, on the island known as Polydorus, for the sea battle, and the second for the infantry engagement, at the spot where they first turned the enemy to flight. [8] Both the Peloponnesians in the city and all survivors from the battle fled to Pharnabazus' camp; and the Athenian generals, having simultaneously vanquished two such substantial forces, captured all their ships, besides rounding up numerous prisoners and an incalculable amount of booty.[56]

52. When word of this victory [Mar./Apr. 410] reached Athens, the people, faced with the good fortune that had befallen the city on the heels of earlier disasters, were exultant over their successes, and all together made sacrifice to the gods and held various festivities. They also selected for the campaign a thousand of their most physically robust hoplites, together with a hundred cavalry; in addition to these they sent out thirty triremes to Alcibiades and his force, so that now they had the mastery at sea, they might with impunity despoil those cities that supported the Lacedaemonians. [2] The Lacedaemonians themselves, however, when they heard about the disaster that had befallen them at Cyzicus, sent ambassadors to Athens to negotiate for peace, their ambassador-in-chief being Endius. On being granted permission, he came forward and spoke in a succinct, "laconic" manner: this is why I decided not to omit his speech just as it was delivered:[57]

---

56. The victory at Cyzicus gave Athens back dominance in the Aegean, recovered control of the vital supply line via Euboea and Oropus, made victory once again look possible, and dealt a severe blow to Spartan morale. A captured Spartan dispatch reporting the defeat (Xen. *Hell.* 1.1.23; Plut. *Alcib.* 28.6) consisted of the stark laconic message: "Ships lost. Mindarus dead. Men starving. At a loss what to do."

57. Cf. Just. 5.4.4 and Nep. *Alcib.* 5.5. The philo-Laconian Xenophon tactfully makes no mention of this (unsuccessful) approach. Despite Diodorus' assurances, it is very unlikely that Endius' speech is a direct report, though its contents are plausible. Endius

[3] "Men of Athens, we want to make peace with you, [on these terms]: that each of us keep what cities we now possess; that the strongholds we maintain in one another's territories be abandoned; and that our prisoners of war be ransomed by exchange, one Laconian for one Athenian. We are not unaware that this war is harmful to us both, though far more so to you. [4] Don't bother with my arguments, though: just look at the facts. We have the whole of the Peloponnese to cultivate, but you, [now], only a small part of Attica [<9.2]. The war has brought us Laconians many allies, but from you Athenians it has taken as many as it has presented to your enemies.[58] We have the wealthiest of all monarchs in the known world to meet our expenses in this war [<36.5], whereas you are dependent on its most indigent inhabitants. [5] Thus our troops, in view of their ample pay, serve with enthusiasm; whereas yours, who have to meet war taxes from their own resources, have no stomach either for the hardships of war or for its high costs. [6] Furthermore, when we carry on the war at sea, the only state resources we risk losing are hulls, while most of the personnel you have aboard are citizens.[59] Most important of all, even if we are defeated in a naval campaign, we still retain our acknowledged supremacy on land, since a Spartan infantryman doesn't even know what flight means. But once <you're driven>[60] from the sea, it's not for supremacy that you contend on land but to stave off destruction.

[7] "It remains for me to show you why, when we have so many substantial advantages in this war, we still call on you to make peace. I'm not saying that Sparta is benefiting from hostilities, simply that she's suffering less damage than Athens. Only madmen would feel good about sharing their enemy's misfortunes when it was open to them to have no experience of misfortune whatsoever. Destruction of the enemy brings no joy so great that it can match the wretchedness of one's own people. [8] Nor are these the only reasons why we wish to come to terms with you: it is also because we cherish our ancestral customs. When we contemplate the bitter rivalries inherent in warfare, and the varieties of awful suffering to which they give rise, we feel we should make it clear to all, to both gods and mortals, that of all men we are least to blame for such things."

---

himself was an old friend of Alcibiades and had served on such missions before (Thuc. 5.44.3, 8.6.3).

58. E.g., Miletus, Rhodes, Chios, Ephesus, Thasos, and, above all, Euboea.

59. A tantalizing remark: who in fact *did* crew the Lacedaemonian triremes? Helots? Messenians? Hired rowers?

60. A participle has clearly fallen out of the Greek here, as Vogel saw: the verb must be "driven out" or the equivalent. I translate Reiske's *ekblēthentes.*

53. After the Laconian had advanced these and other similar arguments, the most reasonable-minded among the Athenians were leaning in their opinions towards the idea of peace; but the habitual warmongers, who made a practice of turning civic disturbances to their own profit, rather chose war. [2] One adherent of this attitude was Cleophon, the most prominent populist leader of the day.[61] He now came forward and addressed the issue at length in his own peculiar manner. By stressing the magnitude of their [recent military] successes—as though Fortune were not in the habit of handing out prizes for primacy to all sides in turn—he whipped up public excitement. [3] So the Athenians were talked into a flawed decision of which they repented too late for any good it might do them, and they were deceived by mere flattery into so thoroughgoing a blunder that never thereafter at any time could they really recover from its effects. [4] These events, which took place somewhat later, however, will be discussed in the period to which they belong. At the time, the Athenians—being elated by their successes and cherishing many grandiose hopes because of having Alcibiades as their commander-in-chief—imagined they had already recovered their supremacy.

54. When the events of this year reached their conclusion, in Athens Diocles took over as archon [409/08], while in Rome [Varr. 412] the consulship was held by Quintus Fabius [Ambustus Vibulanus] and Gaius Furius [Pacilus]. About this time [spring 409] Hannibal, the Carthaginian general, assembled the Iberian mercenaries he had hired, together with the soldiers he had recruited in Libya [<44.4–6], manned sixty warships, and also got ready some 1,500 transports. [2] On to these he loaded troops, siege equipment, missiles, and all the rest of his stores. After crossing the Libyan Sea with his fleet, he made landfall in Sicily at the promontory called Lilybaeum, directly opposite Libya. [3] At the time, some Selinuntine cavalrymen were on patrol in the area, and on observing the great size of the fleet putting in to shore, with all speed reported the presence of hostile forces to their fellow-citizens. The Selinuntines at once sent off dispatch riders to Syracuse, with a request for help. [4] Hannibal meanwhile disembarked his troops and set up a camp, beginning at the well to which, at the time, the name "Lilybaeum" was attached (even when, many years later, a city was founded nearby, it was the well

---

61. Cleophon son of Cleïppides, reputedly a lyre maker, introduced some kind of (much-debated) two-obol dole in 410, the *diobelia*. He persisted in opposing peace after both Arginusae in 406 (Arist. *Ath. Pol.* 34.1), when he spoke in the Assembly drunk and wearing a breastplate, and the final defeat at Aegospotami a year later (Lys. 13.8). He was executed in 404. Diodorus, despite the promise of 53.4, never refers to him again.

that gave the city its name). [5] Hannibal's total forces, according to Ephorus, consisted of 200,000 infantry and 4,000 cavalry; but Timaeus reckons he had not much over 100,000 men all told.[62] Every one of his ships he hauled ashore in the bay of Motya, being anxious to give the Syracusans the impression that he had not come there to make war on them or even to sail round the coast with his fleet to Syracuse. [6] After adding to his forces troops from Egesta and his other allies, he struck camp and marched from Lilybaeum towards Selinus. When he arrived at the Mazarus River, he found a trading station on its bank, which he took without any trouble. On reaching Selinus, he divided his army into two corps, after which he invested the city, brought up his siege engines, and began an energetic assault. [7] He set up six towers of remarkable height and brought forward the same number of iron-shod battering rams against the walls; in addition to these, he used great numbers of archers and slingers to drive back the combatants on the battlements.

55. The Selinuntines had for a long while now lacked experience of sieges; they had also been the only Sicilian Greeks to fight on the Carthaginian side in the war against Gelon and had never expected to be so terrorized by those whom they had befriended. [2] But when they contemplated the size of the siege engines, and the vast numbers of the enemy, they became exceedingly afraid and were dumbfounded by the magnitude of the danger facing them. [3] They did not, however, entirely give up hope of rescue. In the expectation that they would shortly get relief from the Syracusans and their other allies, they turned out in force to drive back the enemy from their walls. [4] All the men of military age were under arms and engaged in the struggle, while their elders took care of supplies for them, and as they went around the wall begged the young not to let them fall into the hands of the enemy. Women and children too kept bringing food and missiles to those fighting for their fatherland, paying no heed to the decent modesty they observed in peacetime. [5] Such was the degree of panic that the magnitude of the crisis required the assistance even of women.

Hannibal, who had promised his soldiers that he would give them the city to plunder, advanced his siege engines and attacked the walls with successive

---

62. Even Timaeus' estimate, based on Xen. *Hell.* 1.1.37, looks suspiciously high. See 16.77.4 (cf. Plut. *Tim.* 25.1), where against Timoleon the Carthaginians reportedly put 80,000 men into the field (even this may be an exaggerated figure to enhance the triumph of Timoleon). More realistic is Diodorus' estimate at 23.8, where Hanno in 262/1 faced two Roman consular armies (Polyb. 1.17.6) with 56,000 men. It would be surprising if Hannibal's force numbered even 50,000.

relays of his best troops. [6] The trumpets all together sounded the attack, and at the one word of command the entire Carthaginian host raised the battle yell: the walls shook under the onslaught of the rams, while the height of the towers enabled the fighters stationed on them to kill large numbers of the Selinuntines. [7] Because of the long years of peace they had lived through, the latter had not paid the slightest attention even to their walls and so were easily overcome, since the wooden towers stood far higher. When the wall collapsed, the Campanians, in their zeal to accomplish some outstanding deed, quickly plunged into the city. [8] At first they terrified the few defenders there to resist them; but very soon, when large numbers hurried to the rescue, they were driven back out, with heavy losses: for since they had forced their way in before the wall had been completely cleared off, and during their assault had been blocked by difficult ground, they were easily overcome. When night fell, the Carthaginians called off their attack.

56. The Selinuntines selected their best horsemen and sent them off at once, under cover of darkness, some to Acragas, others to Gela and Syracuse, asking for immediate help, since their city could not hold out against this powerful foe much longer. [2] The Acragantines and the men of Gela were waiting for the Syracusans, since they wanted to lead a united force against the Carthaginians. The Syracusans, when they heard about the siege, broke off the war they were conducting against the Chalcidians and then began at a leisurely pace to round up troops from the countryside and make elaborate preparations, convinced that while Selinus might [eventually] be reduced by siege, it would not be taken by storm.

[3] When the night was over, Hannibal at dawn launched attacks from every quarter, and the part of the city wall that had already collapsed, together with the stretch adjacent to it, he demolished with his siege engines. [4] He then cleared away the rubble where the wall had fallen, and pushing the assault forward with relays of his best troops, gradually forced the Selinuntines out. Even so, it was not possible simply to overpower men who were fighting for their very existence. [5] Many were killed on both sides; but fresh troops kept taking over the brunt of the battle for the Carthaginians, whereas the Selinuntines had none to relieve them. The siege went on for nine days, with unsurpassed obduracy, the Carthaginians both inflicting and suffering the most fearful injuries. [6] When the Iberians swarmed up over the breach in the wall, the women on the rooftops cried out, and the Selinuntines, thinking the city was being taken, in high alarm abandoned the walls and packed the entrances to the narrow alleys. This attempt to barricade the streets held off the enemy for a considerable time. [7] As the Carthaginians forced their

way forward, the bulk of the women and children fled to the housetops, from where they hurled stones and roof tiles down on the enemy. For a long while the Carthaginians had a rough time of it. Because of the house walls they could not surround the men in the alleys, and because of the missiles coming at them from the rooftops they could not decide the issue on equal terms. [8] As the struggle dragged on till late afternoon, however, the fighters on the rooftops ran out of missiles, while on the Carthaginian side, hard-pressed troops were regularly relieved, and their replacements carried on the struggle with fresh energy. Finally, since the defending force continued to be reduced in numbers, and more and more of the enemy came crowding into the city, the Selinuntines were forced to abandon the alleys.

57. So, all the time the city was being taken, tears and lamentation could be observed among the Greeks, but on the barbarian side, loud war cries and confused shouting. The former, as they witnessed the enormity of the disaster that had engulfed them, were consumed with fear, while the latter, elated by success, were urging each other on to a killing spree. [2] The Selinuntines now converged on the marketplace, and those who made a stand there were slaughtered to the last man. The *barbaroi* spread throughout the city and plundered the houses of their valuables. Any occupants they found still in them they burned along with their homes. Those who forced their way out into the street they butchered without the least hint of compassion—children, babies, women, old men, making no distinction of age or sex. [3] In accordance with their national custom they even lopped the extremities off corpses: some carried severed hands strung round their waists, others brandished heads spitted on their assegais and hunting spears. Any women they found to have sought refuge with their children in temples, however, they ordered not to be killed, and these were the only persons to whom they gave assurances to that effect. [4] They did so, however, not because they pitied such unfortunates but out of concern lest the women, abandoning all hope of survival, might burn down the temples—thus depriving them of the opportunity to pillage the rich dedications stored inside. [5] To such an extent did these *barbaroi* outdo all other men in sheer savagery, that whereas the rest of mankind spare the lives of those who seek sanctuary in temples in order to avoid an impious offense against divinity, these Carthaginians, on the contrary, would keep their hands off an enemy in order to plunder the temples of their gods. [6] By the time it was dark the city had been sacked: of the houses some had been burned and others demolished, and the whole place was full of blood and corpses. The number of the fallen was afterwards found to be some 16,000, besides which more than 5,000 were taken prisoner.

58. The Greeks who were there as allies of the Carthaginians,[63] thus confronted with the transformation in the lives of these wretched people, could not but feel pity for their fate. The women, deprived of the luxury to which they were accustomed, passed their nights exposed to the lust of their enemies, suffering fearful indignities. Some, indeed, were forced to look on while their nubile daughters suffered outrages that had no place in a young girl's life: [2] the brutal nature of the *barbaroi* spared neither freeborn youths nor virgins, subjecting these unhappy victims to the most appalling experiences. Consequently, the women, brooding on the slavery that would be their fate in Libya, pictured themselves and their children leading an existence deprived of all human rights and forced to endure insulting treatment at the hands of their masters. Being aware, too, that these [masters] spoke an unintelligible language and had bestial habits, they mourned those of their children who still lived, with every individual outrage committed against them like a dagger piercing their hearts. This drove them to an extremity of grief and agonized lamentation over their own fate. Their fathers and brothers, however, who had died fighting for their country, they held blessed, in that these had witnessed no spectacle unworthy of their own valor.

[3] Those Selinuntines who evaded capture, some 2,600 in number, got safely to Acragas and received every sort of kindness there: the Acragantines issued rations to them at public expense and billeted them out in private homes, urging the householders—who were only too willing—to furnish them with every necessity for daily life.

59. While these events were unfolding, there arrived in Acragas 3,000 crack troops from Syracuse, who had been sent on in advance with all speed as a relief force. When they heard about the fall of Selinus, they sent ambassadors to Hannibal, urging him to ransom the prisoners and spare the temples of the gods. [2] Hannibal's response was that since the Selinuntines could not preserve their own freedom, they would now get a taste of slavery; and that the gods had abandoned Selinus out of disgust at its inhabitants. [3] The fugitives, however, had sent Empedion as their ambassador, and to him Hannibal restored his possessions, since he had consistently supported Carthaginian policies, and before the siege had advised the Selinuntines not to go to war with Carthage. Hannibal also, as a special favor, released to him any kin of his who were among the captives, and to the Selinuntines who had got away

63. Presumably the Egestans, though strictly speaking they were not Greek (43.2 and n. 43).

he gave permission, provided they paid the Carthaginians tribute, to live in the city and to farm its land.

[4] At the time of its capture, this city had been continuously occupied for two hundred and forty-two years since its foundation [651].[64] After demolishing the walls of Selinus, Hannibal marched with his entire field force against Himera. This city above all he longed to destroy utterly, [5] since it was responsible for his father's exile [<43.5], and it was in fighting against it that his grandfather Hamilcar, outgeneraled by Gelon, had been killed, as were 150,000 of his troops, with as many again being taken prisoner [<11.20.1–23.2]. [6] It was for these reasons that Hannibal was bent on revenge. He pitched camp with 40,000 men on some hills not far from the city. With the rest of his force, augmented by 20,000 additional troops from the Sicels and Sicans, he laid the city itself under siege. [7] He positioned his siege engines and began to batter the walls at a number of points: he also launched assaults with relays of shock troops and thus slowly wore down the defenders, helped by the confidence generated in his soldiers as a result of their successes. [8] He also undermined the fortifications, shored up [his tunnels] with wooden pit props, and then set these on fire: as a result, a large section of the wall very quickly collapsed. A desperately fought battle now took place, with one side exerting all its strength to get inside the wall, and the other in terror of suffering the same fate as the Selinuntines. [9] Because of this, with the defenders waging an all-out battle for the sake of children, parents, and the fatherland that all men fight to defend, the *barbaroi* were driven back, and the gap in the wall was quickly repaired. There also now rallied to their support both the Syracusans from Acragas, and a relief force from their other allies, some four thousand troops all told, under the command of Diocles the Syracusan [<34.6].

60. At this point, however, night cut short any continuation of the conflict, and [the attackers] broke off their assault. When day dawned, the men of Himera determined not to let themselves be ignominiously boxed in, like the Selinuntines: instead, they posted guards on the walls, and then with the rest of their troops and those allies who had joined them, some ten thousand men in all, they charged out [from the city]. [2] So unexpected an attack on the enemy dumbfounded the *barbaroi*, who thought these were allies arriving to relieve the besieged. Now, since [the Himerans] far excelled their

64. Diodorus' date for the foundation of Selinus gets some support from pottery; but Thucydides' (6.4.2) alternative date (628) better matches the earliest remains on the acropolis.

opponents in both daring and military expertise, and, most important of all, because their sole hope of survival depended on victory in this battle, the first opponents they met they rapidly dispatched. [3] Indeed, with the main mass of the barbarian host flocking together in great confusion (since they never would have expected those under siege to risk such a move), they were at no small disadvantage, since 80,000 men converging in complete disorder meant that the *barbaroi* suffered more from attacks on one another than from the enemy. [4] The Himerans had parents, children, and every sort of relative watching them from the walls and thus hazarded their lives unstintingly for the common salvation of all. [5] So brilliantly did they fight that the *barbaroi*, stunned by their unexpected daring, turned and fled, in utter disorder, to the corps encamped on the hills, while the Himerans pressed hard on their heels, calling out to one another to take no prisoners. According to Timaeus, they slaughtered more than 6,000; Ephorus says 20,000. [6] Hannibal, perceiving that these men were on their last legs, brought down his troops from their hilltop encampment and threw them in as relief for their beaten comrades, catching the Himerans in no sort of order as they continued the pursuit. [7] A tough battle followed, and the greater number of the Himerans turned and ran. Three thousand of them, however, who made a stand against the Carthaginian army, and fought valiantly, were killed to the last man.

61. This battle was already at its end when there reached Himera twenty-five triremes from the Sicilian Greeks, which had been sent out earlier to support the Lacedaemonians [<34.4], but were now back from that campaign.[65] [2] A rumor, further, spread through the city that the Syracusans, in full force and accompanied by their allies, were on the march to bring relief to Himera; also that Hannibal intended to man his triremes at Motya with the pick of his troops, sail to Syracuse, and capture the city while it was short of defenders. [3] Accordingly, Diocles, the [Syracusan] commander in Himera,

---

65. The Syracusan triremes at Cyzicus had been burnt by their crews after the battle (Mar./Apr. 410) to prevent their falling into Athenian hands (Xen. *Hell.* 1.1.18). Pharnabazus funded a building program to replace the vessels thus lost (Xen. *Hell.* 1.1.24–26), and when the democratic replacements for Hermocrates and his fellow-generals arrived, still in 410 (Xen. *Hell.* 1.1.29), these ships were ready. We get a glimpse of the new squadron, twenty-five strong, in action in the fall of 409 (Xen. *Hell.* 1.2.12). Hannibal's invasion of Sicily had come at the start of the 409 campaigning season (54.1), i.e., late March or early April, and ended with the capture of Himera three months later (Xen. *Hell.* 1.1.37), i.e., at some point in July. Thus, either the squadron in the Hellespont was recalled in the emergency, and returned to the eastern Aegean in the fall (the likeliest explanation), or else Pharnabazus' munificence paid for fifty triremes rather than twenty-five.

advised the flotilla captains to make for Syracuse with all speed, lest it should happen that the city was taken by assault. [4] Therefore, since their best troops had perished in the battle, they decided that the best plan would be to pull out from Himera, evacuating half the population aboard the triremes—these would convey them to a point beyond Himeran territory—and leaving the other half to keep watch until the triremes returned. [5] When the Himerans were told this, they expostulated vehemently; but since there was no other option available, the triremes were hurriedly loaded by night with a mixed crowd of women and children, and some other inhabitants also, who traveled aboard them as far as Messene. [6] Diocles now also, taking his own troops with him but leaving behind the bodies of those who had died in the fighting [>75.3–5], set out on his long march home. Many Himerans, together with their wives and children, went along in his company, since there was not room aboard the triremes for the entire populace.

62. Those left behind in the city spent the night armed and on the walls. From daybreak on the Carthaginians surrounded the city and launched assaults thick and fast. The remaining Himerans, who were expecting the fleet's return, spared themselves nothing in the struggle. [2] For the whole of that day, then, they held out stubbornly. But on the next, with the triremes already clear in view, the siege engines began to bring down the wall, and a mass of Iberians charged through the breach. Some of the *barbaroi* fought off those Himerans who came to the rescue, while others, clambering on to the walls, would help their comrades through. [3] Thus the city was taken by storm, and for a long time the *barbaroi* went on mercilessly butchering anyone they caught. When Hannibal gave orders to take prisoners, the killing stopped, and they started looting the riches from private homes. [4] Hannibal despoiled the temples, dragged out the suppliants who had sought refuge in them, and set them on fire. The city itself, two hundred and forty years after its founding, he razed to its foundations. Of the captives, the women and children he distributed throughout the army to be kept under guard; but the male prisoners, numbering about 3,000, he brought to the place where long ago his grandfather Hamilcar had been slain by Gelon [<11.22.1] and had them all tortured and executed there. [5] This done, he dismissed part of his army, sending the allies from Sicily back to their several homelands. With them went the Campanians, who had been making angry complaints to the Carthaginians: though the various successes, they claimed, been chiefly due to them, they had not received adequate recompense for their achievements. [6] Hannibal now put his expeditionary force aboard the warships and merchantmen; then, leaving behind sufficient troops [to protect] his allies, he set

sail from Sicily [Aug. 409]. When he reached Carthage with his ample spoils, everyone came out to meet him, welcoming and honoring him as one who in a brief period had achieved more than any previous general.

63. Hermocrates of Syracuse now [? Aug./Sept. 409] sailed home to Sicily, a man who, as general in the war against Athens, had done his country much good service and thus gained great influence among the Syracusans. Later, however, after he had been sent out to join the Lacedaemonian alliance, as admiral commanding thirty-five triremes [<34.4], he was removed from power [in his absence] by a cabal of his political opponents, sentenced to exile, and required to turn over his squadron <in the Hellespont>[66] to those sent out as his designated successors [Xen. *Hell.* 1.1.27–29]. [2] Since in consequence of his campaign he was now on friendly terms with the Persian satrap Pharnabazus, he obtained substantial funds from him, which, after putting in at Messene, he used to build five triremes and hire a thousand mercenaries.[67] [3] He added to this force about a thousand of the dispossessed Himerans and then made an attempt, with the cooperation of his friends, to engineer his return to Syracuse. Failing in this plan,[68] he marched his force through the interior to Selinus, which he occupied. He then restored part of the city wall and sent out a general appeal for any Selinuntines who were still alive to join him. [4] Many others besides he welcomed into the area; and in this way he collected a force of 6,000 first-class fighters.

From [Selinus] he then proceeded to launch a series of attacks. First, he ravaged the territory of the Motyans: those who sallied out of the city against him he defeated with heavy losses, and the remainder he drove back within

---

66. Diodorus' MSS read, nonsensically, "in the Peloponnese," which Wesseling, with the theater of war in mind, emended to "in the Hellespont." Xenophon, a contemporary witness, states specifically (*Hell.* 1.1.32) that the transfer took place at Miletus, and there is no reason to disbelieve him. I therefore use Wesseling's emendation and translate accordingly.

67. Taking the average cost of a trireme as one talent, and the average daily pay of a mercenary as two drachmas, for a month-long campaign Pharnabazus must have dispensed at least fifteen talents, and probably nearer twenty if Hermocrates was also to be responsible for the fitting out, upkeep, and pay of the ships and their crews.

68. His return was clearly blocked by the new democratic radicals headed by Diocles, scared that his outstanding military reputation (which contrasted impressively with Diocles' own) and strong aristocratic, conservative bias might well be used to overturn the reforms of 412. Hermocrates' military actions on return, all pointing towards the undoing of Hannibal's conquests and the ultimate dismantling of the Carthaginian domain in western Sicily, must have powerfully strengthened the move to recall him.

their walls. Next, he raided the countryside around Panormus [Palermo] and acquired an immense amount of booty. When the inhabitants of the city came out in full force to do battle with him, he slaughtered about five hundred of them and, [again], boxed up the rest inside their fortifications. [5] In similar fashion he proceeded to lay waste all the rest of the territory held by the Carthaginians, which won him the approbation of the Sicilian Greeks. This also very quickly caused most of the Syracusans to have a change of heart [? winter 409/8], with the realization that Hermocrates' exile was an unworthy response to his excellent and courageous record. [6] So, after a considerable debate regarding him in successive meetings of the assembly, it became clear that the *demos* wanted him recalled; and Hermocrates, on learning of this discussion concerning himself in Syracuse, began to make very careful plans for his return from exile, well aware that his political opponents would work against it.

Such were the events that took place in Sicily.

64. In Greece [<53.4] <Thrasyllus>,[69] who had been sent out by the Athenians with thirty ships, a large number of hoplites, and a hundred cavalrymen, made landfall at Ephesus [summer 409]. After disembarking his troops at two separate landing points, he launched assaults on the city [*Hell. Oxy.* 30–33]. Those within the walls came out against them, and a hard-fought battle took place. Since the Ephesians were engaged in full force, four hundred Athenians lost their lives: the remainder <Thrasyllus> got aboard his ships and then set sail for Lesbos [Plut. *Alcib.* 29.1; Xen. *Hell.* 1.2.7–10]. [2] The Athenian generals [operating] in the Cyzicus area now sailed to Chalcedon, where they established the fortress of Chrysopolis and left a sufficient force there to garrison it. Those in command they instructed to impose a ten-percent tariff on all traffic from the Black Sea. [3] After this they split their forces. Theramenes was left behind with fifty vessels to besiege Chalcedon and Byzantium. Thrasybulus was dispatched to the Thraceward regions, where he set about bringing over the local cities. [4] Alcibiades now sent <Thrasyllus>[70] and his thirty

69. Diodorus' MSS name the general as Thrasybulus; but from Xen. *Hell.* 1.2.6 it is clear that Thrasyllus was in command. Diodorus (or his source) similarly confuses the two at 39.4, just as at 37.4 (see n. 35 there) and elsewhere he mixes up the two satraps Tissaphernes and Pharnabazus.

70. Thrasyllus had not left Lesbos and joined his fellow-commanders till c. Nov. 409; when he did, Alcibiades' men, undefeated themselves, at first flatly refused to serve with the new arrivals after their crushing defeat at Ephesus (Xen. *Hell.* 1.2.15; Plut. *Alcib.* 29.1–2). Alcibiades was not overall commander: he and Thrasyllus will have operated separately

ships on separately, and sailed to the territory held by Pharnabazus. Working together, they laid waste a great deal of it: as a result, they glutted their troops with plunder but also themselves amassed money from the spoils, since they were anxious to relieve the [Athenian] people of the burden of war taxes [winter 409/8].

[5] When the Lacedaemonians realized that all Athenian forces were now deployed in the Hellespontine area, they made an expedition against Pylos, held with a garrison by the Messenians. They did this with eleven ships by sea (five from Sicily, six crewed by their own citizens), while they had also as-sembled ground forces in adequate numbers. After investing the fortress, they <enforced their siege>[71] by both land and sea. [6] The moment the Athenian *demos* got the news, it sent out thirty ships under Anytus son of Anthemion[72] to relieve the besieged. Anytus duly sailed, but because of storms was unable to round Cape Malea and so returned to Athens. This so angered the *demos* that it charged him with treason and put him on trial. In this perilous situ-ation Anytus saved his neck by laying out cash and appears to have been the first Athenian actually to bribe a jury [Arist. *Ath. Pol.* 27.5]. [7] For quite a while the Messenians in Pylos continued to hold out, in the expectation of relief from the Athenians; but what with the enemy's endless round of as-saults, and the fact that of their own number those who were not dying from their wounds had been reduced to desperate straits through lack of food, they finally evacuated the position under truce. This, then, was how the Lace-daemonians regained control of Pylos, after a fifteen-year occupation by the Athenians, beginning with Demosthenes' fortification of the site.[73]

65. While these events were taking place, the Megarians seized [their port of] Nisaea, which at the time was in Athenian hands, and the Athenians sent

---

(until the reconciliation of their troops, Xen. *Hell.* 1.2.17; Plut. *Alcib.* 29.2) by mutual agreement.

71. Accepting, as does Oldfather 1950, Post's emendation of *epoliorkoun* for the reading of the MSS, *eporthoun* ("continued ravaging").

72. A lover of Alcibiades (Plut. *Alcib.* 4.4–5) and the future accuser of Socrates (Plat. *Apol.* 18b).

73. Demosthenes occupied Pylos in 425 (12.63.5), and this would date its reoccupa-tion by Sparta to 410/09. This episode, the Megarian seizure of Nisaea (65.1–4), and the Athenian attack on Chalcedon (66.1–2, firmly datable to early spring 408), however, are all correlated chronologically, and on balance it seems likelier that Diodorus either took the fifteen-year estimate from another source, or miscounted, rather than narrating the recapture of Pylos out of context. This error should thus not be a factor in determining the overall chronology of the period 411–406 (see 68.1 and n. 75).

out against them Leotrophides and Timarchus, with a thousand infantry and four hundred cavalry. The Megarians came out to confront them under arms and in full force, and after augmenting their numbers with some of the forces from Sicily, they formed their battle line near the hills known as The Horns [*Hell. Oxy.* 36–37]. [2] The Athenians fought brilliantly and routed an enemy who greatly outnumbered them. Large numbers of Megarians perished, but no more than twenty Lacedaemonians, since the Athenians, who had been infuriated by the seizure of Nisaea, did not pursue the Lacedaemonians but inflicted heavy casualties on the Megarians out of pure resentment.[74]

[3] The Lacedaemonians now appointed Cratesippidas admiral, manned twenty-five of their own vessels with allied crews, and ordered them out to the assistance of their allies [in the eastern Aegean]. Cratesippidas spent some while off the Ionian coast without accomplishing anything worthy of note; later, however, in return for a cash payment furnished by the exiles from Chios, he reinstated them and captured the Chian acropolis. [4] These Chian returnees now in their turn banished the political opponents who had been responsible for exiling them, to a total of about six hundred. The latter seized a place called Atarneus on the mainland opposite, a stronghold of extreme natural ruggedness, and from then on used it as a base for conducting guerilla warfare against those in power on Chios.

66. While these events were taking place, Alcibiades and <Thrasyllus> fortified Lampsacus, left a sufficient garrison there, and themselves sailed with their forces to join Theramenes, who with seventy ships and 5,000 troops was ravaging [the territory of] Chalcedon [spring 408]. When their fleets and armies were united in the one location, they invested the city from sea to sea with a wooden stockade [Xen. *Hell.* 1.3.1–8; Plut. *Alcib.* 29.3–30.1]. [2] Hippocrates, the man stationed in the city by the Lacedaemonians as commander (what Laconians referred to as a "harmost"), led out against them both his own troops and all the Chalcedonians. A fierce battle ensued, in which Alcibiades' troops fought with great bravery. Hippocrates himself was killed. Of his troops some perished, while the severely wounded all sought refuge inside the city.

[3] After this, Alcibiades sailed down to the Hellespont and the Chersonese, his object being to collect cash payments, while Theramenes and his

---

74. For the importance of Nisaea to Athens, see 11.79.2 and n. 106. Since Diodorus mentions only Megarian and Sicilian troops before the skirmish, Vogel wants to emend "Lacedaemonians" to "Sicilians." But it is very likely that Lacedaemonians were present, if only in an advisory capacity, and this is confirmed by *Hell. Oxy.* 36–37 (Florence fr. 11).

staff made an agreement with the citizens of Chalcedon that they should pay
the same amount of tribute [to Athens] as they had done previously. From
there he took his forces across to Byzantium and laid that city under siege,
beginning the investment with great speed and energy. [4] Alcibiades, after
collecting his payments, persuaded a good number of the Thracians to join
the campaign under him and also attracted a mass enlistment from the Chersonese. He then set out with his entire force. First, he captured Selymbria
by betrayal, mulcted the Selymbrians of a large sum of money, and imposed
a garrison on them [Plut. *Alcib.* 30.2–5]. He then moved on quickly to join
Theramenes at Byzantium. [5] When their forces were united, they began
making preparations for a siege, [in the knowledge that] they intended to conquer a city of great substance that was crammed with defenders: apart from
the Byzantines themselves, of whom there were many, the Lacedaemonian
harmost Clearchus [<40.6; Thuc. 8.80.3] had numerous Peloponnesians and
mercenaries on hand. [6] Thus, though they continued to make assaults for
some while, during this period they did no serious damage to the defenders.
But as soon as the governor [Clearchus] left to get funds from Pharnabazus,
certain Byzantines, who detested the severity with which he exercised his
office (Clearchus was indeed a stern authoritarian) betrayed the city to Alcibiades and his colleagues [Xen. *Hell.* 1.3.14–22; Plut. *Alcib.* 31.2–4].

67. The latter sailed out that afternoon with their entire fleet and also
marched their ground forces some distance away, as though they meant to
raise the siege and remove their armaments to Ionia; but as soon as it got dark
they returned, reaching the city about midnight. They then sent the triremes
with orders to start hauling away the [Byzantines'] merchantmen and to make
as much noise as possible, as though the entire force was there. They themselves meanwhile stood ready with their land forces before the walls, watching
for the agreed-on signal from those who were to surrender the city.
[2] So those aboard the triremes carried out their instructions, slamming
into some of the vessels with their rams, trying to tear others loose by means
of grappling irons, and all the time keeping up a tremendous hullabaloo.
At this the Peloponnesians in the city—and everyone else unaware of the
deception—rushed down to the harbors to save the situation. [3] Those betraying the city now raised their signal from the wall and let Alcibiades and
his men in by means of ladders—a completely safe move, since the bulk of
the populace was down at the harbor. [4] But when the Peloponnesians discovered what had happened, to begin with, they left half their number at the
harbor, and with the rest came running back to recover the captured walls;
[5] and although almost the entire Athenian force was now inside the city,

they were not dismayed but kept up their resistance for a long time, they and the Byzantines battling the Athenians together. Indeed, in the end the Athenians would never have reduced the city by force of arms had not Alcibiades, seeing his chance, proclaimed that the Byzantines were to suffer no improper treatment: this was what made the citizen body change sides and turn against the Peloponnesians. [6] Most of the latter, as a result, fell fighting gallantly, while the survivors, about five hundred in number, sought refuge at the altars in the temples. [7] The Athenians returned their city to the Byzantines, after first making them allies, and then came to an agreement with the suppliants at the altars: they would remove their arms, convey their persons to Athens, and turn them over to the *demos* for a decision regarding them [May/June 408].

68. When the year had run its course, the Athenians conferred the archonship upon Euctemon [408/7], the Romans elected [Varr. 411] as consuls Marcus Papirius [Mugillanus] and Spurius Nautius [Rutilus], and the 93rd Olympiad was celebrated, in which Eubatus of Cyrene won the *stadion*. About this time[75] the Athenian generals, now that they were masters of Byzantium, made for the Hellespont and took every city along it except for Abydos. [2] Then,[76] leaving Diodorus and Mantitheus in charge there with a sufficient force, they themselves sailed to Athens with the ships and the spoils, having accomplished many notable deeds for their country. When they were nearly there, the whole populace came out to meet them, overjoyed at their

---

75. The chronology is doubtful, largely because Xenophon failed to mark the beginning of one year (which one remains uncertain) during the period 411–406: for a clear exposition of the problem see Krentz 1989, 11–14. For the most part, with modifications, I adhere to the oldest solution, which brings Alcibiades back home in 407: this squares with more of the evidence than other theories since proposed, though it creates the assumption that Diodorus antedates these particular events by at least a year.

76. Xenophon (*Hell.* 1.4.8–12) makes it clear that a considerable amount of activity took place before the return to Athens and suggests strongly that the generals did not all return together. Alcibiades spent long enough in Caria to collect a hundred talents, a very considerable sum. Thrasybulus systematically recaptured Thasos and all other Thracian cities that had gone over to Sparta. (Diodorus misplaces this: 72.1–2.) These actions will have more than filled the rest of the 408 campaigning season. The campaign in the Hellespont will have followed (as Diodorus reports) in the spring of 407. Thrasyllus then (? June 407) returned to Athens with the rest of the fleet while both his fellow-generals were still absent (§10). It was only after his election by the *demos* (together with Thrasybulus and Conon) as general, that Alcibiades made his own cautious return, perhaps in company with Thrasybulus, in ? July 407 (archonship of Antigenes, 407/6: schol. Aristoph. *Frogs* 1422). Diodorus has run two separate homecomings into one.

successes, and great numbers of aliens too, as well as women and children, all thronged down to Piraeus. [3] For this return of the generals gave ample scope for astonishment, seeing that they brought with them no less than two hundred captured ships, together with a vast quantity of prisoners and spoils of war. Their own triremes they had taken much trouble to decorate with gilded arms and wreaths, as well as with items of booty and every other kind of adornment.

But most people had hastened down to the harbor to catch a glimpse of Alcibiades, slaves and free vying with one another, so that the city was completely deserted [Xen. *Hell.* 1.4.13–19; Plut. *Alcib.* 32.1–5; Nep. *Alcib.* 6.1–3]. [4] For by now this man had come to be so admired that the more prominent Athenians thought they had finally found a strong man who could oppose the people openly and boldly, while the indigent figured they would have in him a first-rate champion, who would heedlessly throw the city into turmoil to relieve their penury. [5] In boldness he far outstripped all others; he was an immensely clever speaker, unrivaled as a general, his daring marked by practical success. Over and above this he was quite extraordinarily handsome in appearance, with a brilliant mind and a spirit bent on high endeavors. [6] In short, almost everyone nursed such lofty assumptions concerning him as to be convinced that with his return, good fortune in their public affairs had likewise come back to the city. In addition, just as the Lacedaemonians had been ahead of the game while he was on their side, so [the Athenians] expected that they too would enjoy success with this man as an ally.

69. So, when the fleet came into harbor, the crowd turned towards Alcibiades' ship, and as he stepped from it everyone welcomed him, congratulating him on his successes but also on his return from exile. He greeted the crowds warmly and [later] called a meeting of the assembly, at which he made a lengthy defense of his personal actions. This generated such goodwill towards him in the masses that all agreed it was the city that had been at fault as regards the decrees voted against him. [2] As a result, his property, which had been impounded by the state, was returned to him, and in addition they threw into the sea the stelae on which his sentence and the other verdicts against him had been inscribed. They also passed a vote that the Eumolpidae[77] should revoke the curse they pronounced against him at the time when he was believed to have profaned the [Eleusinian] Mysteries. [3] Finally, they appointed him supreme commander on land and at sea, entrusting all their armaments to him.

77. The Eleusinian priestly clan in charge of the Mysteries.

They also elected as his fellow-generals those whom he wanted, Adeimantos and Thrasybulus.

[4] Alcibiades manned a hundred ships and sailed to Andros [Oct. 407], where he seized a stronghold called <Gaurium>[78] and fortified it. When the Andrians came out against him in full force, together with the Peloponnesians guarding the city, a battle took place which the Athenians won. Of those from the city, many were killed, and of those who survived, some scattered across the countryside, while others sought refuge within the walls. [5] Alcibiades made some attacks on the city but then left a sufficient garrison in the position he had fortified, appointed Thrasybulus its commander, and then himself sailed on to Cos and Rhodes, both of which he plundered, collecting ample booty for the maintenance of his troops.

70. Though the Lacedaemonians had lost their entire naval force, together with its commander Mindarus, they nevertheless did not sink into despair. They now chose as admiral Lysander, reputed to surpass all others in strategic skill and possessed of a daring that could deal successfully with any situation.[79] On assuming the command he set about enrolling an adequate number of troops from the Peloponnese and manned as many ships as he was able to. [2] He then sailed to Rhodes, where he augmented his squadron with all the ships available from the various Rhodian cities. From there he moved on to Ephesus and Miletus. After fitting out the triremes in these cities, he requisitioned those from Chios and thus made ready at Ephesus a fleet consisting of some seventy vessels. [3] On hearing that King Darius' son Cyrus[80] had been dispatched by his father to support the Lacedaemonian war effort,

---

78. Rhodoman's emendation—based on Xen. *Hell.* 1.4.2 and accepted by Vogel 1893 and Oldfather 1950—of the otherwise unknown *Katrion* of Diodorus' MSS.

79. There was some mystery about Lysander's (c. 455–395) birth: his father was an aristocrat, but it is possible that his mother was a helot. He was thus socially handicapped as to status, being what was known at Sparta as a *mothax*. Diplomatic and military talent, plus high-level patronage, nevertheless ensured his successful career. He was also the lover of Archidamus II's younger son, the lame (and subsequently famous) Agesilaus, whose succession he helped secure at the expense of Agis II's son Leotychidas, suspected of being Alcibiades' bastard (Plut. *Alcib.* 23.7–8, *Lys.* 22.4–6).

80. Cyrus (c. 425–401) was the younger son of Darius II by his queen Parysatis, who promoted him against his older siblings, including his brother and heir Artaxerxes II Mnemon (108.1). It was by her influence that in 407 he succeeded Tissaphernes (now relegated to Caria) as satrap of all western Asia Minor, while still under seventeen years of age. From the beginning he had his sights set on the throne: for his unsuccessful attempt to overthrow Artaxerxes at Cunaxa, see 14.22.4–24.7.

he traveled to Sardis to meet him. To such an extent did he sharpen the young man's enthusiasm for the war against the Athenians that he got ten thousand darics[81] from him, there and then, as pay for his troops; and for the future, Cyrus bade him make his requests without reserve, since he had instructions from his father to furnish the Lacedaemonians with anything they might require [Xen. *Hell.* 1.5.1–9; Plut. *Lys.* 9.1–2]. [4] Lysander then returned to Ephesus and summoned the most powerful men from the cities [of Ionia], with whom he set up political groups, promising them that if his plans were successful, he would place them in charge of their several cities. As a result, these men competed with one another to provide greater aid than had been demanded of them; and so very soon, against all expectations, Lysander came to have an abundance of every kind of supply useful for warfare [Plut. *Lys.* 5.3–5].

71. When Alcibiades heard that Lysander was fitting out his fleet at Ephesus, he set sail thither with his entire fleet. He cruised in close to the harbors, but when no one came out against him, he brought most of his ships to Notium and left them anchored there, entrusting the command of them to his personal steersman Antiochus, with orders not to risk a sea battle during his absence; he himself meanwhile [? Dec. 407] took the troop transports and sailed with all speed to Clazomenae, since this city, an ally of Athens, was suffering from incursions by some of its exiles.[82] [2] Antiochus, however, being impetuous by nature and eager to bring off some brilliant coup on his own account, ignored what Alcibiades told him. Manning ten of the best ships, and ordering the captains of the remainder to keep them ready for action

---

81. The Persian daric was a gold coin that weighed 2 Attic drachmas. The ratio in price of gold to silver at this time was 13:1. Thus, a daric was the rough equivalent in value of 26 silver drachmas. There were 6,000 drachmas to the talent: thus, 10,000 darics would represent about 43.3 talents. But according to Xenophon (*Hell.* 1.5.3), Cyrus told Lysander that he had available no less than 500 talents and was prepared to spend them, and more if need be. This was a huge sum, almost as much as Athens' tribute from the subject-allies in a year. Either Diodorus' 10,000 darics was simply an initial down payment or (more probably) Cyrus was making extravagant promises in his quest for supporters.

82. Sources disagree on the cause of Alcibiades' fatal absence. Xenophon (*Hell.* 1.5.11) and Plutarch (*Lys.* 5.1) report him as joining Thrasybulus in the blockade of Phocaea. This, taken with Diodorus' reference to Clazomenae, would suggest a general campaign to secure the coastal cities of Ionia. Plutarch (*Alcib.* 35.4) claims that Lysander's higher pay to his sailors (from Cyrus' bounty), by provoking mass desertions of rowers (Plut. *Lys.* 4.4), forced Alcibiades back to Caria to raise more cash. Lysander had good reason to play a waiting game.

should there be need for them to join in, he sailed up close to the enemy and challenged them to battle.[83] [3] Lysander, who had learned, from some deserters, about Alcibiades' departure with the best of his troops, figured that this was a good moment to accomplish something worthy of Sparta. He therefore put out in response to the challenge with all his ships. The leading [Athenian] ship, on which Antiochus had stationed himself for the engagement, he sank; the rest he put to flight and pursued, until the Athenian captains manned the rest of their vessels and rallied in support, though with no kind of ordered formation. [4] A sea battle developed close inshore between this crowded mass of ships, in which the Athenians, because of their disorder, got the worst of it and lost twenty-two vessels. Very few of their crew members, however, were taken prisoner: for the most part they swam safely ashore. When Alcibiades heard what had happened, he hastened back to Notium, manned all his triremes, and sailed up to the enemy-held harbors; but Lysander would not venture out against him, and so he [gave up and] set course for Samos.

72. While these events were taking place, the Athenian general Thrasybulus sailed against Thasos with fifteen ships. He fought and defeated those who made a sally from the city, killing about two hundred of them; he then laid siege to the city itself, boxing in its inhabitants. [In this way] he forced them to take back their exiles (who were those supporting the Athenians), to accept a garrison, and to become allies of Athens. [2] After this he sailed to Abdera, at that time one of the most powerful cities in Thrace, and brought it over [to the Athenian side]. These, then, were the accomplishments of the Athenian generals after setting out from home.

[3] King Agis of Sparta happened to be in Deceleia [<9.2] with his army [at this time], and on finding out that the best of the Athenians were on campaign with Alcibiades, he picked a moonless night and marched his force to Athens. [4] He had with him 28,000 infantry, half of them select hoplites and the rest light-armed troops; there were also in his train some 1,200 cavalry, of whom the Boeotians provided nine hundred and Peloponnesian [cities], the remainder. When he got near the city, he overran the outposts before they realized he was there: because he had caught them unawares he scattered them easily, killing a few and chasing the rest to the shelter of the walls. [5] When the Athenians heard what had happened, they issued orders

83. Xen. *Hell.* 1.5.11–14; Plut. *Alcib.* 35.5–6, *Lys.* 5.1–2; *Hell. Oxy.* 40–43 (IV.1–4). Antiochus himself was killed at the first onset; why Alcibiades had appointed a steersman (however well regarded, even with instructions to do nothing) remains an unresolved question.

for all the older men and the biggest boys to stand to under arms. These promptly obeyed the summons, so that the circuit of the [city wall] was fully manned by those who had hurried together to meet the common danger. [6] At daybreak the Athenian generals observed the enemy forces in extended array, forming a line four men deep and eight *stadioi* [just under a mile] long. This for the moment disconcerted them, since they could see that roughly two-thirds of the ramparts were thus covered by the enemy. [7] They then sent out their horsemen, however, who in numbers were roughly an equal match for their opponents. These engaged in a cavalry battle outside the city, which was fiercely fought and went on for some time. (The infantry line had been drawn up about five *stadioi* [slightly over half a mile] from the city wall, whereas the cavalry had engaged and were fighting right outside the ramparts themselves.) [8] The Boeotians, who had previously defeated the Athenians unaided at Delium [<12.69.1–70.6], thought it would be a terrible thing if they were [now] revealed as inferior to those they once had defeated; while the Athenians—with spectators on the walls, to whom every man of them was known, as witnesses to their valor in battle—were determined to hold fast come what might for the sake of victory. [9] [It was the Athenians who] finally broke their opponents, killed large numbers of them, and pursued the rest as far as the infantry line. At this point the infantry advanced against them, and they withdrew into the city.

73. Agis for the moment decided against a siege, and pitched his camp in the Academy.[84] The next day the Athenians set up a trophy. Agis then paraded his army in battle order and challenged the troops in the city to do battle with him for possession of this trophy. [2] When the Athenians led out their troops and formed them up under the ramparts, at first the Lacedaemonians advanced to start the battle, but such a vast number of missiles were cast at them from the walls that they withdrew their forces from the city, and after ravaging the rest of Attica returned to the Peloponnese.[85]

[3] Alcibiades put to sea with all his ships and made for Cyme [? Jan. 406]. He then proceeded to bring false accusations against the Cymaeans, since he wanted an excuse for despoiling their territory. To begin with, he rounded up large numbers of prisoners and was taking them back to his ships; [4] but those in the city came out to the rescue in full force and fell on him unex-

---

84. The pleasant grove of olive trees rather less than a mile north-northwest of Athens' Dipylon Gate, site of a public gymnasium and, from the early 4th century, of Plato's famous philosophical school.

85. Diodorus is the only source for this alarming assault by Agis.

pectedly. For a while he and his troops put up a strong resistance, but then large numbers from city and countryside alike flocked to the support of the Cymaeans, so that [the Athenians] were forced to abandon their prisoners and run for it to the ships [Nep. *Alcib.* 7.1–2]. [5] Alcibiades, much distressed by these setbacks, sent to Mytilene for his hoplites, drew up his forces before the city, and challenged the Cymaeans to battle. When no one came out, he laid waste their territory, and then set sail for Mytilene. [6] The Cymaeans now dispatched an embassy to Athens, which accused Alcibiades of having laid waste an allied city that had done no wrong. There were also many other charges brought against him. Some of the troops at Samos, who had their differences with Alcibiades, sailed to Athens and denounced him in the assembly as pro-Lacedaemonian—and for cultivating the friendship of Pharnabazus with an eye to getting the mastery over his fellow-citizens once the war had ended [Xen. *Hell.* 1.6.16; Plut. *Alcib.* 36.1–2; Nep. *Alcib.* 7.2–3].

74. Alcibiades' reputation was badly enough damaged by the reverse he had suffered in the sea battle and the offenses he had committed with regard to Cyme; but since these [other] accusations had very soon come to be generally believed, the Athenian *demos,* viewing the man's brashness with some suspicion, elected [Mar. 406] as their ten generals Conon, Lysias, Diomedon, and Pericles, together with Erasinides, Aristocrates, Archestratus, Protomachus, <Thrasyllus> [n. 118 below], and Aristogenes. Of these their first choice was Conon, and they at once sent him out to take over the fleet from Alcibiades.[86] [2] Alcibiades duly ceded the command to Conon and handed over his forces. After this he dismissed the idea of returning to Athens, and taking one trireme only, withdrew to Pactyë in Thrace, since in addition to the anger of the public, he was worried by the lawsuits that had been filed against him. [3] Many individuals, observing how powerfully he was resented, had made him the object of numerous charges: the most serious of these was the one to do with the horses, the sum involved being estimated at eight talents. Diomedes, a friend of his, had sent a four-horse team with him to Olympia [416]. Alcibiades, however, when recording the entry in the usual way, listed the horses as his own. Having won the four-horse race, he then took all the

---

86. The narrative here (and in Xen. *Hell.* 1.5.16 and Plut. *Alcib.* 36.3) suggests that Alcibiades was simply not reelected; but Plutarch (*Lys.* 5.2) and Nepos (*Alcib.* 7.3) make it clear that he was in fact deposed from office before the year was up, so that Conon would have taken over from him in late Jan. or Feb., prior to his own election as general for 406. Alcibiades now retreated to a private stronghold in Thrace that he had cannily set up against just such an eventuality.

prestige of the victory for himself and did not [even] return the horses to the man who had trusted him with them [Isocr. 16; Plut. *Alcib.* 12.2–3]. [4] Reflecting on all these matters, he was afraid that the Athenians would pick a good opportunity to exact retribution from him for all the wrongs he had done them. He therefore of his own accord imposed upon himself the penalty of exile [Xen. *Hell.* 1.5.17; Plut. *Alcib.* 36.2–3].

75. During this same Olympiad [the 93rd: 408–405], the chariot race for pairs was first introduced. In Sparta King Pleistoanax died [408] after a reign of fifty years and was succeeded by Pausanias, who ruled for fourteen years.[87] Those inhabitants of the island of Rhodes from Ialysus, Lindus, and Cameirus resettled themselves [408/7] in one city, today itself known as Rhodes.

[2] Hermocrates of Syracuse [<63.1–6] mustered the troops serving with him and marched from Selinus [? spring 408]. When he reached Himera, he pitched camp in the suburbs of the ruined city. He then searched for and found the place where the Syracusans had made their last stand, and gathered up the bones of the dead. These he had escorted to Syracuse on wagons specially prepared and extravagantly decorated. [3] Hermocrates himself waited at the frontier, since exiles were debarred by law from <crossing it>;[88] but he sent on some of the men with him, and they accompanied the wagons into Syracuse. [4] Hermocrates did all this so that Diocles—who both opposed his recall and was thought to be responsible for having left the dead unburied [<61.6]—might lose the approval of the populace; whereas he, by his humane concern for the slain, would regain the public goodwill that he had previously enjoyed. [5] When the bones had been conveyed [into the city], dissension arose between Diocles and the public, since he objected to their burial, while most people were in favor of it. In the end the Syracusans buried the remains and indeed turned out in full force to pay their respects during the procession [to the grave site]. They also banished Diocles—yet even so they did not allow Hermocrates to return. They were suspicious of his daring,

---

87. Pleistoanax, of the Agiad line, eldest son of Pausanias, the victor of Plataea (11.33.1), succeeded as a minor in 458 but spent the years 445–426 in exile on suspicion of having been bribed by Pericles to withdraw prematurely from an invasion of Attica (Thuc. 2.21.1), during which time his own son Pausanias ruled (also as a minor: Diodorus does not record this part of his reign). Pausanias succeeded on Pleistoanax's death in 408, but in 395/4 himself fled into exile after arraignment for failing to rescue Lysander, and died c. 385.

88. Diodorus' MSS read *synienai* ("accompany"); since clearly the generic law regarding exiles did not specifically forbid them to escort the bones of the dead but simply to enter Syracusan territory, I accept Wesseling's emendation *eisienai* ("enter").

on the grounds that he might, once he was in a position of leadership, proclaim himself *tyrannos*.

[6] So Hermocrates, seeing that this was not an opportune moment to force matters, went back to Selinus. Some while afterwards [? summer 408], however, his friends sent for him, and he set out with 3,000 troops, traveling [to Syracuse] through the territory of Gela and reaching the appointed rendezvous at night. [7] Not all his force was able to keep up with him, and he was accompanied by only a few of them when he arrived at the postern gate opening on to [the quarter of] Achradina. On discovering that some of his friends had already taken over the area, however, he decided to wait and pick up the stragglers. [8] The Syracusans quickly found out what had happened, and assembled in the marketplace under arms; it was here, after showing up in vast numbers, that they killed Hermocrates and most of his supporters. Those who survived the fighting they brought to trial and sentenced to exile. [9] As a result, some of those who had been severely wounded were given out by their relatives as having died, to avoid abandoning them to the anger of the common people. Amongst them was that Dionysius who afterwards [>95.3] became *tyrannos* of Syracuse.

76. When this year's events drew to a close, in Athens Antigenes succeeded to the archonship [407/6], and the Romans elected [Varr. 410] as consuls †Gaius† Manius Aemilius [Mamercinus] and Gaius Valerius [Potitus Volusus]. About this time [? Mar. 406] the Athenian general Conon, after taking over the forces based on Samos [<74.1], fitted out all vessels there present and in addition called in those of the allies, being determined to make his fleet a match for the ships of the enemy. [2] The Spartans, meanwhile, since Lysander's term as admiral had expired, sent out Callicratidas[89] to succeed him [Xen. *Hell.* 1.6.1–2]: a very young man, of unblemished and straightforward character, but as yet lacking experience in foreign ways, and of all the Spartans the most law-abiding [Plut. *Lys.* 5.5]. (It is generally agreed that during his period of command he committed no injustices against either cities or individuals and indeed dealt severely with those who attempted to bribe him,

---

89. Like Lysander (70.1, n. 79) and Gylippus (7.2), Callicratidas was a *mothax,* i.e., born to a helot mother (Ael. *VH* 12.43), with the inevitable chip on his shoulder in consequence. Lysander's local allies (70.4) admired Callicratidas' virtues but resented his replacing Lysander, not least since he may well have belonged to the moderate group favoring peace with Athens (Kagan 1987, 327–329). Furthermore, Lysander not only organized a chorus of damaging complaints against his replacement (Xen. *Hell.* 1.6.4, 10; Plut. *Lys.* 6.1) but deliberately left him without funds by returning his own unspent surplus to Cyrus.

taking punitive action against them.) [3] He it was who now [Mar. 406] sailed to Ephesus and took over the fleet. When he had called in all contingents, his total command, including those he took over from Lysander, numbered one hundred and forty vessels. Since the Athenians controlled Delphinium in Chian territory, he sailed against them there with his entire fleet and set about besieging the place. [4] The Athenian [garrison], about five hundred in number, took fright at the great size of his force and abandoned their position, passing through the enemy lines under a truce. Callicratidas took over the fortress and demolished it. Then he sailed against the Teïans, got inside their walls at night, and plundered the city. [5] After this he sailed to Lesbos with his armada and attacked Methymna, which had an Athenian garrison. He organized continuous assaults, yet to begin with got nowhere. But not long afterwards, certain individuals betrayed the city to him, and he slipped [his troops] inside the walls. Though he despoiled the city of its possessions, he spared its men and returned it to the Methymnaeans.[90] [6] This done, he made for Mytilene, turning over the hoplites to Thorax the Lacedaemonian, with orders to force-march there as fast as might be, while he himself sailed down the coast.

77. The Athenian general Conon had seventy ships, fitted out for naval warfare in a manner that no earlier general had ever equaled as regards preparation. He took all these ships when he sailed to the relief of Methymna. [2] On learning that the city had already fallen, however, he then bivouacked on one of the so-called Hundred Islands.[91] At daybreak, seeing the enemy squadrons approaching [Xen. *Hell.* 1.6.16–18], he decided it would be dangerous to risk a full-scale engagement there, against double his own number of triremes. Instead, he planned to avoid battle by sailing outside [the islands] and then to draw some of the enemy triremes after him towards Mytilene, where he would engage them. In this way, he reckoned, if he won, he could put about for the pursuit, but if defeated, seek refuge in the harbor. [3] So,

---

90. Urged to sell his Methymnaean captives as booty, he refused, declaring that "while he was in command, to the best of his ability no Greek would be sold into slavery" (Xen. *Hell.* 1.6.14–15). This was good propaganda to Athens' former subject-allies, but he had no qualms about selling off the Athenian garrison. He also sent a startling message to Conon, telling him to "stop playing the adulterer with the sea," the implication being that the Aegean now legitimately belonged to Sparta.

91. These islands, the Hecatonnesoi, lay across the strait from northeast Lesbos, close to modern Ayvalik. Despite their name (*hekatón* = 100), Strabo (13.2.5, C.618) calls them the islands of Apollo, *hekatós* (short for *hekatebólos*, "far-darting"), being here an epithet of Apollo. In any case, there are less than twenty of them.

after embarking his troops, he put to sea, setting a leisurely pace for his oars-
men, so as to give the Peloponnesian ships time to get near him. As the Lacedaemonians approached, they kept pushing their craft faster and faster, in the
hoping of overtaking the rearmost enemy vessels. [4] As Conon continued
to retreat, those with the best of the Peloponnesian ships stepped up their
pursuit, exhausting their rowers through this sustained labor at the oars, and
getting a very considerable distance ahead of the rest. Conon duly observed
this, and when his ships were close to Mytilene, ran up a red pennant from
his own vessel: this was the signal to his captains. [5] In response, just as the
enemy was close-hauling them, they suddenly and simultaneously put about:
the rank and file raised the battle paean, and the trumpeters sounded the
attack. The Peloponnesians, dumbfounded by this new move, made a hasty
attempt to get their ships into defensive line; but as they had no time to put
about, and the slower ships behind them had abandoned their usual formation, they fell into a state of noisy disorder.

78. Conon exploited his opportunity with some skill, closing in on them
promptly and making it impossible for them to establish a battle line. Some of
their vessels he holed [by ramming], while shearing off the oar banks of others. Of those ships facing Conon, not one turned to flight: they all continued
to back water while waiting for their own stragglers. [2] The Athenians on the
left wing, however, did put their opponents to flight, pressing ever harder on
their heels and pursuing them for a considerable time. But when the Peloponnesians finally got all their ships together, Conon, in concern at the enemy's
numbers, broke off the chase and set course for Mytilene with forty vessels.
[3] The Athenians who had been in pursuit now found themselves, to their
great alarm, completely surrounded by the entire Peloponnesian fleet. Their
retreat to the city thus cut off, they were forced to run their ships ashore. The
Peloponnesians pressed them hard with every trireme they had, so that the
Athenians, seeing no other way of escape open to them, made for dry land,
abandoned their vessels, and sought refuge in Mytilene.
[4] By capturing thirty of their ships, Callicratidas realized, he had dealt a
crippling blow to his enemies' naval power; but as he foresaw, the struggle on
land still remained [Xen. *Hell.* 1.6.17–23].[92] He therefore sailed on to Myt-

---

92. Xenophon's account differs substantially from Diodorus', very much in favor of
Callicratidas (whom he reports as reaching the Mytilene harbor simultaneously with
Conon) and to the disadvantage of Conon, whose brilliant tactics (as related by Diodorus)
are nowhere to be seen. But that Conon was fighting, at best, a defensive action until
help arrived from Athens seems clear. He was heavily outnumbered (170 vessels to 70); he

ilene himself. Meanwhile Conon, who the moment he got there took steps to anticipate the siege he saw coming, set about preparatory defenses at the harbor entrance. In the shallows he sank small boats weighted down with rocks; where the water was deeper he anchored stone-carrying merchantmen.[93] [5] So the Athenians—together with a large crowd of Mytilenaeans, who because of the war had come in to the city from the fields—quickly completed their preparations for the siege. Callicratidas now disembarked his troops on the beach near the city, made a camp, and set up a trophy for the sea battle. Next day he picked the best of his ships, and (after instructing them not to get separated from his own vessel) put to sea, determined to smash through the enemy's barrier and force his way into the harbor. [6] Conon meanwhile put some of his troops aboard the triremes (which he stationed with prows facing the open entrance), and others on the big merchantmen; others again he posted to the harbor breakwaters, to ensure that the harbor was protected on all sides, by both land and sea. [7] Conon himself, with his triremes, then got ready for battle, blocking the open space between the barriers. The men stationed on the merchantmen dropped their great stones from the yardarms on the enemy's ships, while those lining the breakwaters stood off any bold attempts to force a landing.

79. The Peloponnesians, however, were in no way outdone by the Athenians when it came to competitive zeal. They advanced [on the harbor] in close formation, with their best fighting men stationed on the quarterdecks, and thus made this naval engagement also an infantry battle. When [their ships] crashed into those of their opponents, they boldly jumped aboard the latter's prows, confident that men who had just been defeated would not hold firm against terrifying violence. [2] The Athenians and Mytilenaians, however, seeing that their only hope of survival lay in victory, were determined to meet a gallant death rather than break ranks. With this unsurpassable emulation possessing both sides, a huge death toll resulted, since everyone exposed

---

could not hope to hold his exposed position off the Hecatonnesoi; his only chance (thus Diodorus) was to run for Mytilene and use every device to stall his pursuers while getting there, including a harbor-mouth battle where numbers would not count. The result (whether Callicratidas caught up with him or not) was a complete blockade by land (76.6) as well as by sea.

93. This odd but effective technique involved attaching heavy weights to the yardarms and releasing them as an enemy vessel passed below. The missile of choice was a metal "dolphin," the nose of which was intended to smash clean through the hull: Thuc. 7.41.2. How supplies of "huge stones" were raised to the yardarms, or deployed there for use (79.3), is not at all clear: perhaps in rope nets, by block-and-tackle?

their bodies unstintingly to the perils of combat. [3] Those on the quarter-decks suffered continual hurt from the mass of missiles coming at them: some fell into the sea, mortally wounded, while others, so long as their wounds were still fresh, fought on without being conscious of them. Large numbers were finished off by the bombardment from the yardarms, since the Athenians up aloft kept lobbing down these huge stones. [4] The fighting nevertheless went on for a long time, with heavy casualties on both sides, until Callicratidas, wanting to give his troops some respite, had the trumpeters sound the recall. [5] After a while he manned his ships once more and renewed the struggle. Finally, after a protracted struggle, he just managed, through the great number of his ships and the physical toughness of his marines, to force the Athenians back from their position. When the latter fled for safety to the inner basin, Callicratidas brought his ships through the barriers and dropped anchor close in to the city. [6] The entrance for the control of which they had fought had a good harbor, which was nevertheless outside the city; for the ancient city is a small island, and the later foundation lies opposite it on Lesbos itself, while between the two runs a narrow strait that increases the city's strength. [7] Callicratidas now disembarked his forces, invested Mytilene, and made assaults on it from all quarters.

This, then, was the situation at Mytilene.

[8] In Sicily [<62.6] the Syracusans sent ambassadors to Carthage [? spring 406], putting the responsibility for the war on the Carthaginians and demanding that for the future they give up their quarrel. The Carthaginians returned them ambivalent answers, since they were preparing a large-scale expeditionary force in Libya and had their minds set on enslaving every Sicilian city.[94] Before ferrying their armies across, however, they selected volunteers from among their own citizen body and the other Libyans and founded in Sicily, close to the thermal springs, a city to which they gave the name of Therma.

80. When the events that took place during this year came to an end, in Athens Callias took over the archonship [406/5], and in Rome there succeeded to the consulship Lucius Furius [Medullinus] and Gnaeus <Cornelius> [Cossus]. At this time the Carthaginians—elated by their successes in Sicily and eager to take over the entire island—voted for the preparation of major

---

94. This decision must surely have been stimulated by Hermocrates' alarmingly successful campaign in western Sicily, including the recovery of the half-destroyed (57.6, 59.4) city of Selinus: 63.2–5. Therma, significantly, was only a little to the west of the leveled site of Himera (62.4), thus advancing the frontier of Carthaginian influence some way eastward.

armaments, electing as general that Hannibal who had demolished both Selinus and Himera and entrusting to him overall authority for the campaign.
[2] When he asked to be excused on the grounds of age, they appointed in addition to him a second general, Himilco son of Hanno, from the same family.
After public consultation, these [commanders] sent out certain men in high
repute among the Carthaginians, carrying large sums of money, some to Iberia, others to the Balearic Islands, with instructions to hire all the mercenaries
they could find. [3] They themselves went round Libya, signing up Libyans
and Phoenicians and the fittest of their own citizens, as well as calling in
troops from the tribes and kings allied to them—Maurusians, Nomads, and
some of those inhabiting the regions out towards Cyrene. [4] They also hired
Campanians from Italy and shipped them across to Libya, in the knowledge
that their employment would be of the greatest help—but also because they
knew that the Campanians left in Sicily after their quarrel with the Carthaginians [<62.5] would certainly side with the Sicilian Greeks.[95] [5] When these
forces were finally assembled at Carthage, the total muster of troops, cavalry
included, was not much more than 120,000, according to Timaeus, though
Ephorus puts it at 300,000.

In preparation for their sea crossing, the Carthaginians fitted out all their
triremes and also assembled more than a thousand freighters.[96] [6] They also
sent an advance force of forty triremes to Sicily; and to this the Syracusans
quickly responded with a squadron of about the same size, that showed up
off Eryx. A lengthy naval engagement took place, during which fifteen of the
Phoenician ships were destroyed, and the rest, as night came on, fled out to
sea. [7] When news of this defeat reached Carthage, Hannibal the general
put to sea with fifty ships, determined both to prevent the Syracusans from
making use of their advantage and to secure a safe landing point for his own
forces.

81. When news of this advance force of Hannibal's spread through the
island, everyone expected the main armada to follow immediately. When the

---

95. They also sent an embassy to Athens, presumably to make sure that Athens did not
come to terms with Sparta and Corinth, thus freeing them to help the Syracusans. Athens'
hatred of Syracuse got this embassy a favorable hearing, and a return visit in 406 produced
an alliance (Fornara, no. 165).

96. As elsewhere, these figures are wildly exaggerated. Diodorus clearly disbelieves
Ephorus. The number of freighters will have been increased to accommodate Timaeus'
estimate. On the other hand, the number of Carthaginian triremes (50 + 40) is reasonable.
Hannibal is unlikely to have had a task force of more than 60,000 at most (Caven, 46).

cities heard about the scale of the enterprise, they became highly alarmed, realizing that the struggle would be a life-or-death matter. [2] The Syracusans accordingly approached both the Greeks in Italy and the Lacedaemonians about an alliance and kept sending agents round the cities of Sicily to urge people at large to join the battle for their common freedom. [3] The Acragantines, who shared a frontier with the Carthaginian possessions [in Sicily], anticipated (what in fact happened) that the weight of the war would fall on them first of all. They therefore voted to bring inside their city walls from the countryside not only the grain and other crops but also all their possessions.

[4] During this period, as it happened, both the city and territory of Acragas were enjoying a period of great prosperity, which, I think, it would not be inapposite for me to describe. Their vineyards were quite exceptional for both size and beauty, and the greater part of their land was planted with olive trees, the abundant crop from which they sold to Carthage; [5] for at the time Libya had no such cultivated trees,[97] so that the Acragantine landowners got the wealth of Libya in exchange for their exports and thus accumulated fortunes of quite incredible size. Many signs of this wealth still survive among them, concerning which a brief digression will not be out of place.

82. The building style of their sacred edifices, above all [that of] the temple of Zeus, reveals the lofty concepts inspiring the men of this period. Of the other shrines, some were burned out, and some completely destroyed through the city having been so often taken [by enemies]; but the Olympieum was complete, except for its roof, the addition of which this war made impossible. Indeed, since the city was leveled, never thereafter could the Acragantines muster sufficient resources to complete their building program. [2] This temple is three hundred and forty feet long, <one hundred and> sixty wide, and one hundred and twenty high, not counting the foundation. Since it is the largest temple in Sicily, it might not unreasonably be compared, at least as regards the size of its groundplan, with temples outside Sicily: for even though in the end the design failed to reach completion, its original concept remains clear. [3] Further, though temples elsewhere are built either with <enceinte walls> or else with columns surrounding their <inner sanctuaries>, this one embodies both plans, since the columns were engaged with the walls, being rounded externally but cut square inside the temple. The surface measurement of their external portion is twenty feet, and there is room for a man's

---

97. Diodorus perhaps forgets that at 4.17.4 he has described how Heracles introduced the vine and olive to Libya.

body in the fluting; that of the inner part is twelve feet. [4] The porticoes were both huge and amazingly high. On the east [pediment] they portrayed, in sculptures of exceptional size and beauty, the Battle of Gods and Giants, and on the west, the Capture of Troy, where each of the heroes can be seen represented in a pose appropriate to his situation.[98] [5] At that time there was also, outside the city, an artificial lake, seven *stadioi* [c. ¼ mile] in circumference and twenty cubits [about twenty-five feet] deep, fed with piped water. Very ingeniously, they contrived to stock it with an abundance of every sort of fish for their public feasts. Besides the fish, it was home to swans and a vast number of other birds, so that it offered great enjoyment to the spectator. [6] Further evidence of Acragantine luxury is provided by the costly extravagance of their [funerary] monuments (which they adorned variously with such things as [sculptures of] their racehorses or of the little pet birds that young girls and boys kept in their homes): these Timaeus is on record as saying he saw surviving even during his own lifetime. [7] Also, in the Olympiad before the one presently under discussion—that is, the 92nd—when Exaenetus of Acragas won the *stadion* [412: <34.1],[99] they brought him into the city in a chariot; and the escorting procession included (among other things) three hundred chariots drawn by pairs of white horses, all provided by Acragantine citizens. [8] In sum, they enjoyed a luxurious lifestyle from childhood onwards: their clothes were extraordinarily soft and delicate, they wore gold ornaments, and even the scrapers and oil flasks they used were of gold or silver.

83. Possibly the wealthiest of the Acragantines at this time was one Tellias, who had large numbers of guestrooms in his house, and used to keep servants stationed at his gates, with instructions to invite every [passing] stranger to accept his hospitality. Many other Acragantines did something of the sort, pursuing a kind of old-fashioned and open-handed social intercourse, which is why Empedocles describes them as

---

98. The groundplan of the Olympian temple of Zeus at Acragas (Agrigento) in fact measures about 361 x 171 ft. At some point, "one hundred and" was clearly lost from the description of the temple's width in Diodorus' MS tradition. The description of the temple in general is textually uncertain at several points. "With enceinte walls" (*meta periteichōn*) is an emendation by Capps, and "inner sanctuaries" (*sēkous*) is Reiske's suggestion, both accepted by Oldfather 1950, and the second by Vogel 1893. The technical name for the arrangement of half-columns and curtain walls described by Diodorus is pseudoperipteral. The building was begun some sixty to eighty years before the sack of the city in 406; ironically, much of the work had been done by Carthaginian slave labor (11.25.2–5).

99. He had won also during the previous (91st) Olympiad of 416: 12.82.

For strangers havens of reverence, in evil unpracticed.[100]

[2] On one occasion, indeed, as Timaeus says in his fifteenth book, when a cavalry unit five hundred strong arrived from Gela in the middle of a winter storm, Tellias entertained them all, providing them immediately on arrival with mantles and tunics fetched from his personal reserves. [3] Polyclitus too, in his *Histories,* has a description of the wine cellar in Tellias' house, claiming that it still existed when he was in Acragas as a soldier and that he inspected it himself. It contained, he says, three hundred jar-shaped tanks hewn out of the solid rock, each with a capacity of one hundred amphoras;[101] and beside these stood a giant stucco-lined vat that could hold one thousand amphoras, from which [wine] flowed into the tanks. [4] It is also recorded that Tellias was quite unremarkable in appearance but endowed with an extraordinary character. Once he was sent on an embassy to Centuripe, and when he appeared before the assembly, people burst out laughing in an unseemly manner, as they saw how far he fell short of their expectations. He, however, cut them short with an admonition not to be surprised, since the Acragantines were in the habit of sending their handsomest citizens to famous cities, but to insignificant and wholly unremarkable ones, men of like nature.

84. Tellias was not the only instance of such magnificence of wealth: there were many others like him in Acragas. Take the case of Antisthenes, known as Rhodos ["Pinky"]. When he was celebrating his daughter's wedding, he provided a feast for every individual citizen in the various alleys and courtyards where they lived, and more than eight hundred chariots and pairs followed the bride in procession: furthermore, not just the city's own cavalry corps but also many [cavalrymen] who had been invited to the wedding from neighboring areas amalgamated to form the bridal escort. [2] The most extravagant thing of all, it is said, however, was the arrangement made for the lighting. Every altar in the city, in temples and alleyways, he loaded with firewood, and to shopowners he distributed faggots and kindling, with instructions that when [they saw] a fire kindled on the acropolis, they should all do likewise. [3] They duly carried out their orders, [given] as the bride was being brought to her [new] home. Since there were also numerous torchbearers in the procession,

---

100. This line, unknown elsewhere, is often inserted by editors as the third line of Empedocles' poem *On Purifications,* beginning: "Friends, who in the great township by the tawny Acragas [river] / dwell up on the city's heights, occupied with good actions . . . (Diels[5] fr. 112).

101. The standard amphora held 8.58 gallons.

the city was filled with light, while the main streets that formed the route could not accommodate the accompanying crowds, so eager was everyone to ape Antisthenes' lavishness. For in those days the Acragantines numbered more than 20,000, and with resident aliens included, not less than 200,000.[102] [4] It is said that Antisthenes once saw his son doing battle with a poor local farmer, putting pressure on the man to sell him his little tract of land. For a while he merely reproved the boy; but when the latter's greed grew more intense, he told him he should not be trying to beggar his neighbor but on the contrary to see he got rich, for then the man would want a bigger estate, and when he failed to buy additional land from his neighbor, he would sell what he now had.

[5] Because of the general degree of prosperity throughout the city, the Acragantines came to enjoy such luxury that somewhat later, when the city was under siege, they made a decree concerning guards who spent the whole night at their posts, restricting them to one mattress, one cover, one sheepskin, and two pillows. [6] If this was their toughest notion of bedding, one can imagine the luxury that marked their general lifestyle.

We wished neither to bypass these matters altogether nor yet to go on about them at such excessive length that we would fail to include more important events.

85. The Carthaginians, after ferrying their forces across to Sicily [May 406], marched against Acragas and made two camps: one on certain hills, where they posted the Iberians and some Libyans, up to 40,000 men in all; and the other not far from the city, surrounding it with a deep ditch and a palisade. [2] First of all they sent ambassadors to the Acragantines, asking them, for choice, to ally themselves with Carthage; or, failing that, to stay neutral and keep the peace by maintaining friendly relations with the Carthaginians. When those in the city refused to accept such terms, the siege was at once set in action. [3] The Acragantines now armed all those of [military] age, paraded them, and stationed one group on the walls, holding the rest in reserve as re-

102. Though population figures in the classical Greek world are notoriously untrustworthy, and such little evidence as there is does suggest higher numbers for the Greek cities of Sicily, this estimate for Acragas still gives one pause. To make sense of it, we have to assume that the figure of 20,000 refers to adult enfranchised males only: multiply by 4 to include women and children, and we still reach no more than 80,000. Athens in the late 4th century (the only comparable figures available) had half as many resident aliens as male citizens. Even if we double that number for Acragas, that brings us to only 100,000. The only way to reach Diodorus' total is by invoking Acragantine luxury and assuming one slave for every free body *and* every resident alien.

placements for them when they became exhausted. Fighting alongside them was also Dexippus the Lacedaemonian, lately arrived from Gela with 1,500 mercenaries: for at that time, as Timaeus records, he was staying in Gela and highly thought of there by reason of his nationality. [4] Because of this, the Acragantines invited him to hire as many mercenaries as possible and bring them to Acragas; there were also hired with them the eight hundred-odd Campanians who had previously served under Hannibal [<44.1, 62.5]. These mercenaries occupied and held the height above Acragas known as "Athenian Hill," which overlooks the city from an excellent strategic position. [5] Himilco and Hannibal, the Carthaginian generals, examined the fortifications and perceived that at one point the city was highly vulnerable to attack. They then moved up two gigantic towers against the walls. Throughout that first day they conducted the siege from these and took many lives before calling off the combatants by trumpet. After darkness had fallen, however, those in the city sallied out and burned the siege equipment.

86. Hannibal and his staff were anxious to make assaults from a greater number of points: they therefore ordered their troops to demolish the grave monuments and [using this material] to build a series of mounds up under the walls. This work, through the abundance of labor available, was very soon completed. But then a wave of superstitious terror spread through the army. [2] It so happened that the tomb of Theron—a quite unusually large one— was struck by lightning, and consequently when it was being torn down, certain seers, who foresaw the future, forbade this. A plague, too, promptly broke out among the troops and caused many deaths, while not a few suffered agonies and were in great distress. [3] Among those who succumbed was Hannibal the general; and some of those sent out on sentry duty reported that during the night, ghosts of the dead had been sighted. Himilco's first act, on observing the rank and file thus consumed by superstitious dread, was to stop the destruction of the monuments. He then proceeded to supplicate the gods in accordance with ancestral custom by sacrificing a young boy to Cronos, and by drowning a large number of sacrificial animals in honor of Poseidon. At the same time he did not abandon his siege works. After damming up, for the extent of the walls, the river that ran alongside the city, he brought up all his siege engines and began to make daily assaults.

[4] The Syracusans, whose observation of the siege of Acragas left them anxious lest the besieged might meet with the same fate as the Selinuntines and Himerans, had been wanting to send them aid from very early on. When at this point the allied contingents from Italy and Messene arrived, they chose Daphnaeus [>96.3] as general, mustered their forces, picked up detachments

from Camarina and Gela en route, called in some troops from the peoples of the interior, and made for Acragas, with thirty of their ships coasting along beside them. They had all told more than 30,000 infantry, and of cavalry not less than 5,000.[103]

87. When Himilco learned of the enemy's approach, he sent out to meet them the Iberians, the Campanians, and of the rest not less than 40,000. The Syracusans had already crossed the Himera River when they and the *barbaroi* came face to face. The battle that followed was of long duration, and the Syracusans were victorious, killing more than 6,000. [2] They would have utterly crushed the entire army and have chased it all the way back to Acragas, had it not been for the fact that the troops engaged in the pursuit were in wild disorder, and their general—well aware that this was how the Himerans had been annihilated—was worried that Himilco might show up with the rest of his army and retrieve the defeat. Nevertheless, while the *barbaroi* were fleeing to their camp before Acragas, the soldiers in the city, observing the Carthaginian defeat, called on their generals to lead them out, declaring that the moment was ripe to destroy the enemy's forces. [3] The generals, however—whether, as was rumored, because they had been bribed or in fear that Himilco might seize the city if it was emptied of its defenders—put a curb on their men's enthusiasm, thereby enabling the fugitives to reach their camp outside the city in safety.

When Daphnaeus and his army reached the campsite that the enemy had abandoned, he took it over. [4] The soldiers from the city, along with [their commander] Dexippus, at once came out and mingled with them. The populace hurriedly met in assembly: everyone was infuriated that the opportunity had been let slip and that when they had the *barbaroi* in their power, they had not exacted due retribution from them. On the contrary: though the generals had been in a position to sally from the city and wipe out the enemy, they had let all those thousands of men slip away. [5] While the assembly was in a state of uproar, with everyone shouting, Menes of Camarina, who had been appointed to the leadership, came forward and denounced the Acragantine generals. This got everyone so worked up that when the accused attempted to speak in their own defense, no one would listen, and the crowd began to throw stones at them. Four of them they actually stoned to death; the fifth, Argeius, a much younger man, they let go. Dexippus the Lacedaemonian also

---

103. They also had Dionysius, the future *tyrannos*, who was a trained scribe, serving as secretary to Daphnaeus and his fellow-commanders (Polyaen. 5.2.2).

incurred their abuse, since although an appointed commander and obviously not lacking in military experience, he had acted as he did, [they claimed], with a view to betraying them.

88. After the assembly, Daphnaeus and his staff led his forces out and attempted to besiege the Carthaginian encampment; but when he saw how elaborately it had been fortified, he gave up that idea. Nevertheless, by patrolling the roads with his cavalry, he both picked up foraging parties and cut off the [Carthaginians'] supply convoys, thus reducing them to a state of serious deprivation. [2] What with not daring to fight a formal engagement, and being hard-pressed by lack of food, the Carthaginians were in deep trouble. Many of the soldiers were actually starving to death, while the Campanians, along with almost all the other mercenaries, forced their way into Himilco's tent and demanded the rations that had been agreed on previously, failing which they threatened to defect to the enemy. [3] Himilco, however, had heard from someone that the Syracusans were bringing in a huge cargo of grain to Acragas by sea. So, this being his one chance of survival, he talked the mercenaries into hanging on for a few more days, giving them by way of pledge the drinking cups belonging to the contingent from Carthage. [4] He then personally sent for forty triremes from Panormus and Motya and planned an attack on those bringing in the supplies. Since prior to this the *barbaroi* had withdrawn from the sea, and winter had already set in, the Syracusans scorned the Carthaginians, confident that they would not dare to man their triremes again. [5] For this reason they were very lax in their convoying of the supplies, so that Himilco, putting out suddenly with his forty triremes, sank eight of their warships and pursued the rest to the shore; and by capturing all the merchantmen, he so completely reversed the hopes of both sides that the Campanians in service with Acragas wrote off the Greeks as a lost cause. Fifteen talents sufficed to buy their allegiance and bring them over to the Carthaginians.

[6] At the beginning, when the Carthaginians were doing badly, the citizens of Acragas had run through their food and other supplies without restriction, in the ongoing expectation that the siege would very soon be lifted. But when the expectations of the *barbaroi* got this boost, the presence of so many tens of thousands of human beings crowded into the one city meant that food supplies were exhausted before they realized. [7] It is also reported that Dexippus the Lacedaemonian succumbed to a fifteen-talent bribe, since he at once replied, to [a question from] the generals of the Italian Greeks, that, yes, it would be better for the war to be continued in some other place, since their provisioning had failed. Thereupon the generals, claiming by way of excuse

that their agreed period of service had elapsed, took off with their troops to the straits. [8] After this withdrawal, the generals conferred with the elected leaders and decided to check the amount of grain left in the city. Finding it very low, they were faced with the necessity of evacuation. They therefore at once issued orders that everyone was to move out the following night [mid Dec. 406: >91.1].

89. With such a multitude of men, women, and children leaving the city, a sudden wave of weeping and lamentation filled people's homes. Fear of the enemy transfixed them; but at the same time, because of the sudden emergency, they were also forced to leave behind, as spoils for the *barbaroi,* all those things that had contributed to their happiness. With fate now depriving them of their domestic treasures, they concluded that they should be glad at least to be saving their skins. [2] Nor was it only the wealth of this great city that was now being visibly abandoned but also a great number of human beings. Those suffering from illnesses were ignored by their relatives, since everyone was thinking about his own survival, while those far advanced in years were left behind because of the weakness of old age. Many, indeed, regarding removal from their native city as the equivalent of death, laid violent hands upon themselves so that they might breathe their last in their ancestral homes. [3] At least the great crowd now making its exodus from the city was provided by the troops with an armed escort as far as Gela. The main road and all parts of the countryside on the way to Geloan territory were crowded with a confused mass of wives, children, daughters, who, exchanging the spoiled existence to which they were used for an exhausting march and extreme hardships, nevertheless, with fear stiffening their resolve, toughed it out to the end. [4] These [refugees] reached Gela in safety and later were resettled in Leontini, after the Syracusans offered them that city as their new home.

90. At dawn Himilco brought his forces inside the walls and put to death almost all who had been left behind: even those who had taken refuge in the temples the Carthaginians dragged out and slaughtered. [2] It is said that Tellias, the foremost citizen as regards both wealth and gentlemanly character, shared in the misfortune of his country: he and some others had decided to take refuge in the temple of Athena, supposing that the Carthaginians would abstain from criminal acts against the gods. But when he witnessed their impious behavior, he set fire to the temple and burned himself along with the dedicatory offerings in it. By this one act he reckoned he would keep the gods immune from impiety, deprive the enemy of a rich haul of plunder,

and (most important of all) save himself from assured physical maltreatment. [3] Himilco pillaged temples and private houses alike, ransacking them methodically. In this way he amassed as much spoils as a city was likely to contain that boasted a population of 200,000 [< n. 102], had never been sacked since its foundation, and was almost the wealthiest Greek city of its day—besides having its occupants' love of beauty manifest itself in the acquisition of every kind of costly objet d'art. [4] Thus the treasures found included an enormous number of exquisitely executed drawings and paintings, as well as innumerable statues of every sort, that likewise revealed the most consummate artistry. The most valuable of these works [Himilco] accordingly sent back to Carthage, while the rest of the spoils he sold as booty. Among the former, as it turned out, was the bull of Phalaris.[104] [5] This bull Timaeus, in his *Histories,* alleges never to have existed at all. He has, however, been refuted by Fortune herself: for about two hundred and sixty years after the fall of Acragas, Scipio sacked Carthage and restored to the Acragantines (among other surviving possessions of theirs in Carthaginian hands) this same bull, which was still in Acragas while the present history was being written.

[6] I have been impelled to discuss this matter with a certain warmth since Timaeus[105]—a most virulent critic of his literary predecessors, and one who showed no mercy to other historians—is here himself caught out in an improvisation, and that in an area where he most stresses the accuracy of his narrative. [7] [Historical] writers, in my opinion, should be forgiven their moments of ignorance, since they are only human, and the truth regarding bygone ages is hard to discover; but those who by deliberate choice avoid exactitude most properly invite censure, whether it be through flattery of individuals or overharsh criticism inspired by personal enmity that they diverge from the truth.

---

104. Phalaris of Acragas, one of the first Sicilian *tyrannoi* (early to mid 6th century), was notorious for cruelty: the bull referred to here was made of bronze and hollow; Phalaris reputedly used to shut his enemies in it, light a fire underneath, and roast them to death. Diodorus describes this instrument of torture at 9.18–19: its first victim was said to have been Perilaüs, the sculptor who made it.

105. Timaeus of Tauromenium (Taormina), c. 350–c. 260, son of Andromachus (16.7.1), was the most influential of the western Greek historians: his *Sicilian History* in 38 books remained the standard account throughout antiquity. His innovative technique of using Olympiads as chronological markers was adopted by Diodorus, along with his practice of using historical events to exemplify divine retribution overtaking the wicked. But he had his bitter critics, above all Polybius, who faulted him, inter alia, for vulgar superstition, fictional speeches, lack of autopsy, and military and geographical ignorance (12.3–4, 25–28).

91. Himilco had besieged the city for eight months and captured it shortly before the winter solstice [22 Dec. 406]. In order, therefore, that his forces could use the houses as winter billets, he refrained from demolishing it immediately. But when the disaster that had overtaken Acragas became public knowledge, such panic swept the island that some of the Sicilian Greeks moved to Syracuse, while others actually emigrated, with wives, children, and all their possessions, to Italy. [2] Those Acragantines who had escaped capture denounced their generals when they arrived in Syracuse, claiming that it was through their treachery that Acragas had been destroyed. The Syracusans too incurred criticism from the rest of the Sicilian Greeks for choosing the kind of leaders that put all Sicily at risk of destruction. [3] Yet even so, when a meeting of the assembly was called in Syracuse [? Jan. 405], and despite the great fears that overshadowed them, not one person dared to speak up with advice regarding the war. Then, while everyone was still at a loss [what to do], Dionysius son of Hermocrat<u>s[106] came forward, accused the generals of betraying their cause to the Carthaginians, and whipped up his audience to exact retribution, urging them not to wait for what the law allotted but to impose their penalty out of hand. [4] When the magistrates, in compliance with the laws, fined Dionysius for creating a disturbance, Philistus,[107] an extremely wealthy man who afterwards wrote the history [of Sicily: >103.3], paid the fine and told Dionysius to say whatever he wanted, adding that if they wanted to fine him all day long, he, Philistus, would furnish the money on his behalf. From that moment Dionysius took heart: he kept stirring up the common people, and threw the assembly into confusion by his denunciations of the generals, saying they had been bribed to disregard the safeguarding of the Acragantines. At the same time, he leveled charges at the rest of [Syracuse's] most distinguished citizens, claiming that they were oligarchic

106. All ancient literary sources describe Dionysius as the son of Hermocrates, but without comment: had his father really been the famous aristocratic general and statesman, this would certainly have attracted attention, if only as to how the son succeeded where the father failed. In fact, as we know from an inscription of 369/8 (Rhodes-Osborne, no. 33, lines 20–21), Dionysius' son, and therefore in all likelihood his father too, was named Hermocrit<u>os</u> (Latinized as -<u>us</u>). But the inevitable unconscious association with Hermocrates was too strong for the MS tradition.

107. Philistus of Syracuse (c. 430–356), historian, general, and steadfast supporter of Dionysius I, who nevertheless twice exiled him, first to Thurii c. 386, then again later, *sine die,* for personal reasons (15.7.4; Plut. *Dion* 11.5–7). Recalled c. 367 by Dionysius II to serve as adviser and admiral, he either committed suicide (16.16.1–4) or was butchered on capture (Plut. *Dion* 35.3–6) in 356 after a defeat by the Syracusans. For his historical work, see 103.3 and n. 119.

sympathizers.[108] [5] He therefore counseled [the assembly] to choose as their generals not the most powerful citizens but rather the most accommodating and popular. The former, [he argued,] since they ruled their fellow-citizens in a despotic fashion, regarded the many with contempt, and the misfortunes of their own country as a source of private income; whereas those of lower degree would do none of these things, since they feared their own inherent weakness.

92. By thus suiting his speech in every way both to the prejudices of his audience and to his own personal aims, he aroused the anger of the assembly to no small extent, since the people had for some while now nursed resentment against the generals for what was seen as their inept handling of the war and now found their anger exacerbated by what they were being told. They therefore removed some of them from office on the spot and appointed other generals, including Dionysius himself, who was much admired by the Syracusans for the outstanding bravery he was reputed to have shown in the battles against the Carthaginians. [2] So, having had his hopes raised in this fashion, he tried every trick he knew to become *tyrannos* of his native city. After assuming office, he neither took part in the generals' meetings nor associated with them in any way; and while acting thus he spread the rumor that they were in communication with the enemy. This, he reckoned, was how he might best whittle away their power and invest himself alone with the generalship.

[3] Such conduct on his part led the most respectable citizens to suspect what was going on, and at every public meeting they maligned him; whereas the populace, knowing nothing of his intentions, sang his praises, saying that in him the city had found a reliable leader, and not before time. [4] Despite this, during the numerous meetings of the assembly to consider preparations for war, Dionysius, noting that fear of the enemy had reduced the Syracusans to a state of abject terror, kept counseling them to recall their exiles; [5] for, said he, it was ridiculous to solicit aid from other states in Italy or the Peloponnese, yet refuse to enlist the support of fellow-citizens to confront one's own dangers—citizens who were promised great rewards by the enemy if they would fight on their side, yet still preferred to die as wanderers in foreign countries rather than compass any hostile act against their own country. [6] Indeed, there were those at present in exile, as a result of episodes of civil dissension that had taken place in the city, who—should they be granted this benefaction—would be only too eager to fight, as a way of expressing thanks

108. Including Daphnaeus (86.4): Arist. *Pol.* 1305A.26.

to their benefactors [<75.7–9]. With repeated arguments relative to the occasion that supported his proposal, he won over the Syracusans' votes. None of his fellow-officials dared to speak against him in this matter, partly on account of his audience's general enthusiasm, and partly because they saw that all they would get if they did would be hatred, whereas he would have the gratitude of those whom he had befriended. [7] Dionysius acted thus in the hope that he would have the exiles as his supporters, these being men who were eager for change, and would be well disposed towards the establishment of a *tyrannis*—would, indeed, take much pleasure in seeing their enemies murdered and their wealth impounded, not to mention the restoration to themselves of their own property. When, finally, the proposal regarding the exiles was ratified, they returned very promptly.

93. It was the arrival of a letter from Gela [? March 405], containing a request for the dispatch of additional troops, that gave Dionysius a good opening for the implementation of his own plan. Sent out himself, at the head of 2,000 infantry and four hundred cavalry, he lost no time in getting to Gela, at that time under the protective watch of Dexippus the Lacedaemonian, who had been appointed to that position by the Syracusans. [2] Dionysius, finding the wealthiest citizens at loggerheads with the common people, denounced them in a meeting of the assembly and got them condemned. He then put them to death and impounded their property.[109] Out of these funds he paid the city garrison commanded by Dexippus the wages owed them. At the same time, he promised his own troops, those that had accompanied him from Syracuse, that he would double the rate of pay laid down for them by the city. [3] In this way he secured the loyalty both of the troops in Gela and of those he had brought with him. He also won the praise of the Geloan common people, as having been responsible for winning their freedom; for in their envy of the most powerful citizens, they cried down the superiority of these men as a despotism over themselves. [4] They therefore sent ambassadors who sang his praises in Syracuse and brought with them decrees honoring him with rich gifts. Dionysius also made an attempt to talk Dexippus into associating himself with his undertaking; but Dexippus would not agree to commit himself, and Dionysius was all set to take his troops and go back to Syracuse. [5] The Geloans, however, on learning that the Carthaginians, with their entire expe-

---

109. On what authority? Presumably in collusion with the populists in the Geloan *demos:* this was very close to Corcyraean-style *stasis* (Thuc. 3.82). It is noteworthy that Dexippus, though glad enough to have his troops paid, refused to become associated with Dionysius (§4), and would seem to have summed him up with some percipience, as Dionysius himself realized (96.1).

ditionary force, planned to make Gela their first target for attack, begged Dionysius to stay and not to look on and do nothing while they suffered the same fate as the Acragantines. Dionysius reassured them that he would very soon be back with a larger force, and then set out from Gela with his own troops.

94. A play was being put on in Syracuse, and he reached the city just as the audience was leaving the theater. When a crowd gathered round him with questions about the Carthaginians, he told them that though they failed to realize it, they had more dangerous foes at home than any abroad—the ones in charge of their public affairs. These were the men the citizens relied on while they kept holiday; yet they were also the ones who let the soldiers go unpaid while embezzling public funds themselves. Further, though the enemy was preparing for war on an unrivaled scale and about to launch an expeditionary force against Syracuse, the generals were paying not the slightest heed to such matters. [2] The reason for such behavior he had known earlier, but now he had clearer information. Himilco, he said, had sent a herald to him: ostensibly on the subject of prisoners of war, but in fact, since he, Dionysius, was refusing to collaborate, to urge him—now that the bulk of his colleagues had agreed not to interfere with what was going on—at least not to offer active opposition. [3] As a result, [Dionysius continued], he had no desire to serve any longer as general and was in Syracuse to lay down his office. It was intolerable, when his other colleagues were selling out their country, that he should be the only one to face the peril with his fellow-citizens and to risk the [later] assumption that he had shared in the betrayal.

[4] Though people had been fired by his words, and what he said had quickly spread through the entire army, at this point every individual departed to his house in an agony of anxiety. But the following day [another] assembly was convened, during which, by making numerous accusations against the magistrates, and stirring up the *demos* against the generals, Dionysius gained no small measure of approval. [5] Finally, some of his listeners called loudly for his [immediate] appointment as general plenipotentiary rather than waiting until the enemy was assaulting their walls. The magnitude of the war, [they argued], made such an office essential: only thus was it possible for their affairs to prosper. The matter of the traitors could be thrashed out in another assembly meeting: it was not relevant to the present crisis. There was, too, a precedent: with Gelon as general plenipotentiary,[110] 300,000 Carthaginians had been beaten at Himera.

110. This is possible, but the passages cited in favor of it (11.22, 26.5–6) do not in fact say so.

95. The many, in their usual fashion, quickly veered towards the worse decision, and Dionysius was duly appointed general with supreme authority.[111] Since his position now matched his desires, he proposed a decree doubling the pay of the mercenaries. If this were to be done, he said, they would also be much keener for the struggle ahead; and regarding the funds, he told them not to trouble themselves, since to raise such a sum would be an easy matter.

[2] When the assembly dispersed, quite a number of the Syracusans found fault with what had been done, as though it had not been they themselves who ratified the decision; for as their thinking came round to their own state, they had a shrewd notion of the arbitrary rule to come. In their wish to guarantee their freedom, these men had, without realizing it, set a despot in power over their country. [3] Dionysius, anxious to anticipate any change of mind among the populace, kept looking for some way in which he could [plausibly] ask for a bodyguard, since once this was granted him he would easily be able to lay firm hold on the *tyrannis*. He therefore promptly issued orders that all men younger than forty should take thirty days' rations and rendezvous under arms in Leontini, at the time a Syracusan [frontier] stronghold, full of exiles and foreigners. Dionysius hoped to get these latter groups on his side, since change was what they most wanted; he was also betting that most of the Syracusans would not even show up in Leontini. [4] Regardless, while he was encamped at night out in the countryside, he pretended to be the victim of a plot, and by means of his personal servants contrived to raise a great shouting and hullabaloo. After so doing, he took refuge on the acropolis [of Leontini] and passed the rest of the night there, burning bonfires and sending for the most staunchly loyal of his troops. [5] At dawn, when the populace thronged into Leontini, he spoke plausibly and at length in furtherance of his plan, and persuaded this crowd to grant him a bodyguard of six hundred soldiers, whom he could choose for himself. It is said that Dionysius acted thus in imitation of Peisistratus the Athenian, [6] who, the story goes, inflicted wounds on himself and then appeared before the assembly, claiming to be the victim of a conspiracy: as a result, he was granted a bodyguard by his fellow-citizens and used this to set himself up as *tyrannos*.[112] So now Dionysius, after hood-

---

111. If Dionysius was in fact appointed general plenipotentiary (*stratēgós autokrátōr*) it was probably in the first instance with one or two colleagues who shared his authority, as Hermocrates had proposed (Thuc. 6.72.5), and perhaps with Hipparinus as an elder adviser (Plat. *Ep.* 8.353A; cf. Arist. *Pol.* 1306A1).

112. In 560/59: cf. Hdt. 1.59; Arist. *Ath. Pol.* 14.1;, Plut. *Sol.* 30; Polyaen. 1.23.1. Dionysius carefully picked the number of 600 (Arist. *Pol.* 1286B35–40) since this was the regular size of Syracuse's special guards regiment (11.76.2; cf. Thuc. 6.96.3).

winking the populace by a very similar device, established the basis of his own *tyrannis*.

96. He now at once chose over a thousand individuals who were without property but daring in spirit, provided them with expensive weapons and armor, and raised their hopes with the most generous promises; the mercenaries too he made his own by calling them in for friendly discussions. He also made changes in the military command structure, transferring key appointments to his most trusted associates; Dexippus the Lacedaemonian he relieved of his post and sent back to Greece, since this was a man he felt he had to watch carefully, in case he seized the opportunity to give the Syracusans back their freedom. [2] He also summoned the mercenaries in Gela, and indeed collected fugitives and impious characters from all quarters, in the expectation that his *tyrannis* would derive its most solid support from such people. Even so, after openly declaring himself *tyrannos,* he camped out in the naval station when he came into Syracuse. Though the Syracusans resented him, they were forced to hold their peace, since there was nothing they could do now: the city was full of armed mercenaries, and everyone was scared of the Carthaginians and their formidable military strength. [3] Dionysius also lost no time in marrying the daughter of that Hermocrates who had defeated the Athenians, as well as giving his own sister in marriage to Polyxenus, the brother of Hermocrates' wife. This he did because he wanted to establish a family connection with a famous house and thus set his *tyrannis* on a solid basis. He then summoned an assembly and had his most powerful opponents, Daphnaeus and Demarchus, put to death.

[4] From a clerk and an ordinary private citizen Dionysius had [risen to] become *tyrannos* of the greatest city in the Greek world: moreover, he maintained his rule until the day he died, continuing as *tyrannos* for thirty-eight years [405–367]. We shall give a detailed description of his various actions and the expansion of his power at the appropriate chronological junctures, since it would appear that this man, through his own unaided efforts, established what was both the greatest and the longest-lasting *tyrannis* in all recorded history.

[5] The Carthaginians, after their capture of Acragas, conveyed to Carthage the dedicatory offerings, the statues, and anything else of exceptional value. Having burned down the temples and pillaged the city, they then passed the winter there. When spring returned, they set about getting ready every kind of siege engine and missile, with the intention of first investing the city of Gela.

97. While these events were going on [? spring 406], the Athenians [<79.7], who had suffered a continuous series of reverses, made citizens of

the metics and any other foreigners willing to join their struggle. In this way, a great crowd of new citizens was rapidly put on the rolls, and the generals kept calling up for active service all of them who were fit. They put sixty ships into commission, fitting them out at great expense, and then sailed for Samos. Here they found the other generals, who had collected eighty triremes from the surrounding islands. [2] They had also asked the Samians to man ten additional triremes. It was thus with one hundred and fifty ships in all that they put to sea and dropped anchor at the Arginusae Islands, with the firm intention of raising the siege of Mytilene [Xen. *Hell.* 1.6.24–25]. [3] When Callicratidas, the Lacedaemonian admiral, learned that these ships were approaching, he left Eteonicus and the ground forces to take care of the siege, while he himself manned one hundred and forty ships and hastily put to sea on the other side of the Arginusae. These islands (which were then inhabited, with a small Aeolian township) lie between Mytilene and Cyme, close in to the mainland by the Cane promontory.

[4] The Athenians immediately took note of the enemy's approach, since they were anchored at no great distance from them. On account of the strong winds, however, they refused battle, instead making preparations for an engagement on the following day. The Lacedaemonians did likewise, though the seers on both sides were against it. [5] On the Lacedaemonian side, the head of a victim, which was lying on the beach, vanished from sight when a wave broke over it, and this led the seer to forecast the death of the admiral in action. It is said that when Callicratidas heard his prophecy, he remarked that if he did die during the battle, he would do nothing to lessen Sparta's good name. [6] As for the Athenians, their general <Thrasyllus>, who held the supreme command for that day, had the following dream the night before. He seemed to be in Athens, at the theater, which was crowded, and he, with six of the other generals, was acting in Euripides' tragedy *The Phoenician Women,* while their competitors were performing *The Suppliants.* The result, in his dream, was a "Cadmean victory"[113] for them, and they all died, thus repeating the fate of those who marched against Thebes. [7] On hearing this, the seer revealed that seven of the generals would lose their lives. Since the sacrificial omens indicated victory, the generals banned any public reference to their own demise but had the victory announced by the omens proclaimed throughout their entire force.

---

113. I.e., a victory in which the victors suffer as much as the vanquished: the reference to Cadmus probably recalls the dragon's teeth he sowed, which then sprouted as armed soldiers who killed each other.

98. The admiral Callicratidas assembled his rank and file and encouraged them with words appropriate to the occasion, concluding as follows: "I am so eager to face this challenge for my country that even with the seer foretelling, from the sacrificial victims, victory for you, but death for me, I am nevertheless ready to die. So, aware as I am that after a commander's death his forces are prone to confusion, I now hereby designate as admiral, should I meet with some mishap, Clearchus, a man of proven experience in the business of warfare." [2] By speaking thus, Callicratidas caused not a few to emulate his valor and themselves become more eager for the battle. So the Lacedaemonians, with words of encouragement one to another, went aboard their ships. Meanwhile, the Athenians (after being exhorted by their generals to go [bravely] into the conflict ahead of them) hastily manned the triremes, after which all of them took up their positions [Xen. *Hell.* 1.6.29–35]. [3] The right wing was commanded by Thrasyllus, together with Pericles (the son [by Aspasia] of that other Pericles who because of his authority was known as "The Olympian"[<12.40.6]). Thrasyllus also coopted Theramenes—who was serving on this campaign in the ranks—into a command on the right wing, since previously he had often commanded armaments. The remaining generals he stationed at intervals along his entire battle line. This line covered the whole extent of the Arginusae Islands, since he was anxious to spread his ships as widely as possible.[114] [4] Callicratidas now put to sea. He himself was in command of his right wing, while the left he had allotted to the Boeotians, under the Theban Thrasondas. Being unable to equal the enemy's line in length (the islands extended a very considerable distance) he instead divided his fleet, forming it into two separate squadrons, and fought a double engagement, one on each wing. [5] His move caused considerable amazement all around to those watching, since there were in effect four fleets battling each other, and the total number of ships gathered into the one area was not far short of three hundred. This is the largest sea battle on record fought by Greeks against Greeks.

99. The admirals gave the order for the trumpeters to sound [the attack]; and at the same moment, the war cry was raised in turn by the entire force on either side, making a quite extraordinary din. All the rowers drove vigorously at the waves, vying one with another, each eager to be the first to begin the battle. [2] Most of them, indeed, because of the length of the war, had considerable battle experience, and they brought to the occasion unsurpassed

---

114. I.e., he used the islands themselves as blocks in his line, advancing by squadrons between them.

enthusiasm, since it was the cream of the forces [but see <97.1] that had come together for this decisive conflict, and all of them assumed that those who won the battle would finish off the war. [3] Callicratidas in particular, having heard from the seer the end that would be his, was determined to claim for himself the most glorious death possible. He was thus the first to attack the ship of Lysias the general,[115] which he, along with the triremes accompanying him, stove in at the initial onset, and sank. Of the remaining vessels [opposed to him] he rammed some, rendering them unseaworthy, and sheared off the oar banks of others, which incapacitated them for combat. [4] Finally, he rammed Pericles' trireme with great violence, opening up a great hole in its side; but the beak of the ram jammed in the gap, so that [the crew] were unable to back away again. At this Pericles threw a grappling iron on to Callicratidas' vessel, and once it had a firm hold the Athenians crowded round and sprang aboard, overwhelming the crew and butchering them all. [5] It was at this point, they say, that Callicratidas, after fighting brilliantly and holding his own for a long while, was finally worn down by the number of his attackers, who dealt him wounds from all quarters. When their admiral's defeat became generally known, the Peloponnesians panicked and gave way. [6] But although the Peloponnesian right wing was routed, the Boeotians on their left continued to put up a vigorous fight for a considerable time, since not only they but also the Euboeans alongside them—and indeed all those who had defected from Athens—were scared that the Athenians, should they recover their position of authority, would exact retribution from them for their revolt. However, on seeing that most of their ships had sustained damage, and that the bulk of the victorious fleet was now coming about to deal with them, they were forced to flee. Of the Peloponnesians some got safely to Chios, and others, to Cyme.

100. The Athenians pursued their beaten opponents for a good distance, littering the entire adjacent area of the sea with corpses and wrecked ships. After this some of the generals thought that they should pick up the dead, since the Athenians took an extremely harsh view of those who left corpses unburied; others, however, said they should sail to Mytilene and raise the siege as quickly as possible. [2] But then a huge storm[116] developed, so that

---

115. According to Xenophon (1.6.30–31), both Callicratidas and Lysias were stationed on the right wings of their respective fleets, though both he and Diodorus agree that Pericles was on the left. Xenophon also states (§33) that Callicratidas was thrown overboard and vanished when his trireme rammed an enemy vessel.

116. This area of the Gulf of Adramyttium, between Lesbos and Ayvalik in Turkey, is subject (as I have personally witnessed) to storms of a peculiar violence and intensity, with

the triremes were tossed about, and the rank and file, both as a result of their grueling experience in the battle and because of the size of the waves, were against picking up the dead. [3] Finally, as the storm grew more violent, they neither sailed to Mytilene nor stopped to pick up the dead but were forced by the winds to put in at the Arginusae. In this battle [? Sept. 406] the Athenians lost twenty-five ships, together with most of their crews, and the Peloponnesians, seventy-seven; [4] and because so many vessels had gone down, along with those who manned them, the whole coast from Cyme to Phocaea was strewn with corpses and wreckage.

[5] When Eteonicus, still besieging Mytilene, heard from someone about the Peloponnesian defeat, he sent his ships to Chios, but himself, with his ground forces, withdrew to the city of Pyrrha, which was an ally; for he was afraid that, if the Athenians brought up their fleet against him and the besieged then made a sortie from the city, he risked losing his entire force. [6] In fact the Athenian generals, after sailing to Mytilene and collecting Conon and his forty ships, put in at Samos, from where they carried out destructive raids on enemy territory [Xen. *Hell.* 1.6.36–38]. [7] After this[117] [winter 406/5], those dwelling in the Aeolid and Ionia and such islands as were allied with the Lacedaemonians met in Ephesus, and as a result of their deliberations resolved to send to Sparta and ask for Lysander as admiral; for during his term as supreme naval commander he had accomplished a great deal and was thought to surpass all others in strategic skill. [8] The Lacedaemonians, however, had a law against sending the same man out twice, and they were not ready to break with ancestral custom. They therefore chose Aracus as admiral but sent Lysander with him as a private citizen, instructing Aracus to accept his advice in all matters. So these two, on being sent out to assume command, began to assemble as many triremes as they could, both from the Peloponnese and from their allies [Xen. *Hell.* 2.1.6–7; Plut. *Lys.* 7.1–2].

101. When the Athenians heard of their success off the Arginusae, they congratulated the generals on the victory but took it ill that men who died fighting for Athenian supremacy should have been left unburied [Xen. *Hell.* 1.7.1–35]. [2] Now since Theramenes and Thrasybulus had returned to Athens ahead of the rest, the generals assumed it was they who had brought charges before the populace regarding the dead and therefore sent letters against them to the *demos,* explaining that it was in fact they who had been ordered to pick up corpses

high winds, known locally as *phourtounes.* The sailors knew very well what they were up against, and the final decision was amply justified.

117. The victory at Arginusae had been followed by yet another Spartan peace proposal (Arist. *Ath. Pol.* 34.1), rejected out of hand by Athens.

[Xen. *Hell.* 1.6.35]. This, however, became the main cause of their undoing. [3] They could have had the powerful assistance in their trial of Theramenes and his group: men who were skilled speakers, who had numerous friends, and, best of all, had participated with them in the events surrounding the battle; but now, on the contrary, they had them as adversaries and bitter accusers. [4] For when the letters were read before the *demos,* the immediate reaction of that body was anger at Theramenes and his friends; but after these had spoken on their own behalf, this anger was redirected against the generals. [5] As a result, the *demos* notified them that they would be required to stand trial and instructed them to turn over command of their forces to Conon, whom they cleared of responsibility in the matter. The rest of them, they decreed, were to return as soon as possible. Of these, Aristogenes and Protomachus, fearing the wrath of the masses, fled; but Thrasyllus, <Diomedon>,[118] and Calliades, as well as Lysias, Pericles, and Aristocrates, sailed back to Athens with the bulk of their ships, hoping that they would have the help of their crews—a sizable body—during their trial. [6] When the populace gathered in assembly, however, they listened to the charge, and those whose words were calculated to please them, but the defendants they shouted down and would not let speak [but see Xen. *Hell.* 1.7.16–33]. Also, no little damage was done the latter by the relatives of the deceased, who appeared before the assembly in mourning, and begged the *demos* to punish the men guilty of leaving unburied those who had been happy to die for their country. [7] Finally, then, the friends of the bereaved, together with Theramenes' partisans (of whom there were many) got their way, and the upshot was that the generals were condemned to death, with the forfeiture of their property to the state.

102. When the matter had been thus decided, and they were about to be led off to death by the public executioners, Diomedon, one of the generals, stepped forward: a man both active in the prosecution of the war and regarded as a paragon of righteousness and every other virtue. [2] Everyone fell silent. He said: "Men of Athens, may the decision taken concerning us turn out auspiciously for the city. Regarding the vows we made for victory: since Fortune has prevented our discharging them—and it would be well that you give them your consideration—do you pay [what is due] to Zeus the Savior and Apollo and the Hallowed Goddesses [i.e., the Furies], since it was to them

---

118. Clearly (see 102.1–3) this name at some point was lost from the MS tradition. The full list of ten generals at 74.1 includes Diomedon but contains two names—Erasinides and Archestratus—unaccounted for here, while incorrectly including Thrasybulus (here listed as returning early to Athens) rather than Thrasyllus (the corrected reading in my translation). Neither Calliades nor Theramenes figures on the earlier list.

we made our vows before we won our victory at sea." [3] After Diomedon
made this statement, he was led away with the other generals to the execution
decreed for them, though among all decent citizens he had aroused tears and
much compassion: that a man about to meet an unjust end should make no
mention at all of his own misfortune but rather, on behalf of the city that
was doing him wrong, should ask for his vows to the gods to be paid—this
seemed the act of a pious and high-minded man, one who little merited the
fate awaiting him. [4] So these men were put to death by the eleven magistrates legally appointed for that purpose, though not only had they committed no offense against the city but had won the greatest naval engagement ever
fought by Greeks against Greeks, besides distinguishing themselves brilliantly
in other battles and, because of their personal acts of valor, setting up trophies
over their [defeated] enemies. [5] To such a degree at this time were the people
out of their right minds, and unjustly spurred on by their populist leaders,
that they took out their anger on men who deserved, not punishment, but
much praise and many decorations.

103. Very soon, however, persuaders and persuaded alike had cause to be
sorry for what they had done, since it was as though heaven itself had decided
to exact retribution from them. Those who had been gulled were paid out
for their ignorance not all that long afterwards, when they were subjected
to the power not of one despot, but of thirty [>14.3.5–5.7]; [2] and their
deceiver, Callixenus, being also the motion's proposer [Xen. *Hell.* 1.7.9–10],
was brought to trial as soon as the commons repented, on a charge of deceiving the *demos*. Without being allowed a defense, he was pinioned and thrown
into the public jail. He managed, without being observed and in the company
of several others, however, to dig his way out of prison and make his way to
the enemy at Deceleia. As a result, he escaped death; but for the rest of his
natural life, the shameful thing he had done meant that not in Athens alone,
but among Greeks everywhere, he always had to face the pointing fingers of
contempt [Xen. *Hell.* 1.7.35].

[3] Such then, more or less, were the events that took place during this
year. Of the [historical] writers, Philistus[119] brought his first survey of Sicilian

———————

119. Cf. 91.4 and n. 107. The second part of the *Sicilian History* covered Dionysius I's
rule from 406/5 until his death in 368/7 (15.73.5); he also wrote two more books on Dionysius II, bringing the narrative down to 363/2. Notoriously, but not surprisingly, Philistus
showed himself proauthoritarian in his judgments as a historian: Plutarch, commenting
on his sympathy for all aspects of *tyrannis* (*Dion* 36.3), calls him *philotyrannōtatos*. As later
critics (Cicero included, e.g., *De Orat.* 2.57) stressed, he sought, not without some success,
to emulate Thucydides. The failure of his work to survive is a serious loss, but his vivid

affairs down to this point, concluding with the capture of Acragas and covering a period of more than eight hundred years in seven books. He began his
second survey, in four books, from where the first left off.

[4] About this same time [? fall 406] Sophocles son of Sophilus, the tragic
playwright, died at the age of ninety, after winning first prize eighteen times.
The story goes that when he put on his very last tragedy and won with it, his
immoderate transports of delight were also the cause of his death. [5] Apollodorus, the author of the *Chronological Survey*,[120] states that Euripides died
during the same year. Some sources, however, place his death at a slightly
earlier date [correctly: 407/6]. While living [at the court of] King Archelaus
of Macedon, they say, he made a trip into the countryside and was there set
upon and torn to pieces by dogs.

104. When this year had run its course, Alexias was archon in Athens
[405/4], and in Rome [Varr. 408] in lieu of consuls three military tribunes
were appointed: Gaius Julius [Vopisci Iullus], Publius Cornelius [Cossus],
and Gaius Servilius [Ahala]. At a time when these had already entered office, and after the execution of the generals, the Athenians put Philocles in
command, turned the fleet over to him, and sent him out to Conon, with
instructions that the two of them were to share the overall command. [2] After he had joined Conon on Samos, he put the entire fleet into commission,
one hundred and seventy-three ships in all. Of these, Conon and Philocles
decided to leave twenty behind; and with all the rest they—exercising their
joint command—set course for the Hellespont.

[3] Lysander, the Lacedaemonian admiral [in effect: but see <100.8], after
collecting thirty-five ships from nearby allies in the Peloponnese, sailed for
Ephesus. Here he also called in the squadron from Chios and put it in readiness. Next he traveled up-country to see King Darius' son Cyrus, and obtained
from him ample funds for the maintenance of his soldiers. [4] Since Cyrus was
being summoned back to Persia by his father,[121] he transferred to Lysander his
authority over the cities subject to him and instructed them to pay Lysander

first-hand testimony can be glimpsed at intervals throughout Diodorus' Sicilian narrative, e.g., during the final sea battle between Syracuse and Athens in the Great Harbor of
Syracuse (15.3–17.5).

120. Apollodorus of Athens (*fl.* 2nd century BCE) composed his *Chronological Survey*
in verse for mnemonic purposes, drawing inter alia on archon lists to produce a survey
ranging from 1184 (the "late date" for the fall of Troy) to 110/9.

121. During the previous winter Cyrus had executed two of his cousins for alleged
lèse-majesté, and their parents had lodged a strong complaint with the Great King: Xen.
Hell. 2.1.8–9.

their tribute. After thus acquiring every possible resource for prosecuting the war, Lysander returned to Ephesus [Xen. *Hell.* 2.1.10–14; Plut. *Lys.* 9.1–2].

[5] At this time also certain men in Miletus, who were aiming at an oligarchy, with the assistance of the Lacedaemonians[122] put an end to democratic government there. First of all, during the Dionysia they went to the homes of their chief opponents, seized them, carried them off (they were about forty in number), and butchered them all. Then, [at midmorning] when the marketplace was full, they picked off three hundred of the richest citizens and killed them too. [6] The most respectable of those citizens who supported the democracy, over a thousand all told, in alarm at their situation fled to Pharnabazus the satrap. He gave them a kindly welcome, presented each of them with a gold stater, and settled them at Blauda, a stronghold in Lydia.

[7] Lysander now sailed with the larger part of his fleet against Iasus in Caria. This city, which was an ally of Athens, he took by storm, butchering all adult males, to a total of eight hundred, selling the women and children as spoils of war and leveling the city. [8] After this he sailed against Attica and many other places [Xen. *Hell.* 2.1.15; Plut. *Lys.* 9.2–3] but accomplished nothing substantial or worth recording, for which reason we have not taken the trouble to record these matters. Finally, however, he captured Lampsacus. He let the Athenian garrison withdraw under truce and returned the city to its citizens, but only after seizing their property [Xen. *Hell.* 2.1.18–19; Plut. *Lys.* 9.4].

105. When the Athenian generals heard that the Lacedaemonians were besieging Lampsacus in full force, they got their triremes together from all quarters and hastily put to sea against them with one hundred and eighty vessels. [2] Finding the city already taken, they instead dropped anchor at Aegospotami ["The Goat's Rivers"] and from this base sailed out daily against the enemy, challenging them to a battle. But the Peloponnesians steadfastly refused to come out and face them, and this left the Athenians at a loss what to do in the circumstances, since they were running out of rations with no prospect of further supplies on site. [3] It was now that Alcibiades came to them with a proposition.[123] Medocus and Seuthes, he said, the kings of the Thra-

---

122. For Lysander's devious role in this affair, see Plut. *Lys.* 8.1–3.

123. This famous last-minute intervention by Alcibiades from his nearby stronghold of Pactyes was widely reported: Xen. *Hell.* 2.1.25–26; Plut. *Alcib.* 36.5–37.2; Nepos, *Alcib.* 8.1–6. Xenophon and Nepos both mention something that Diodorus does not: Alcibiades' sensible recommendation that the Athenians should shift their base to Sestos, where (even if further away from Lysander) they would have both a harbor and available supplies. His proposed strategy (forcing a combined land and sea operation, as at Cyzicus) had much to be said for it. Ironically, his own reputation ensured its rejection.

cians, were his friends and had agreed to provide him with a large force if he wanted to finish off the war against the Lacedaemonians. He therefore invited [the Athenians] to give him a share of the command, promising them one of two things: he would either force the enemy to fight them at sea or else fight them himself on land along with the Thracians. [4] This proposal Alcibiades made because of the longing he had to achieve, through his personal efforts, some major success for his country and thus, by his benefactions, to bring the people back to their former friendly regard for him. The Athenian generals, however, figuring that they would incur the blame for a defeat, whereas everyone would attribute any success to Alcibiades, told him to take himself off double-quick and never come near the camp again.

106. Since the enemy continued to refuse a naval engagement, and the troops were on the verge of starvation, Philocles (who held the command that day) ordered the other captains to man their triremes and follow on, while he, with thirty ships that were then ready, set out ahead of them.[124] [2] Lysander, who had learned about this [plan] from some deserters, now stood out to sea with his entire fleet, put Philocles to flight, and chased him back in the direction of the other ships. [3] These Athenian triremes had not yet been manned, and everyone was thrown into confusion by the unexpected appearance of the enemy. [4] Lysander, perceiving the hullabaloo and disorder among his opponents, promptly disembarked Eteonicus and those troops of his who were used to fighting on dry land. Eteonicus, losing no time, seized his chance and overran part of the [Athenian] camp. Lysander himself meanwhile sailed up with all his triremes ready for battle and, by throwing out grappling irons, began to drag off the ships that were moored inshore. [5] The Athenians, dumbfounded by this unexpected action, had no chance to get their vessels afloat, and they were unable to fight it out ashore. After a brief resistance they were routed. Immediately—some deserting the ships, and the rest the camp—they took to flight, in whatever direction each individual hoped escape might lie. [6] Of the triremes, ten only got away. One of these belonged to Conon the general, who, fearing the fury of the *demos,* abandoned any thought of returning to Athens: instead he fled to Cyprus and sought refuge with its ruler Evagoras, with whom he was on terms of friendship. Most of the troops retreated overland and got safely to Sestos. [7] The

---

124. What Philocles hoped to achieve by this maneuver is hard to figure: it may well be that Lysander's tactics simply forced him to take action or face mutiny. Xenophon's account (*Hell.* 2.1.27–29) of the battle (if it merits that title) is a wholly incredible episode designed solely to glorify Lysander.

rest of the ships Lysander captured; and having taken Philocles, the general, prisoner, he conveyed him to Lampsacus and there executed him.[125]

After this [Sept. 405] he put messengers aboard his fastest trireme and sent them to Lacedaemon to bring news of the victory, decorating the vessel with the most valuable arms and spoils. [8] He then moved against the Athenians who had taken refuge in Sestos, capturing the city but allowing the Athenians to withdraw under truce. Immediately thereafter he embarked his troops and made for Samos. He himself embarked on the siege of the city but dispatched to Sparta Gylippus (the same man who had taken a squadron to fight alongside the Syracusans in Sicily [<13.7.2]) as escort for the booty, and with it 1,500 talents of silver. [9] The money was in small sacks, each of which also contained a tally stick[126] with a note of the amount. Gylippus, unaware of this [precaution], secretly opened up the sacks and skimmed off three hundred talents. The notes gave him away to the ephors: he fled the country and was condemned to death [Plut. *Lys.* 16.1–17.1]. [10] Something very similar happened to Gylippus' father <Cleandridas>,[127] who at an earlier time also went into exile, when he was suspected of having been bribed by Pericles not to carry out a raid into Attica. He too was condemned to death, fled to Thurii in Italy, and stayed there [Plut. *Per.* 22.2–3; cf. Thuc. 2.21.1]. So these men, who were otherwise thought well of, by acting in such a manner clouded the remainder of their lives with shame.

107. When the Athenians heard about the destruction of their forces,[128] they gave up their attempts to win control of the sea and instead turned

---

125. With good reason: see Xen. *Hell.* 2.1.31–32; Plut. *Lys.* 9.5, 13.1–2. Philocles had proposed a motion, passed by the Assembly, that in future after a victory each captive should have either his right thumb or his whole right hand cut off; he had also thrown overboard the entire crews of two captured triremes. In the desperate atmosphere of looming defeat and numerous desertions, atrocities were becoming the order of the day,

126. This was the *skytale,* a primitive Spartan encoding device. Two matching cylinders or staffs were kept, one by the home authorities, the other by a commander abroad. A strip of papyrus was wound round one of these slantwise, and a message inscribed on it. It was then unwound and regarded as unreadable until rewound on the other. Few things so bring it home to us that this was, still, primarily an oral culture.

127. Diodorus' MSS call him Clearchus: corrected from Thuc. 6.93.2 and Plut. *Per.* 22.2.

128. Brilliantly described by Xenophon in a justly famous passage (*Hell.* 2.1.3–4), recounting how "the wailing ran up the Long Walls from Piraeus to the city . . . and that night no one slept, grieving not only for the dead, but—far more—for themselves, in the belief that they too would suffer what they had inflicted on the Melians . . . and many other Greek peoples."

to such matters as repairing their fortifications and blocking their harbors, anticipating (what in fact was very probable) that a siege was imminent. [2] The two Lacedaemonian kings, Agis and Pausanias, invaded Attica with a large army and camped before the walls, while Lysander arrived at Piraeus with more than two hundred triremes [Xen. *Hell.* 2.2.7–9; Plut. *Lys.* 14.1]. The Athenians, though in dire straits, nevertheless continued to resist, and for some time found it easy enough to defend the city. [3] Since the siege was proving a tough option, the Peloponnesians decided to withdraw their ground forces from Attica and instead to enforce a blockade from a distance with their ships, to prevent any grain getting through. [4] When this was done, the Athenians were reduced to a dire lack of all commodities but in particular of food, since this had always been brought in by sea [Xen. *Hell.* 2.2.11]. As the crisis grew daily more acute, and the city filled up with corpses, those who were left sent ambassadors [mid March 404] and made peace with the Lacedaemonians, the terms being that they should break down their Long Walls and the fortifications of Piraeus, retain no more than ten warships, remove [their officers] from all the cities, and accept Lacedaemonian hegemony.[129] Thus the Peloponnesian War, the longest of any known to us, after lasting for twenty-seven years came to an end in the manner described above.

108. A little after the peace [early Apr. 404] Darius, the Great King of Asia, died after a reign of nineteen years, and his eldest son Artaxerxes [II Mnemon] succeeded to the throne and reigned for forty-three years [>15.93.1]. During this same period, according to Apollodorus the Athenian [<103.5], the poet Antimachus[130] flourished.

[2] In Sicily, Himilco, the Carthaginian commander, about the beginning of summer [405] leveled the city of Acragas; and anything in those temples that he felt had not been well and truly destroyed by fire, such as the sculptures and works of fine art, he defaced. This done, he mustered his entire force and invaded the territory of Gela. [3] In his progress through this territory and that of Camarina, he gave his army its fill of every kind of spoils.

---

129. Cf. Plut. *Lys.* 14.4 (the purported Spartan ephors' decree), Xen. *Hell.* 2.2.15, 20 (10 *stadia* only of the Long Walls to be destroyed, Athens' exiles to be repatriated). A full list of the terms, with sources, in Green 2004, 148–149. Lysander sailed into Piraeus, and the demolition of the walls began, on 16 Mounychion = 22/23 Apr. 404 (Plut. *Lys.* 15.1–4; Xen. *Hell.* 2.2.23).

130. Antimachus of Colophon (*fl.* c. 400), epic and elegiac poet, editor of Homer, friend of Plato. He wrote a *Thebaid*, and his elegiac work *Lyde* was composed to celebrate his deceased wife: Callimachus later described it, or her, as "fat and crass."

He then marched on Gela itself, skirting the river of the same name, and pitched camp. [4] Outside their city the Geloans had a gigantic bronze statue of Apollo, which the Carthaginians seized and sent off to Tyre. The Geloans had erected it in obedience to a divine oracular response; and the Tyrians of a later day, when under siege by Alexander of Macedon [>17.41.7], gave [the god] short shrift, on the grounds that he was fighting on the side of their enemies. But after Alexander took the city—as Timaeus says, on the identically named day, and at the same hour, as the Carthaginians had carried off the Apollo from Gela—then the god was honored by the Greeks with the most elaborate sacrifices and processions, as having been the cause of Tyre's capture. [5] Thus, though these events took place at different periods, we thought it not inappropriate (they being so extraordinary) to cite them side by side.

The Carthaginians felled trees in the surrounding countryside and dug a ditch all round their encampment, since they were expecting Dionysius to appear with a strong force to bring relief to the besieged in their peril. [6] At first the citizens of Gela voted, because of the magnitude of the danger they anticipated, to evacuate their women and children to safety in Syracuse; but when the women rushed to the altars in the marketplace, and begged to share the same fortune as their menfolk, they agreed to their request. [7] They then organized their troops into numerous detachments, which they sent out in turn to scour the countryside. Since these knew the lay of the land, they regularly picked off enemy stragglers, of whom they killed not a few, and every day brought back large numbers alive. [8] Despite the Carthaginians' relays of assaults on the city, and the damage done to the walls by their battering rams, the Geloans put up a gallant defense; for the sections of the walls that fell during the day they rebuilt at night, with the help of their women and children. All the men who were young and fit were under arms and constantly engaged in the fighting; thus it was the remainder of the population that, with immense enthusiasm, stood ready to take care of repair work and the maintenance of supplies. [9] In short, they resisted the Carthaginian onslaught with such stubborn determination, that even though their city was not fortified and they were without allies—besides being able to see their walls crumbling at a number of points—they still remained undismayed by the dangers encompassing them.

109. Dionysius, the *tyrannos* of Syracuse, after summoning support from the Greeks of Italy and his other allies, got his army on the road. He also called up the greater number of those Syracusans of military age and drafted the mercenaries into his regular forces. [2] He had in all (according to some

sources) 50,000 men [under arms], though Timaeus puts his numbers at
30,000 infantry, <4,000> cavalry,[131] and fifty decked vessels. It was with this
very considerable body that he marched out to the relief of Gela [? June 405].
When he got near the city, he pitched camp by the sea. [3] His plan was not
to divide his forces, but to use the same base for carrying out attacks, both
by land and by sea. With his light-armed troops he harried the enemy and
prevented them from foraging in the countryside. Meanwhile, he employed
both his cavalry and his ships in an attempt to debar the Carthaginians from
receiving the supplies brought in to them from areas under their control.
[4] For twenty days they waited, accomplishing nothing worthy of note. But
then Dionysius divided his infantry into three groups: one of these divisions,
comprising the Sicilian Greeks, he ordered to advance against their adversary's
palisaded trench, keeping the city on their left flank; the second, mustered
from the allies, he commanded to thrust forward along the shoreline, with
the city to their right; he himself meanwhile, with the [third] division, consisting of the mercenaries, advanced through the city to the point where the
Carthaginian siege engines stood. [5] His instructions to the cavalry were that
the moment they saw the infantry advancing, they were to cross the river and
spread out across the plain: if they saw their side winning, they should join
in the fighting, but if they saw them losing, they should rescue any of them
who were hard pressed. Those aboard the ships he ordered to bear down on
the enemy camp as soon as the Italian Greeks attacked.

110. This last order was carried out at just the right moment, so that the
Carthaginians came hurrying across to help at the point of attack, in an effort
to hold off those now swarming ashore from the ships. In point of fact the
area of the actual encampment, all along the beach, was completely unfortified. [2] Simultaneously the Italian Greeks—who had come the entire way
hugging the shoreline and found now that the bulk of the defenders had gone
to help stand off the attack from the ships—routed such troops as had been
left behind here and went charging into the camp itself. [3] At this the greater
part of the Carthaginian defense force turned about, and engaged in a lengthy
struggle with the attackers that had got past the ditch, finally, and with great
difficulty, managing to force them out. So the Italian Greeks, overwhelmed
by the sheer numbers of the *barbaroi*, in the course of their retreat found
themselves driven into the acute angle of the palisade, with no relief in sight:

131. Diodorus' MSS read *chilious* ("one thousand"), an extraordinarily small number:
Daphnaeus took 5,000 cavalry to the relief of Acragas (86.5). I agree with Caven (62) that
the true figure has been corrupted in transmission. This would be easy: /Δ (4,000) could
easily be misread as /A (1,000), and I emend the text accordingly.

[4] for the Sicilian Greeks advancing across the plain arrived too late, while the mercenaries accompanying Dionysius had problems in getting through the streets of the city and could not move as fast as they had planned on doing. The Geloans made a sortie for some way from the city but could give help to the Italian Greeks only over a limited area, since they were afraid to abandon the defense of the walls: the result was that they accomplished too little too late. [5] The Iberians and Campanians serving with the Carthaginians pressed hard on the Italian Greeks and slaughtered over a thousand of them. Since the crews of the ships held off further pursuit with volleys of arrows, however, the remainder got safely back to the city. [6] On the other front the Sicilian Greeks set about the Libyans who opposed them, killing large numbers and pursuing the rest to the encampment; when not only the Iberians and Campanians, but also the Carthaginians came to the Libyans' aid, however, they withdrew to the city, with the loss of about six hundred men. [7] The cavalry too, after seeing their side worsted, likewise pulled back to the city, with the enemy hot on their heels. Dionysius, having with difficulty made his way through Gela, thus found his forces defeated, and for the moment fell back within the walls.

III. At this point he called a meeting of his friends and sought their advice regarding the war. When they all agreed that the place was ill suited to a final battle with the enemy, he sent out a herald towards evening about the matter of taking up the dead on the following day. Then, about the first watch of the night, he had the main body of the populace leave the city; he himself set out around midnight, leaving behind some two thousand of his light-armed troops. [2] These had orders to keep fires burning all night and to make plenty of noise, so that the Carthaginians would be led to suppose he was still in the city. As dawn was breaking these troops set off to join Dionysius, and the Carthaginians, on discovering what had happened, moved their quarters into Gela and pillaged anything that had been left behind in the houses.

[3] When Dionysius reached Camarina, he made its citizens likewise take their wives and children and leave for Syracuse. Fear left no room for delay: some collected their silver and gold and anything that could easily be carried, while others left taking only their parents and children and babies, with no regard for their valuables. Some, who were very old or handicapped by disease, were left behind for lack of relatives or friends, since the Carthaginians were expected to arrive at any moment. [4] People were terrified by the disaster that had befallen Selinus and Himera and Acragas, and everyone thought of Carthaginian brutality as though it was something to which they themselves had been eyewitnesses. With the Carthaginians there was no sparing of captives: for such unfortunate wretches they were wholly lacking in compassion,

crucifying some and subjecting others to intolerable outrage. [5] Even so, the evacuation of both cities meant that the countryside was now full of women and children and every kind of riff-raff. When the troops saw all this they were angry with Dionysius and filled with compassion for the misfortunes of these luckless victims; [6] for they saw freeborn boys and girls of marriageable age hurrying wildly along the road in a manner ill befitting their age, since the crisis had stripped them of that serious dignity and restraint that should be shown in the presence of strangers. In the same way they sympathized with the plight of the elderly, seeing them pushed beyond their natural limits in the struggle to keep up with those still in their prime.

112. It was for such reasons that the hatred against Dionysius was now catching fire. Moreover, people assumed that he had acted as he did quite deliberately, his plan being to get control of the remaining cities without risk by exploiting the fear of Carthage. [2] They adduced various arguments: his dilatoriness in bringing aid; the absence of casualties among his mercenaries; his retreat without cause, since no serious setback had befallen him; and, most important, the way that not one single enemy soldier had troubled to pursue him. Thus, for those who had already been looking for the right moment to revolt, everything—as though by the gods' foreknowledge—[seemed to be] working towards the overthrow of his rule.

[3] The Italian Greeks deserted Dionysius and made their way home by way of the interior, while the Syracusan cavalry at first kept watch to see whether it might prove possible to make away with the *tyrannos* on the highway. When they saw that the mercenaries were not abandoning him, however, with one accord they rode off back to Syracuse. [4] When they found that the guards at the dockyards knew nothing of what had been going on at Gela, they went in unopposed and pillaged Dionysius' house, which was full of silver and gold and every kind of costly luxury. They also seized his wife and treated her so appallingly[132] as to ensure that the *tyrannos'* fury would never be appeased, figuring that their revenge on her would create the strongest bond between them all for their rebellion against him. [5] Dionysius, surmising while still on the way what had happened, picked out the most loyal of his cavalry and infantry, and with them pressed on towards Syracuse, never slackening speed; for he reckoned that his only chance to get the upper hand over the cavalry was through swift action, which he duly took. If he could only make his arrival even more unexpected than theirs, he was confident of being able to carry out his plan; and that is what happened. [6] The cavalry assumed that

132. She was gang raped and as a result committed suicide: Plut. *Dion* 3.1–2.

Dionysius would neither return to Syracuse nor remain with his army; so, in the belief that they had succeeded in their design, they said that he had pretended to be giving the Carthaginians the slip in leaving Gela, whereas the actual truth was that he had given the slip to the Syracusans.

113. After covering four hundred *stadia* [almost fifty miles], Dionysius reached the Achradina Gate about midnight with a hundred cavalry and six hundred infantry. Finding the gates closed, he stacked against them a pile of reeds fetched from the marshes, the kind used by the Syracusans for binding their plaster. While the gates were burning down, he marshaled the stragglers as they came in. [2] When the fire had consumed the gates, he and his followers advanced through Achradina. The toughest of the cavalrymen, on hearing what had happened—without waiting for the main body, and few though they were—at once rushed out to resist them. They were in the area of the marketplace, and here they were surrounded by the mercenaries and dispatched to the last man in a hail of javelins. [3] Dionysius then worked his way through the city, mopping up random patches of resistance and going the rounds of his opponents, from house to house, killing some and running others out of town. The main cavalry corps, or what remained of it, fled the city and occupied what is now known as Aetna. [4] At daybreak the bulk of the mercenaries and the army of the Sicilian Greeks reached Syracuse. The men of Gela and Camarina, however, who bore a grudge against Dionysius, now left for Leontini.

114. . . . .[133] As a result, Himilco, under the force of circumstance, sent a herald to Syracuse, calling on the vanquished to come to terms. Dionysius was only too glad to do so, and they made peace on these conditions: "To the Carthaginians shall belong the Elymi and the Sicans,[134] together with their original colonists. The citizens of Selinus, Acragas, Himera, Gela, and Camarina may occupy their cities, these being unfortified, but shall pay tribute to the Carthaginians. The Leontines, Messenians, and Sicels shall all live under

---

133. Dindorf correctly noted a sizable lacuna in the text here. It is generally assumed that the Carthaginians were hit by another outbreak of plague, Syracuse remained dauntingly powerful, and the obviously imminent final collapse of Athens would leave too many powerful cities free to intervene in Sicily: Caven, 74–75. In any case, Dionysius too was ready for peace: he needed time and money to build up a strong army capable (he hoped) of dealing with the Carthaginian problem once and for all.

134. The Sicans were generally believed to be indigenous to Sicily (D.S. 5.2.4, 6.1), whereas the Sicels (D.S. 5.6.3–4) were early immigrants from Italy who occupied territory abandoned by the Sicans and subsequently fought them for further *Lebensland.*

their own laws. The Syracusans shall be subject to Dionysius. Those in possession of captives and ships shall return them to those who lost them."

[2] When this treaty had been implemented, the Carthaginians sailed back to Libya, having lost more than half their troops to the plague; but this pestilence continued unabated in Libya, so that huge numbers both of the Carthaginians themselves and of their allies perished.

[3] Now that we have reached the conclusion of these wars—in Greece, in the Peloponnese, and in Sicily, the first between the Carthaginians and Dionysius—we are of the opinion, since the task we proposed is complete, that we should set down subsequent events in the next book.

BOOK 14.1–34: 404–401 B.C.E.

1. All men—possibly by nature—object to hearing hostile criticism of themselves. Even those whose wickedness is so entirely manifest that it cannot even be denied nevertheless resent it when they incur obloquy and make every effort to counter the accusation. For this reason, we should all take the greatest possible care to avoid base actions, especially those of us who cherish ambitions for high office or have received some notable favor from Fortune. [2] The life of such men is, of course, a matter of public record, and because of its exposure in every detail, cannot conceal any personal lapses. Thus no one who has attained any measure of eminence should assume, if he is guilty of serious crimes, that he will finally get off undetected and free of censure. For even if he escapes a harsh verdict during his own lifetime, he must expect that at some later date the truth will catch up with him, freely trumpeting abroad matters long kept silent. [3] Thus it is the hard lot of the bad man to leave behind, after his own death, a kind of indestructible image of his entire life for posterity; for even if matters subsequent to our death in no way concern us (a popular slogan with certain philosophers),[1] nevertheless that prior life becomes far worse for all <eternity>[2] as a result of the ill deeds embodied in our public remembrance of it. Clear instances of this can be found by readers of the detailed narrative in the following book.

2. Thus, in Athens thirty men who out of personal greed became *tyrannoi* both plunged their country into great misfortunes and themselves very soon fell from power, leaving to posterity the undying memory of their disgrace

---

1. Diodorus will have had in mind, primarily, the materialist philosophy of Democritus (whose death he notes: 11.5) and the Epicureans.

2. Reading Dobree's emendation *aiôna* ("eternity") for *bion* ("life") of Diodorus' MSS. This reading is accepted by Oldfather 1894. Bonnet, in the Budé edition, prefers Dindorf's *chronon* ("time"). Vogel 1893 retains the reading of the MSS.

[>3.2–6.3, 32–33]. The Lacedaemonians secured for themselves undisputed domination over Greece but lost it when they started engaging in improper activities against their allies; for the authority of rulers is maintained through benevolence and justice but undermined by acts of wrongdoing, and the resultant hatred towards them of their subjects [>10.1–2, 13.1, 17.6, 38.4–5]. [2] The same is true of Dionysius, the *tyrannos* of Syracuse [>7.1–9.9, etc.]. Though he was the most successful of such dynasts, he never ceased to be plotted against while alive [>7, 96.2], was forced by fear always to wear an iron cuirass over his tunic, and, once dead, left his life as a prime example, for all time, of the power of public condemnation.

[3] But we shall discuss each of these examples more fully in its appropriate context. For now we shall pick up the thread of our narrative where we abandoned it, pausing only to list the periods treated. [4] In the books preceding this one, we recorded events from the capture of Troy down to the end of the Peloponnesian War and the Athenian hegemony, covering in all seven hundred and seventy-nine years [1184–405]. In the present book we shall continue this sequence of events, beginning with the establishment in Athens of the Thirty *Tyrannoi* and ending with the capture of Rome by the Gauls, encompassing a period of eighteen years [404–386].

3. In the seven hundred and eightieth year after the capture of Troy [404/3], there was no archon[3] in Athens because of the defeat of the city as an independent power, while at Rome [Varr. 407] four military tribunes—†Gaius Fulvius†, Gaius Servilius [Ahala], Gaius Valerius [Potitus Volusus], and Numerius Fabius [Vibulanus]—assumed consular powers, and during this year the 94th Olympiad was held, in which C<ru>cinas of Larissa won [the *stadion*]. [2] About this time the Athenians, finally worn out, made a treaty with the Lacedaemonians [<13.107.4], by the terms of which they were required to demolish their city walls and to adopt their "ancestral constitution" (*patrios politeia*). The walls they removed,[4] but differences of opinion arose concerning the form of government. [3] For those who inclined towards oligarchy argued for undertaking between them that former system by which a very small

---

3. There was in fact an archon, Pythodorus; but since he was not elected in due democratic form, it was later officially determined that the year should be regarded as one of *anarchia* (Xen. *Hell.* 2.3.1).

4. Xen. *Hell.* 2.2.15 and the archaeological evidence (Green 2004, 153) indicate that the demolition was limited to 10 *stadia* (just over a mile) of the walls, plus the fortifications of Piraeus. Even this took at least four months and may in fact never have been completely carried out.

group represented the whole citizen body; on the other hand, the majority, as committed democrats, recommended the "government of their fathers," asserting that this, as all agreed, was true democracy.[5]

[4] When the dispute on this point had continued for some days, those favoring oligarchy dispatched envoys to Lysander the Spartan—since after the war he had been sent out to organize the administration of the cities, and in most of them oligarchies had been established—hoping as a result, very plausibly, that he would support their scheme. They therefore crossed over to Samos, since Lysander, after his recent capture of the city, was still in residence there.[6] [5] When they solicited his aid, he agreed to cooperate with them [>10.1]. He appointed the Spartan Thorax as governor of Samos, and himself, with a hundred ships, sailed into Piraeus [Apr. 404]. He then summoned an assembly, and advised the Athenians to choose thirty men to run the government and manage all the affairs of the city. [6] When Theramenes spoke against this and read out the clause in the treaty agreeing to the adoption of the ancestral constitution, saying that it would be an outrage if they were robbed of their freedom in contravention of a sworn agreement, Lysander retorted that it was the Athenians who had broken the terms of the armistice, by pulling down their walls later than the agreed date. He also threatened Theramenes with the direst consequences, saying that if he did not stop his opposition to the Lacedaemonians, he would be put to death. [7] As a result, Theramenes and those assembled with him were forced, out of sheer terror, into abolishing the democracy on a show of hands. Thirty men were then chosen to direct the public business of the city: officially as "governors," in fact as *tyrannoi*.[7]

4. The people, aware of Theramenes' reasonable nature and convinced that his high principles would act to some degree as a brake on the cupidity of their

5. As Bonnet rightly comments (156), the *patrios politeia* was a handy term used by all political groups, particularly oligarchs (Arist. *Ath. Pol.* 31.1; Xen. *Hell.* 2.3.2): ancestral tradition could be invoked by right and left alike. Diodorus ignores the middle way of moderate oligarchy promoted during the 411 revolution (cf. Arist. *Ath. Pol.* 34.3).

6. The embassy (led by Theramenes) arrived about the end of Nov. 405, while Lysander was in fact still besieging Samos, and was detained by him there for over three months.

7. Late September 404 (Green 2004, 159). Theramenes: resistance hero or quisling? Diodorus and Aristotle (*Ath. Pol.* 34.2–3) see him as the first, Xenophon (*Hell.* 2.2.16) and Lysias (12.68–70, 73), as the second. In fact he was a realist: he negotiated as good a surrender as Athens could hope for, the acceptance of which was proposed by Dracontides and ratified by formal vote. Ten of the Thirty were nominated by Theramenes himself (Lys. 12.76).

new leaders, included him in their vote as one of the Thirty. Those elected were required to appoint a Council and the various other officials and to draft the laws by which they would govern.[8] [2] The business of lawmaking they continually put off, always proffering plausible excuses; while the Council and other official vacancies they filled from the ranks of their personal friends, so that while these had the name of magistrates, they were in fact mere lackeys of the Thirty. To begin with, they brought to trial the city's most notorious malefactors and condemned them to death; and so far what was going on met with even the most reasonable citizens' approval.

[3] But after this, since they were planning more violent (and illegal) activities, they requested a garrison from the Lacedaemonians, promising to establish a regime in Sparta's best interests. This was because they knew that without foreign arms they would be unable to carry out any murders, since all citizens would combine to ensure their own common security. [4] When the Lacedaemonians sent them a garrison, with Callibius as its commander, the Thirty first won over the garrison-commander with bribes and various other favors; then, picking out from among the wealthy citizens those that suited their plans, they proceeded to arrest them as revolutionaries, put them to death, and confiscate their possessions.

[5] When Theramenes opposed his fellow-officials and threatened to join the resistance group insisting on general security, the Thirty called a meeting of the Council. Critias, as their spokesman, brought numerous charges against Theramenes, accusing him of betraying this government in which he himself had chosen to serve; but Theramenes then took the floor, rebutted the charges in detail, and got the entire Council on his side. [6] Critias and his supporters, scared that this was a man who might at some point get rid of the oligarchy, threw a cordon of soldiers with drawn swords around him, and set about his arrest. [7] But Theramenes, anticipating this, sprang up towards the altar of Hestia of the Council, exclaiming that he was taking refuge with the gods, not because he thought this would save him but in his determination to make his killers also involve themselves in an act of impiety against the gods.

5. When the officers came up and dragged him away, Theramenes bore his ill fortune nobly, since he had partaken of philosophy to no small degree

---

8. For a detailed account of the activities of the Thirty (including versions of the speeches made by Critias and Theramenes at the latter's arraignment), see Xen. *Hell.* 2.3.11–4.1.

in the company of Socrates; but the crowd as a whole, though feeling pity for Theramenes' distress, dared not come to his rescue because of the strong armed guard surrounding him. [2] Socrates the philosopher and two of his close friends rushed forward and attempted to check the officers. Theramenes, however, urged them not to do any such thing. While he had only praise (he said) for their friendship and courage, it would be the greatest misfortune for him should he prove the cause of death to such intimate associates. [3] Socrates and his companions, since they had no support from anyone else, and saw that the threatening attitude of those in authority was intensifying, kept quiet. Then those who had been so ordered tore Theramenes away from the altar and dragged him through the middle of the marketplace to his death. [4] The populace, cowed by the arms of the garrison, felt a common pity for him in his distress, and wept not only for his sorry fate but for their own enslavement, since every one of these wretches, on seeing the high virtues of Theramenes thus contemptuously treated, realized that in their weakness they would be sacrificed without a moment's thought.

[5] After Theramenes' death,[9] the Thirty continued to pick off wealthy citizens, bring false charges against them, put them to death, and plunder their estates. Those they executed included Niceratus, son of that Nicias who had been a general at Syracuse [<13.33.1]: a man of moderate and kindly behavior to everyone, and for wealth and reputation first, or nearly so, among all Athenians. [6] In consequence, every household joined in lamenting the fate of this fine man, and the recollection of his decency brought tears to their eyes. Nor did the *tyrannoi* abate their lawless conduct; on the contrary, their madness so increased that they slaughtered the sixty wealthiest foreign residents to get possession of their property. With citizens being executed daily, almost all the well-to-do fled the city. [7] Amongst others they did away with Autolycus, a notably outspoken man, and in general they concentrated on the most distinguished individuals. To such an extent did they wreak destruction on the city that over half the Athenian population fled.[10]

---

9. Both Xenophon (*Hell.* 2.3.39) and Aristotle (*Ath. Pol.* 37.1) place Theramenes' execution later, after the arrest of Niceratus (Xen.) or even later than the occupation of Phyle (winter 404: 32.1–2) by the democrats (Arist.).

10. Xenophon (*Hell.* 2.3.39) states that each of the Thirty was required to arrest one resident alien: i.e., his total is half Diodorus'. Autolycus was also an Olympic victor in the *pancration* (an almost-no-holds-barred mixture of boxing and wrestling). Pausanias (9.32.8) reports his execution as an act of personal revenge on the part of the Spartan garrison commander Callibius. According to Isocrates (7.67), more than 5,000 Athenians fled the city: a substantial number, but scarcely over half the population.

6. The Lacedaemonians, who were keeping a watch on the city of Athens, in the determination that the Athenians should never regain their old power, were very pleased, and made their attitude quite clear by voting that Athenian exiles anywhere in Greece should be compulsorily returned to the Thirty, and that anyone who sought to prevent this should be liable to a fine of five talents. [2] Though the decree was an outrage, the other cities, terrified by the solid power of the Spartans, complied with it. The sole exception was Argos, whose citizens were the first to offer these fugitives compassionate asylum—moved by hatred of Lacedaemonian cruelty as well as by pity for the fate of the unfortunate. [3] The Thebans, too, voted [Plut. *Lys.* 27.6] that anyone who witnessed an exile being arrested, and did not offer him all possible assistance, should incur a fine.

This, then, was the situation in Athens.

7. In Sicily, Dionysius, the *tyrannos* of the Sicels,[11] after making peace with Carthage, had it in mind to concern himself with the future safeguarding of his *tyrannis,* since he figured that the Syracusans, now they were finished with the war, would have time to pursue the recovery of their freedom. [2] Observing that the Island [of Ortygia] was the strongest quarter and could easily be defended, he separated it from the rest of the city by a costly rampart, along which he built, at close intervals, a series of high towers. In front of this he constructed counting houses and covered colonnades capable of accommodating large crowds of people. [3] He also created on the Island, at vast expense, a fortified citadel to serve as a retreat in any sudden emergency, extending its wall to include the dockyards belonging to the small harbor known as Laccion. These had berths for sixty triremes and a restricted entrance through which no more than one vessel could pass at a time. [4] He reserved the best areas of [Syracusan] territory as gifts for his friends and those appointed to high command and divided up the rest equally between outsiders and citizens, including in the latter category freed slaves, whom he referred to as "new citizens." [5] He also distributed the houses among the population at large, with the exception of those on the Island: these he made over to his friends and the mercenaries.

When he felt he had done all that was necessary for the safeguarding of his

---

11. This appellation appears only here and at 18.1. Diodorus' normal (and accurate) title for Dionysius was "*tyrannos* of the Syracusans." The Sicels were early, though not indigenous, colonizers of Sicily (5.2.1). It is possible that Dionysius, who at this point spent a good deal of time fighting and using them (7.5, 53.5, 78.7, etc.), promoted himself briefly as "Lord of the Sicels."

tyrannis, he took the field against the Sicels. He was determined to bring all the independent peoples under his domination, but these in particular because of their earlier alliance with the Carthaginians. [6] He therefore encamped before the city of Herbessus and prepared to besiege it. But the Syracusans serving under him, now that they were armed, got together in groups and reproached one another for not having joined the cavalry in their bid [405: <13.113.3] to overthrow the *tyrannos.* The officer appointed by Dionysius as troop commander first threatened one of these outspoken individuals and then, when the man answered him back brashly, made as though to strike him. [7] This so enraged the troops that they killed the officer, whose name was Doricus. Then, loudly calling on the citizens to rally for freedom, they sent messengers to bring in the cavalry from Aetna, since these last had been exiled at the beginning of the *tyrannis* and were occupying a stronghold there.

8. Dionysius, taken aback by this revolt of the Syracusans, broke off the siege and hurried back to Syracuse, in haste to occupy the city. After his flight, the ringleaders of the revolt chose as generals those who had killed his troop commander, joined up with the cavalry from Aetna, established a camp on the so-called heights of Epipolae, directly opposite the *tyrannos'* defenses [<11.73.2], and cut him off from any access to the countryside. [2] They also at once dispatched ambassadors to the Messenians and Rhegians, asking them to support their struggle for freedom by means of naval action, since at the time those cities habitually kept a minimum of eighty triremes manned and ready, which now—so zealous were they in the cause of freedom—they did send out [to their assistance]. [3] [The rebels] also offered, by proclamation, a large cash reward to anyone who killed the *tyrannos* and promised citizenship to any mercenaries who changed sides and joined them. They also set up siege engines, with the object of weakening and ultimately breaching the walls, made daily assaults on the Island, and gave a special welcome to any mercenaries who came over to them.

[4] Dionysius was now cut off from the countryside, while desertions by the mercenaries continued. He therefore got his friends together to discuss the situation. He so completely despaired of recovering power that he was no longer looking for a way to defeat the Syracusans but rather for the kind of death that would let him end his rule in a not wholly ignoble manner. [5] Now Heloris, one of his friends (or, according to some, his adoptive father), quoted the saying to him that "a *tyrannis* makes a fine shroud." But Polyxenus, his brother-in-law [<13.96.3], was of the opinion that he should take the fastest horse available and ride off into Carthaginian-controlled territory, to the Campanians (whom Himilco [actually Hannibal: <13.62.5] had left

behind to guard various positions in Sicily). Philistus, who composed his *Histories* after these events, spoke out against Polyxenus, saying that rather than skip out of a *tyrannis* on a horse at the gallop, one should have to be dragged out of it by one leg. [6] Dionysius agreed with him and made up his mind to submit to anything rather than relinquish power voluntarily. He therefore sent ambassadors to the rebels, asking them to give him and his companions safe conduct out of the city, while at the same time secretly getting in touch with the Campanians and agreeing to give them whatever pay they might demand for [their support during] the siege.

9. After these events the Syracusans allowed the *tyrannos* to put to sea with five ships and from that moment somewhat relaxed their vigilance. The cavalry they discharged, as being of no use for a siege, while most of the infantry, assuming that the *tyrannis* was already ended, now dispersed into the countryside. [2] The Campanians, however, much elated by the promises made to them, first made their way to Agyrium, where they left their baggage in the keeping of Agyris, the local ruler [>95.4–7]. They then—a body of twelve hundred cavalry—set out, riding light, for Syracuse. [3] Speedily completing their journey, they took the Syracusans completely by surprise, killed a good many of them, and forced their way through to Dionysius. At the same time, three hundred mercenaries also sailed in to assist the *tyrannos,* so that his hopes began to revive. [4] With this renewal of the regime's strength, the Syracusans split into factions, one group saying they should stay put and maintain the siege, another that they should dismiss the troops and abandon the city.

[5] On learning of this, Dionysius led his forces out against them, and falling upon them in the quarter known as the New City, while they were in this state of confusion, easily put them to flight. Not many of them were killed, however, for Dionysius rode around, stopping his men from slaughtering the fugitives. The Syracusans now scattered across the countryside, but shortly afterwards more than seven thousand of them flocked to join the cavalry at Aetna. [6] Dionysius buried the Syracusan dead and then sent envoys to Aetna, inviting the exiles to be reconciled on terms and to return to live in their native land, giving his sworn word that he would bear them no malice. [7] Some of them, who had left wives and children behind, of necessity accepted his offer; but the rest, when the envoys cited Dionysius' good service in his burial of the fallen, said he deserved to get a like favor, and they prayed the gods to let them see him get it, as soon as possible. [8] So these men, being in no way willing to trust the *tyrannos,* stayed there in Aetna, waiting for a propitious moment to strike at him. Those exiles who did come back Dio-

nysius treated with every kindness, hoping thus to induce the others to return to their homeland too. The Campanians he rewarded with the gifts agreed upon, and then packed them off out of the city, since he regarded them as thoroughly untrustworthy [78.1]. [9] They made their way to Entella, where they talked the citizens into accepting them as fellow-inhabitants; then they set upon them by night, slaughtered the adult males, married the wives of the men they had betrayed, and took over the city [>21.18.2–3].

10. In Greece the Lacedaemonians, having successfully concluded the Peloponnesian War, were by common consent agreed to hold supreme power both on land and at sea. They now appointed Lysander naval commander and commissioned him to make a tour of the cities, setting up in each of them the officials they call harmosts; for the Lacedaemonians, being opposed to democracies, wanted the cities to be governed by oligarchs. [2] They also imposed tribute on those they had defeated; and although prior to this they had not used coined money, from now on they collected more than a thousand talents annually in the form of tribute.[12]

When they had settled the affairs of Greece to their own satisfaction, they sent out to Syracuse one of their most distinguished men, Aristus by name [or Aretes: >70.3]: ostensibly (they pretended) to end dynastic rule, whereas in actual fact they were eager to strengthen the *tyrannis*. What they hoped was that by establishing Dionysius' rule more firmly, they would, in return for services rendered, have him as an obedient ally. [3] So Aristus sailed to Syracuse, where he held secret discussions with the *tyrannos* about these matters, while at the same time stirring up the Syracusans with promises to restore their freedom. He assassinated Nicoteles the Corinthian, a Syracusan leader, and by betraying those who had put their trust in him, strengthened the *tyrannos'* position: through these actions he brought dishonor both on himself and on his country. [4] Dionysius got the Syracusans out to harvest their crops, whereupon he raided their homes and removed all their weapons [>15.1]. He then built a second wall round the citadel, fitted out warships, rounded up a large number of mercenaries, and took all other measures necessary for the safeguarding of his *tyrannis,* having learned by hard experience that the Syracusans would stick at nothing to escape slavery.

---

12. Lysander had already been appointed naval commander (*nauarchos*) in 408/7 and could not hold this office twice (13.100.8; Xen. *Hell.* 2.1.7): he thus officially served as *epistoleus* or "secretary" (not "vice-admiral," as LSJ s.v. *epistoleus* II wrongly rationalizes) but retained the real power. The figure of over 1,000 talents for the tribute the Spartans collected is surely much exaggerated.

11. At the same time as these events, Pharnabazus, Darius the [Great] King's satrap, out of a desire to build credit with the Lacedaemonians, arrested Alcibiades the Athenian and put him to death. Since Ephorus' account states that he was plotted against for other reasons, however, I think it may not be unprofitable to set down here the plot against Alcibiades as presented by this historian. [2] In his 17th book he says that Cyrus and the Lacedaemonians were planning secretly to make war together against Cyrus' brother Artaxerxes; and that Alcibiades, having learned of Cyrus' intentions from certain informants, went to Pharnabazus and gave him a detailed account of them. He then asked him for safe conduct to Artaxerxes, eager to be the first to reveal this conspiracy to the King. [3] Pharnabazus, however, on hearing his story, appropriated the report himself and dispatched confidants of his own to inform the King of the matter. So, when Pharnabazus would not give him an escort to the King, Ephorus says, Alcibiades set off to the satrap of Paphlagonia, in the hope of journeying upcountry with his help instead. But Pharnabazus, scared lest the King should get wind of the truth about this business, sent men to kill Alcibiades on the road. [4] They caught up with him at a village in Phrygia where he had found shelter for the night, and stacked kindling all around [the house]. When they set it ablaze, Alcibiades tried to defend himself, but was overcome by the flames and the javelins cast at him, and so met his end.[13]

[5] About the same time, the philosopher Democritus died, at the age of ninety.[14] Lasthenes of Thebes, a victor in this year's Olympic games, is said to have competed against a racehorse, the course being from Coroneia to Thebes [c. 20 miles], and to have won the race.

[6] In Italy the Romans garrisoning Erruca [Verrugo], a city of the Volsci, were attacked by enemy forces, who captured the city and killed most of the garrison [Liv. 6.58.3].

---

13. Pharnabazus, hereditary satrap of Hellespontine Phrygia and future son-in-law of Artaxerxes II, had had earlier dealings with Alcibiades (13, 73.6). The facts of the latter's death are more or less consistent in our other accounts (Plut. *Alcib.* 39.1–4; Nep. *Alcib.* 10.1–6), but the motives vary. Nepos largely agrees with Diodorus but (with Plutarch) also asserts that pressure was put on Pharnabazus by Lysander, after the latter had had anxious representations from Critias, the leader of the Thirty in Athens.

14. This cannot be right. The chronographer Apollodorus, cited at Diog. Laert. 9.41, dates his birth in the 80th Olympiad (460–457). Whether he lived to be ninety (so Diodorus) or a hundred and nine (Hipparchus ap. Diog. Laert. 9.43), he lived on for a good half-century after 404/3. Diodorus must have mistaken his *floruit* (Greek *akmé*, regularly set at the age of forty) for his date of death.

12. When this year's events were concluded, the archon in Athens was Eu-
cleides [403/2], while in Rome consular powers were assumed [Varr. 406] by
four military tribunes: Publius Cornelius [Rutilus Cossus], Numerius Fabius
[Ambustus], Lucius Valerius [Potitus], and †Terentius Maximus†. [2] While
these men were in office, the Byzantines, being both split by factional strife
and also at war with their Thracian neighbors, found themselves in serious
trouble. Since they were unable to resolve their internal rivalries, they asked
the Lacedaemonians for a general. To restore order in their city, the Spartans
sent them Clearchus [<13.66.5–6]. [3] Entrusted by the Byzantines with authority in all matters, he proceeded to enroll large numbers of mercenaries, so
that he was their protector no longer but rather their *tyrannos*. First, he invited
their leading officials to some festival or other and put them all to death. This
left the city without a governing body. In its absence, he rounded up thirty of
the most prominent Byzantines, put cords round their necks, and strangled
them, after which he appropriated all their property for himself. He then
made a list of the wealthiest citizens and brought various false charges against
them. Some he executed, others he exiled. In this way he got possession of a
great deal of money, which he used to hire numerous mercenaries and thus
safeguard his authority.

[4] When his savagery and tyrannical power became matters of public
knowledge, the Lacedaemonians first of all sent representatives to him to persuade him to give up his dictatorial rule; but since he took no notice of their
request, they then sent an expeditionary force against him, with Panthoedas
as its commander. [5] On learning of his approach, Clearchus removed his
own troops to Selymbria, another city under his control, figuring that, with
his record of offenses against the Byzantines, he would have not only the Lacedaemonians but every man in the city as his enemy. [6] So, having decided
that Selymbria would make a safer base from which to conduct the war, he
transferred both his funds and his armed forces there. On being informed
that the Lacedaemonians were near at hand, he went out to meet them and
fought an engagement with the force led by Panthoedas near what is known
as "The Ford" (*poros*). [7] The battle went on for a long time, but the Lacedaemonians fought brilliantly, and the forces of the *tyrannos* were destroyed.
Clearchus himself, with a few comrades, at first took refuge in Selymbria and
was besieged there; but after a while he became scared, slipped out by night,
and sailed away to Ionia, where he became a close friend of Cyrus, the Great
King's brother, and got to command his troops [>19.8]. [8] Cyrus, who had
been designated as commander-in-chief of the maritime satrapies, was full
of ambition, and indeed had plans to lead an expedition against his brother

Artaxerxes. [9] So, seeing that Clearchus was a man of bold and natural audacity, Cyrus provided him with cash and gave him the job of enlisting as many mercenaries as he could, convinced that in him he would have an apt partner for his daring enterprise.

13. Lysander the Spartan had by now reorganized all the cities subject to the Lacedaemonians in accordance with the policy of the ephors, establishing decarchies [ruling bodies of ten men] in some and oligarchies in others. He was accordingly a man very much in the public eye at Sparta, especially since by winding up the Peloponnesian War, he had brought his country to a position of uncontested supremacy by both land and sea. [2] As a result, he had become swollen with pride, and had in mind a scheme for terminating the kingship of the Heracleidae[15] and electing the kings from the whole Spartan citizen body, convinced that the royal mandate would very soon fall on him because of his great and illustrious accomplishments. [3] Being aware of the close attention paid by the Lacedaemonians to oracles, he attempted to bribe the prophetess at Delphi, in the belief that if he got an oracular response supporting his private designs, his plans would be accomplished without trouble. [4] However, when over a long period his offers of bribes to the staff of the oracle found no takers, he transferred his attention to the priestesses of the sanctuary at Dodona, using as his intermediary one Pherecrates, an Apollonian by birth who was well known to the sanctuary's personnel.

[5] Getting nowhere here either, he took a trip abroad to Cyrene, ostensibly to discharge a vow to Ammon but actually with the intention of bribing the oracle;[16] he had brought along vast sums of money, with which he hoped to corrupt the shrine's attendants. [6] Moreover, the king of that region, Libys, was a guest-friend of his father, and indeed it so happened that Lysander's brother had been named Libys as a tribute to their friendship. [7] With this connection, then, and the money he had brought, Lysander hoped to get his way. Yet he not only failed in his attempt, but the administrators of the shrine sent official delegates to charge him with attempted bribery of the oracle. So, when Lysander returned to Lacedaemon, this charge was brought against him, but he made a convincing speech in his own defense. [8] At the time, the Lacedaemonians knew nothing of Lysander's plan to abolish the royal line

---

15. I.e., the Spartan dual hereditary kingship held by two aristocratic families, the Agiads and the Eurypontids, who traced their ancestry from (alleged) twin descendants of Heracles (Hdt. 6.52).

16. This was the oracle of Zeus Ammon in the Siwah Oasis, most notable for its consultation by Alexander III of Macedon (332/1: 17.51.1–4).

of descent from Heracles; but some time later, after his death, a search in his house for certain public documents also brought to light a speech, commissioned at considerable expense and written for public delivery, arguing that kings should be elected from the citizen body at large.[17]

14. When Dionysius, the *tyrannos* of Syracuse, had made peace with Carthage [405/4: <13.114.1–2] and got rid of civil uprisings in the city, he was determined to bring under his control the neighboring Chalcidic cities of Naxos, Catana, and Leontini. [2] His eagerness to make himself master of them was due to their abutting on Syracusan territory and offering numerous resources for the extension of his sovereignty. He began by marching on Aetna and taking over its stronghold [>58.2], the exiles there being no match for so large a force. [3] He then moved his troops off to Leontini and pitched camp near the city, beside the Terias River. His opening gambit here was to draw up his army in battle order and send a herald to the citizens of Leontini with orders to turn the city over to him, figuring that he had already sufficiently terrified the inhabitants. [4] The Leontines, however, ignored this request and made full preparations to withstand a siege. Since Dionysius had no assault engines, he abandoned the idea of a siege for the time being but laid waste all the surrounding countryside. [5] He and his army next moved into Sicel territory, under the pretence of launching a campaign against them, his object being to make the Catanians and the Naxians somewhat less vigilant in guarding their cities. [6] While encamped near Enna, he persuaded Aeimnestus, a native of that city, to try and set himself up as *tyrannos,* promising to support him in his endeavor. [7] The fellow's coup was successful, but he then refused to admit Dionysius to the city. Dionysius, infuriated, switched sides and called on the citizens of Enna to overthrow the *tyrannos.* They armed themselves and came flocking into the marketplace, so that the whole city was in an uproar. [8] When he learned of this uprising, Dionysius took his light-armed troops, quickly broke into the city at an unguarded spot, arrested Aeimnestus, and handed him over to the men of Enna for punishment. He then left town without getting involved in any wrongdoing [>78.7]. He acted thus not out of any concern for what was right but from a desire to encourage the other cities to trust him.

15. From Enna he marched to Herbita and attempted to sack it, but when his assault got nowhere, he made peace with the inhabitants and led his army

---

17. The speech was composed by a famous sophist, Cleon of Halicarnassus, whose services (like those of Isocrates) did not come cheap: Plut. *Lys.* 25.1, 30.3–4; Nep. *Lys.* 3.5.

off to Catana, since Arcesilaus, the Catanian general, had promised to betray this city to him. Accordingly, he was smuggled in by this man about midnight, and thus became master of Catana. He then stripped the citizens of their arms and put in a strong garrison. [2] After this, Procles, the leader of the Naxians, seduced by the lavishness of Dionysius' promises, handed over his native city to him. Dionysius paid this traitor all the gifts he had promised him and released his relatives to him as a special favor. He then sold the remaining inhabitants into slavery, turned their property over to his troops to plunder, and demolished both walls and houses. [3] He treated the Catanians in much the same way, selling the prisoners he took as booty in Syracuse. The territory of the Naxians he made over as a gift to their Sicel neighbors, while the city of Catana he gave as a dwelling place to the Campanians [>58.2].[18] [4] Next, he marched out in full force against Leontini and put the city under siege. He then sent an embassy to the Leontines, with orders to hand over their city and accept citizenship in Syracuse. The Leontines, who had no expectation of help, and drew their own conclusions from the misfortunes of the Naxians and Catanians, were terrified that they too might suffer the same fate. They therefore yielded to immediate urgent need and agreed to the proposal, abandoning their own city and relocating to Syracuse.

16. After the peace made between the Herbitan *demos* and Dionysius, Archonidas [<12.8.2], the president of Herbita, decided to found a [new] city. He had a large number of mercenaries, as well as a mixed crowd that had flocked to the city at the time of the war against Dionysius, while many of Herbita's impoverished citizens promised to join the colony. [2] So he took this accumulated mass of people and occupied one of the hills lying eight *stadioi* [just under a mile] from the sea, on which he founded the city of Alaesa (since there were other cities of that name in Sicily, he called it Alaesa Archonidius after himself). [3] When in later times this city experienced considerable growth due to its maritime trade and the tax-exempt status granted it by the Romans [263/2], the Alaesians denied any kinship with the inhabitants of Herbita, since they thought it socially demeaning to be regarded as colonists from a poorer city. [4] Nevertheless, numerous family ties still survive on both sides down to the present day, and they employ an identical ritual when offering sacrifice in the sanctuary of Apollo. Some, however, claim that Alaesa was founded by the Carthaginians, about the time that Himilco made peace with Dionysius [405: <13.114.1].

---

18. For the earlier employment of Campanian mercenaries in Sicily, see 13.44.2, 80.4. They were also regularly hired by Carthage: 13.44.1, 55.7–8, 62.5, 85.4, 88.2–5.

[5] In Italy, war broke out between Rome and <Veii> for the following reasons <. . . . .> [Liv. 4.58.1–10]. This was the first occasion on which the Romans voted an annual payment to their troops to cover their expenses on active service [Liv. 4.59.11]. They also reduced by siege that city of the Volsci which at the time was called Anxur but now is named Terracina [Liv. 4.59.3–4].

17. When the year had run its course, Micon became archon in Athens [402/1], while in Rome consular powers were taken over [Varr. 405] by three[19] military tribunes, Titus Quinctius [Capitolinus Barbatus], Gaius Julius [Vopisci Iullus], and Aulus Manlius [Vulso Capitolinus]. After they had entered on their term of office, the inhabitants of Oropos, torn by civil factionalism, exiled a number of their citizens. [2] For a while the exiles worked to secure their return by their own efforts; but when in the end they proved unable to carry out their plan, they persuaded the Thebans to send a force to help them. [3] The Thebans then marched against Oropos, took control of the city, and resettled its inhabitants seven *stadioi* [about ¾ mile] inland.[20] For a while they let them govern themselves, but then gave them [Theban] citizenship and annexed their territory to Boeotia.

[4] At the same time as these events,[21] the Lacedaemonians lodged numerous complaints against the Eleians, chief among them that they had stopped the [Spartan] king Pausanias from sacrificing to the god and also because they had not allowed the Lacedaemonians to compete in the Olympic Games [420/19]. [5] As a result, they decided to go to war with [the Eleians], and sent them ten ambassadors, who were to order them to grant their dependent townships autonomy, and require of them their agreed contribution to the cost of the war against the Athenians. [6] They acted thus in pursuit of pretexts that put them in a good light, and of convincing reasons for going to war. But when the Eleians not only took no notice but actually accused them of enslaving the Greeks, they sent out Pausanias, one of their two kings, against them, with 4,000 soldiers. [7] There accompanied him also numerous

---

19. There were in fact six military tribunes, and one branch of Diodorus' MS tradition (MF) records this fact, though without giving names. The three omitted are Q. Quinctius Cincinnatus, L. Furius Medullinus, and M. Aemilius Mamercinus (Broughton, 80).

20. Thus seriously hampering their use of their port for the benefit of Athens (Bonnet, 168).

21. I.e., in 402. Xenophon (*Hell.* 3.2.21; cf. Thuc. 5.49–50.2) correlates these Lacedaemonian complaints with the actions of Dercyllidas in Asia Minor (399), but this is almost certainly wrong (Tuplin 1993, 201–205; Krentz 1995, 171), and Diodorus' chronology of the war (402–400) is to be preferred. Both sources are highly selective: Diodorus highlights Sparta's less successful ventures (e.g., 17.8–12) and is clearly using another source besides Xenophon.

troops from almost all the allies, except the Boeotians and the Corinthians: they, out of disgust at the Lacedaemonians' behavior, would not take part in this campaign against Elis.

[8] So Pausanias, invading Elis by way of Arcadia, quickly overran the frontier post of Lasion. Then he led his troops through [the district of] Acroreia, where he won over four cities: Thraestus, Halion, Epitalion, and Opus. [9] From here he marched on Pylos. This position too, which was about seventy *stadioi* [c. 7¾ miles] from Elis, he captured in short order. He then advanced on Elis itself and encamped on the hills across the river. Shortly before this the Eleians had received allied support in the shape of a thousand picked troops from the Aetolians and had assigned them the area around the public gymnasium to guard. [10] Now this was the point at which Pausanias had begun to establish his siege, with contemptuous carelessness, convinced that the Eleians would never dare make a sortie against him. But suddenly the Aetolians, together with a mass of citizens, came charging out from the city, terrifying the Lacedaemonians and killing about thirty of them. [11] At this point Pausanias raised the siege. Then, realizing that the city itself would be hard work to capture, he made his way through Eleian territory, ravaging and looting as he went—consecrated land though it was—and amassed vast amounts of booty.[22] [12] With winter now imminent, he built fortified guard posts in Elis, left adequate forces to man them, and himself with the remainder of his army went into winter quarters at Dyme.

18. In Sicily, Dionysius, the *tyrannos* of the Sicels [<7.1], now that his dynastic ambitions were progressing according to plan, had it in mind to launch a campaign against the Carthaginians. Since he was not yet adequately equipped for this, however, he kept his project secret while he made essential preparations for the conflict that lay ahead. [2] Knowing as he did that during the war with Athens the city had been walled off from sea to sea [<13.7.4], he was determined, should he ever suffer a similar setback, not to be cut off from access to the countryside, since he saw that the plateau known as Epipolae naturally dominated the city of Syracuse. [3] He therefore consulted his architects, and on the basis of their advice decided he had to fortify Epipolae, [beginning] at the point[23] where the present wall abuts on the Six Gates

22. Largely in the form of winter provisions (Xen. *Hell.* 3.2.26); Elis was rich and fertile (Polyb. 4.73.4).

23. Modern Scala Greca, on the north side of Epipolae, and the terminus of the coastal road to Leontini and Catana. Dionysius completed all his preparations by 398/7 (46.5); this included the south wall, enclosing the quarters of Neapolis and Achradina.

(*Hexapyloi*). [4] This part faces north, is sheer throughout and so rugged as virtually to bar access from the outside. Wanting to make a quick job of erecting the walls, he assembled the whole population of the countryside, selected the free men best suited for the work, to the number of some sixty thousand, and shared out the area to be walled between them. [5] At intervals of one *stadion* he stationed an architect, and at intervals of one *plethron* [about 100 ft.] he placed builders, with a *corvée* of two hundred laborers per *plethron* to carry out the work for them. Over and above all these, there were huge numbers of workers quarrying rough blocks of stone, and six thousand yoke of oxen to deliver the blocks where they were needed. [6] The cumulative activity of all these workers, and their eagerness to complete the tasks allotted them, filled those who observed the scene with amazement. In fact Dionysius, to whet his vast task force's enthusiasm, was offering rich prizes to all those who finished first: one lot for the architects, another for the builders, and still more for the actual laborers. Furthermore, he, along with his friends, spent long hours, day after day, supervising the various works, putting in an appearance everywhere, and constantly lending a hand to those hardest pressed. [7] By and large he laid aside the dignity of his office and came across as an ordinary individual, buckling down to the toughest chores and enduring the same hardships as the rest. This generated such competitive activity that some even worked on for part of the night after putting in a full day, which shows the kind of enthusiasm animating this vast corps of workers. [8] As a result, and contrary to expectation, the wall was completed in twenty days. It was thirty *stadioi* [over 3⅓ miles] long, and of proportionate height, so that with the natural strength of the position reinforcing the wall, it stood impregnable against any assault: for there were high towers along it at close intervals, built of four-foot stone blocks, fitted together with great precision.

19. When this year came to an end, <Xen>aenetus was archon in Athens [401/0], while in Rome consular powers were assumed [Varr. 404] by six military tribunes: Publius Cornelius [Maluginensis], Caeso Fabius [Ambustus], Spurius Nautius [Rutilus], Gaius Valerius [Potitus Volusus], Manius Sergius [Fidenas], and <Cn. Cornelius Cossus>. [2] About this time Cyrus, the commander-in-chief of the maritime satrapies [<12.8], was implementing a long-meditated scheme to take the field against his brother Artaxerxes.[24]

---

24. From here to ch. 31, Diodorus' narrative should be read in conjunction with the detailed (and largely eyewitness) account of these events provided by Xenophon in his *Anabasis*.

A highly ambitious young man, he had a by no means ineffectual appetite for the contests of war. [3] When an adequate corps of mercenaries had been assembled, and all preparations for the campaign were in place, he still did not tell his troops the truth but said he was taking this force to Cilicia to deal with the *tyrannoi* who had revolted against the King. [4] He also sent ambassadors to the Lacedaemonians, to remind them of the service he had rendered them during their war against the Athenians [407/6, <13.70.3] and to solicit their alliance. The Lacedaemonians, reckoning that this war would be to their advantage, decided to support Cyrus and at once sent envoys to Samos,[25] their admiral, instructing him to do whatever Cyrus might ask of him. [5] Samos had twenty-five triremes, with which he sailed to Ephesus, to Cyrus' admiral, prepared for any kind of joint action with him. They also dispatched a force of eight hundred infantry under the command of Cheirisophus. The commander of the barbarian fleet, Tamōs, had fifty magnificently equipped triremes; when the Lacedaemonians arrived, they all put to sea together, setting course for Cilicia.

[6] Cyrus, meanwhile, assembled in Sardis both the contingents from Asia and 13,000 mercenaries. As governors of Lydia and Phrygia he appointed Persian kinsmen of his, but for Ionia, the Aeolid, and surrounding regions he chose Tamōs [>35.3], his trusted friend and a native of Memphis. He himself and his army set out as though making for Cilicia and Pisidia, spreading the word that certain inhabitants of these regions were in revolt. [7] From Asia he had a total of 70,000 troops, including 3,000 cavalry; from the Peloponnese and the rest of the Greek mainland, the 13,000 mercenaries. [8] The troops from the Peloponnese, except for the Achaeans, were commanded by Clearchus the Lacedaemonian; those from Boeotia, by Proxenus of Thebes; the Achaeans, by an Achaean, Socrates; and the Thessalian contingent, by Menôn of Larissa. [9] The junior officers of the *barbaroi* were Persians, while Cyrus himself was commander-in-chief of the entire force. By now he had revealed to his senior commanders that this expedition was in fact directed against his brother, but he still kept the troops at large in the dark,[26] fearing that the vast scale of the campaign might drive them to abandon his undertaking. Consequently, with an eye to future events, he went out of his way

---

25. Called Samios in Xen. *Hell.* 3.1.1, and Pythagoras (sic) at *Anab.* 1.4.2, where Xenophon also differs on the number of Lacedaemonian triremes (35) and troops (700), besides giving Tamōs a smaller fleet (25 triremes).

26. Including the Greek mercenaries: Clearchus (Xen. *Anab.* 1.3.1–21) seems to have been the only one among them privy to Cyrus' plans.

on the march to keep the rank and file happy, treating them courteously and ensuring that they were well provisioned.

20. After traversing Lydia and Phrygia and the regions bordering on Cilicia, he reached the frontier of Cilicia itself, the defile at the Cilician Gates. This defile is both narrow and precipitous, some twenty *stadioi* [about 2¼ miles] long, closely flanked on both sides by exceptionally high and impenetrable mountains. Walls, again on both sides, run down from the mountains to the road, on which gates have also been constructed. [2] Cyrus led his army through the defile and debouched on what is, without exception, the most beautiful plain in Asia. Across this plain he advanced to Tarsus, the largest city in Cilicia, which he quickly occupied. When Syennesis, the ruler of Cilicia, heard reports of the size of the enemy forces, he was in something of a quandary, being no match for them if it came to a fight. [3] So, when Cyrus sent for him, with pledges of safe conduct, he went. On learning the truth about the war, he undertook to ally himself with Cyrus against Artaxerxes and sent one of his sons, together with a sizable contingent of Cilicians, to join the expedition. Being a crafty rogue by nature, he insured himself against the uncertainties of Fortune by secretly dispatching his other son to the King, to report on the forces massed against him and to explain that he, Syennesis, was allied with Cyrus only out of necessity, that he was actually a loyal subject still, and that when an opportunity arose, he would desert Cyrus and join the King's forces.[27]

[4] Cyrus rested his troops in Tarsus for twenty days. But when he then struck camp, the rank and file suspected that the expedition was really aimed at Artaxerxes. As each man calculated the distances to be covered, and the number of hostile tribes through whose territory they would have to make their way, he became acutely worried, for the word had got around that it was a four months' march for an army to Bactria and that more than 400,000 troops had been mustered to serve the King. [5] They were thoroughly scared, and this made them resentful. Indeed, they became so furious with the way they had been treacherously deceived, that they were all set to murder the leaders responsible. However, when Cyrus made an urgent appeal to them all, and assured them that he was leading the army, not against Artaxerxes but to deal with a satrap in Syria [Abrocomas: Xen. *Anab.* 1.3.20], the troops were

---

27. Xenophon (*Anab.* 1.2.12, 26–27) gives further details of Syennesis' double-dealing, reporting inter alia that he sent his wife Epyaxa to Cyrus before Cyrus reached the Cilician Gates, with back pay for his troops and herself (it was widely believed) for his bed.

convinced and—after receiving a pay raise—resumed their original goodwill towards him.

21. After traversing Cilicia, Cyrus reached Issus, which is by the sea and the last city in Cilicia. About the same time, the Lacedaemonian fleet also put in there. They went ashore, met with Cyrus, and informed him of the Spartans' favorable reaction to his plans. They also disembarked the eight hundred foot soldiers who had come with Cheirosphos and turned them over to him. [2] They pretended that it was Cyrus' friends who had sent these mercenaries, but in actual fact everything had been done with the approval of the ephors. The Lacedaemonians were not yet openly committed to this war, but they still kept their intentions secret, waiting on the turn of events.

Cyrus struck camp and set out with his army, making for Syria and ordering his naval commanders to accompany him by sea, with the entire fleet. [3] When he reached what are known as "The Gates" and found the place unguarded, he was overjoyed, having had serious concerns that troops might have already occupied it. The site is a narrow and precipitous pass, easily guarded by a few men. [4] The mountains [on either side of it] lie close to each other, the one being rugged, with beetling crags, while the other—<the largest> in the region, called <Am>anus, and running the whole length of Phoenicia—comes right down to the road. The open space between the mountains is about three *stadioi* [c. ⅓ of a mile] in length, walled throughout, and with gates so designed as to leave only a narrow opening.[28] [5] After passing through the Gates unopposed, Cyrus sent back to Ephesus the part of the fleet that had accompanied him; since he was about to strike inland, he would no longer have any use for it. A twenty days' march brought him to Thapsacus, a city on the Euphrates River. [6] Here he stopped for five days, and after ingratiating himself with the troops by a generous distribution of provisions and booty from foraging, he summoned them to an assembly and disclosed the true purpose of the expedition. When the soldiers reacted to his speech with hostility, he begged them all not to desert him and promised (among other munificent rewards) that when he got to Babylon, he would give every man there five silver minas [= 500 drachmas]. Elated by this prospect, the rank and file were persuaded to follow him [Xen. *Anab.* 1.4.11–18]. [7] When Cyrus

28. This, the modern Bahçe pass, known in antiquity as the Amanic Gates, was used by Darius III to come down in Alexander's rear and cut off his line of retreat before the battle of Issus (fall 333): cf. D.S. 17.32.1–4 and Green 1991, 221–226 with notes. I accept Vogel's emendation *megiston* ("largest") for the (in context) meaningless reading of Diodorus' MSS, and Wesseling's topographically acute Amanos for the MS reading Libanos.

had crossed the Euphrates with his army, he force-marched nonstop until he reached the frontier of Babylonia, and there he rested his troops.

22. King Artaxerxes had been informed earlier by Pharnabazus that Cyrus was covertly assembling an army with which to attack him; and now, on hearing he had set out for the interior, the King summoned contingents from every quarter of the empire to Ecbatana in Media. [2] When those from the Indians and certain other peoples were slow in arriving because of the distance they had to travel, he set out to confront Cyrus with such troops as were already mustered. He had in all, according to Ephorus, not less than 400,000 men, cavalry included. [3] On reaching the Babylonian plain, he pitched camp along one bank of the Euphrates, with the intention of leaving his baggage there: he had heard that the enemy forces were not far off, and [reports of] their dangerous recklessness made him nervous. [4] He therefore had a protective ditch dug, sixty feet wide and ten deep, and encircled [his camp] with the covered wagons that accompanied him, like a rampart. Then, leaving behind in camp both the baggage and a crowd of noncombatants, together with an adequate detachment to guard them, he set out at the head of his army, marching light, to meet an enemy that was now close at hand.[29]

[5] When Cyrus saw the King's forces approaching, he at once drew up his own troops in battle order. His right wing, flanking the Euphrates, was held by the Lacedaemonian infantry and some of the mercenaries, under the general command of Clearchus the Lacedaemonian, and supported by the cavalry contingent from Paphlagonia, a thousand and more strong. The other wing consisted of troops from Phrygia and Lydia, together with about a thousand cavalry under the command of Arrhidaeus. [6] Cyrus stationed himself in the center of the phalanx, with the finest troops of the Persians and other *barbaroi,* some ten thousand in number. Deployed in front of him was a crack cavalry regiment, a thousand strong, splendidly equipped with Greek cuirasses and dirks [7] Artaxerxes stationed large numbers of scythed chariots along the entire front of his phalanx, at the midpoint of which he took up his own position, having at his command not less than 50,000 picked troops.

23. When the armies were about three *stadioi* [c. 580 yds.] apart, the Greeks launched into their paean, and to begin with advanced at an easy pace; but as

29. For a full eyewitness account of the battle of Cunaxa (name of site preserved by Plut. *Artax.* 8.2), see Xen. *Anab.* 1.7.14–8.29, 10.1–16, on which Diodorus' narrative largely relies, with additional details from Ephorus and Ctesias.

they came within bowshot range they broke into a fast run. They had been ordered to do this by Clearchus the Lacedaemonian, his idea being that not running for too great a distance would keep the combatants physically fresh for battle, while moving in at the double when at close quarters would cause arrows and other missiles to fly over them. [2] And indeed, as Cyrus's troops drew near the King's army, they became the target for such a volley of missiles as one might well expect from a horde 400,000 strong. Nevertheless, they spent comparatively little time fighting with javelins, after which they battled it out hand to hand. [3] From the very first moment of engagement, the Lacedaemonians and the other mercenaries astounded the *barbaroi* arrayed against them both by the excellence of their equipment and by their evident expertise, [4] since the *barbaroi* themselves were protected only by small bucklers, and most of their divisions were light-armed troops. Furthermore, they were not battle hardened; whereas the Greeks, because of the length of the Peloponnesian War, had been engaged in nonstop fighting and thus were experienced veterans by comparison. As a result, they routed the *barbaroi* straight off and killed large numbers of them during the subsequent pursuit. [5] It also so happened[30] that both men competing for the kingdom had taken up a position in mid-phalanx, so that when they realized this fact, they made for each other, in an ardent desire to decide the outcome of the battle by themselves. Fortune, it would seem, was bringing the brothers' rivalry for supreme power to the test of single combat, as though in imitation of that braggart encounter long ago—the theme of so many tragedies[31]—between Eteocles and Polyneices. [6] Cyrus made the first move. He hurled his javelin from a distance, hit the King, and laid him low; but Artaxerxes' attendants quickly picked him up and carried him away, out of the battle. The Persian warrior Tissaphernes at once took over the King's command, rallied the rank and file, and himself fought heroically, making good the setback caused by the King's elimination, showing up everywhere with his elite troops and killing large numbers of the enemy, so that his presence was noted even at a distance. [7] Cyrus, elated by the success of his troops, charged impetuously into the thick of the enemy, and at first, thanks to his boundless daring, slew many of them. But then, exposing himself too recklessly, he was struck by a common Persian soldier and fell, mortally wounded. With his death, the King's men regained confidence

---

30. In fact this was a well-established Persian tradition: Xen. *Anab.* 1.8.22.

31. Best known today from Aeschylus' *Seven Against Thebes.* On the Theban cycle, see Gantz 1993, ch. 14, in particular 510–518. Eteocles and Polyneices were two sons of Oedipus who engaged in a fratricidal civil war over the succession, killing one another in the battle for Thebes.

for the fight. In the end, through a mixture of resolute courage and superior numbers, they overwhelmed their opponents.

24. On the other wing Arrhidaeus—Cyrus' satrap who had been appointed to that command—to begin with, vigorously withstood the attacks of the *barbaroi;* but later, hemmed in by their extended battle line and learning of Cyrus's death, he withdrew, with his own troops, to one of his earlier way stations, which provided a passable refuge for them. [2] Clearchus, observing that not only the allies' center but the rest of their line had been routed, stopped the pursuit, recalled his troops, and deployed them in battle order, fearing that the entire enemy force might now descend on the Greeks, encircle them, and wipe them out to the last man. [3] The King's troops, after routing their opponents, first pillaged Cyrus' baggage train and then, night already having fallen, launched a general assault on the Greeks; but when the latter stoutly fought off the attack, the *barbaroi* resisted for a short while only, and very soon turned and fled, overcome by the Greeks' daring and expertise. [4] Clearchus' troops slaughtered a good many of the *barbaroi,* and then, it now being dark, retired and set up a trophy. At some time around the second watch,[32] they made it safely back to their camp.

[5] Such was the outcome of this battle. The losses of the King's army totaled more than 15,000, most of them killed by the Lacedaemonians and mercenaries with Clearchus. [6] On the other side, of Cyrus' troops there fell about 3,000, while not a single Greek (we are told) was killed, and only a few were wounded. When the night ended, Arrhidaeus (he who had withdrawn to the way station) sent word to Clearchus, inviting him to bring his troops over, so that together they could get safely through to the coast. Now that Cyrus was dead, and the King's forces everywhere in the ascendancy, acute anxiety afflicted all those who had had the temerity to join an expedition for the object of overthrowing Artaxerxes' royal power.

25. Clearchus now called a meeting of generals and other commanders to discuss the current situation. While they were about this business, there arrived an embassy from the King, in which the chief ambassador was a Greek named Phalynus [Xen. *Anab.* 2.1.7], a Zacynthian by birth. Introduced into the meeting, they reported King Artaxerxes' words as follows: "Since I

32. The Greeks divided the night, from dusk to dawn, into five watches (*phylakai*). These varied in length according to the time of year. Cunaxa was fought in late summer, when dusk fell about 9:00 p.m. and the sun rose soon after 5:00 a.m. The second watch would then begin a little before 10:30 p.m.

have defeated and killed Cyrus, surrender your arms, make your way to my doors, and find out how you may win my favor and thus get some benefit." [2] To this pronouncement each of the generals gave a reply much like that of Leonidas, made when he was guarding the pass of Thermopylae, and Xerxes sent messengers ordering him to lay down his arms. [3] At that time Leonidas told them to take this message back to the King: "We are of the opinion that, even should we become friends to Xerxes, we shall be better allies with our arms in our possession; and if we are forced to fight him, we shall, likewise, fight better if armed" [<11.5.5]. [4] After Clearchus had made a very similar response, Proxenus the Theban said: "We have now lost virtually everything else, save only our valor and our arms. So we believe that if we hang on to the latter, our valor, too, will be of some use to us, whereas if we surrender them, valor alone will avail us nothing." He therefore told them to take this message back to the King: "If he is planning some kind of trouble for us, we will use our arms to contend with him for our common good." [5] One of the commanders, Sophilus, is also on record as having said he was surprised at the King's words, "for if he thinks himself more than a match for the Greeks, let him come here with his army and take our arms from us; but if he prefers persuasion, let him state what favor he will grant us that is a fair return for them." [6] Next after these, Socrates the Achaean said that he found the King's behavior in their regard quite extraordinary, "since what he wants of us he demands on the spot, whereas what will be given to us in return he orders us to enquire of him later. In brief, then: if it's in ignorance of who actually won that he's telling us to obey his orders as though we were the losers, let him bring his vast host here and find out whose the victory was; but if he's lying to us in full awareness that we were the victors, then how can we trust any future promises he may make?"[33]

[7] On getting these responses, the messengers departed, and Clearchus marched his men to the way station where those troops that escaped the battle

---

33. Diodorus' account of this exchange differs in several respects from Xenophon's. The speech that the latter attributes to Theopompus Diodorus gives to Proxenus; that of Proxenus in the *Anabasis* Diodorus puts in the mouth of Sophilus; and he adds an intervention by Socrates the Achaean. Neither of these last two figures in Xenophon's account. Bonnet (xxvi) points out that Diodorus' version (unlike Xenophon's) claims knowledge of events on the Persian side (22.1–4, 24.5–6, 26.4–5). Though Diodorus clearly drew on Xenophon (for a striking instance, see 30.1–2 = *Anab.* 4.8.20–21), he also, equally clearly, had access to a version (? that of his fellow-commander Sophaenetus, now lost) that remembered the meeting differently and could draw on Persian-controlled sources.

in safety had found refuge. When the entire force was assembled there, they deliberated together about how they were to manage their retreat to the sea and what route they should take. [8] They decided that they should not return the same way as they had come, since much of it was barren countryside where they could not expect to find provisions, especially with a hostile army in pursuit of them. They therefore determined to make for Paphlagonia, and the whole force accordingly set out in that direction, traveling at an easy pace, to let them procure provisions en route.

26. The King was by now somewhat recovered from his wound, and when he learned of the enemy's retreat, he got the impression that they were in flight and hastened to pursue them with his own forces. [2] Since they were making slow progress, he soon caught up with them. But by then night had fallen, so he encamped nearby. When day broke, and the Greeks began to array their forces for battle, he sent messengers to them and arranged a temporary three-day truce. [3] During this period, they reached an agreement. He would arrange a peaceful passage through his territory to the sea for them and furnish them with guides to that end, while the mercenaries under Clearchus and all the troops commanded by Arrhidaeus would commit no offenses in the course of their march.[34] [4] After this the Greeks took to the road, and the King led his army back to Babylon. There he fittingly honored each individual who had distinguished himself in the battle and judged Tissaphernes to have been the most courageous of them all. So he gave him rich rewards in recompense, as well as his own daughter in marriage, and from then on continued to treat him as his most faithful friend. He also gave him the command that Cyrus had held over the maritime satrapies.[35]

[5] Tissaphernes, observing the King's fury at the Greeks, offered to destroy them all for him, provided he gave him the men to do it, and made a deal with Arrhidaeus, being convinced that this was a man who would betray the Greeks during the course of their march [he was right: *Anab.* 2.6.35–40]. The

---

34. Diodorus has run two stages of the negotiations into one. The three-day truce was to let the Greeks seek provisions in the villages (*Anab.* 2.3.1–16); there followed a longer discussion, with Tissaphernes as broker, to set up guidelines for the march north (*Anab.* 2.3.17–29).

35. Though he became Cyrus' virtual successor in Asia Minor (Xen. *Hell.* 3.1.3), Tissaphernes did not marry Artaxerxes' daughter (Diodorus here confuses him with his colleague Orontas, the satrap of eastern Armenia, *Anab.* 2.4.8), and after his defeat by Agesilaus at Sardis in 395, he was summarily executed (80.6–8).

King received this proposal with pleasure, and let Tissaphernes select, from the whole of his army, as many of the top warriors as he might need for his project. [6] <Tissaphernes then proposed to Clearchus and>[36] the other leaders that they should come and discuss matters with him in person. So almost all the generals, together with Clearchus and a score or so of captains, went to meet Tissaphernes, and there followed them some two hundred soldiers who wanted to visit the market. [7] Tissaphernes invited the general into his tent, while the captains waited outside. After a little while a red flag was hoisted from Tissaphernes' tent: he had the generals inside arrested, while a specially assigned group descended on the captains and killed them, and others finished off those soldiers who had come for the market, all except for one man who got away back to camp with news of the disaster.

27. On learning what had happened, the troops were momentarily panic stricken. They all hastened to arm themselves, but in great disorder, since they had no commanders. When no one came to trouble them, however, they chose a number of generals and gave the supreme command to Cheirisophus the Lacedaemonian. [2] These men organized the army as seemed best to them for the march and pushed on towards Paphlagonia.

Tissaphernes handcuffed the generals and sent them off to Artaxerxes, who had them all executed, with the single exception of Menōn, since he alone, because of his disagreements with his allies, was thought to have been ready to betray the Greeks.[37] [3] Tissaphernes and his forces followed close on the heels of the Greeks, yet he dared not engage them face to face in battle, from fear of the crazy recklessness of desperate men. Though ready to harass them when the terrain was advantageous, he could not do them any serious harm but simply kept in pursuit, inflicting minimal damage, as far as the country of a people called the Carduchi, at which point, [4] unable to do anything further, he and his army took off for Ionia.

It took the Greeks seven days to cross the mountain passes of the Carduchi, during which they suffered a great deal from the attentions of the local inhabitants, who were both aggressive and familiar with the terrain. [5] They

---

36. There is a lacuna in the MSS here, though the sense (as inserted) remains clear enough. Diodorus' account of the episode that follows is narrated at great length by Xenophon: *Anab.* 2.5.2–27.

37. A view shared by Xenophon: *Anab.* 2.5.8, 6.29. This is the same person as the Meno who figures as the protagonist in Plato's dialogue of that name, where his guest-friendship with the Great King is mentioned (78D).

were an independent tribe, hostile to the Great King, and well practiced in military matters: in particular, they trained themselves to use exceptionally large stones as missiles for their slings, as well as large arrows. Employing these, they kept up a lethal fusillade against the Greeks from high ground, killing large numbers of them and seriously injuring not a few others. [6] For their arrows, more than two cubits [three feet] long, penetrated both shields and cuirasses, and no defensive armor could withstand their force. The arrows they used, it is said, were so large that the Greeks wound thongs round spent ones and threw them back, treating them like javelins [Xen. *Anab.* 4.2.27–28]. [7] Having thus with much difficulty made their way through the aforesaid country, they reached the Centrites River, and by crossing it entered [western] Armenia. The satrap there was Tiribazus: they made a treaty with him and passed through his territory as friends.

28. As they were negotiating the mountain passes of Armenia, they were caught in a heavy snowstorm and barely escaped perishing to the last man. When the air was disturbed, to begin with, the snow fell so lightly from the sky that the progress of the march was in no way hampered; but then a wind arose, and the snowfall became heavier and heavier, blanketing the ground until not only the road but every landmark was completely invisible. [2] Discouragement and fear now spread among the rank and file. No one wanted to turn back, which meant certain destruction; yet because of the massive snowfall, further progress was impossible. As the storm gathered intensity, there came fierce gusts of wind and heavy hail, blowing directly into their faces and bringing the entire column to a halt. Each individual, unable to endure the hardships of this march any further, was stopped dead in his tracks, wherever he happened to be. [3] Though all lacked even the barest necessities, they endured the rest of that day and the following night in the open, suffering intensely. The unending snowfall covered up their weapons, and their bodies were chilled through by the freezing air. The hardships they endured were such that they got no sleep all night. Some managed to light fires and found a measure of relief from that; but others were so chilled throughout their bodies, with almost all their extremities frostbitten, that they gave up any hope of rescue. [4] Thus, when the night was over it turned out that most of the beasts of burden had perished, while of the men many were dead, a considerable number, though still conscious, could not move their frozen bodies, and some were blinded because of the cold and the reflected glare off the snow. [5] Undoubtedly they would all have perished had they not gone on a little further and found villages with supplies in abundance. These villages had spe-

cial underground entry tunnels for the beasts of burden, and others, with ladders, for the inhabitants. . . . <In the>[38] houses the cattle were provided with
fodder, while their owners had a plentiful store of all the necessities of life.

29. After spending eight days in these villages, they pressed on to the Phasis
River, where they stopped for another four days. They then passed through
the territory of the Taochi and the Phasians. When the local inhabitants attacked them, they defeated them in battle, killing a good many. They then
occupied their properties, which had good things in plenty, and spent fifteen
days there. [2] Marching on from there, they passed through the territory
known as that of the Chaldaeans in seven days and reached the Harpagus
River, which is four *plethra* [c. 400 ft.] wide. Their route then took them
through the territory of the Scytini, across a plain where they rested for three
days, enjoying every necessity in abundance. After this they marched on, and
by the fourth day reached a large town called †Gymnasia† [? Gizenenica].
[3] At this point the local ruler made an agreement with them and provided
them with guides as far as the sea.

After fifteen days they reached Mt. Chenion, and when those at the head
of the column glimpsed the sea, in their delight they raised such a hullabaloo
that the rearguard assumed there had been an enemy attack, and rushed to
arms.[39] [4] But when they had all got up to the point from which the sea was
visible, they raised their arms to the gods in gratitude, convinced that they
now had reached safety. They gathered a great mass of stones and built them
into two huge cairns, on which they dedicated spoils taken from the *barbaroi,*
being determined to leave behind an undying memorial of their expedition.

Their guide they presented with a silver bowl and a Persian robe; and he,
after showing them the road to the Macrones, took his leave. [5] The Greeks
then entered the territory of the Macrones, with whom they concluded an
agreement. As a pledge of good faith, they received from them a native spear
and gave them a Greek one in exchange. The *barbaroi* assured them that this
tradition, handed down to them from their forefathers, was the strongest
known guarantee of good faith. On leaving the frontiers of this people, they
found themselves in the country of the Colchians. [6] When the local inhabit-

---

38. Another textual lacuna: the sense is clear from the parallel description by Xenophon: *Anab.* 4.5.25.

39. The occasion is famous from Xen. *Anab.* 4.7.21–26 ("Thalassa! Thalassa!"), yet its
details remain obscure: e.g., the identity and precise location of the mountain ("Thēchēs"
in Xenophon) are still uncertain, though the arguments of Manfredi in Tuplin 2004,
319–323, in favor of Deveboynu Tepe, close to Maden Hanlary, are very plausible.

ants banded together against them, they defeated them in battle, killed large numbers of them, and seized a hilltop stronghold from which they plundered the surrounding territory. The booty thus acquired they brought back to the stronghold, and rested themselves in the midst of plenty.

30. In this region there were to be found vast numbers of beehives [Xen. *Anab.* 4.8.20–21], which yielded a rare and costly kind of honey. But all those who sampled it experienced the strangest affliction: after eating some they lost consciousness, fell down, and lay on the ground like so many corpses.[40] [2] Since its special sweetness had led many to try it, the number of the fallen soon came to resemble the victims of a military rout. For the rest of that day the troops were much disheartened, taken aback both by the strangeness of the incident and by the multitude of those affected. But next day, at about the same time, they all came round, gradually regained their faculties, and got to their feet: their physical state resembled that of someone recovering from a dose of poison.

[3] After three days' recuperation, they marched on [May/June 400] to the Greek city of Trapezus [modern Trebizond], a colony of the Sinopians located within Colchian territory. There they stayed for thirty days, entertained splendidly by the local inhabitants. They offered sacrifices to Heracles and Zeus the Deliverer and held a gymnastic contest at the place where, it is said, Argo put in with Jason and his crew.[41] [4] From here they sent off their leader Cheirisophus to Byzantium to obtain transport vessels and triremes, since he reckoned himself a friend of Anaxibius, the Byzantine naval commander. Him they dispatched in a light craft, and then, taking over a couple of oared skiffs from the men of Trapezus, they proceeded to despoil the neighboring *barbaroi* by both land and sea.

[5] So, for thirty days they awaited Cheirisophus' return, but when he still delayed, and provisions for the men were running short, they left Trapezus, and two days later reached the Greek city of Cerasus, a colony of the Sinopians. After stopping there for a few days they moved on into the territory of the Mossynician tribe [Xen. *Anab.* 5.4.1–26]. [6] When these *barbaroi* gathered to attack them, they defeated them in battle with great slaughter. The Mossy-

---

40. The local bees harvested the blossoms of the yellow-flowered rhododendron luteum; the resultant honey, when still fresh in the comb, would produce just the toxic effect described by Diodorus and Xenophon: Lane Fox, 35–39.

41. Diodorus here confuses the Colchis at the eastern extremity of the Black Sea (which was where Jason reputedly landed) with the territory of the Colchians immediately to the south of Trapezus.

nicians then retreated to a stronghold where they resided, and had a number of wooden towers seven stories high. The Greeks launched a series of assaults on it and took it by storm. This stronghold was the capital of all their other defensive positions, and in it, at its very summit, their king had his dwelling. [7] They have a traditional custom that the king must stay in it for his entire life and issue his edicts to the masses from there. The troops declared that this was the most barbarous tribe they had ever encountered, reporting that the men had congress with their women in public; that even the wealthiest people's offspring were fed on boiled nuts; and that they were all, as children, tattooed with various designs on both back and breast.

The Greeks got through this region in eight days, and the next, called Tibarene, in three.

31. From there they came to a Greek city called Cotyora, a colony of the Sinopians. They spent fifty days there, raiding the Paphlagonians and other *barbaroi* in the area. The inhabitants of Heracleia and Sinope sent them transport vessels in which they and their baggage-animals were ferried over [to Sinope]. [2] Sinope, a colony of the Milesians situated in Paphlagonia, had the greatest renown of any city in the area and was where, in our own times, that Mithradates who fought the Romans had his largest palace.[42] [3] Another arrival there was Cheirisophus, whose mission to secure triremes had come to nothing. The Sinopians nevertheless entertained them all generously and sent them on by sea to Heracleia, a colony of the Megarians. The entire convoy anchored off the peninsula of Acheron, where (the story goes) Heracles brought Cerberus up from Hades. [4] From here they made their way overland through Bithynia, at some risk to themselves, since the local inhabitants kept harassing them for the whole course of their march. So it was with difficulty that these survivors of the Ten Thousand, now some 8,300 in number, made it through to the Chalcedonian city of Chrysopolis. [5] From there on, further travel was easy, and some got safely home to their own countries; but the remainder assembled in the Chersonese and plundered the adjacent territory of the Thracians. This, then, was the conclusion of Cyrus' campaign against Artaxerxes.[43]

---

42. Mithradates VI (120–63) of Pontus (of which Sinope was the capital) fought two major wars against Rome (89–85, defeated by Sulla; 73–66, defeated by Lucullus and Pompey).

43. This chapter is a perfunctory note covering events that take up the whole of Books 6 and 7 in Xenophon's *Anabasis*. With the conclusion of the affairs of the Ten Thousand,

32. The Thirty *Tyrannoi,* now [winter 404/3] in control of affairs in Athens, never let up on their daily round of exilings and executions. The Thebans, angered by what was going on, made the exiles welcome; and Thrasybulus, known [from his deme] as "the Steirian," an Athenian who had been banished by the Thirty, succeeded—with the covert assistance of the Thebans—in capturing a place in Attica called Phyle. This outpost was both strongly forti-fied and located only a hundred *stadioi* [c. 11 miles] from Athens, thus offer-ing them numerous opportunities for attacks.[44] [2] The Thirty *Tyrannoi,* on learning what had happened, first led out their forces against them with the intention of besieging the place; but while they were encamped near Phyle, a heavy snowfall took place [Feb./Mar. 403]. [3] When some of the troops set about shifting their tents, the main body got the impression that this was a retreat and that some hostile force was nearby. A wave of so-called panic fear swept through the army, and they struck camp and moved to another site.

[4] The Thirty, perceiving that those citizens in Athens who had no part in the regime of the Three Thousand[45] were elated by the possibility of over-throwing the current government, relocated them to Piraeus and maintained their control of the city by means of armed mercenaries. They also accused the inhabitants of Eleusis and Salamis of abetting the exiles, and slaughtered them all. [5] While this was going on, many of the exiles flocked in to join Thrasybulus. <The Thirty also dispatched an embassy to him>,[46] ostensibly to discuss the fate of certain prisoners but privately to urge him to break up the group of exiles, and instead to join them, the Thirty, in the running of the city, as the elected replacement for Theramenes. He would, they added, have the authority to bring back into the country any ten exiles he chose. [6] Thra-sybulus replied that he preferred his current exile to power with the Thirty and, further, that he would not stop fighting until every citizen was repatri-ated, and the people got back their ancestral constitution. The Thirty—con-scious that many were rebelling against them out of hatred, while the exiles'

Diodorus picks up the narrative of the Thirty again from ch. 6, so that ch. 32 reverts in time to 404–403.

44. Phyle was a minor Attic deme most notable for its frontier fortress (4th-century portions of which still survive) controlling the main pass to Boeotia over Mt. Parnes.

45. This was the body of citizens entitled, under the Thirty, to take part in public life (Xen. *Hell.* 2.3.18–19; Arist. *Ath. Pol.* 36.1–2; cf. Bonnet, 158). Diodorus implies its exis-tence at 4.5 without actually naming it.

46. The sense of the text missing in the lacuna of the MSS is reasonably clear, and Wes-seling's supplement, used here, is plausible. The Thirty's actions at Eleusis were designed to secure the place as a safe retreat in case of need (Xen. *Hell.* 2.4.8; D.S. 33.5).

numbers continued to grow—sent envoys to Sparta soliciting aid, and themselves, after mustering all the troops they could raise, pitched camp in open country near the deme known as Acharnae [May 403].

33. Thrasybulus, leaving behind a sufficient guard for his base [at Phyle], led out the exiles, some 1,200 in number, and made a surprise night attack on the enemy's camp. He killed large numbers of them, spread terror through the rest by this unforeseen move, and forced them to retreat to Athens. [2] After the battle Thrasybulus at once force-marched to Piraeus and occupied Munychia, a bare, easily defendable hilltop. The *tyrannoi,* under the command of Critias, then descended on Piraeus with their full force and assaulted Munychia. The battle lasted a long time and was sharply contested, with the Thirty having the advantage of numbers, and the exiles that of the natural strength of their position. [3] But finally, after Critias fell,[47] the troops with the Thirty, terror struck, backed off to more level ground, where the exiles dared not venture down against them. Subsequently, large numbers [of the Thirty's forces] deserted and joined the exiles: Thrasybulus and his men then launched a sudden attack on the enemy, won the ensuing battle, and thus gained control of Piraeus. [4] Straight away many up in Athens, eager to be rid of the *tyrannis,* flocked down to Piraeus from every quarter; and all the exiles, then dispersed among various cities, on hearing of Thrasybulus' successes made for Piraeus too, so that from now on the exiles' forces were far superior, and as a result, they embarked on a siege of the city.

[5] Those still in Athens now deposed the Thirty from power and expelled them from the city [late May 403]. They then appointed ten men with full authority to bring the war, if they could, to an amicable conclusion. But on assuming power, these men ignored their commission, revealed themselves as *tyrannoi* [Lys. 12.55–57], and sent a request to Lacedaemon for forty ships and a thousand troops, under the command of Lysander. [6] But Pausanias, the king of the Lacedaemonians, who was envious of Lysander and saw that Sparta had become highly unpopular in the Greek world, marched out at the head of a large army, and on arriving in Athens successfully reconciled those in the city with the exiles [June 403: Arist. *Ath. Pol.* 39.1]. Thus the Athenians regained their own country and from now on governed it in accordance with

47. His friends put up a monument to him, which showed Oligarchy, personified, putting a torch to Democracy, with the inscription: "This memorial is for the gallant gentlemen who briefly held back the damned Athenian mob from their insolence" (schol. Aeschin. 1.39). Few texts so well convey the bitter class hatred that permeated that traditional home of democracy.

their own laws; and those who feared retribution for their endless series of crimes they allowed to take up residence in Eleusis.

34. The men of Elis, scared by the Lacedaemonians' superior power, terminated their war against them,[48] the conditions being that they should surrender their triremes to the Lacedaemonians and leave their outlying cities independent. [2] Now that the Lacedaemonians had concluded their wars and were unoccupied, they launched a campaign against the Messenians, some of whom were occupying a stronghold on Cephallenia, while others were settled in Naupactus (which the Athenians had given them [<11.84.7]), in the territory of the western Locrians. After expelling them from both these positions, the Lacedaemonians returned the one to the Cephallenians, and the other to the Locrians. [3] The Messenians, being thus driven out from all quarters because of the ancient hatred between them and the Spartans, took their arms and departed from Greece. Some sailed to Sicily and became mercenaries under Dionysius [>78.5–6]; another group—about three thousand in number—took ship for Cyrene and joined up with the exiles there [Paus. 4.26.2]. [4] At that time Cyrene was in a state of political upheaval. A group led by Ariston had seized control of the city: five hundred of the most influential Cyrenaeans had been executed, and of the rest, the most reputable had all been banished. [5] Nevertheless, the exiles, their numbers now reinforced by the Messenians, fought it out with those who had taken over the city. Many of the Cyrenaeans, on both sides, lost their lives, and the Messenians were wiped out almost to the last man. [6] After this engagement the Cyrenaeans exchanged representatives and became reconciled with one another, taking an immediate oath banning reprisals, after which they all lived together in the city.

[7] During the same period, the Romans added more colonists to the town of Velitrae.

---

48. Diodorus here resumes the narrative abandoned at 17.12, so that after a lengthy excursus we are back in the archonship of Exaenetus (401/0). The war was terminated in 400 (n. 21).

BIBLIOGRAPHY

TEXTS, TRANSLATIONS, AND COMMENTARIES

Ambaglio, D., F. Landucci, and L. Bravi. 2008. *Diodoro Siculo, Biblioteca Storica. Libro XII: Commento storico.* Milan.

Bonnet, M., and E. R. Bennett. 1997. *Diodore de Sicile: Bibliothèque Historique. Livre XIV.* Budé edition. Paris.

Casevitz, M. 1972. *Diodore de Sicile: Bibliothèque Historique. Livre XII.* Budé edition. Paris.

Cawkwell, G., ed. 1978. *Xenophon: A History of My Times* (Hellenica). Translated by Rex Warner. Harmondsworth.

Fornara, C. W. 1983. *Translated Documents of Greece and Rome 1: Archaic Times to the End of the Peloponnesian War.* 2nd ed. Cambridge.

French, A. 1971. *The Athenian Half Century: Thucydides I 89–118 Translation and Commentary.* Sydney.

Gagarin, M., and D. MacDowell, trans. 1998. *Antiphon and Andocides.* Austin, Tex.

Gomme, A. W. 1945. *A Historical Commentary on Thucydides.* Vol. 1. Oxford. (Corr. ed. 1959.)

———. 1956a. *A Historical Commentary on Thucydides.* Vol. 2. Oxford. (Corr. ed. 1962.)

———. 1956b. *A Historical Commentary on Thucydides.* Vol. 3. Oxford. (Corr. ed. 1962.)

Gomme, A. W., A. Andrewes, and K. J. Dover. 1970. *A Historical Commentary on Thucydides.* Vol. 4. Oxford.

———. 1981. *A Historical Commentary on Thucydides.* Vol. 5. Oxford.

Green, P. M. 2006. *Diodorus Siculus, Books 11–12.37.1: Greek History, 480–431 BC, The Alternative Version.* Austin, Tex.

Haillet, J. 2001. *Diodore de Sicile: Bibliothèque Historique, Livre XI.* Budé edition. Paris.

Hornblower, S. 1991. *A Commentary on Thucydides.* Vol. 1, *Books I–III.* Oxford.

———. 1996. *A Commentary on Thucydides.* Vol. 2, *Books IV–V.24.* Oxford.

How, W. W., and J. Wells. 1912. *A Commentary on Herodotus.* 2 vols. Oxford.

Krentz, P. 1989. *Xenophon:* Hellenika *I–II.3.10.* Warminster.

———. 1995. *Xenophon:* Hellenika *II.3.11–IV.2.8.* Warminster.

Lattimore, S. 1998. *Thucydides: The Peloponnesian War.* Indianapolis, Ind.

Lenfant, D. 2004. *Ctésias de Cnide: La Perse, L'Inde, Autres Fragments.* Budé edition. Paris.

Macan, R. W. 1895. *Herodotus: The Fourth, Fifth, and Sixth Books.* 2 vols. London. (Repr. New York 1973.)

———. 1908. *Herodotus: The Seventh, Eighth, and Ninth Books.* 2 vols. London. (Repr. New York 1973.)

Maidment, K. 1941. *Minor Attic Orators.* Vol. 1, *Antiphon and Andocides.* Cambridge, Mass.

Marincola, J., ed. 2003. *Herodotus: The Histories.* Trans. A. De Sélincourt. London.

McKechnie, P. R., and S. J. Kern, trans. and comm. 1988. *Hellenica Oxyrhynchia.* Warminster.

Meiggs, R., and D. M. Lewis. 1988. *A Selection of Greek Historical Inscriptions to the End of the Fifth Century B.C.* Rev. Ed. Oxford.

Oldfather, C. H. 1946. *Diodorus of Sicily, Vol. IV: Books IX–XII.40.* Cambridge, Mass.

———. 1950. *Diodorus of Sicily, Vol. V: Books XII.41–XIII.* Cambridge, Mass.

———. 1954. *Diodorus of Sicily, Vol. VI: Books XIV–XV.19.* Cambridge, Mass.

Rhodes, P. J., and R. Osborne. 2003. *Greek Historical Inscriptions 404–323 BC.* Oxford.

Vogel, F. 1890–93. *Diodori Bibliotheca Historica.* Vols. 2–3. Leipzig.

Wesseling, P., and J. N. Eyring, 1793–1807. *Bibliothecae historicae libri qui supersunt e recensione Petri Wesselingi, cum interpretatione Latina Laur. Rhodomani atque annotationibus variorum integris indicibusque locupletissimis. Nova editio cum commentationibus III Chr. Gotte. Heynii et cum argumentis disputationibusque Ier. Nic. Eyringii.* 11 vols. Amsterdam.

Yardley, J. C., and R. Develin. 1994. *Justin: Epitome of the Philippic History of Pompeius Trogus.* Atlanta, Ga.

GENERAL

Ambaglio, D. 2002. "Diodoro Siculo." *Storici Greci d'Occidente,* ed. R. Vattuone, 301–338. Bologna.

Badian, E. 1993. *From Plataea to Potidaea: Studies in the History and Historiography of the Pentecontaetia.* Baltimore.

Briant, P. 2002. *From Cyrus to Alexander: A History of the Persian Empire.* Trans. P. T. Daniels. Winona Lake, Ind.

Broughton, T. R. S. 1951. *The Magistrates of the Roman Republic.* Vol. 1, *509 B.C.–100 B.C.* New York.

Burn, A. R. 1984. *Persia and the Greeks: The Defence of the West, c. 546–478 B.C.* 2nd ed. London.

Cambridge Ancient History. 1988. 2nd ed. Vol. 4, *Persia, Greece, and the Western Mediterranean, c. 525–479 B.C.* Ed. J. Boardman et al. Cambridge.

———. 1992. 2nd ed. Vol. 5, *The Fifth Century B.C.* Ed. D. M. Lewis et al. Cambridge.

Cartledge, P. 2006. *Thermopylae: The Battle That Changed the World.* London.

Casevitz, M. 2003. "Le temps chez Diodore de Sicile: Grecs et Romains aux prises avec l'histoire." In: *Grecs et Romains aux prises avec l'histoire: representations, récits et idéologie,* ed. G. Lachenaud and D. Longrée, 2 vols. Vol. 1: 15–19. Rennes.

Caven, B. 1990. *Dionysius I, Warlord of Sicily.* New Haven, Conn.

Feeney, D. 2007. *Caesar's Calendar: Ancient Time and the Beginnings of History.* Berkeley.

Finley, M. I. 1968. *A History of Sicily.* Vol. 1, *Ancient Sicily.* London.

Freeman, E. A. 1891–1894. *The History of Sicily from the Earliest Times.* 4 vols. Oxford.

Frost, F. J. 1998. *Plutarch's Themistocles: A Historical Commentary.* Rev. ed. Chicago.

Furley, W. D. 1996. *Andokides and the Herms: A Study of Crisis in Fifth-Century Athenian Religion. BICS* Supplement 65. London.

Gantz, T. 1993. *Early Greek Myth: A Guide to the Literary and Artistic Sources.* Baltimore.

Gray, V. J. 1987. "The Value of Diodorus Siculus for the Years 411–386 BC." *Hermes* 115: 72–89.

Green, P. M. 1971. *Armada from Athens.* London.

———. 1991. *Alexander of Macedon, 356–323 B.C.: A Historical Biography.* Berkeley.

———. 1996. *The Greco-Persian Wars.* Rev. ed. Berkeley.

———. 2004. *From Ikaria to the Stars: Classical Mythification, Ancient and Modern.* Austin, Tex.

Grundy, G. B. 1901. *The Great Persian War and Its Preliminaries: A Study of the Evidence, Literary and Topographical.* London. (Repr. New York 1969.)

Hignett, C. 1963. *Xerxes' Invasion of Greece.* Oxford.

Holland, T. 2005. *Persian Fire: The First World Empire and the Battle for the West.* London.

Hornblower, S. 1987. *Thucydides.* Baltimore.

Kagan, D. 1969. *The Outbreak of the Peloponnesian War.* Ithaca, N.Y.

———. 1974. *The Archidamian War.* Ithaca, N.Y.

———. 1981. *The Peace of Nicias and the Sicilian Expedition.* Ithaca, N.Y.

———. 1987. *The Fall of the Athenian Empire.* Ithaca, N.Y.

Krentz, P. 1982. *The Thirty at Athens.* Ithaca, N.Y.

Kuhrt, A. 1995. *The Ancient Near East, c. 3000–330 BC* Vol. 2. London.

La Genière, J. de. 2001. "Xenoi en Sicile dans la première moitié du Ve siècle: Diod. XI.72.3." *REG* 114: 24–36.

Lane Fox, R. 2004. *The Long March: Xenophon and the Ten Thousand.* New Haven, Conn.

Lapini, W. 1997. "Le strade di Turii (Diod. 12.10.7)." *RSA* 27: 7–20.

Lazenby, J. F. 1993. *The Defence of Greece, 490–479 B.C.* Warminster.

Lévy, E. 2001. "Diodore de Sicile récrivant Thucydide (D.S. XII.62.6–7 et 67.3–5 versus Thuc. IV.12.3 et 80)." *Ktéma* 26: 333–341.

Manfredi, V. 2004. "The Identification of Mount Theches in the Itinerary of the Ten Thousand: A New Hypothesis." In *Xenophon and His World: Papers from a Conference Held in Liverpool in July 1999,* ed. C. J. Tuplin, 319–324, Stuttgart.

Meiggs, R. 1972. *The Athenian Empire.* Oxford.

Munn, M. 2000. T*he School of History: Athens in the Age of Socrates,* Berkeley.

O'Sullivan, J. N. 2000. "Heniochoi kai parabatai." *Philologus* 144: 383–385.

Podlecki, A. J. 1998. *Perikles and His Circle.* London.

Robinson, E. 2000. "Democracy in Syracuse 466–412 B.C." *HSCPh* 100: 189–205.

Rubincam, C. I. R. 1998. "How Many Books Did Diodorus Siculus Originally Intend to Write?" *CQ* 48: 229–233.

Sacks, K. S. 1990. *Diodorus Siculus and the First Century.* Princeton.

———. 1998. "Dating Diodorus's *Bibliotheke.*" *Mediterraneo Antico* 1.2: 437–442.

Strauss, B. S. 1987. *Athens after the Peloponnesian War: Class, Faction and Policy 403–386 BC.* Ithaca, N.Y.

———. 2004. *The Battle of Salamis: The Naval Encounter That Saved Greece—and Western Civilization.* New York.

Tuplin, C. J. 1993. *The Failings of Empire: A Reading of Xenophon* Hellenica *2.3.11–7.5.17.* Stuttgart.

———, ed. 2004. *Xenophon and His World: Papers from a Conference Held in Liverpool in July 1999.* Stuttgart.

Wentker, H. 1956. *Sizilien und Athen: Die Begegnung der attischen Macht mit den Westgriechen.* Heidelberg.

INDEX

All locators designate page numbers. Those in *italics* refer to maps.

Locators with suffixed n indicate material mentioned in footnotes but not in the corresponding page of the translation.

Arrangement of material within entries is predominantly chronological, though some material of a topical nature is alphabetically ordered; the first line of each alphabetical section is marked by an em dash —.

Naxos, island of, *42*, 89
Naxos, Sicily, 54–55, *164*, 167, 283, 284
Nemea, *10*
  Games, 68
Niceratus son of Nicias (Athenian general), 275
Nicias son of Niceratus (Athenian general)
  expeditions in Archidamian War, 145–146
  Peace of, 153–154
  campaigns in Cythera, Nisaea and Melos, 159
  advises against Sicilian Expedition, 162, 186
  command in Sicily, 162, 165, 169, 171, 174, 176, 179
  Syracusan debate on treatment, 186–187, 190
  death, 191
—conservatism, 162n, 165n
  Syracusan *proxenos* in Athens, 186
Nicolaüs (Syracusan citizen), 180–187
Nicomedes son of Cleomenes (Spartan general), 82
Nicostratus (Athenian general), 157–158
Nicoteles the Corinthian, 279
Nisaea, *10*, *26*, 81n, 98n, 147, 159, 222–223
Nomads, 238
Nomae, battle of, 91
Notium, battle of, *42*, 228–229

Octavian (C. Octavius, later Augustus), 2, 3, 5
Odrysian kingdom, 133–134
Oeniadae, *10*, 86, 88–89, 132
Oenoë, 80n, 129n
Oenophyta, battle(s) of, *10*, 83–84
Oesyme, 148
Oetaea, 140
oligarchy
  Argive Thousand, 159
  Corcyrean party favoring, 206–287
  Spartans establish in Greek cities, 158n, 261, 273, 279, 282
  See also Athens (Four Hundred; Thirty; Ten)

Olympia, *10*, 93n, *115*
Olympic festivals
  chronology, 4, 231–232, 285
  victors. *See beginning of each passage on a particular year*
Olynthos, *10*, 119, 131, 156
omens, 254
Opus, 286
oracles
  and Athenian treatment of Delos, 140, 156
  Lysander's unsuccessful attempts to bribe, 282
  Spartan, on "lame leadership," 55
  See also under Delphi
oral culture, 191n, 263n
oratory, 93, 94, 134–135
Orchomenus, *10*, 149, 157–158
Orneae, 160
Oropus, *10*
  Athenian control, 145, 150, 210n
  naval battle, 192, 194, 196n
  civil war and Theban annexation, 285
orphans, law on guardianship of, 105
ostracism, 59, 84n, 87–88
Ovid (P. Ovidius Naso), 6
Oxyrhynchus Historian, 198n, 208n

Paches son of Epicurus (Athenian general), 137
Pactyë, Alcibiades in, 231, 261n
Pagasae, *10*, 49n
Pagondas (Boeotian general): 149
Palermo. *See* Panormus
Palice, 89–90, *164*
Pallene, battle of, *10*, 119
Pamphylia, 11, 13, 28, *42*
Panhellenism, 5, 100n, 101
Panormos (Palermo), 29n, *115*, *164*, 221, 245
Panthoedas (Spartan commander), 281
Paphlagonia, 291, 295, 298–300
Parnassus region, *10*, 82
Paros, *42*, 206
  Marmor Parium, 4
Patrae, *10*, 132
patricians, Roman, 111